Chief Loco

The Civilization of the American Indian Series

Chief Loco
Apache Peacemaker

Bud Shapard

University of Oklahoma Press : Norman

Library of Congress Cataloging-in-Publication Data

Shapard, Bud, 1937-
    Chief Loco : Apache peacemaker / Bud Shapard.
        p   cm. — (Civilization of the American Indian ; v. 260)
    Includes bibliographical references and index.
    ISBN 978-0-8061-4047-6 (hardcover : alk. paper) 1. Loco, Chief, 1823–1905.
2. Chiricahua Indians—Kings and rulers—Biography. 3. Chiricahua Indians—Wars.
4. Chiricahua Indians—Government relations. 5. Indians, Treatment of—United
States—History—19th century. I. Title.
    E99.C68L637 2010
    976.6'4800497256—dc22
    [B]

                                                                    2008050117

Chief Loco: Apache Peacemaker is Volume 260 in The Civilization of the American
Indian Series.

The paper in this book meets the guidelines for permanence and durability of the
Committee on Production Guidelines for Book Longevity of the Council on
Library Resources, Inc. ∞

1 2 3 4 5 6 7 8 9 10

For the descendants of Chief Loco
especially his great–great grandsons
John Loco Shapard and Jeff Loco Shapard

Contents

List of Illustrations   ix

Preface   xi

Introduction   3

1.   Loco   7
2.   In Search of a Good Peace   22
3.   Chaos at Cañada Alamosa   32
4.   Forced to Tularosa   42
5.   "We Are Dying Here"   55
6.   The Ghosts of Tularosa   64
7.   Gunfight at Victorio's   72
8.   "We Are Good Indians"   86
9.   A Run for Home   101
10.   Final Removal from Ojo Caliente   112
11.   Loco's Dilemma   139
12.   The "Loco Outbreak"   152
13.   Ambushed at Sierra Enmedio   164
14.   Ghastly Scenes at Alisos Creek   176

15. Chiz-odle-netln's Escape   187

16. Returned to San Carlos   198

17. Loco Saves the Chihennes   209

18. Exiled to the East   219

19. Fort Marion, Florida, 1886–1887   250

20. Life at Fort Marion   259

21. Mount Vernon, Alabama, 1887–1894   272

22. The Dark Side of Mount Vernon   284

23. "Loco Died, Causes Unknown"   295

Notes   307

Bibliography   341

Index   351

Illustrations

Maps

Loco's country   8–9
Apaches' escape route, 1882   151

Photographs

Chief Loco with children   126
Loco at San Carlos, 1883   127
Loco, 1883   128
Nana   129
John P. Clum, 1876   130
Geronimo, about 1905   131
Mariana, Navajo chief, 1874   132
Loco's wife Chiz-pah-odlee, 1886   133
Captain Tillius C. Tupper, about 1883   134
Loco's wife Chiz-odle-netln, 1886   135
General Nelson Miles, about 1895   136
Chief Loco in Washington, D.C., 1886   137
Chatto in Washington, D.C., 1886   138
Fort Marion, Florida   233
Loomis L. Langdon, about 1865   234
Children sent to Carlisle, Pennsylvania, from Fort Marion, 1887   235
Herbert Welsh, Indian rights activist, about 1910   236

First Apache village at Mount Vernon, Alabama, about 1890   237
Marion Juan Loco, Chief Loco's daughter-in-law, 1910   238
Loco and other Apache leaders at Mount Vernon,
    about 1889   239
Geronimo, 1904   240
Captain William W. Wotherspoon, about 1894   241
Members of Company I, Twelfth Infantry, about 1892   242
Apache baseball players, Mount Vernon, Alabama, about 1890   243
Loco at Mount Vernon, Alabama, about 1892   244
Second Apache village at Mount Vernon, Alabama, about 1892   245
Apache gambling circle, Mount Vernon, Alabama, about 1890   246
Apache notables at Mount Vernon, Alabama, about 1890   247
John and Marion Loco, prisoners of war, 1912   248
Chiricahua survivors, 1913   249

Preface

Historians and writers dealing with Apaches have focused their attention almost entirely on the Indians' tough-fisted nature and their feats as a warrior society. In this book I have done the opposite. I have followed the life of Chief Loco and his Warm Springs people, the most amicable of the Chiricahua Apaches. Little has been written about Loco's search for a peaceful life. He generally has been banished to brief passages and footnotes. Here, I bring him to the fore. The tale is not without violence and heartbreak, but I have attempted to present the other half of the Apaches' story—their efforts to make peace.

A book such as this would be impossible without the help of many knowledgeable people. They are too numerous to list individually, but I gratefully acknowledge their help. Among the ranks of volunteers, I want to single out the following for special appreciation.

My wife, Beth, acted as editor and proofreader. She watched patiently as I galloped off daily for seven years to adventure with Chief Loco and his Apaches, repeatedly proofread the manuscript, and offered countless suggestions to improve the story. Her insight and guidance have been invaluable.

My deepest appreciation goes to my former father-in-law, the late Raymond Loco, who was Chief Loco's grandson, to other Loco descendants, and to members of the Fort Sill Apache Tribe, who generously furnished material about Chief Loco's life that is unavailable anywhere else. This work fulfills a promise I made to Raymond almost fifty years ago. He always believed the history of the Chiricahua Apaches was incomplete unless Chief Loco's story was told.

My profound gratitude also goes to Edwin R. Sweeney, who knows more about Chiricahua and Warm Springs Apache history than any other person alive. Ed freely shared his personal research and historical documents on Loco and Loco's times and provided crucial advice along the way. Special thanks to Alicia Delgadillo and Miriam Perrette for their advice on photographs and for their genealogical expertise. Alexandra Keraudran of Scottsdale, Arizona, has my heartfelt appreciation for freely donating her extraordinary talent for photography and photographic restoration. In my opinion, Alex is one of the better photographers in Arizona. Thanks also to Carl and Joyce Bornfriend of the Frisco Native American Museum. This museum, in Frisco, North Carolina, holds one of the largest collections of Apache photographs in the country. Thanks also to Marcy Thompson of the Transylvania County, North Carolina, Public Library, who located countless obscure volumes for my research. My special appreciation goes to members of the University of Oklahoma Press: Alessandra Jacobi Tamulevich, acquisitions editor; Emmy Ezzell, production manager; and Alice Stanton, special projects editor, all of whom guided me through different stages of the publishing process. They are professionals and diplomats.

Chief Loco

Introduction

When the United States assumed control of land that the Chiricahua Apaches believed was theirs, a rancorous clash between cultures followed for nearly seven decades. By the time the conflict ended, 91 percent of the Chiricahua population of 1848 had died or been killed. At the conclusion of the saga in April 1913, the once powerful Chiricahua and Warm Springs tribes had been reduced to a mere 274 survivors.

Modern aficionados of Apaches euphemistically describe raiding and warfare as mainstays of the traditional Chiricahua economy. Plainly speaking, "raiding" meant stealing, and "warfare" meant murdering anyone who resisted the robbery, especially anyone who killed an Apache while defending his property. There was no morality attached. It was nothing personal, just business. The Apaches had operated this way long before the Americans or even the Mexicans arrived on the scene, taking life's necessities from neighboring Indian tribes. The Apache culture was not one that easily reconciled with its neighbors.[1]

The Americans, however, imbued with their manifest destiny, were determined to own or control every inch of land from the Atlantic to the Pacific. It was America's business to settle and civilize the country. There was a nation to build, with no place in it for wild Indians who stood in the way of progress. Roads had to be cut, fields cleared, and communications established. Above all, the biggest obstacle, Indians living on the land, had to be put aside, stashed away in some godforsaken place, or, if necessary, just done away with. If the Apaches would not make way and let the Americans have the land, give up their primitive lifestyle, and assume a less than second-class citizenship, no one should feel any compunction about killing them. It was the right thing to do. It was what God wanted.

Complicating the inevitable conflict that arose between these two cultures was an assembly of inept, malfeasant bureaucrats, army officers, and politicians who had neither the foresight nor the inclination to work out a peaceful solution with the Indians. Further, a few influential citizens living in Apachería—Apache country—found that war with the Apaches was a profitable business, so they promoted the conflict.

Conversely, few Apache leaders could imagine a peaceful coexistence with the white man in which they would be unable to take at least some of life's necessaries in the traditional manner. It was a lifestyle handed down by their fathers, and their fathers' fathers before them. Apache raiding was not a heroic defense of the homeland. It was simply a never-ending quest for groceries. Apaches considered peace agreements to be tactical maneuvers providing short respites from the rigors of their rob-and-run lifestyle. The chiefs Victorio, Juh, Naiche, and even the belligerent Geronimo made brief, tentative gestures toward peace over the years, only to return quickly to their pillaging lifestyle.[2]

Although both sides avowed that they wanted peace, both received peacemakers poorly. After a massacre of 144 unarmed Apaches near Camp Grant (later Fort Grant), Arizona, by 140 drunken citizens from Tucson in April 1871 and a subsequent outcry from eastern liberals, President Ulysses S. Grant initiated a controversial peace policy with the Indians. His representatives, sent to implement a peaceful approach with the Apaches, were quickly undermined by the local press and citizens. The first emissary, Vincent Colyer, scathed by vitriolic attacks in the territorial newspapers, soon exited the scene, completely unsuccessful among both the settlers and the Chiricahuas. Colyer's successor, General Oliver ("Bible Toting") Howard, had some success with Cochise and his Central Chiricahuas but duped Loco's Warm Springs people out of a reservation in the process. General George Crook is usually credited with finally bringing peace to Apachería, but that happened only after he used Apache scouts to run ragged the few remaining hang-tough hostiles.

The Apaches' legendary leader Mangas Coloradas was murdered for his efforts by the men to whom he extended the hand of friendship. The famous Cochise worked a deal with General Howard, but it was regional and excluded any relief for residents of Mexico, whom he would still be free to raid. The passing of Cochise ended that effort.

Chief Loco of the Warm Springs Chiricahuas was among a minority of Apache visionaries who recognized that the Apaches would have to change to accommodate the Americans. As a band leader in his early thirties, he made his first peaceful overtures to the Americans in 1855. His unflagging struggle for peace continued through fifty turbulent years until his death in 1905. Unfortunately, Loco was ahead of his time. Initially, few of his friends and compatriots could grasp the concept of life on a reservation without raiding.

Loco was caught between two fractious worlds. The Americans tended to discredit or ignore his gestures for peace. They focused on the troublemakers. When there were problems, Loco's band often drew the blame, mostly because they were stationary and easy to find, and the Apache firebrands habitually ran for the protection of Loco's camps on the reservation. Conversely, some Apaches criticized Loco because they believed he was afraid to fight, or possibly crazy. They claimed his attitude was certainly not Chiricahua-like.

Ironically, Chief Loco's motivation to remain at peace stemmed largely from a deep-rooted tradition among the Chiricahuas, the love of their children. Affection and concern for the band's youngsters stood as an important feature of Chiricahua society. Adults were deeply devoted to the rearing and training of their children. This affection was the basis of dozens of rituals employed to shield a child from harm that began as soon as the mother learned she was pregnant. The rituals continued until the youngster was well into his or her teens. All of Loco's descendants emphasized that the chief's intense affinity for the children's safety often affected his decisions and the subsequent course of events.[3]

Loco was among the first Apache leaders to recognize—and probably the only one initially to comprehend—that to continue the old Apache way at any level would lead to certain annihilation of the entire Warm Springs band.[4] Nevertheless, when he worked a successful peace deal with the Americans in 1869, more Apaches from all bands gathered under his leadership at Ojo Caliente, New Mexico, than under any leader before or after, with the possible exceptions of Mangas Coloradas and Cochise. The Apache wars would have ended there except for a complex tangle of inept or corrupt bureaucrats, bad luck, and a few intractable Apaches who continued to stir up the Americans with their raiding.

Despite this, by early 1886 most of the Chiricahuas understood that a continuation of their ancestral lifestyle would lead to their destruction, and they were following Loco's example by settling peacefully on the reservation. Some Apaches, to be sure—especially Geronimo—never adjusted to the idea of settling down and continued to raid in spite of the odds. Geronimo was not the last standing Apache paladin of home-land defense, as he has been pictured. Nevertheless, by 1886 most of the Chiricahuas were quietly farming on the reservation, and Geronimo was virtually a loner. No evidence suggests that his actions had anything to do with restoring the motherland to the Apaches. It was his refusal to settle on the reservation and his persistent raiding that finally ended any opportunity for peace, dashed hopes for a Chiricahua reservation in Apachería, and landed the entire tribe in prison for twenty-seven years.[5]

Whatever the Indians' culpability in their own decline, even the most cynical readers must shake their heads in disbelief at the governmental treachery and bureaucratic buffoonery that repeatedly undercut Loco's efforts for peace. Despite the continuing burlesque of blunders and perfidy that systematically frustrated his every effort, Loco continued his struggle for "a good peace with no lie" until he died at the age of eighty-two.[6] This is Chief Loco's story.

CHAPTER ONE

Loco

Apaches take great pride in their personal names. A name is considered valuable individual property of the bearer and is often derived from a significant event in the owner's life. The meaningful event for Chief Loco took place during a raid in the late 1840s. A small Warm Springs Apache raiding party was driving a few stolen cattle northward toward its home camp near Ojo Caliente in southwestern New Mexico. Concurrently, a company of Mexican infantry was tramping south on a collision course with the Apaches. The Mexicans spotted the Indians first and set an ambush near a dusty patch that would soon become Mesilla, New Mexico.[1]

When the raiders bumbled directly into the trap, the Mexican troopers let loose a volley that decimated the Apaches. In the blistering crossfire that followed, the survivors made a headlong dash for safety. According to Chief Loco's descendants, one young warrior in his late twenties lay low over his horse and was racing through the firestorm when he heard a wounded relative shout his name and plead for help. He skidded his mount to a stop, lifted his cousin aboard the horse, and continued his dash to safety as Mexican marksmen poured fire onto the two. The event inspired the Apaches to rename the warrior "Jlin-tay-i-tith," or "Stops-His-Horse." The Mexicans called the lucky fellow "Apache Loco"—Crazy Apache. The Apaches quickly picked up on the Mexican moniker and began calling him Loco.[2]

Loco disclosed his Apache name to John Bourke, a captain in the U.S. Army and an ethnographer, in 1886, but he apparently did not tell Bourke

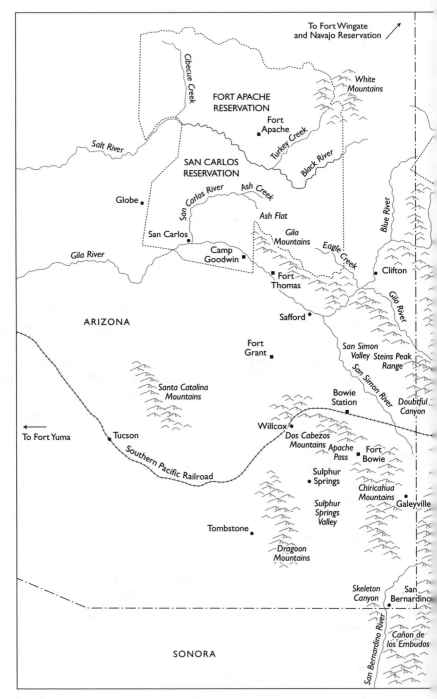

Loco's country

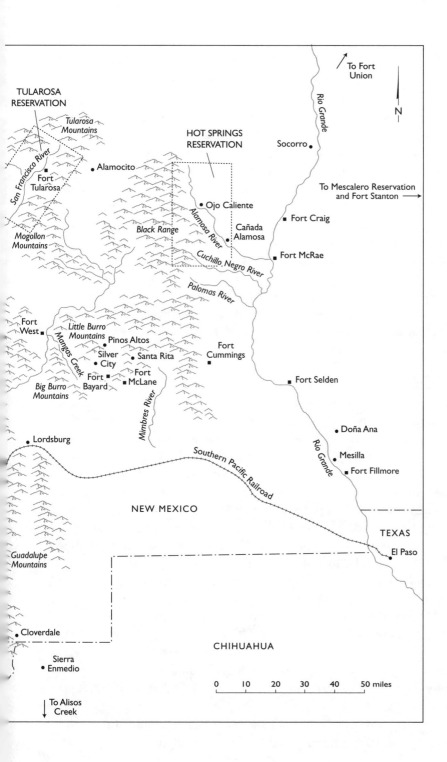

TULAROSA
RESERVATION

Tularosa Mountains

San Francisco River

Fort
Tularosa

• Alamocito

Mogollon Mountains

HOT SPRINGS
RESERVATION

Black Range

Alamosa River

• Ojo Caliente

Cañada
Alamosa

Cuchillo Negro River

Palomas River

To Fort
Union

Rio Grande

N

Socorro •

To Mescalero Reservation
and Fort Stanton ➔

■ Fort Craig

■ Fort McRae

Fort
West ■

Little Burro Mountains

Pinos Altos

Silver
• City

• Santa Rita

Fort ■
Bayard

Mangas Creek

Big Burro Mountains

■ Fort
McLane

Fort
Cummings
■

■ Fort Selden

Mimbres River

• Lordsburg

Southern Pacific Railroad

• Doña Ana

Rio Grande

• Mesilla

■ Fort Fillmore

NEW MEXICO

TEXAS

El Paso •

Guadalupe Mountains

• Cloverdale

CHIHUAHUA

Sierra
• Enmedio

0   10   20   30   40   50 miles

↓ To Alisos
  Creek

the story behind it. Balatchu, an Apache contemporary of Loco's, said Loco's Apache name was "Lidayisil" but translated it the same way, as Stops-His-Horse. Anthropologist Morris Opler's study of the Apaches' use of names during emergencies further validates the account given by Loco's descendants. Opler's informants said that ordinarily it was rude to speak a person's name in his presence, but in times of dire need, the use of one's name would bring immediate help. "A man is willing to do anything for another if he calls him by name."[3]

A number of writers and later-generation Apaches have erroneously asserted that Loco received the name because he trusted whites and repeatedly made peace with the Americans. These accounts lack credit because Loco already sported the name when he was mentioned for being absent during the signing of the first Apache peace treaty with the Americans at Acoma, New Mexico, in 1852. He was also one of the signers of the 1855 Fort Thorn treaty, under the name "Losho"—the name apparently recorded that way as the result of a glitch in translation. The idea that he received the name Loco solely because of his penchant for peaceful relations with the whites is incorrect, but no doubt a few years after the Stops-His-Horse incident, some tribal wag connected the name with his efforts for peace.[4]

Loco was born during the hot months of 1823 in the Black Range of southwestern New Mexico, somewhere near the Alamosa River. He entered the world as a member of what anthropologists have defined as the Eastern Chiricahua group, one of three divisions of the Chiricahua tribe. Loco's band occupied most of southwestern New Mexico. The Americans referred to the Eastern Chiricahuas as the Mimbres, Gila, Copper Mine, Mogollon, Mimbreño, and Ojo Caliente, or Warm Springs, Apaches. These people called themselves Chihennes, the Red Paint People, and painted a red stripe across their faces. The other two divisions of the tribe were the Central Chiricahuas, who lived primarily in southeastern Arizona, and the Southern Chiricahuas, who lived almost exclusively in northeastern Chihuahua and northwestern Sonora, Mexico. The Central Chiricahuas were often referred to as the Cochise Chiricahuas, but they called themselves Chokonen. The Southern Chiricahuas were known as Mexican or Pinary Apaches but called themselves Nednai.[5] The Chiricahuas recognized a fourth band, the Bedonkohe, but this band apparently disappeared in the 1860s, having been killed off or integrated into other bands.[6]

Loco's family was associated with the band of Chihennes under the leadership of Cuchillo Negro, which tended to be the most peaceful of the Chiricahua bands. Its peoples were a little more sedentary and did a bit more small-patch farming than the others. That is not to say they did not follow the Apaches' traditional pillage-and-plunder lifestyle. As Mexicans and Americans moved into their territories, game became scarce. Accordingly, raiding became increasingly important, not to drive out the new immigrants or defend the homeland but to find food.

Loco's father was probably the headman of a local group associated with Cuchillo Negro's band. Apache leaders often came from the wealthier "better families," headed by brighter men who were effective leaders. Their children, who grew up surrounded by upper-crust models, naturally became successful leaders. When his name first appeared in official American records, Loco, at the age of thirty, was already the leader of a small local group.[7]

Physically, Loco was smaller than most of the well-known Apache leaders. In 1872, General Howard wrote that he was "a little smaller" than another Chihenne chief, Victorio, whom Howard described as five feet ten inches tall. In later life Loco enlisted as a scout on three separate occasions at Fort Sill, Oklahoma. His height was listed differently for each enlistment, at five feet two, five feet four, and five feet six inches. Analysis of photographs of Loco standing beside other Apaches of known heights, such as Naiche, who was five feet eleven, indicate that he was about five feet four inches tall.[8]

Despite Loco's being physically small, oral history accounts from his descendants indicate that as a young adult, he more than met the expectations of traditional tribal culture. His successes as a rising Apache warrior soon attracted a small following of relatives and friends. That he was a physically powerful man may have sped his selection as a leader.

His strength with his bow and arrow is legendary. Loco purportedly owned bows so stout that only a few men in the band were able to draw the strings. He was known for his prowess with the bow. Once, in a clash with a small group of Navajos, Loco fell into an archery duel with the Navajo leader. In an effort to avoid Loco's arrows, the Navajo repeatedly dived forward, exposing his shoulder. One of Loco's arrows struck the Navajo just behind the collar bone, traveled diagonally through the entire length of the poor fellow's body, and exited from his thigh, just below the buttock. According to the story, the other Navajo warriors took that as a cue to abandon the fight. Jason Betzinez, a member of Loco's band and eventually a follower of Geronimo, marveled that Loco and Nana, another Chihenne leader, could each slaughter steers on ration issue day at the Warm Springs Indian agency with one arrow that went entirely through the animal's body. Years later, in his seventies, the old chief still slaughtered cattle this way on ration day at Fort Sill.[9]

Loco's prodigious strength once saved his life, but the incident left him marked with distinctive scars. The episode probably happened in the 1860s. The affair began with a fight between two old women. As village headman, it fell to Loco to separate the two and settle the squabble. He pulled the brawlers apart and slung the more aggressive contender into her wickiup. As he left the scene, the woman shouted, "I hope a bear chews your leg off."[10]

A few days later Loco took his young son hunting in the Black Range. In those days, grizzly bears were so plentiful there that even a short stroll in the mountains was dangerous. Apaches believed the grizzly had strong evil powers. One of Opler's informants warned that "if you come in contact with a bear by smell or touch, you can get sick. Bear sickness often shows up in a deformity, in a crooked arm or leg."[11]

Unfortunately, the two stumbled across a large grizzly during their outing. Loco pushed the boy up into a tree and turned to deal with the bear, simultaneously trying to load his musket. The muzzle-loader, its wooden ramrod still in the barrel, was knocked from his hands as the bear slammed into him. Loco pulled a hunting knife, and the two went about the deadly business of carving each other up. Ultimately, the bear quit the fight, but not before it took a large bite out of Loco's right thigh and swiped a paw across his face, leaving gashes in several places around his left eye. As the bear ran off, Loco scooped up his gun, the ramrod still in the barrel, and fired it at the bear. The ramrod shattered harmlessly on the bear's back. As the legend goes, Loco then hobbled after the animal, waving his knife and shouting for the grizzly to come back and finish its meal, if it dared. When he finally caught up with the animal, it was dead.

The people from his village carried Loco back to the camp. As Loco passed the wickiup of the woman who cursed him, he allegedly shouted from his stretcher, "I hope you are satisfied, old woman." Loco collected an impressive set of scars about his left eye from the incident and, as Opler's informant warned, a deformed leg. If there was any doubt that the woman was a witch and a menace to the community, it was dispelled by this affair. The modern family version discretely does not mention the fate of the witch.[12]

One Apache writer suggests that Loco acquired "bear power" after the fight and became a medicine man. Betzinez and a descendant of Victorio's imply that he later wore a necklace of bear claws. Loco's descendants reported no knowledge of his being a medicine man or having "bear power." No pictures exist showing him wearing a bear claw necklace. It is unlikely that he did, because Loco was apparently a popular fellow. Any man wearing a bear claw necklace would have attracted few friends and certainly no following.[13]

Most of Loco's non-Indian contemporaries and subsequent writers ascribe his facial injuries and his bad eye to a bear attack, as do some Apaches. Everyone agrees that the bear damaged his face and leg. Some of Loco's descendants deny that the scuffle with the grizzly had anything to do with his blind eye. An analysis of a photographic enlargement of the injured area on Loco's face shows deep scars above and to the left of the eye and on his cheek. The eyelid, however, seems to be normal and undamaged. A claw might have damaged nerves to the eyelid, but it appears unlikely that a claw tore through it. The actual incident in which Loco's sight was impaired was recounted by Raymond Loco as it was told to him by his father, John Loco, the chief's son.

In that account, Mexican soldiers attacked an Apache camp by surprise. As the Mexicans began firing into the camp, the Indians scattered in all directions in the predawn darkness. In an effort to save a prized saddle, Loco threw it over his shoulder as he dashed to escape. Running in the dark, he raced over the edge of a rocky arroyo, landed on his face, and permanently damaged his eye. Another of Loco's grandsons, Moses, said Loco had "some vision left in his eye," but probably no more than being able to see light and form. Britton Davis, an officer in the Third Cavalry who was heavily involved in Apache matters during the period, observed that a cataract had formed over the eye. Loco's eyelid drooped over the eye and had to be held open with a finger for him to see at all.[14]

His facial disfigurement "gave him a sinister appearance entirely foreign to his nature." General Howard noted that he had "a pleasant smile." Britton Davis wrote that Loco, among others, made frequent visits to Davis's tent at Fort Apache for "friendly or business talks."[15]

Charles Clark, a telegraph operator at the San Carlos Indian agency, Arizona, in the summer of 1881, became good friends with Loco. Clark described Loco as "a short, fat, big-paunched Apache who had lost one eye." They met when Loco's band came to the agency for its weekly rations. The Indians came to the agency by noon on Thursdays to be counted, but the rations were not issued until Friday, forcing the Apaches to loll about the area throughout Thursday afternoons. "Loco made the front of the telegraph office his loafing place and all of Thursday afternoons could be found lying half against the front wall of the office, watching my work in which he took interest. During these visits I kept him supplied with 'the makings' [of cigarettes] and we became quite friendly."

Clark had heard about the Apaches' "ceremonial dances" and wanted to see one. He asked Loco on two occasions for the opportunity to attend, to which Loco replied, "Poco tiempo," meaning, "Soon." Eventually Clark was invited to a social dance and was allowed to bring two couples along. The group arrived at the dance scene just after nine o'clock in the evening, led by a youngster, probably Loco's son. "We were welcomed by Loco in person and conducted to seats on the ground at the edge of the large circle formed by the spectators," wrote Clark.

In addition to being good-natured, Loco was a bit of a jokester. After Clark and his friends had been at the dance for some time, Clark recalled:

> Loco walked over to me and saying something I did not understand took my arm and walked me onto the dance floor stopping in front of two squaws. He hooked their arms within mine, facing the squaws in one direction and myself in the opposite. Then the orchestra struck up and the dance commenced. . . . [After a while] I considered I contributed much toward the entertainment of the evening as any of the devils [masked dancers] so I broke holds and sat down. The two women laughed over my weakness and signaled another buck in the circle, who jumped in to help with a yell, ran to where the women stood waiting, and hooking arms with them cut up more didos and coming than I could ever thought of. The two squaws telling him what a weakling I was, I suppose, for they would look at me and then throw a fit.[16]

Generally speaking, most Americans and most Apaches who knew Loco liked him. Loco himself noted that white people "seemed to like to have me near them." Even his harshest critics, the descendants of Victorio, admit that Loco was usually good-natured, although they also claim he was a "gruff man" with a "reputation for sudden bursts of temper." The fact was that the two leaders seldom saw eye-to-eye. Although supposedly cousins, and cohorts in a few misadventures when they were younger, Loco and Victorio were a fractious twosome, often vying for control of the Chihennes. They argued over which other Apaches should be allowed on the reservation. Victorio almost always favored a traditional raiding lifestyle and was inclined to allow militant bands to move in with the Chihennes. Loco invariably favored peace and modernization, generally trying to exclude hostiles such as Geronimo from the reservation, where they were often confused with the peaceful Chihennes. Perico, an old-time Chihenne warrior and army scout, told anthropologist Sol Tax that "while Victoria [*sic*] was the main chief, the war chief, and Loco the assistant, most of the tribe were 'with' Loco because he always favored peace." White settlers and military officers were also quick to notice and appreciate Loco's preference for peace. Britton Davis wrote that "Loco, while generally acknowledged as chief of the Warm Springs, was [after Victorio's death], like Mangas [the son of Mangas Coloradas], pacifically inclined, but he was a man of greater force and exercised a controlling influence over a considerable number of his people; an influence always in the paths of peace."[17]

Victorio's descendants report that Victorio and Loco never "saw eye-to-eye concerning slaves." Many Apaches kept captives, mostly young boys, girls, and women. Eventually many of these were adopted, married to their captors, or otherwise taken into the tribe, but until then they were slaves, often treated badly and sold or traded readily. Loco was among the Apache slaveholders. It appears from the few available accounts that he often gave his slaves a bad time.[18]

In May 1853, Mangas Coloradas and several other leaders assembled at Fort Webster to clarify and reaffirm the terms of the Treaty of Acoma with Indian Agent Edward Wingfield and Captain Enoch Steen. Reports of the meeting referred to a Chihenne chief, Loshio or Losio, undoubtedly Loco. The Chihennes arrived a few days late, bringing with them four captives, Mexican girls ages six to eleven. The Apaches were apparently expecting to sell or trade the girls to the Americans. Captain Steen was shocked at the captives' condition. "A narrative of their sufferings by the captives is sufficient to shock with horror and chill the blood in the veins of the most degenerated Americans." Backed by the army, Steen took the girls from the unsuspecting Apaches. In exchange, Steen and Wingfield issued the Indians rations, but they observed that the Chihennes "appeared much dissatisfied, displaying signs of belligerent nature" as they left Fort Webster.[19]

Victorio's granddaughter reported an incident in which Loco whipped a captive to death because she ignored his instructions. It might have happened, but there seems to be no corroborating evidence. In a second incident, told by descendants of both Loco and Victorio, Loco killed one of Victorio's slaves. The accounts differ somewhat about the circumstances. According to the Loco family, the chief was at Victorio's camp enjoying an evening of *tiswin,* an Apache beerlike drink, and talk with a few friends. Apparently everyone was in his cups when a favorite slave of Victorio's refused to bring more tiswin and loudly scolded the men for overindulging. Loco, perhaps a bit inebriated at this point, stopped the woman's diatribe by hurling his lance through her chest. In 1879 Lieutenant Thomas Cruse wrote, "From Loco I bought a lance, the blade of which was an officer's sword of 1857, with probably a gruesome history." Perhaps it was the same lance that that killed the unfortunate woman.

The Victorio family suggests that the incident soured Loco and Victorio's friendship, and afterward the two went their separate ways. It appears, however, that Loco and Victorio split up as early as 1873 in a contentious struggle over the leadership of the Chihennes. In any event, more was involved than the death of a single captive.[20]

Both incidents probably happened while Loco was drinking. Like most other Apache leaders of the day, Loco was a hard drinker. Lest one judge him or the other Apaches by today's standards, it should be understood that the scope of Indian drinking during the period paled in comparison with that of non-Indian drinkers in the region. Liquor consumption by white Americans was prodigious. By the 1830s it was estimated that nationwide, every adult over the age of fifteen consumed seven gallons of alcoholic beverages annually. One foreign visitor observed that drunkenness was "everywhere prevalent," and the amounts consumed were "scandalous."[21]

Things were hardly better in the American military. By the 1880s, one in every twenty-five military men was hospitalized as an alcoholic. Those in treatment were only the tip of the iceberg, because only the most serious cases were hospitalized for advanced alcoholism with symptoms such as delirium tremens and cirrhosis. Ironically, the Apaches may have drunk less than their non-Indian counterparts, because of federal policies prohibiting the sale of liquor to Indians.[22]

When Chief Loco and others are mentioned in whisky-related incidents or are recorded as being drunk, their behavior is best viewed as a phenomenon of the era, affecting both whites and Indians. As with most other Apache leaders, drinking did not appear to affect Loco's decision-making or his leadership.

Between 1840 and 1860, the period of Loco's rise to prominence, even the Chihennes under Cuchillo Negro's leadership alternated between making peace deals and making war. For the most part the peace accords failed miserably as a result of bad faith by one side or the other. Even as seven leaders—Mangas Coloradas, Ponce, Cuchillo Negro, Jose Nuevo, Veinte Realles, Rinon, and Corrosero—put their Xs on the Treaty of Acoma on July 11, 1852, several bands under Delgadito, Itan, Laceris,

Loco, and Victorio were either gathering mescal or raiding in Sonora, and probably a little of both.[23]

By the time the Chihennes signed the Acoma treaty, their alternating peace and war gyrations were costing the Apaches dearly. A few months after the treaty was signed, Michael Steck, agent for the Apaches, wrote on August 12, 1853, "White encroachment on their lands and their long war with Mexico has significantly affected their numbers and their ability to make a living." He found each man to have "two to five wives" and reported that "often from ten to fifteen are dependent on a single hunter." Loco took three wives, the second and third both widows. Steck astutely noted the Apaches' dilemma: "The lack of game in their country made it impossible for them to live without raiding. It is plain as the light of day that they must be rationed or a war of extermination commenced if we wish to prevent these depredations. They must steal or starve."[24]

On August 12, 1854, Cuchillo Negro and Josecito met with Steck and "made strong protestations of friendship." Encouraged by the Apaches' apparent interest in a permanent peace, Governor David Meriwether of New Mexico traveled to Fort Thorn to discuss the possibilities with "Losho [Loco], Laceres, Jose Nuevo, Delgadito Janeros, Delgadito, Itan, and Josecito," whom he characterized as "Gila Apaches." He concluded that the meeting was satisfactory and set about drafting a new treaty that was more favorable to the Americans than the Acoma deal had been.[25]

Ten months later, on June 7, 1855, several Chihenne and Nednai leaders signed onto Governor Meriwether's new proposition, the Treaty at Fort Thorn. The signatories included seven Chihenne headmen: Cuchillo Negro, Loco (Losho), Itan, Delgadito, Rinon, Laceres, and Jose Nuevo. Two Nednai leaders also signed. Mangas Coloradas sent word that he was sick and could not attend, but he promised to travel to Santa Fe and sign later. He never did.[26]

Not much changed as a result of the Fort Thorn accord except that the government began a modest rationing system. As more Americans settled in Apachería, more incidents occurred. Things broke for the worse in 1857 when Colonel Benjamin Bonneville, acting commander of the army's Department of New Mexico, launched a nine-hundred-man campaign to punish the Apaches for the murder of Navajo agent Henry Dodge. Western Apaches, probably Coyoteros, had killed Dodge, but Bonneville's expedition managed to dispatch forty-two innocent Chihennes. Significantly, one of the dead was the peaceful Chihenne leader Cuchillo Negro, leaving Victorio, Loco, and Nana as the band's most prominent leaders.[27]

Things worsened after the so-called Bascom affair of 1861, when Cochise, leader of the Central Chiricahuas, was captured under a flag of truce, and Lieutenant George Bascom had three of his relatives hanged following Cochise's escape at Apache Pass, Arizona. In 1863, Mangas Coloradas was captured by miners, turned over to the army at Fort McLane, and shot dead by American troops there. Because of these two events, most if not all the Chihennes under Loco, Victorio, and Nana joined forces with Cochise for a six-year vendetta against the Americans. By end of the 1860s, the Apaches could not have hired an American or Mexican to trust them. After years of on-again-off-again peace deals with the Apaches and Cochise's sustained campaign, cynical suspicion seemed to be sensible thinking in the American mind.[28]

The Indians had their own righteous doubts about peace accords. Nearly all the Apaches' big losses before 1865 came about not in open warfare but during truces. The Johnson bloodbath of 1837 killed more than 20; the Elias Gonzales massacre in 1844 saw 80 dead; the Galena episode of 1846 slaughtered 148; and a poisoned whiskey incident in 1857 murdered approximately 60. These events all happened during agreed-upon truces. Without fail, it was more costly for the Apaches to make treaties than it was to make war. From this perspective, one might understand how a vouchsafe from the Americans or Mexicans carried no currency with the Indians. Any negotiations with the Americans or Mexicans became displays of personal heroism, deeds of desperation, or perhaps both.

So it was unusual, but not a surprise, when Loco, with Victorio looking over his shoulder from a safe distance, made a limited peace in 1867 with the little New Mexico town of Cañada Alamosa. Cañada Alamosa had been settled in 1856 in the heart of Chihenne territory, only a few miles from Ojo Caliente, the hot springs. Two things stand out about the agreement. First, although Victorio was in the area, Loco took the risk of entering the town to negotiate the arrangement. Second, it was purportedly the only peace agreement that was never broken by either side. Betzinez credits Loco for the "treaty."[29]

The affair took place on October 15, 1867, and centered on three friends, American settlers Richard C. Patterson, Sam Creevy, and Joseph D. Emerson. The three had met in 1861 when they joined Company G, First California Volunteers. They came to New Mexico in 1862 with the Volunteers to save Arizona and New Mexico from the Confederates and to keep the Indians in check. When they were discharged, the three settled in Cañada Alamosa, where Patterson bought land and hired Emerson and Creevy to build a house and help run a small farm.

"Very early" on the morning of October 15, Patterson and Creevy went out to Patterson's cornfield, about a half mile from town, to husk and stack corn in "snug piles" to be picked up by a wagon train expected to arrive in a day or so. As the two worked in the field, Emerson stepped from the front door of his house in town. "I saw four mounted Indians ride up to a boy that was picking some ears of green corn; they picked him up and put him on a horse and started off with him." Emerson yelled for help and ran after the kidnappers. He had run only a short distance "when the people in the town halloaed to me to come back; that the whole Indian tribe was coming to town."

When Emerson learned that Patterson and Creevy were alone in the cornfield, he "halloaed" for the citizens to get their guns and follow him. He and a local fellow, Dreyfus, ran toward Patterson's field followed by "12 or 15 Mexicans."

Meanwhile in the cornfield, Patterson and Creevy were shucking and stacking when Patterson spotted a second group of Indians approaching. He shouted to Creevy, "There are Indians. Go for your gun." The two dashed a short distance to a small hillock where they had left their rifles. By this time they were under fire from the advancing Indians. The two began to return the fire, shooting "one at a time to keep one gun loaded." They decided to retreat over the hill, back to town, but when they reached the top, they discovered "a large party of Indians between us and the town, about 15 on horseback," undoubtedly those spotted by Emerson a few minutes before. Then, looking around "across the cornfield," Patterson later testified, "I saw an ox wagon and five Mexicans" surrounded by a third party of about thirty Indians. Creevy and Patterson changed directions and headed across the field to assist the Mexican teamsters. As they crossed the field, they found themselves under fire by a fourth party "on higher ground than those that surrounded the Mexicans." As soon as Patterson and Creevy reached the edge of the field, firing as they went, the Indians surrounding the Mexicans retreated up the hill to join the marksmen there. Patterson reported that several of the Indians were badly hurt and one Mexican wounded.

About this time, Emerson arrived with Dreyfus and the party of Mexicans from town. The Indians withdrew further and raised "a white buckskin flag, up on a lance," about a half mile away. There was "quite a crowd of Indians, about 80 or 100" on the hills a half mile or less from town. They were carrying the flag and had with them the boy who had been captured earlier. They sent the lad with two Indians a little closer to the town, "so we could hear better." According to them, the Indians wanted the boy's father to come and talk. Terrified, the father refused, so they asked for the boy's uncle, José Trujillo, Cañada Alamosa's justice of the peace and mayor.

Eventually, Trujillo, Emerson, and another citizen went "out about half way to where the Indians were." Loco came down with two Indians. One was Francisco, a Mexican and former captive, who did the interpreting. The two sides came within two hundred yards of each other and agreed to lay down their weapons. "We took our guns and stuck them muzzle down in the dirt, and they stuck their lances in the ground and threw off their bows and arrows and started towards us, and we met them about half way."

The group "talked some time," and finally "Loco said they didn't want to fight any more with the people in that town; they said they would go down on the river and kill whoever they pleased; that they wanted to trade with us in Cañada." The deal was that the citizens could have the boy back for forty yards of cotton cloth and three "fanagas" of wheat. The Indians also agreed to return all the horses they had just stolen for six dollars each. Trujillo suggested that they could come in near the town, but only a few could enter the town at one time, and the trading could take place there. For the Indians, this was the dangerous part. Nevertheless, Loco and the others came in, and the agreement was finalized. The town got the boy and the horses back and the Apaches got their calico, corn, and wheat. Most of the Indians remained until "nearly dark, then they left except one or two that stayed in town over night," but Patterson noted that "the hills in the neighborhood of my cornfield showed that there was a large number of Indians in that neighborhood." So began Loco's "cornfield treaty" with Cañada Alamosa.[30]

Betzinez, who would have been about seven years old at the time of the cornfield affair, suggests a different version. He wrote that the arrangement between the Indians and the town began in about 1856, before his birth, when the citizens of Cañada Alamosa captured Nah-thle-tla, the wife of an important Chihenne leader, Tudeevia (Delgadito). Actually, Nah-thle-tla was married first to a man called Shnowin, who was killed in northern Chihuahua, Mexico, in 1855 during a fight in which she was captured, presumably by Mexicans. She escaped a year later, made it back to her relatives at Ojo Caliente, and married Tudeevia's son, Non-i-thian, "the Limper." Apparently lucky in love but slow afoot, she was captured again, this time by the citizens of Cañada Alamosa. According to Betzinez, town officials sent her to contact Loco, who was known to be receptive to peaceful approaches and who had recently signed the peace treaty at Fort

Craig in 1855. Loco and the citizens of the town then negotiated a successful treaty.

Aside from his confusion over the players, the problem with Betzinez's account is that if the agreement with Cañada Alamosa was made in 1856, then the 1867 attack on the town would fly in the face of Betzinez's statement that the treaty was never broken. Nah–thle–tla's tribulations probably took place, and they might have paved the way for the cornfield peace agreement ten years later, but the incident does not appear to have been the basis for Loco's treaty with Cañada Alamosa "that was never broken."[31]

Whatever the circumstances of its origin, the treaty was successful, not because the citizens of Cañada and the Apaches liked or trusted each other but because of the economics of it. The Indians needed a safe place to sell their stolen goods and livestock, and the people of the town made remarkable profits on the deals. About two years later Lieutenant Henry Leggett wrote from nearby Fort McRae, "I was informed that a party of 15 Apaches, mostly squaws, had been in town trading with people. . . . In my opinion the native Mexican citizens of Cañada Alamosa are carrying on an illicit trade with the Apaches by procuring ammunition at Fort Craig or other posts ostensibly to defend themselves [and] this they are trading with the Indians." The cornfield treaty was holding, but the trade in stolen goods and whiskey was about to cause headaches for the army and problems for both the town's citizens and Loco's Apaches.[32]

CHAPTER TWO

In Search of a Good Peace

For the Apaches, it was a time for desperate measures. By the spring of 1869, Loco's people were decimated and demoralized. Almost every family had lost relatives. Uncounted Chiricahua women and children were living as slaves from Santa Fe to Quintana Roo, Mexico. Many of the best men were dead or crippled from wounds. It was common to find a single warrior and hunter supporting ten or more dependents. Armies on both sides of the U.S.-Mexico border were devoted to making the Chiricahuas' lives miserable. Traditional hunting grounds were used up. Ancient homelands were now overcrowded with new settlers. Shattered fragments of Chiricahua bands were mixing with the dispirited remnants of other bands for survival, ignoring old social boundaries between the Chihennes, Nednais, Bedonkohes, and Chokonens. Life as the Apaches had known it was on its last legs.[1]

It is not surprising that Chief Loco rode into Fort Craig, New Mexico, in 1869 with his small band of 100 to 150 Chihennes, asking for sanctuary and something to eat. It was not the chief's intention to set into motion a grand plan to bring the Apache nation and the Americans together in peaceful coexistence. He was a relatively unknown leader of a small group, whose followers were beset by hard times. They had been run ragged, some were hurt, and all were hungry. Loco came in hoping for a permanent peace for his small band of Chihennes.

The Apaches who came in with Loco were probably the survivors of an ambush that took place about a month before they arrived at Fort Craig. Around the middle of March 1869, Captain Henry Corbin and troopers from the Thirty-eighth Infantry tracked an Apache group for five days and then attacked their small *rancheria* while "their fires were still burning, with beef and mescal . . . cooking." The captain reported that he found "a quantity of leather and approximately five hundred pounds of beef, dried and being dried . . . all of which we destroyed." Corbin also noted that his men could find no dead or wounded Apaches but discovered blood in several places.[2]

It is a good bet that it was Loco's rancheria. When Lieutenant Charles Drew later met with Loco's Chihennes, he noted that some of the Indians were still nursing wounds. In their haste to escape, the band abandoned its entire food supply and a stockpile of leather meant to be used to make clothes for the coming winter. Loco's people were destitute.

The incident, or one like it, may have been the last straw for Loco, the one that inspired his decision to make a permanent peace. Captain John Gilmore, commanding Fort McRae, twenty miles south of Fort Craig, doubted it was an honest offer: "I have very little confidence in his [Loco's] sincerity. It is thought that a party of these same Indians might be those committing depredations between Ft. Bowie and Ft. Cummings." Many other Apaches had little confidence in Loco's peace overture. Cochise, Lopez, and Victorio all admitted that they wanted to see how Loco fared before they risked their own skins.[3]

Lieutenant Colonel Cuvier Grover, commanding Fort Craig, found the small, ragged group no cause for concern. On June 2, Grover made an offhand mention of Loco's arrival in a letter to Colonel George Getty, commanding the District of New Mexico. "An Apache Indian named Locs," he wrote, "the chief of two small rancherias numbering 20 men able to carry arms and heretofore hostile," had come into the post proposing a peace deal. Five days later Grover again wrote to Getty, providing a detail not included in his June 2 letter. The Apaches wanted out of the fray and onto a reservation. "The Brevet major directs me to inform you that a small rancheria of Apache Indians, numbering about 20 warriors, and headed by their chief Loco, have offered to surrender themselves to the Commanding Officer at Fort Craig with a view of them being placed on an Indian reservation." There was no response from Getty.

Without instructions for dealing with peaceful Indians, Grover declined Loco's offer to surrender. Accepting a surrender would have forced Grover to feed the Indians as prisoners, something he was unwilling to do even though Fort Craig was a major supply depot. He told Loco that if he stayed out of mischief, he need not worry about attacks from the army.

He sent the chief and his famished band packing, with neither rations nor sympathy.

By the time Grover mailed his letters to Colonel Getty in Santa Fe, Loco was making a similar offer to Captain Gilmore at Fort McRae. Gilmore was more sympathetic to the starving Indians and gave Loco a little food, but he wanted authorization from his superiors before he started a wholesale feeding program. He wrote to Getty on June 22 that "two parties of Apaches" (Loco and Loco's son-in-law, Salvador) were camping across the river from Fort McRae and seeking peace. "I request information as to what will be done with the Miembres [sic] Apaches who visited this post peaceably, requesting to be furnished with rations. I have on two occasions issued rations to nine of them. . . . They state their desire to remain in camp opposite this post on the west side of the Rio Grande. If they do so, I expect they will be constantly after rations and respectfully request information as to whether I shall supply them." He was right. Loco returned to the post asking for food twice in the following month. Again, Colonel Getty did not respond.[4]

By May 1869 the word was out that Loco was surrendering. Loco's Warm Springs band, which had been unable to draw a raised eyebrow from Colonel Grover at Fort Craig, suddenly became the focus of national attention. The *Santa Fe New Mexican* published two articles announcing the news: "The mail rider going south reports that Salvador (son of Mangas Coloradas) and another chief of the Mimbres Apaches [undoubtedly Loco] with a detachment of their followers were at the town of Cañada Alamosa, on the Rio Grande and said they were going to Fort Craig to ask for peace and that they would assemble the tribe with the view of bringing them in." The second article announced Loco's arrival at Craig: "We hear the Indians are trying to make peace at Fort Craig."[5]

Although Getty did not bother to respond to any of the dispatches regarding the Indians' surrender, Gilmore's letter of June 22 drew his immediate attention—especially the part about Loco's Apaches wanting peace on a reservation. On July 3, 1869, Getty notified Major William Clinton, New Mexico's superintendent of Indian affairs, that the army had some peaceful Apaches camped at Fort McRae, and he requested that someone from "the Indian Department be sent to induce them to remove to a permanent reservation." In turn, Clinton quickly advised the commissioner of Indian affairs, Ely Parker. In an unusual burst of speed, Parker designated First Lieutenant Charles E. Drew as the new agent for the Southern Apaches. By July 20, Drew was on his way to the territories with orders to proceed to Fort Bayard and "endeavor to communicate with the Southern Apache Tribes of Indians." He arrived in Apache country about the third week in August, authorized "to stop at any place on the road to Fort Bayard, providing I could enter into communications with the Indians."[6]

The government's extraordinary excitement was the result of a bureaucratic furor that was taking place in Washington at the time of Loco's surrender. In a happy coincidence for the Apaches, when Ulysses S. Grant assumed the presidency on March 4, 1869, he immediately established an Indian peace policy. A bitter fracas over the administration of the policy followed. While Loco was looking for victuals at Forts Craig and McRae, the Board of Indian Commissioners was embroiled in an ugly quarrel with the Indian Office over control of Grant's new peace plan. Ironically, peace with the Indians, in one form or another, was on everyone's mind at the very time Loco came in to talk peace.[7]

If he knew, Colonel Getty did not notify Captain Gilmore that his letter had started a rush to make a deal with Loco, and apparently he did not let Gilmore know that Drew was on the way. On August 12, just before Drew arrived, Gilmore sent another letter to remind Getty he had some starving Apaches on his hands: "Loco, the chief of the Miembres Apaches has been in this post twice [more], he is now located on the Cuchillo Negro about ten miles from this post with 13 women and children and 17 men [probably Loco's immediate family]. . . . He states through an interpreter that he is anxious and desirous to be placed on a reservation."[8]

Meanwhile, Drew reached the vicinity of Forts Craig and McRae. When he found Loco's peaceful Indians camped near the fort, munching short rations (about half the soldiers' fare) and requesting a reservation, he reckoned that McRae was an excellent place "to communicate with the Southern Apache Tribes of Indians." Nevertheless, he hesitated to drop in unannounced on the tough-looking group across the river. "In my opinion no better place could be had to negotiate with them than this (Ft. McRae); [but] should you go out to them with troops, they will hide, and if you go alone you are not apt to return." He checked in with Captain Gilmore. The captain found a few Mexicans who were willing to take a request for Loco to come in for talks with the new agent.[9]

It took three days for Loco to respond. He probably needed the delay to assess his support and to gauge what other leaders in the vicinity might do. At this point, no one trusted anyone. But despite the prevailing paranoia, the meeting with Drew came off without a hitch. Loco arrived accompanied by three men and four women. Through interpreters, he emphasized that he was willing to stop all raiding and that he could speak for "all his tribe." It is unclear whether he meant all the Chihennes or just his Warm Springs people. He told Drew that the group wanted "peace, and a good peace, and no lie." He reported that others would come in as soon as they saw "what becomes of Loco." Drew wrote to Commissioner Parker that "Loco promised to remain camped where he now is, until I hear from this letter and know your wishes."

Of greater interest to Drew were Loco's comments about Cochise, whom Drew described as "the most daring robber and bloodthirsty of the Apaches." Loco reported that the famous leader "said he would come in and join him [Loco] as soon as a treaty was made but he wished to be satisfied that there is no treachery about it, and that if he comes in he will not be betrayed and killed as his people have been in times past."[10]

During the meeting, Loco told Drew that the Apaches needed a protected reservation if the Americans wanted to settle the conflict with them. Drew included Loco's proposition in his September 3 letter to the commissioner:

> In speaking of what they wanted, Loco says they want to plant near the Cuchillo Negro, where they used to plant before they were driven away; also to hunt on the east side of the Mimbres mountains as far south as old Fort Thorn, and as far as the mountains east of the Rio Grande, known as the Sierra de Caballos [just east of the river], and to a distance of 20 miles north of Fort McRae. They want the fort left here for their protection. They appear very willing to make peace, and I think that with proper care and by treating them honestly and justly, the whole of the Apache tribes may be brought in from the warpath . . .[11]

At first blush, Loco's proposed reservation appears to be sizable, approximately forty by sixty miles. However, when Victorio's and Lopez's bands joined the Warm Springs band in November, the head count went into the neighborhood of four hundred. Furthermore, Apaches from all over liked what they saw happening in Loco's territory and began to move into the area. A year after the chief's first meeting with Drew, the commissioner of Indian affairs reported to Congress that fifteen hundred formerly hostile Apaches were camped peacefully with Loco's people. Such estimates were often inflated in order to justify larger ration issues; in reality there were probably no more than thirteen hundred

Chihennes and Chokonens together in 1869. But even with half that population on the reservation proposed by Loco, the Apaches could not survive without hefty government subsidies. On short rations and with no sundries in sight, Drew noted that six months after the chief's band arrived at Fort McRae, the groups were already beginning to scatter in a hunt for game to supplement the scanty rations he was able to issue. "The Indians remained in camp near Cañada Alamosa with the exception of a few under Victorio that have gone to the Rio Cuchillo Negro to hunt and Loco says they were compelled to separate in order to find game enough to sustain themselves as the amount issued by the government is insufficient."

Even before additional bands began moving into the area, things were tight for Loco's Chihennes. Drew, in his letter to Commissioner Parker of September 3, 1869, reported that Loco "says he is contented to wait a month [until October] to hear from the Great Father. . . . I would beg that if anything is to be done with them, it be done as soon as possible." Time was critical for the Apaches. October marked the onset of colder weather, and the Indians were still in their summer clothing when Loco brought up the deadline. The Apache lifestyle did not afford the luxury of storing winter garb for the next season. With the late summer raiding parties canceled or failed, the Apaches needed cold-weather gear and blankets and, more urgently, something to eat. By this time in the season, the band should have had several hundred pounds of dried meat stored to supplement its winter hunting, and enough tanned leather to provide winter clothing. Captain Corbin and the Thirty-eighth Infantry's attack in March had destroyed all that.[12]

Drew's correspondence in late September had a ring of desperation: "Since my arrival here I have had two interviews with three of their chiefs, Loco, Victorio, and Lopez. They are willing to go on a reservation . . . [but] it will be necessary for me to give them bread and meat. They are now hunting near Hot Springs. . . . it is necessary for something to be done for them. They are destitute of clothing."[13]

September came and went. Still Drew received neither instructions for himself nor so much as a hardtack biscuit for the Indians. Consequently, on October 10 he held a meeting at Cañada Alamosa to reassure the Chihenne leaders, Loco, Victorio, Lopez, and Chastine. The meeting got off to a bad start. Just as the lieutenant spotted the leaders with forty warriors about a mile from town, a posse of armed citizens blundered into Cañada Alamosa, searching for Indians who had recently killed a woman and child near Pinos Altos, a village to the southwest. They admitted they had not tracked the killers but had assumed it was the Apaches around Warm Springs.

After Drew insisted, the disgruntled posse withdrew from town without incident. To save the day, Drew and his interpreter rode out to the forty Apaches, who were poised to fight or scatter, and invited them to come in for the parley, but "I could not get them into town." Even after the vigilantes left, "the Indians took every precaution to prevent a surprise and were very restless. . . . It is impossible to get near them with soldiers, they are so suspicious. . . . All the warriors I have seen are young and hardy and a great many of them have been wounded."[14]

At the enlarged meeting on the outskirts of town, Drew observed that Loco did all the talking. The purpose of the meeting was apparently to reassure the Apaches that food and blankets were on the way and to convince the Indians to hang around a bit longer. Loco again extended the deadline, this time until January 10, and threw in an additional incentive: "All will come in from the warpath if their Great Father will give them food and clothing." But he warned, "I must hear pretty soon." Drew had nothing to offer the chief in return and was hard pressed to explain the government's inaction.[15]

After the meeting, Drew once again wrote to Clinton: "Loco says he will keep what there now is [of the Apaches] together where they now are . . . and will also try and get as many more of them as he can. I am certain Loco means peace, but he will have hard work to keep some of them [at peace], as I believe Victorio is not disposed to do if he can keep enough warriors with him. At present he has a very small band, and can do nothing unless some of the others get discontented. . . . A beginning must be made if anything is to be done, and . . . now is the time to do it."[16]

Still there came no reply from Getty, Clinton, Parker, or anyone else in the government. The Indians' condition was worsening by the day. At the end of his string, an anxious Drew penned another note on December 1: "I hardly know what to do. It is certain they must be fed regularly, or they must steal or starve. I believe they would do as near right as any of them do if placed on a reservation. The position I am in is very unpleasant, not being able to promise them anything. . . . I would respectfully request that you lay this matter before the Department with the request that some action be taken immediately. . . . I have given them some corn but as yet no meat."[17]

Again there was no reply. After waiting another twenty-five days, Drew sought help from an old friend, the new commandant at Fort McRae,

Captain George Shorkley. He convinced Shorkley to write Colonel Getty. Shorkley's note pointed out that Drew had negotiated a peace deal with Loco and other leaders, had straightaway reported the terms to Clinton and Parker, and had asked for instructions and supplies to complete the bargain. He emphasized that Drew had repeatedly requested instructions, but "he informs me that he has not received even an acknowledgment of the receipt of his communications, much less the instructions asked for."[18] He applauded Drew's efforts, remarking that Drew had acted "with a most commendable zeal [and] has repeatedly visited them [the Apaches] and remained over night in their camp or village, and has so far kept them in patient waiting, although they have greatly needed these issues." Shorkley even praised the Apaches, noting that they "have faithfully kept every condition of the agreement . . . but they expect issues of clothing, blankets &s., as agreed upon."[19]

By January 1, 1870, Drew again visited the Indian camp and estimated that the number of Apaches had dropped to about three hundred, under the leadership of Loco and a few others. All expressed a willingness to do whatever was required, but just before he left to meet with the leaders, a problem developed. Drew was informed that stock had been stolen from San José, in Grant County. The citizens blamed Loco's band.

"I informed Loco of the fact," Drew later wrote to Clinton. "He denied any knowledge . . . and sent Salvadore . . . and ten or twelve others to look for the trail." On the following day, Salvador reported that he had tracked the stolen cattle and that Navajos or Mexicans were the culprits. He also offered to lead Drew or someone else to track down the rustlers and prove that the Apaches were innocent. Relieved, Drew complained that "Mexican thieves are continually stealing from the citizens along the Rio Grande and then start in pursuit of the Indians. This is a notorious fact."[20]

Despite Shorkley's appeal to Colonel Getty on Drew's behalf, still no supplies arrived for the Apaches, and still Drew received no orders. As Loco's January 10 deadline approached, Drew gave it one last try. On January 5 he wrote once more to Superintendent Clinton, emphasizing that he had received no instructions, blankets, or food to keep the Apaches in place after the tenth. "Most of those found in camp are women and children, and their destitute condition should not fail to excite the commiseration of any who see them."[21]

At the last moment, just after Drew wrote his letter, the financial cavalry arrived. Drew received a niggardly $2,800 to feed, clothe, and otherwise supply approximately three hundred Apaches. It was just enough to prevent what might have been a rousing outbreak from the camp. Although most of the Apaches remained in the Cañada Alamosa area, they were a disgruntled lot. The outlook for a long-standing peace was diminished, and the Americans' resolve was called into question. Yet at this point the Apaches probably had little choice except to remain at Ojo Caliente, at least until spring. On the basis of promises of food, clothing, and other items, they had delayed their usual raiding trips to Mexico. By the time the Loco-Drew deal had apparently failed, it was well into winter. The Indians were without food. They had no warm clothes, blankets, or four-footed transportation—they had eaten their mules and horses. For all practical purposes, the option of leaving Fort McRae for better pickings was gone by December.

Whatever the Apaches' reasons for staying—whether a sincere desire for peace, Loco's charisma, or lack of choice—stay they did, hungry, freezing, and unhappy. For twenty-one years the Americans had sought to put the Apaches in the mood to make peace. When Loco dropped the opportunity into their laps in May 1869, the government lapsed into tight-lipped inaction, apparently neither able to do the deal nor willing to explain its inertia.[22]

To understand the situation, it is necessary to leave the dusty New Mexico countryside and venture into the sinister streets of New York. Blame for the army and Indian Office's inaction falls directly on the doorstep of two New York millionaires who knew nothing about Lieutenant Drew's problems at Fort McRae, had no interest in the Indian Office or its predicament, and knew little or nothing about Chiricahuas.

When President Grant took office, federal finances were in a mess. "Greenback dollars," first issued as an emergency war measure in 1861, were immensely unpopular. The public generally considered paper money to be all but worthless. The country was wobbling toward bankruptcy. The urgency was such that Grant's first act as president was to sign legislation to pay off federal bonds and redeem the greenbacks in gold or its equivalent.

On that news, railroad tycoons Jay Gould and Jim Fisk developed a grandiose gambit to amass as much gold as possible at the lowest conceivable price, drive up the value, and then sell it to the government at the inflated stock exchange price. On September 20, 1869, with gold selling for around $125 an ounce, Gould and Fisk began an awe-inspiring forty-million-dollar buying spree that shot gold prices into the neighborhood of $162 within days. Droves of speculators joined in an unbridled buying frenzy.

Secretary of the Treasury George Boutwell spotted the frenetic activity in the market, recognized what Gould and Fisk were up to, and informed Grant. The president quickly ordered up to $4 million in gold reserves unloaded onto the market. When word hit the Wall Street Gold Room, the price of gold plummeted to $133 in a matter of minutes. In the ensuing Panic of 1869, thousands of investors lost everything, several brokerage firms went bankrupt, businesses all over the country failed, banks were mobbed and closed, and suicides were rampant. The federal government teetered on insolvency.[23]

The "Black Friday" market collapse took place on September 24, 1869, just three weeks after Charles Drew penned his first request for food and supplies to seal the peace deal with Loco. Black Friday and the subsequent financial disaster brought all government business to an immediate halt. Neither expenditures nor payments were approved. A congressional committee investigating the panic later concluded that "for many weeks the business of the whole country was paralyzed." With no money on which to operate, the army and Indian Office lapsed into a catatonic paralysis and suspended any shipment of supplies to back up the peace deal with Loco. There was simply no money with which Drew might buy food and blankets, and no one in Washington could tell Getty, Clinton, Parker, or Drew when there would be. Aside from nearly collapsing the government and ruining thousands of American business-men and farmers, the Gould and Fisk scheme practically starved four hundred Apaches and almost wrecked the country's fledgling peace ini-tiative with the Chiricahuas.[24]

As a result of Loco's dogged determination to remain at peace despite the food crisis, he would henceforth be known as the Apaches' primary proponent of peace. Nevertheless, by the time the federal bureaucrats caught their breath and sent the $2,800 to bail out Drew and Loco, support for Loco's peace plan had waned among the Chiricahuas. The more militant leaders regained some of their following, and everyone looked suspiciously at peace with the Americans. Although many of the Indians remained in place near Fort McRae, they never fully trusted the government again.

CHAPTER THREE

Chaos at Cañada Alamosa

Contrary to the government's best intentions, Chief Loco and Charles Drew's agreement set off a period of chaos in southwestern New Mexico and turned the area around Cañada Alamosa into a hotbed of criminal activity. News that the Warm Springs band and other Chiricahuas were peacefully settled near Fort McRae attracted a seedy collection of whiskey sellers, bounty hunters, and toughs looking for trouble. Unscrupulous land speculators, oft-bumbling bureaucrats, and uninformed do-gooders added to the pandemonium. They all, good and bad alike, wanted to do something to, for, with, or about the formerly fierce Apaches.

Ironically, horse thieves after Indian livestock were among the first troublemakers to collect near Cañada Alamosa. Drew wrote: "These [Mexican and American] thieves hang around the camp of the Indians to see what marks and brands are on their animals, and then claim them as their property. This trick has been exposed on two occasions, and gives me a great deal of trouble . . . to keep down misunderstanding [on the part of the Indians]."[1]

A more serious variety of trouble came from Chihuahua, Mexico, where a cash-for-scalps policy remained in effect. Bounty hunters began making for Alamosa, where they viewed the encamped Indians as easy targets. These mercenaries kept the Apaches justifiably edgy and raised the hackles of American officials who were on the verge of convincing the Indians that settling down was a safe thing to do. Drew complained about the hostile incursions: "Scouting parties from Chihuahua who are paid a premium for Indian scalps are also allowed to hunt for Indians in the Territory [New Mexico]. . . . People, too, [presumably white Americans] hunt Indians only for a few paltry dollars they receive for the scalps. . . . A friendly Indian [scalp] is worth as much as . . . any others."[2]

Probably more concerned about American sovereignty than Apache scalps, headquarters in Santa Fe responded to Drew's letter with orders to commanders of all southwestern posts, including Forts McRae, Cummings, Bayard, and Selden, that "armed parties of Mexicans entering the United States for any purpose whatever . . . will be arrested and disarmed."[3]

Illegal traders added to the disorder. It had been illegal to trade with Apaches without a federal license since the 1850s. The purpose of the license was to keep men of bad repute from trading contraband goods to the Apaches—guns, lead for bullets, powder, liquor, and most anything else the Indians fancied. Putting the kindest possible face on these restrictions, they also prevented the scoundrels from cheating Indians. More significantly from the government's viewpoint, the regulations hampered the Indians' ability to sell booty stolen on raids—rustled cattle and horses, captives, and other valuables. Government officials saw illegal traders as archfiends, much the way drug dealers are viewed today, but the Apaches loved these men. The traders made literally anything the average Chihenne might want available at some of the best bargains in the illegal trading business. The trade in illegal merchandise was also a good deal for the local townspeople. Lieutenant Argalus Hennisee, who later replaced Drew, observed, "I think that I can safely say that nearly every Mexican on the Rio Grande between Socorro and Mesilla who has much property has made it by trading with Indians."[4]

Probably nothing caused more trouble than the government's close-fisted rationing program. Food was the keynote issue for the Apaches when Loco initially surrendered at Fort Craig. Craig had been a center for distributing military supplies since the Civil War and was overflowing with one hundred thousand daily rations at the time of Loco's visit. Victuals would be a determining factor in the course of events for the next two years and arguably for the next forty.[5]

When the Indian Office finally decided that it was legal to feed the Apaches, desk-bound officials in Washington dismissed warnings that the Apaches "could not hunt much for fear of being killed by whites" and ordered field officers to continue issuing half rations. A half ration amounted to the equivalent of two present-day McDonald's "quarter pounders," without trimmings, and one-half loaf of bread per week. It was not much. It was inferior food, and it would not keep the Apaches happy for long. It did, however, prevent a full-fledged uprising, at least for a while.[6]

Complicating the dietary picture was the fact that the mainstay of military rations during the 1860s and 1870s was salted pork. The Chiricahuas, especially the Warm Springs band, refused to allow a dollop of pig meat to pass their lips. They had seen wild peccaries dining on snakes, and anything that ate snakes would never see the inside of an Apache. It was a lesson that officials never seemed to learn. After receiving rations, the Chihennes would leave piles of bacon, salt-cured hamhocks, and other salted pork products on the wayside to be scooped up by civilians and troops who were not so particular. Eventually, their agents adjusted to the Chiricahuas' dietary quirks and began issuing beef-only rations, but until then the Americans' lack of cultural awareness heightened tension at the early critical stages of the peace.[7]

The army and the Indian Office kept the Apaches on half rations for almost eighteen months, in part because little public sentiment, if any, existed in favor of feeding the Indians at all. With the national economy teetering on collapse, the public viewed with enormous contempt the idea of feeding Indians to keep them from stealing. After all, the financial crash of 1869 left thousands of white Americans without work and with no inkling of where their next meal was coming from. No one in the government was offering to feed the unemployed even half rations. Feeding the Apaches any amount, therefore, seemed more than generous.[8]

Consequently, while both Apaches and Americans avowed their good intentions, American penny-pinching on food and clothing led some of the Indians in Loco's camp back to raiding for the necessities of life. Notwithstanding the chief's best efforts, many who would have preferred peace slipped away from Fort McRae, including members of Loco's family. The chief's son-in-law, Salvador, and several friends joined Cochise on an extended raiding venture in November 1870. In February 1871, Salvador was with another raiding party that stole sixteen horses from the Fort Bayard community.[9] Things turned sour after the February raid when thirty citizens armed with army-issued rifles chased down the raiders and killed fourteen, including Salvador and two others from Loco's group. Despite such losses, raiding parties continued to draw some participants from Loco's band.[10]

It appears that few Chihennes were involved in the slash-and-burn raids, though. More often, individuals and families did little more than swipe a few vegetables from local gardens. Richard Patterson, the central figure in the cornfield treaty of 1867, complained that Indians were once again damaging his fields. Patterson took Hennisee on a tour of his plundered acreage. Hennisee found that "a large quantity of corn had been taken, and . . . I was convinced that it had been taken by the Indians." Later, when Hennisee returned to the fields, he "saw Chief Victorio and his family, about fifty yards from one of the fields, cooking and eating corn which evidently had just been taken from the field that morning." Cornfield robberies became so rampant that farmers encouraged the Indians to steal from their neighbors in the hope of saving their own crops. This encouragement only boosted the number of vegetable raids.[11]

In the fall of 1870, during a visit by Special Agent William Arny, Hennisee questioned Loco, Victorio, Cochise, and several other leaders about these indiscretions and specifically asked about recent minor stock thefts in the vicinity. Flatly denying any illegal conduct, Loco blamed Nednai raiders from Mexico. He finally confessed that "peaceful" Apaches had occasionally left the Cañada Alamosa area to raid, but he pointed to paltry rations and hunger as the problem.

Hennisee asked Loco and Victorio if they had not stolen some mules from Mesilla about three months earlier. Loco responded, "Three young fellows from below [Mexico] stole the animals from below and sold them to the Apaches here, and Apaches sold them to the Mexicans at that town." Hennisee asked, "What do you get from the Mexicans for animals?" Loco replied, "Corn, wheat, manta [a rough cotton cloth]."

At this point one might think the Americans should have connected the Indians' raiding with the need for food (corn and wheat) and clothing (manta). Instead, Hennisee switched to his personal obsession, Indian drinking and illegal traders. "Don't you also get whiskey?" he asked. "No," Loco lied—the Apaches were getting hard liquor on demand at Cañada Alamosa. Hennisee: "I saw an Indian drunk this morning." Loco: "He got drunk on tiswin and not whiskey." Perhaps it was true, but the illegal whiskey vendors in the area were doing a booming business around the Indian camps.

At the conclusion of the conference, Loco admitted to the stock thefts but again explained the need for extra food. Hennisee wrote, "They said the stolen stock was eaten because they were hungry, or traded to the Mexicans for something to cover their nakedness; that they did not have any of the stolen animals in their possession, and asked that it should be forgotten in that they intended to behave better in the future."[12]

The meeting with Loco, Victorio, and Cochise convinced Arny that the government's half-ration policy and the Indians' raiding were related.

Just after his visit to Cañada Alamosa in late 1870, he reported the Apaches' condition to Vincent Colyer, corresponding secretary for the Board of Indian Commissioners. Colyer declared to Secretary of the Interior Columbus Delano that Hennisee's success in collecting Apaches at Fort McRae, even at half rations, proved "beyond question" that with larger appropriations, "the whole of the Apaches might long before this, have been brought into peaceful relations with the government."

Secretary Delano was convinced and requested $30,000 to "subsist, maintain peace, and promote civilization among them." As usual, the Indian Office groused about budget shortages and failed to provide any funds. Colyer then asked whether the War Department "cannot promptly issue an order for their officers commanding the Department of New Mexico to subsist the Apache Indians. . . . The President says the War Department has the power to issue such an order." Consequently, President Grant shifted the feeding of the Apaches back to the army. The Indians with Loco started receiving increased rations in January 1871. "The ration issue to adult Indians will consist of one pound of meat and one pound of breadstuff, two quarts of salt to each hundred rations, and four pounds of soap to a hundred rations once a week." It was an improvement, but it was still less than a full ration of food for a soldier.[13]

Despite the skimpy rations, when Hennisee replaced Drew in early July 1870, approximately 360 Chihennes were camped near Fort McRae. Orlando Piper took over the agency from Hennisee in late October 1870. By March 1871, only five months later, and three months after the start of better rations, the new agent claimed that the number had grown to more than a thousand. Piper probably exaggerated the count to get more rations for the Indians. Still, the number of Apaches wanting in on Loco's peace was increasing daily. Hennisee believed that additional rations would entice even more Apaches, possibly even Cochise himself. Piper's announcement about the larger number inspired General John Pope, commanding the Department of the Missouri, to tell Loco, Nana, and Victorio in April 1871 that he "was prepared to feed all Apaches who might come in . . . also that they would be cared for and protected."[14]

For a while after January 1871, the increased food was enough to keep the Apaches' disgruntlement at manageable proportions, but it was too little to stop their raiding entirely. If the only raids in New Mexico and Arizona had originated from the camps around Cañada Alamosa, then they might have been curtailed by the increased rations. But even if Agent Piper was correct in reporting the astonishing head count of nineteen hundred Indians at Cañada Alamosa in the fall of 1871—and he undoubtedly was not—some three thousand to four thousand Western and Southern Apaches were still living free in New Mexico, Arizona, and Mexico. Nathaniel Pope, superintendent of Indian affairs for New Mexico, observed that "a great many of the depredations charged to the Apaches of New Mexico are committed by White Mountain, Coyotero, and Tonto Apaches of Arizona and the Sonora Apaches of Old Mexico and by Mexicans." Also, even though Cochise was still dabbling in affairs at Cañada Alamosa, his Chokonens continued with their busy raiding schedule. Depredations by these roaming bands, unaffiliated with Loco, further served to unsettle the already turbulent circumstances near Cañada. The footloose raiders struck and vanished into the mountains, leaving the victims to cast hard looks at the Apaches camped with Loco. Additionally confusing the issue of who was doing what, the outside bands often drifted into and out of Loco's camp to visit relatives, receive a few rations, and assess the Chihennes' state of affairs. Many of the transient guests also raided a ranch or two on the way over and brought along their spoils, leaving tracks of stolen stock leading directly into the Chihenne camps.[15]

Most Americans, who could not distinguish one band of Apaches from another, believed that any raid by any band, anywhere, implicated all Apaches. The petty filching by Loco's Apaches, combined with the continued raiding by other bands, led citizens in the territory to conclude that the Cañada Alamosa reserve was a "feeding station" for the raiders.[16] In July 1871, Grant County Judge Richard Hudson wrote that "what we want to know is ... if we are to be forever at the mercy of these thieving, murderous Apaches who have a house of refuge at Alamosa ... because the citizens of this country are determined to put a stop to it ... and if they carry out their programme, the Camp Grant Massacre [of April 1871] will be thrown entirely in the shade." It was a constant threat and not one the Apaches could ignore.[17]

Much of the settlers' discontent probably stemmed from the Chokonen rowdies with Cochise. In the ten years since the 1861 Bascom affair, raiding by Apaches under Cochise's leadership had made him a larger-than-life legend. He probably did not commit all the villainy attributed to him, but he was certainly responsible for many attacks on Americans and their property. While Loco negotiated to gain the Americans' trust, Chokonen raiders were on an unprecedented campaign against Americans. Historian Ed Sweeney wrote of the period, "In 1869 and 1870, Cochise spent much of his time in southern Arizona. It was no coincidence that these years were two of the bloodiest in southern Arizona history." A report from one legislative committee bemoaned the fact that Apaches were "now in more active hostility than at any time since the Territory has been under the American flag [1848]."[18]

But at the same time he was raiding, Cochise was also shopping for his own peaceful settlement with the Americans. He had made several overtures in the years since 1868 and showed increased interest after Loco surrendered in 1869. Just as the Chihennes settled in, Cochise began nosing about Cañada Alamosa to see what he might squeeze out of Loco's deal. Government officials saw him in Loco's camp at least ten times between late 1869 and 1872, and sometimes he stayed for months.[19]

The first documented sighting of Cochise came in December 1869, shortly after the Chihennes arrived at Fort McRae. He passed the word then that he would come in if Loco survived the peace experiment. Ultimately, Cochise made a series of trips to the area to keep tabs on Loco's progress and see how the Indians fared. His contacts with Loco were keenly followed and encouraged by the Americans, who hoped that if the influential Cochise came in, others would follow suit. In January 1869, Lieutenant Colonel Thomas Devin candidly expressed his thoughts about the possibility of Cochise's joining Loco: "He [Cochise] is undoubtedly the ablest Indian in Arizona, and could be made very useful [for enticing other Apaches to come in peacefully] if it were found that he could be trusted."[20]

The visiting Chokonens eventually wore out their welcome with their Chihenne cousins. Agent Piper wrote to Major Shorkley at Fort McRae on February 29, 1872, "Things are moderately quiet at the present. We have a 'poco' [small] war. Cochise's band and Loco's band had one or two pitched battles with two or three killed and as many wounded." Cochise hung around for another month or so, but the conflict between in-laws slowed the flow of Chokonen guests into the Chihenne camps. Nevertheless, Cochise's frequent and often publicized stops at Cañada left the impression that the Indians with Loco were part and parcel of the worst rash of raiding in years.[21]

American officials were convinced that the red-hot trade in illegal liquor was the basis for the turmoil that surrounded the Apaches at Ojo Caliente. Except for food, firearms, and ammunition, no other item was more sought after by the Indians, more profitable for illegal businessmen, or a greater cause of concern for the government. Officials believed that the Apaches' fondness for alcohol led to intensified raiding to acquire items to trade for liquor. William Clinton noted, "So long as these people [the Mexicans in Cañada Alamosa] trade with the Indians . . . just so long will the Indians be thieves and uncontrollable by the Agent." Almost anything the Apaches brought in might be traded for a few gulps of whiskey. The profits were huge. Some of the Mexican residents of Cañada Alamosa amassed large herds of horses and cattle or stocked their stores with government-issued blankets, clothes, and tinned goods in exchange for a few bottles of blue ruin.[22]

For the first few months after Loco came in, drinking by the Indians received little official attention. This might have been because Charles Drew was reputed to be a heavy drinker himself and was not entirely convinced that a stiff drink was a bad thing. This changed with the arrival of two federally approved and licensed traders, Thomas Jeffords and Elias Brevoort, in January 1870. A rift quickly developed between the two traders and Lieutenant Drew when Drew attempted to rein in their freewheeling deals with the Apaches. Also, word was out that the agent's position was returning to civilian control in the next few months, and Jeffords might have been attempting to position himself to apply for the job. Whatever the motivation, Jeffords and Brevoort set about to smear Drew's character. In the process they dragged Chief Loco into the dispute.

On March 8, 1870, the two traders sent an inflammatory letter to Lieutenant Drew accusing him not only of supplying Loco with whiskey but also of sharing it with him and several other Apaches. The two claimed that when Loco returned, tipsy and exhausted, to Cañada Alamosa from Fort McRae on March 3, he demanded a drink at Jeffords and Brevoort's trading post. The two storekeepers claimed that what followed implicated the lieutenant in doling out firewater to the Indians. According to the two, when Loco attempted to buy a bottle, they refused him, saying "that if the agent, or great father at Washington knew we gave, or sold him or his tribe whisky we would be removed from here." At that point, the traders claimed, Loco became angry and said he could not understand why they would refuse to get him whiskey when Lieutenant Drew had acquired four bottles of whiskey for him and several other Apaches at Fort McRae the night before, and drank it along with them. "We hope his statement may prove untrue though at the same time, the fact of his becoming so angry and being so much excited is almost proof that his statement is correct."[23]

Drew responded to the allegations quickly, attached the Jeffords-Brevoort letter, and sent the epistles to Superintendent Clinton. "I do not imagine that these gentlemen believe what they say and hence am at a loss to account for their action. I will state to you that there is not the slightest foundation for the story. So far from giving 'Loco' whiskey, I took the trouble to go with him until he passed through Alamsita [*sic*] for the express purpose of preventing him from getting any." Drew concluded with a parting shot: "I . . . am compelled therefore to request that their appointment be revoked." Clinton forwarded the letter to Commissioner of Indian Affairs Ely Parker in Washington, and Parker asked Colonel George Getty to launch an investigation. Getty, in turn, ordered Captain Shorkley at Fort McRae to root out the facts.[24]

Shorkley ran a tough inquiry, obtaining statements from Frank Frenger, the post trader at Fort McRae, and Robert Patterson, who interviewed Loco in Spanish. Frenger said he was the only one selling whiskey legally in the area. He had seen Drew refuse Loco's request for liquor and had heard him warn others, presumably Jeffords and Brevoort, against granting it. Patterson reported that he had gone with Drew to Cañada Alamosa and asked Loco about the matter. "He [Loco] said the statement was false, that he had not said so [asked for liquor] and did not get any whiskey. There was no mistaking his meaning in this, Loco talks very bad Spanish and it is often difficult to understand him."

Shorkley concluded on March 29, 1870: "It seems positive that Loco did not get the whiskey as stated. I saw Loco in the evening of the [March] 3rd instant soon after he came to the post [Fort McRae] and while he was there I thought under the influence of liquor. Agent Drew took him to his quarters and kept him and his party over night. I again saw him the next morning and Loco was entire sober and was so when he left the post. . . . Loco may have been misunderstood by Jeffords and Brevoort as he denies their statement. From my personal knowledge of the condition of Lieut. Drew's Agency I have no hesitancy in stating that I give his statement full credence."

Responding to Drew's recommendation of April 15, about two weeks after receiving Shorkley's report, Clinton issued Order Number 1, revoking Jeffords and Brevoort's trader's license. Brevoort filed an appeal in which he noted, "Lt. Drew personally stated he did not personally like Mr. Brevoort." The appeal was denied.[25]

The controversy over Drew's drinking, his character, and his adminis-tration of the Apaches' affairs was rendered moot during the first few days of June 1870, when William Clinton received a letter from H. D. Hall, a citizen of Paraje, New Mexico. Hall wrote on June 5, 1870:

Lieutenant Drew died this morning under the following circum-stances. The Indians (Mescaleros) run [*sic*] off the herd belonging

to J. H. Whittington's train. Lt. Drew with Lt. Hunter and fifteen
men started after them and when in the mountains could not
find water. Lt. Drew with five men started back for this place.
One of the men was left in the mountains and is supposed to
have perished. All the others came in safe but Drew. He must
have been within eight or ten miles from this place when he
got lost and he has been wandering there for nearly forty
hours. This morning the party sent out to find him, found
him—he was alive but very weak. They gave him water and
stimulants but could not revive him. After carrying him about
four miles, he died in the men's arms. From the time he left the
mountains until this morning (nearly four days) he was without
water. His body was brought in a few minutes ago and will be
sent to Fort Craig for interment. His effects and papers are here
and will be turned over to the Commanding Officer of Fort
Craig. [Signed] H. D. Hall.[26]

Drew's death shocked everyone concerned, but it had virtually no
effect on the subsequent course of events. Even if he had survived, under
the president's new policy of civil administration of Indian affairs, a civilian
would have had his job as agent for the Southern Apaches within four
months. Old Chief Loco later remembered Drew as the best agent the
Apaches ever knew.[27]

CHAPTER FOUR

Forced to Tularosa

In the four-month interlude before the new civilian agent arrived, thirty-one-year-old First Lieutenant Argalus Hennisee was sent to fill Drew's position. During his tenure at Fort McRae, Hennisee dropped the focus on additional food for the Indians and concentrated with missionary zeal on ending the illegal sale of alcohol to his charges.[1]

To stop the manufacture of tiswin, Hennisee issued flour instead of corn. The venture did not stop the flow of tiswin, but it did increase the corn crop robberies. In September 1870, he also moved to end the "illegal traffic in whiskey, powder, lead, percussion caps, manta &c which a large portion of the Mexican population of the country at and within the distance of sixty miles from Cañada Alamosa, N.M., have been engaged in with the Indians under my charge."[2]

When Hennisee learned that "José Trujillo, the Justice of the Peace [and mayor], and Juan Montoya, the constable [for Cañada Alamosa] . . . were the principal [illegal] traders," he raided Trujillo's house, dumped out a thirty-gallon barrel of booze, and arrested the judge and the constable. Unfortunately for Hennisee, his bust went awry. He reported: "Trujillo and Montoya, by virtue of their official positions, summoned a Posse Comitatus of about forty Mexicans, who were at hand for the purpose, and disarmed my party of men, which consisted of my interpreter, three soldiers and Lieut. Thomas Blair." Hennisee later tried to put the best face possible on a bungled operation: "The whole affair appears ridiculous, but as I succeeded in destroying a large portion of whiskey which they had on hand, I would again do as I did."[3]

After Hennisee's party was chased out of town, the lieutenant went directly to the nearest civil court, in the town of Socorro, to get an arrest warrant against Trujillo and Montoya. In response to the lieutenant's writ, Trujillo, a lawyer, filed his own charges for assault against Hennisee in Alamocito, just west of Socorro. According to Hennisee, "I was tried [apparently in absentia], convicted and sentenced to imprisonment in the County Jail for three months." Hennisee appealed the decision, but his conviction stood. At this point, it became personal for the lieutenant. Although the incident left little mark on the lieutenant's military record, it put an ugly bruise on his ego.[4]

Aside from Hennisee's legal problems, affairs at the Southern Apache agency were spinning out of control. Vigilante groups kept the Indians on edge with threats of a massacre. Lowlifes flooded into the area, unleashing their own brand of bedlam. The illegal trading business and liquor sales continued unabated. Despite the government's best efforts, drunkenness remained rampant in the Indian camps and the army garrison alike. Meanwhile, the army and the Indian Office squabbled over the responsibility of caring for the Indians. The count of Indians was escalating beyond all expectations. Although the Americans wanted the Apaches to come in, they had not expected so many. The cost was spiraling out of control. No one was happy with the state of affairs, especially not the Apaches. Loco's peace was in shambles.

On top of this, the government was determined to move the Chiricahuas onto a reservation, but no one could agree on the location. The problems started when Chief Loco "offered to surrender . . . with a view of . . . being placed on an Indian reservation." In his wildest imagination, Loco never contemplated that the reservation would be any place except around Ojo Caliente and Cañada Alamosa. Nevertheless, the army requested in 1869 that "an agent of the Indian Department be sent . . . to induce them to remove to a permanent reservation." The idea of leaving the Chihennes on their own land appears never to have occurred to the government.[5]

William Clinton, the superintendent of Indian affairs for the territory, notified the commissioner of Indian affairs that Loco had requested a reservation and immediately resurrected the Navajo reservation as a site for depositing the Chihennes. Navajo Agent Lorenzo Labadi, who had suffered through the disastrous effort to mix Navajos and Apaches on a reservation at Bosque Redondo, near Fort Sumner, New Mexico, in 1862, immediately rejected the idea. Labadi recommended that Loco's Apaches be moved to Mescalero Apache country, near Fort Stanton in south-central New Mexico.[6]

In mid-October 1870, Special Indian Agent William Arny traveled to Cañada Alamosa to consult with Lieutenant Hennisee and the Apache leaders concerning their placement. Arny had been in the Indian business for ten years, but he had no firsthand experience with the Southern Apaches and knew little about them. During his ten-day visit, he met his first Chiricahuas, conferred with military officers, and parleyed with the Indians, seeking a place to locate the approximately eight hundred Apaches in the area. After viewing the landscape and talking with Hennisee, Arny submitted a list of possible reservation sites for the commissioner's consideration. Because Arny knew nothing about the area and was ignorant of Chiricahua affairs, his list was undoubtedly heavily influenced by Hennisee. Hennisee had been an agent for the Mescaleros for fifteen months before being sent to replace Drew, and he had just spent four months with the Chiricahuas. He was the government's authority on Southern Apache affairs. Evidence indicates that Hennisee used the opportunity to wreak vengeance on José Trujillo for the embarrassment and legal trouble Trujillo had visited on him.[7]

After meeting with Hennisee and the Indians at Cañada Alamosa, Arny sent Commissioner Ely Parker a report on his trip that included a selection of six potential reservation sites. Three of the choices on the list were impractical—Camp Thomas in Arizona; Santa Lucía, an abandoned reserve on the Gila River; and a 225-square-mile site along the Mimbres River that had been proposed in the 1855 Fort Thorn treaty.

Another possibility was the region around Fort Stanton, but that would require mixing the Mescaleros and the Chihennes, or at least putting them in close proximity. The Chihennes were on reasonably good terms with the Mescaleros, but they did not especially relish living with them, and they vehemently resisted moving east of the Rio Grande. Loco argued that they knew little about the country except that it was cold, and he was reluctant to face its biting winters.[8] The notion of a move to the Mescalero area was soon abandoned.

One option on Arny's list, the Ojo Caliente area around Cañada Alamosa, was decidedly Loco's preference, a fact the Indians frequently brought to the attention of anyone who would listen. It was the Chihennes' traditional homeland, and Arny was impressed on his first visit to the hot springs. Just days before he met with Lieutenant Hennisee, he noted, "West of Socorro about 20 miles there is plenty of land, wood, water, and grass to sustain 3,000 Indians. No settlements within 50 miles, and it is, I believe, the best place for a reservation for the Southern Apaches." The area was approximately the same location Chief Loco proposed as a reservation for the Chihennes. Arny estimated that some two thousand acres could be irrigated and another eight hundred acres cultivated without irrigation. Significantly, he added that the area included resources enough to supply "every demand of the whole Southern Apache tribe." He dismissed the only possible objection to locating the reservation near Cañada Alamosa: "There are living on this land 52 families—46 residences, 2 Mexican mills, 193 persons, whose improvements might be purchased for about $11,000 and, since they had no clear title, they could readily be moved away."[9]

Arny had hit upon the one location that would not require moving the Indians, that would be the least expensive for the government to supply, and that included the area the Apache leaders specifically requested. Although Arny enthusiastically described the area as perfect for a Warm Springs reservation, after talking with Hennisee he was suddenly noncommittal about its selection, and conspicuously, he made no mention that the Apaches had passionately and repeatedly asked to remain there.

Finally, Arny listed as one of his options the "Tularosa Valley," which included the valleys along the San Francisco River and its tributary the Tularosa River in New Mexico's Tularosa Mountains. Roughly seventy miles northwest of Loco's camps, it was so remote that Victorio claimed he had never seen the place. Even Cochise was taken aback at the mention of the Tularosa Valley. He was heard to mutter, "That [place] is a long way off." High in the mountains, it was much colder than Ojo Caliente and even Fort Stanton—too cold to be healthy, too cold for farming, and decidedly too cold for the Apaches to find the least bit attractive. The Apaches believed the valley was haunted, and some claimed to have seen ghosts in the area. No Apache in his right mind would set up housekeeping in the Tularosa Valley. The Indians made that crystal clear to Arny. Nonetheless, within thirty days of talking with Hennisee, he recommended the Tularosa Valley as the place in which to establish a reservation for "the Mimbres, Chiricahuas, Coyoteros, Gila and Mogollon Apaches, and for any other Apache bands who by mutual consent may agree to occupy it."[10]

Although Arny recommended it as "the best place for a reservation," he never went nearer to the Tularosa Valley than Warm Springs. He relied entirely on Hennisee for information about the remote valley. On Arny's return trip to Santa Fe, he stopped by the court in Socorro to see what "could be done to relieve" Hennisee from his impending jail sentence for dumping Trujillo's booze. Arny's visit to the Socorro judge suggests that the evils of Cañada Alamosa and its villainous mayor had been thoroughly discussed.[11]

As the government functionaries debated where to relocate the Indians, the Apaches continued to resist any suggestion of removal from Warm Springs. According to Loco's descendants, the chief and other leaders repeatedly made it plain to Hennisee, Arny, and the new agent, Orlando Piper, that the Chihennes would be dissatisfied with any place but where they were. An article in a Las Cruces, New Mexico, newspaper at the time lends credence to the Loco family's recollections. The reporter, who was primarily interested in Cochise, wrote that Cochise's reply to every question the reporter asked him was "coupled with a request that he might live and die there [near Cañada Alamosa and Warm Springs] and not be removed to another reservation. In this expression Loco and Cheever [probably Chiva, another Chihenne leader] joined with him."[12] After receiving Arny's report, Commissioner Parker ignored the special agent's recommendation and out of the blue instructed Nathaniel Pope, superintendent of Indian affairs for New Mexico, to select a tract of land near Fort Stanton for the Southern Apaches.[13]

Piper was dumbfounded at the idea and wrote, "It would be like beginning all over—they would resist, flee to the mountains." He candidly observed that Cañada Alamosa had "wood, water, pasture, and good soil. . . . If the reservation is here, there is no reason why they can't be satisfied." Nevertheless, he made a sincere effort to sell the Apaches on the Fort Stanton option. After a month of trying, Piper wrote in January 1871 that "they positively refuse to go." He again recommended that the reservation lines be drawn around the group where they were already gathered at Cañada Alamosa. Facing the army's reluctance, the Indians' resistance, and the new agent's candor, the Indian Office backed off, and the Fort Stanton plan was scrapped.[14]

That narrowed the options for an Apache reservation down to two, Cañada Alamosa and the Tularosa Valley. A number of officials argued that it would be cheaper, easier, and generally more satisfactory to buy out the residents of Cañada Alamosa and establish a reservation there. Hennisee preferred to remove the Apaches from the "evil influences" around Cañada Alamosa, conforming to the mainstream of current social thinking that Indians should be kept from alcohol and illegal traders at all cost. Unsaid was the fact that by moving the Indian agency and the Indians to another location and reducing the military presence, Hennisee would effectively destroy Cañada Alamosa's booming economy, which was founded on government contracts and illegal trading.[15]

Notwithstanding the bad influences present at Cañada Alamosa, everyone, including Hennisee, knew that the Tularosa Valley was a poor choice and apt to cause trouble. Even Nathaniel Pope thought it might be "cheapest to locate the reservation at Cañada Alamosa, purchase the town and improvements and remove all the white settlers."[16] Despite what appears to have been common knowledge in New Mexico, however, Arny lied in the closing argument of his report to the commissioner and recommended the Tularosa Valley instead of Cañada Alamosa: "The Indians themselves, I believe, would prefer it to any other location." Something beyond the Indians' interests was driving Arny's recommendation.[17]

In the early months of 1871, Congress appropriated $70,000 to "promote peace and civilization" among the Apaches and authorized the creation of protected reservations for them. The Board of Indian Commissioners named the board's venerable secretary, Vincent Colyer, its peace commissioner and directed him to situate the Apaches on suitable reservations, feed and clothe them, and bring them under the civilizing influence of a benevolent Indian Office. The massacre of 144 peaceful Aravaipa Apaches near Camp Grant on April 30, 1871, added urgency to Colyer's mission. Word of the outrage spread quickly to Indian camps all the way from Fort Apache, north of the Salt River in Arizona, to Mescalero, east of the Rio Grande, and left the Indians fearful about the prospect of remaining on even the most protected reserve. The Apaches with Loco near Fort McRae had been repeatedly threatened with attacks similar to the one at Camp Grant and felt especially vulnerable.[18]

Colyer arrived at Fort Craig on August 16, 1871, accompanied by Superintendent Pope and a small escort of troops. After the two-day trip from Santa Fe, Colyer had no doubt been fully familiarized with the proposal to remove the Apaches to the Tularosa Valley. He appears to have decided to move the Indians there before he ever saw the place. Nonetheless, he went through the motions.[19]

Just days before Colyer's visit to Cañada Alamosa, Agent Piper had received a letter from Judge Hudson of Grant County threatening a surprise attack on Loco's Apaches. The well-intentioned but inexperienced Piper called for troops from Fort McRae without informing the Apaches. When the Indians learned that the soldiers had come to protect them from an attack by "the people of Rio Mimbres," they bolted for the mountains, where they remained when Colyer arrived.[20]

By the time Colyer reached Cañada Alamosa on August 17, Piper could produce only a few skittish Indians. A more determined second effort the next day and a ration issue brought in seventy to eighty of an estimated twelve hundred Apaches in the area. Colyer registered his disappointment. "Is it not a shame that a few lawless white men can thus be allowed to overturn all the good work of the Government?" he asked.[21]

Colyer and Pope lingered around Cañada Alamosa for the better part of three days but were unable to ferret out any additional Indians. At that point they withdrew to the more civilized amenities of Fort Craig to regroup. During their absence, Piper scurried about the hills offering gifts and rations to anyone who would come in for a talk with the bigwigs. He had little success.[22]

After a two-day rest at Fort Craig, Colyer and Pope struck out again, this time in an army ambulance, accompanied by twenty soldiers. Colyer noted that they set out to "inspect the upper valley of the Cañada Alamosa beyond the mountains, at Ojo Caliente, and the Tularosa Valley, to ascertain their suitableness for an Indian reservation." By previous arrangement, the Colyer-Pope party linked up at the hot springs with Piper and Trujillo, who were accompanied by Loco and Francisco, a Navajo who interpreted for the chief. Colyer described meeting the two: "Although Agent Piper had promised any and all of the Indians presents who would come out to meet the commissioner from Washington, whom they were eager to see, only two, Loco and Francisco, the Navajo interpreter, could be persuaded to trust themselves, and Loco trembled like a frightened child when they saw us coming."

Colyer was already convinced that Loco's proposed reservation, which included the town of Cañada Alamosa, was unacceptable. Capitalizing on Arny's assessment that it would take $11,000 to purchase the improvements at Cañada Alamosa, Colyer announced, "The valley of Cañada Alamosa (Cottonwood Valley) is beautiful [but] . . . to attempt to buy out the Mexicans, as has been proposed by some, when there are millions of acres of unoccupied land in the immediate neighborhood, I feel would be preposterous." Instead, he would "endeavor, as quickly as possible, to find them another place as near to Cañada Alamosa as practicable." This, of course, meant the Tularosa Valley.

Following Arny's lead of some months earlier, Colyer also considered the area around Warm Springs. After a quick, halfhearted look, he reported that he "examined the neighborhood carefully, and finding the area of land capable of being cultivated far too small for the necessities of a tribe so large as this band, we were very reluctantly compelled to seek further." This was exactly the same land that Arny had described ten months earlier as containing twenty-eight hundred cultivable acres, enough to supply "every demand of the whole Southern Apache tribe." Clearly, the fix was in.[23]

Having dispatched the idea of the hot springs area as a possible reservation site, Colyer wasted no time in making the difficult journey over the mountains to the Tularosa Valley, which by this time was the only remaining option of those on Arny's list. He arrived there on the morning of August 29, 1871, and "carefully inspected the valley and neighborhood of the Tularosa River, and [found] the same to possess most of the requisites necessary for a home for the Indians, it being remote from white settlements, surrounded by mountains not easily crossed, sufficient arable land, good water, and plenty of wood and game." By nightfall Colyer had completed his inspection, "officially notified Colonel Pope that I would designate it as an Indian reservation," and wired Secretary of the Interior Delano what he had done. Probably the best indication that the Tularosa decision was predetermined is that Colyer's one-day visit purportedly covered six hundred square miles in a ponderous army ambulance.[24]

With Colyer's decision announced, and Hennisee out of the picture, Agent Piper was left to carry out the plan. From the first, Piper had been against removal of the Apaches. Nevertheless, he initially raised no objections to the Tularosa Valley decision. Indeed, he made a good-faith effort to sell the program to the Indians. On September 30, a month after Colyer's declaration, he enthusiastically wrote that he foresaw no problems and believed the agency could be transferred to the Tularosa Valley by late October. He changed his tune eleven days later, probably after losing in exchanges with the Apache leadership. On October 9 he wrote to his political sponsor, the Presbyterian Board, that things were not going well, and there might be "trouble in getting the chiefs to consent to remove."[25]

Word that things were not going smoothly quickly reached Santa Fe, and by October 12, 1871, Colonel Gordon Granger, the new military commander in New Mexico, wondered whether it might not be a good idea to "delay establishing a post" in the Tularosa Valley. On the other hand, Superintendent Pope recommended that the government build the agency there; the Indians would come when they wanted food. But he conceded that it might be a good idea to "humor them until spring." He noted that he had met with Loco, Cochise, and Victorio and that they wished to remain at Cañada Alamosa.[26]

At the agency, Piper tried to bribe Loco and Victorio with a horse apiece if they would go along with the government's deal. They rejected the offer. Piper continued to meet with stiff resistance from the two leaders. On October 20 he threatened to stop the rations at Cañada Alamosa and begin issuing them at the Tularosa site, and he told the Apaches who wanted rations to go up there and get them. Still, "they positively refuse to go; saying that I may take the rations and give them to the bears and wolves." At this point Piper recommended that the Tularosa Valley idea be dropped, saving "thousands, probably millions of dollars."[27] About the same time, the press joined a mounting chorus of opponents to the new reservation when the editors of the *Las Cruces Borderer* wrote that if the Apaches were forced to the Tularosa Valley, "one half to two-thirds will take to the mountains, and become more desperate than ever."[28]

Lieutenant Colonel Nelson Davis, who was sent from Leavenworth, Kansas, to "report as accurately as possible" on the situation at Cañada Alamosa, announced that the Apaches "objected to going to Tularosa." He concluded the Indians should be allowed "to remain for the present at Cañada Alamosa as a matter of economy."[29]

By the last week in October, Nathaniel Pope was backing away from his tough stance. He wrote to the commissioner of Indian affairs that the "Apaches positively refuse to go. . . . I don't think it is wise or practicable to move them by force but if the department decides, it would be better to do so now than in the spring." At the same time, Piper was cautioning that the Apaches, if forced to move, "may flee to the mountains of Arizona." For their part, the Indians threatened war if any attempt was made to move them. It appeared that the Apaches might win their case to remain at Cañada Alamosa, just as they had won on the Fort Stanton option, if only they held firm.[30]

Meanwhile, Secretary of the Interior Delano arranged for a meeting in the White House on November 6, 1871, with President Grant, Secretary of War William Belknap, and the Indian Board secretary, Colyer, to clear up the commotion surrounding the Cañada Alamosa Apaches and the proposed new reservation.[31] On Colyer's recommendation, the high-ranking but poorly informed officials at the meeting agreed to transfer the Apaches to the Tularosa Valley as soon as possible but to leave them at Cañada Alamosa until the government could organize the transfer. Colyer wired Superintendent Pope about the decision and advised him to inform the Apaches that their time at Cañada was "limited in duration and that they must prepare to move for Tularosa as soon as possible."[32]

It is difficult to explain Vincent Colyer's apparent enthusiasm for removing the Indians to the Tularosa Valley. He seems to have been sincerely interested in the welfare of the Indians. He created other reservations during the same 1871 swing through the Southwest, and all of them were the Indians' aboriginal homelands. No one had ever questioned that Ojo Caliente was the traditional home of the Chihennes. Even though Arny had recommended the Tularosa Valley, his preference for Warm Springs was transparent in his report. Colyer, however, spent his entire trip in the Cañada Alamosa area with Nathaniel Pope, who had accepted Arny's recommendation at face value and was fed up with the Apaches' resistance: "These Indians have been humored so much of late that they have become very exacting and dictatorial in their intercourse with the Agent. . . . I am loth [sic] to take any action that would furnish the least excuse for them to scatter, but I am as loth to humor them in their frivolous and unreasonable objections to the new Reservation." Pope must have peddled the Tularosa program to Colyer before they arrived at Cañada Alamosa.[33]

Within two weeks after the White House meeting, the secretary of the interior decreed that the Apaches would be moved at the earliest practical date in 1872. By November 20, 1871, General Philip Sheridan, now commanding the military's Department of the Missouri, issued orders declaring the Tularosa Valley an Indian reservation and establishing a military post there, "to be garrisoned this winter by one company of infantry, but to be so placed and planned that the post may be enlarged."[34] Colonel Gordon Granger, commanding the District of New Mexico, was ordered to give the Apaches thirty days "in which to commence their movement," but he was cautioned that the move should be "accomplished peacefully and kindly, and without collision with the Indians."[35]

In the midst of the frenzied planning and preparations, someone realized that if the move was conducted within thirty days, it would take place in the dead of winter. The government officials therefore agreed that it would be impractical to relocate the Indians before spring. Granger moved the target date for the removal to April 1, 1872.[36]

Talk of removing the Apaches dominated the local rumor mill. Agent Piper complained that "evil disposed persons are continually circulating reports that troops are after them [the Apaches] to drive them to Tularosa." As soon as the word leaked to the Indians that the government was not going to back off again as it had with the Fort Stanton proposition, Cochise vanished into the mountains with his followers. Agent Piper observed, "He has not been to the agency since the order for their removal has been made public, [but] he has regularly sent in for rations."[37]

At about the same time that Cochise ran off with his Chokonens, the Chihennes who followed Nana and Horache, another Chihenne leader, headed for Mescalero country in late December 1871.[38] Only Loco, Victorio, Chiva, and another chief named Gordo managed to hold their small bands in place, hoping to convince the Americans to stop the removal. They would continue to argue their case until the Cañada Alamosa agency was closed.

On March 19, 1872, a delegation composed of Superintendent Pope, Colonel Granger, Colonel Irwin Gregg, and Colonel Thomas Devin arrived at Cañada Alamosa to talk the Indian leaders into a meeting with the secretary of the interior and possibly the president in Washington. Two days after the encounter, Pope wrote that Cochise and Loco were afraid to make the trip, but Victorio was willing to chance it. Pope did not think Victorio was important enough to go alone and gave the chiefs six days to decide.[39]

That bit of business done, the military members of the delegation launched into a bootless effort to convince the Apaches to move willingly to the Tularosa Valley. Loco and the other chiefs again offered their best arguments against removal, but in the end the Americans summarily brushed off the Apaches' reasons as insignificant. Nathaniel Pope opined that the Indians' objections were "unimportant and . . . frivolous," and "that all the objections . . . have been suggested and fostered by [Cañada Alamosa's citizens], most of whom are supported indirectly by the Agency business."[40] Granger thought that most of the objections made to the removal "were frivolous. The substance is that they prefer Cañada Alamosa to Tularosa."[41] The chiefs were told to have their people ready to move to the Tularosa Valley by May 1, 1872.

Now convinced that they had no choice but to transfer to the new reservation, Loco and Victorio curiously demanded that efforts be made to persuade Nana and his people to return from the Mescalero area and join them. Piper wrote on March 29 that he had "a long and satisfactory talk" with Victorio and Loco, and although they agreed to the move to the Tularosa Valley, they wanted to see whether they could prevail upon the old Chihenne leader to accompany them. A number of Victorio's and Loco's relatives, including Victorio's wife, were with Nana at the time. Piper agreed to send Loco to Fort Stanton, accompanied by Zeb Streeter, the agency interpreter, to "try and induce Nana and his party to return." However, without notifying the local officials or Streeter, Loco left for Mescalero on April 2, 1872. His unexpected departure sent the Americans into a rash of nervous speculation. Streeter quickly recruited two Mexicans living near Fort McRae to accompany him and set out to catch up with the chief. When Streeter arrived at Fort Stanton, he "learned that . . . about the time, or soon after Loco reached there [Mescalero], the Indians left the reserve," destination unknown. Streeter set out in hot pursuit, but four days later one of his Mexicans returned to Fort McRae with "a note from the interpreter [Streeter] giving this information. It is believed that Loco will not return. He took Victoria's wife with him and it is supposed that Victoria is soon to join them."[42]

Despite Loco's disappearance, Piper remained upbeat about the removal and continued to reassure army and Indian Office officials that "I have every reason to believe they are sincere. Victorio wishes me to say to you that he is talking straight and that they have no intention of going on the war path." Piper's assurances aside, Captain Shorkley at Fort McRae expressed the opinion of most observers on April 18: "I have no doubt that the Indians are lying to the Agent in this. . . . The Mexicans in Cañada Alamosa think that none of the Indians will go to Tularosa and are alarmed for the safety of their stock and are driving it to the river." Word came from Cadette, a Mescalero leader at Fort Stanton, that Loco "means mischief." Pope wrote, "I fear that Agent Piper may have been deceived by Loco and Victoria and that there may be more trouble than was first apprehended."[43]

Piper, however, continued to reassure his superiors: "He [Victorio] still says that he and his people will go with me to Tularosa" and "that he will get all of his and Loco's bands together and then we will decide how they will go. . . . I rejoice at the prospect . . . that something yet may be accomplished to restrain and control these Indians." Piper arrived at the site of the new Tularosa agency on April 29 with not a single Indian in tow. He wrote to Pope that the agency had been moved, but Pope complained that Piper "has failed to notify me how many (if any) Indians accompanied him."[44]

On May 17, 1872, "after the usual delays and finding no other course was open to them," the Apaches "finally agreed to proceed to Tularosa." Colonel Devin and sixteen Eighth Cavalry troopers watched as about sixty of the tribe's "aged and helpless" climbed aboard twenty wagons with the band's earthly possessions and set out for the Tularosa Valley. Accompanied by Zeb Streeter and Tom Jeffords, the former trader at Cañada Alamosa, roughly three hundred "warriors and the great part of their families" moved through the mountains on horseback and afoot. To everyone's surprise except Piper's, they were joined at the Tularosa site by the wandering Loco and his lost entourage on May 24, 1872.[45]

Superintendent Pope wrote that the Apaches were "well pleased" with their new reservation. Devin reported on May 27, 1872, "I have just returned from Tularosa Valley and have the honor to report . . . that the new Apache Reservation is so far a complete success."[46]

One year after the Apaches struck out for the Tularosa Valley, the War Department tried to recover the cost of the removal from the Department of the Interior. Secretary of War Belknap wrote, "I have the honor to transmit herewith statement vouchers and other papers showing the actual expenses incurred by this Department in the removal of the Apache Indians from Cañada Alamosa to the new reservation in the Tularosa Valley, NM to be $18,649.05 and request the amount be refunded to the appropriation for transportation of them." The move alone cost $7,649 more than the $11,000 it would have taken to buy out the property owners in Cañada Alamosa. The expenses would not end there. Henceforth, everything needed to supply the Tularosa agency, the Indians, and the new military post had to be hauled up into the mountains by wagons. Expensive, but worth every penny for Argalus Hennisee to see such an economic calamity befall Mayor Trujillo's town.[47]

CHAPTER FIVE

"We Are Dying Here"

American officials seemed convinced that under Loco's influence the Chihennes posed no threat to the region. Even as the government badgered Loco, Victorio, and company into moving to the Tularosa Valley, it continued to focus on settling things with Cochise and his Chokonens. After years of lethal raiding, Cochise had achieved the status of a sort of superstar scoundrel among the Americans. Mention of the name "Cochise" could raise a grimace anywhere in the country. In May 1871, when Lieutenant Colonel George Crook was transferred to Arizona to deal with the Apache crisis, he announced, "It is against Cochise's band that I propose concentrating all my energies for the present."[1] Even before Loco and his band were forced to the Tularosa reservation, Cochise had become the most sought-after Indian in the country.[2] Thus, in the spring of 1871, officials quickly geared up to arrange a meeting between him and the soon-to-arrive peace commissioner, Vincent Colyer.[3]

Although Cochise—the perceived solution to the "Apache problem"— had moved in and out of the Cañada Alamosa area since October 1870 to keep tabs on Loco, he inconveniently vanished into the state of Sonora, Mexico, not long before Colyer was scheduled to appear in mid-August. Local bureaucrats rushed to reestablish contact with him.[4]

In May 1871, at the direction of Superintendent of Indian Affairs Nathaniel Pope, Agent Orlando Piper contracted with José Trujillo, the Cañada Alamosa mayor, to find Cochise and convince him to meet with the luminary from Washington for talks. Because of his illegal business activities, Trujillo was thought to have a good relationship with Cochise.

The disreputable mayor set out, accompanied by Loco and a couple of associates. Piper submitted a voucher for "presents given to Loco for accompanying José Trujillo to find Cochise"—a coat, a hat, a knife, two pounds of tobacco, two pounds of lead, and a pound of gunpowder. Comparable items in the Sears Roebuck Catalog of 1897 were valued at $16.87. Piper paid Trujillo $1,000 for the trip.

Trujillo and Loco found Cochise's camp around the middle of May and persuaded about one hundred of the Chiricahuas to return with them, but not Cochise. The desire to find, catch, or kill the aging chief had army patrols out in droves, scouring the southern Arizona countryside. Consequently, the ever-wary Cochise declined the invitation to travel cross-country to attend the Cañada Alamosa meeting.[5]

Spurred on by Trujillo and Loco's partial success, Nathaniel Pope and Piper mounted a second expedition to bring in the infamous chief during the first week of June 1871. This time Piper hired the only slightly more reputable Thomas Jeffords, with whom Lieutenant Drew had clashed. Jeffords, too, was promised a $1,000 payment for his effort. He was accompanied by two Mexican mule packers and two unnamed Apache trackers. Jeffords was told "not to return without him [Cochise]," and indeed, he claimed that he found Cochise, but on June 29 he returned empty-handed. Cochise again refused to budge, because "his country was filled with soldiers." Loco had refused to go with Jeffords, whom he now distrusted because of Jeffords's role in the Drew drinking controversy.[6]

With two failures under their belts and with Vincent Colyer expected soon, pressure mounted on Pope and Piper. Despite the cost, they decided to try again with the more successful Trujillo. Trujillo again took along Chief Loco and a mixed bag of Mexicans and Chihennes. They left Cañada Alamosa on July 31, 1871, but not finding the aging chief in the usual haunts, they decided to look around the Fort Apache, Arizona, area, where Cochise had held some encouraging conversations about peace with Major John Green a year earlier.[7]

Meanwhile, Crook, too, had been unsuccessful in his quest for Cochise. After scouring the mountains north of Fort Bowie, Arizona, for a couple of weeks, he took his troop to Fort Apache for rest and resupply. Trujillo and Crook blundered into each other there on August 12, 1871.

As a part of his peace initiative, Vincent Colyer had convinced President Grant to halt all military operations against the Apaches until he could negotiate with them. Crook claimed he did not know about the policy until August 27, eleven days after Colyer arrived at Fort Craig. Trujillo reported that when Crook faced off with him and Loco at Fort Apache,

Crook demanded that they and their party return to Cañada Alamosa immediately. Crook "refused to recognize his [Trujillo's] authority to go to Cochise's camp and threw his letter down in disdain saying that the Superintendent of Indians Affairs of NM nor any of the Indians' agents had any authority to send parties to Arizona. He [Trujillo] also says that they attempted to arrest his Indians, but Lieut. [William] Ross knew Loco and interceded for him. Colonel Crook would not let him get his rations which were at some distance from where he met the party. The gen. told them that they were lucky to get back with their lives without rations."[8]

When he returned to Cañada Alamosa, Trujillo reported the incident to Agent Piper. Piper sent Trujillo's account to Nathaniel Pope, who forwarded it with Piper's letter to the commissioner of Indian affairs with his own comments. Pope complained that Crook had "caused me great inconvenience and delay in the discharge of my duties and will tend to weaken, if not destroy, any influence Agent Piper or myself may have over the Indians."[9] Crook's version was somewhat different. He explained that "two of this party were recognized by several as being Cochise's worst men, and whom they knew to be ringleaders in some of his past outrages. . . . I felt very suspicious they were there in the capacity of spies; but as they could find out nothing of value and I did not want even a semblance of interference with the Peace Department I did not arrest them." Because the Apaches with Trujillo and Loco were Loco's people, not Cochise's, Crook's explanation rings a bit hollow.[10]

Colyer arrived at Fort Craig on August 16, passed quickly through Cañada Alamosa, created the Tularosa fiasco, and left the area for Arizona without ever seeing the "warrior of the age." Colyer was poorly received by the public in the Southwest, did nothing for the Chiricahuas except displace Victorio, Nana, and Loco's Chihennes, and failed to resolve the Cochise problem. Officials in Washington were still convinced that Cochise was the key to peace with the Apaches and immediately set about finding someone to lead another effort to find him. On February 29, 1872, Secretary of the Interior Columbus Delano appointed the one-armed Brigadier General O. O. Howard as the new Indian peace commissioner and announced that the general would have a go at delivering Cochise.

Although General Howard had a reputation for garrulousness and mediocrity as an officer, an empty right sleeve and a series of commendations for bravery during the Civil War bestowed on him a hero status that demanded respect.[11] Immediately after the war, Howard accepted the job of commissioner for the Bureau of Refugees, Freedmen, and Abandoned Lands.[12] The "Freedmen's Bureau" proved to be unpopular with the white American public, and Howard proved to be an incompetent administrator.

By January 1872, things looked bleak for the general. It was obvious that the Freedmen's Bureau was on its last legs. Consequently, Howard was delighted to receive an offer from the secretary of the interior to be the new peace commissioner in Arizona and New Mexico. He left for Arizona in early March 1872.

In his new role as peace commissioner, Howard made two trips to Arizona and New Mexico, both with the primary goal of making "peace with the warlike Chiricahuas under Cochise." His first trip, from March to June 1872, was a self-inflicted failure. In June 1872 he traveled back to Washington with a delegation of ten reservation-bound Western Apaches—no Chiricahuas, no Cochise. Officials in the War Department immediately ordered him back to Arizona to finish the job.[13]

Howard reached Fort Apache for the second time on August 10, 1872. Initially, he intended to mastermind his manhunt for Cochise from Fort Apache. However, after he learned that the only convenient Chiricahuas were those living with Loco on the Tularosa reservation and that Cochise sometimes visited relatives there, he decided to move his search to the vicinity of Loco's camps in New Mexico.[14]

When Howard arrived at Fort Tularosa on September 7, 1872, he found "a small company of infantry of about 40 men, a large part of which had succumbed to the malaria that pervaded the region," and more than three hundred half-sick and restless Apaches on the reservation. The general also found Orlando Piper a nervous wreck—in failing health, suffering from stress, and unable to cope with the demands of the job. Victorio told General Howard, "We mean no disrespect, but that Piper—the agent, is getting old and he had better go home and see his children and take care of them."[15] Other Apaches complained that Piper did not understand their needs. The general described Piper as "an oldish man, lisps a little, has a good heart, tries to do his duty and do right, but the Indians for some unknown cause do not like him."[16]

At the agent's request, Howard granted Piper sick leave and told him that he could extend it if he wished. Howard knew Piper would not return, but he diplomatically suggested that he would ask the commissioner to find "some less arduous work for one so faithful and worthy as yourself." Piper soon went home, retired, and never rejoined the federal service in any capacity.[17]

John Ayres was designated acting agent for about two months after Piper left, until the new man arrived. Benjamin Morris Thomas in turn replaced Ayres in early December 1872, about three months after General Howard departed Tularosa. Thomas was twenty-nine years old when he took the job.[18]

Howard spent his first week at Tularosa dealing with administrative trivia and "lounging about the place . . . visiting the rancherias of the Indians, scattered about, and one day was given to a council with them." He quickly discovered that "all were full of discontent at the transfer [to the Tularosa Valley]. Even the officers of the garrison said that these Apaches had been sorely ill-used." Every Indian he came across pleaded, "Oh, take us back home to Agua Caliente on the Rio Grande! We are dying here." The general "heard the Indians' complaints and promised a visit to that salubrious Cañada." He vowed that he "would carry this petition for the Indians' return to the Rio Grande directly to the President." He further ingratiated himself with his new "friends" when he learned that the Indian Office had once more reduced the Indians' rations, and he directed Pope to increase the issues.[19]

On September 12, 1872 (Howard's aide, Joseph Sladen, said September 11), his last full day at Tularosa, Howard held a formal council with the Chihenne leaders, Loco, Chevo (probably Chiva), Victorio, Nana, Gordo, and Lopez. Howard, Nathaniel Pope, Agent Piper, and Captain Frederick Coleman, commanding Fort Tularosa, represented the Americans.[20] Several officers' wives came to watch the show. During his one-week stay, Howard, the apparently sympathetic "gentleman general," completely won over the Apaches. Victorio opened the meeting by saying, "The sun is shining down upon us." He told Howard, "Every word you say we drink in, for we think you have had a good father and good mother and have been well brought up." Loco added:

Everything Victorio has said is right, and what I would say, but I want to talk a little because I have now met a man I like to talk with. We have always lived in the Mimbres Mountains, were born there, and brought up there, and we made peace there, and our food stays better upon our stomachs there. We want to go back to Cañada Alamosa, which is our home and there we would like to have these ladies come and see us as they have today. We like to see your ladies because they never work and we never work either [perhaps a bit of sarcasm regarding life at Tularosa].

If you will take us back to the Cañada [Alamosa] we will work there where we have always worked, in hunting and obtaining our food. If you will send us back to Cañada, we will plant with a stick in our fashion or if you will give us a plough and other implements of white men, we will try to use them but if the frost comes there as it does here, we shall be discouraged and not plant any more. What do you say?[21]

Throughout the daylong meeting the Indians bombarded Howard with requests to return to Ojo Caliente. When he learned that Charles Drew had promised Loco a reservation at Ojo Caliente in 1869, Howard pledged that he would ask the president to provide a reservation for them in their old homeland. "I will do my best when I get back to Washington to get money appropriated to purchase the land and pay the people for the improvements if I can get all the Apaches to go there. . . . When I get to Washington I will ask the Great Father there to give the Apaches the reservation. All the Apache now here must help me by remaining here till they hear from me again."[22]

At the close of the meeting, Howard asked Loco to show him the Chihennes' old homeland. So with Loco and two Apaches named Dolores and Chie as tour guides, Howard and his entourage spent six days sizing up the Ojo Caliente–Cañada Alamosa area.[23] Howard liked the place, proposed boundaries for a Hot Springs reservation, and even named Thomas Jeffords as the potential agent. Contradicting Hennisee's, Pope's, and Colyer's previous excuses for not selecting Ojo Caliente as the Chihenne reservation, he wrote to the recently appointed commissioner of Indian affairs, Francis Walker, "It is a fine country, just suited to the Indians and the difference of cost of transportation of supplies between Cañada and Tularosa would in four years exceed the purchase of the improvements."[24]

During his stay at Fort Tularosa, Howard scrambled to find the magical combination that would put him in touch with Cochise. On the day after his arrival, the general sent Jake May, his interpreter, to locate Tom Jeffords, "the mysterious white man who had visited Cochise frequently and was on friendly terms with him." By the end of his week at Fort Tularosa, Howard had an agreement with Jeffords to lead him to Cochise, and on October 1, Howard finally met Cochise in the Dragoon Mountains. He tried to convince the old chief to move his people to Ojo Caliente in the hope of consolidating the Chokonens and Chihennes on one reservation. He extolled the Ojo Caliente region's virtues for the chief.[25]

Cochise replied that he liked the Cañada Alamosa area but preferred the traditional Chokonen homeland. He offered a counterproposal: "Why not give me Apache Pass [in the Chiricahua Mountains]? Give me that and I will protect all the roads. I will see that nobody's property is taken by Indians." The general jumped at the idea, abandoned the Ojo Caliente offer, and left the Chihennes stranded at Tularosa. In his mind, the deal completed his main mission—Cochise was at peace on his own reserva- tion. Because Loco's Chihennes were already at peace, the Apache problem was resolved.[26]

After a fashion, Howard did keep his pledges to the Tularosa Indians. He spoke with the president and the secretary of the interior in early November about establishing a reservation for the Chihennes at Ojo Caliente. But he confided to Commissioner Walker, "Had I been able to prevail upon Cochise and his Indians to go to Cañada, I should have recommended strongly a reservation there, [with] the government buying up all the Mexican improvements."[27] The implication is that Howard did not "recommend strongly" that the Chihennes be given a reservation. Indeed, he ignored a condition the Chihennes' had demanded—that they would not abide Cochise's people on the same reserve—and he deliberately discounted the notion of a reservation at Warm Springs without Cochise on it. He went on to tell Walker, "The Indians at Tularosa numbered less than three hundred when I was there. [Actually there were about 350.] We would not be justified with so small a number to ask for the proposed reservation."[28] This argument lacks credibility because Howard had just created a reserve for Cochise's band, which was approximately the same size as Loco's.[29]

Although Howard did not outright lie to the Apaches, his language was laced with bureaucratic subtleties that were impossible for nine- teenth-century Apaches to comprehend.[30] The Indians understood him to promise that the tribe would be moved back to Ojo Caliente by the spring of 1873. Additionally, they thought he promised to return and take a delegation to Washington so that they might plead their case directly to the president. It seemed to Loco that Howard played the Chihennes for fools. Howard also told the Indians that he would remove Agent Piper and replace him with a more acceptable agent. He did release Piper immediately, but the Indians never agreed that the final selection for agent, Benjamin Thomas, was acceptable.[31]

It is certain that Howard knew the Chihennes would feel betrayed over the question of the reservation. After informing Captain Coleman, the commanding officer at Fort Tularosa, that he had successfully installed Cochise on a reservation, he warned Coleman, "I fear your Indians will be discontented at Cochise's decision for they were hoping strongly that he would choose the Cañada Alamosa. I shall lay their [the Chihennes'] request [to move back to Ojo Caliente] before the President and have you all notified of his decision as soon as possible."[32]

From this letter, it seems that Howard deliberately betrayed the Chihennes. Although he talked with the Indians about "all the Apaches" at the September 12 meeting, it appears that he specifically avoided any mention of Cochise. It was obvious from earlier relations between Cochise's people and the Warm Springs band at Cañada Alamosa that the Chihennes were not hoping Cochise would move back in with them at Ojo Caliente. Even when they were later given the opportunity to return to the Warm Springs area, they initially refused because they believed Cochise might join them there. Coleman suggested that Howard might have discussed the Cochise caveat, but only with Victorio: "General Howard had a private talk with Victorio and nobody on the reservation has ever known what was said." Enough Indians made the same claims about Howard's words, however, that it seems certain that they all understood him to promise them their own reservation at Ojo Caliente.[33]

When the only movement the Chihennes saw after four months was the replacement of the temporary agent, John Ayres, with Benjamin Thomas, they became suspicious. The Indians liked Ayres, and when he replaced the disliked Piper, they believed Howard was on the way to keeping his promises. After Ben Thomas arrived in December 1872, the Chihennes began to doubt Howard's word—he had not sent them "an Agent they would like." Captain Coleman wrote, "It seems that the Indians had positively refused to have anything to do with the new agent, unless I was present and had a talk."[34]

Around the middle of January 1873, the new agent, Thomas, wrote to the superintendent of Indian affairs for New Mexico, Edwin Dudley, about the rising discontent on the Tularosa reserve. He asked Dudley to visit the agency and tell the Apaches whether they were going to return to Cañada Alamosa or not.[35] Dudley traveled to the Tularosa agency toward the end of February 1873. Buttressed with a letter from General Howard addressed to Loco, Ponce (another Chihenne leader), and Victorio, he squelched any hope the Indians had of moving back to the Warm Springs area. Howard's letter read in part, "Cachise and his Indians were not willing to go there. The president will not set apart Cañada for a few Indians. Congress will not give the money to buy the land. . . . Victorio knows that I believed Cachise would go to Cañada but he did not go."[36]

Howard's letter left the Apaches disillusioned, but it seemed to solve the problem for Thomas: "The principal cause of congratulation to the agency is the good effect of the recent visit of Superintendent Dudley.

He has virtually settled the very troublesome question of Tulerosa [*sic*] vs. Cañada Alamosa as the permanent home of these Indians. . . . They seem now to have concluded to accept the situation."[37]

Although Thomas may have believed the Apaches were now resigned to living on the Tularosa reservation, officials in the army thought Howard had undermined the potential success of relocating the Apaches there. General John Pope concluded that Howard had apparently "determined the complete abandonment of the Tularosa Reservation."[38]

In Howard's rush to settle with Cochise, his unfulfilled promises to the Chihennes left them more hostile than they had been in years, opened the way for a resumption of raiding, and temporarily suspended the army's policy of driving the Apaches to the reservation. Phil Sheridan complained, "The settlement of these Indians on the Tularosa Reservation was in the process of successful accomplishment when interrupted by General Howard."[39] Furthermore, some officials argued that Howard bungled the Cochise negotiations when he created the new Chiricahua reservation, because its southern boundary coincided with the international border. Although Howard's agreement with Cochise virtually stopped Chiricahua raiding in southern Arizona and New Mexico, it opened a federally protected thoroughfare through the new reservation directly into Sonora, Mexico. Apaches, especially those from the Tularosa Valley, were quick to pick up on the mistake—or the opportunity, depending on one's point of view.[40] Commuting through the new reservation to Mexico became so heavy that both Cochise and Jeffords began telling the travelers from Tularosa that they did not "want them to visit that agency so much . . . on the ground that he [Cochise] has to bear all the blame for all the horse stealing that is done in Sonora from his reservation."[41]

While the vaunted treaty with Cochise might or might not have settled the Chokonens, the fact remained that General Howard, in his single-minded effort to control Cochise at the expense of all else, seemed to scuttle any hope Loco and his people had of an immediate return to a Chihenne-only reservation at Ojo Caliente. On the upside, Howard destroyed the myths created by Hennisee, Arny, and Colyer about the unsuitability of Cañada Alamosa as a reservation and once again put the Ojo Caliente area in the running as the place for Loco's Chihennes—at least in the minds of some important officials in Washington.[42]

CHAPTER SIX

The Ghosts of Tularosa

While General Howard struggled to find Cochise, and the army struggled with Howard's wreckage, Loco's Chihennes struggled with conditions at the Tularosa Valley reservation. In January 1873, approximately 775 Apaches were living around the new Southern Apache agency near the present-day town of Aragon—the largest population in the Tularosa Valley before or since.[1] Contrary to Benjamin Thomas's opinion that "this new reservation of theirs is a very beautiful place and well adapted to the present and future requirements of the Indians," Tularosa turned out to be every bit as bad as the Apaches said it would be.[2] Cochise had not been joking when he said that Tularosa was a long way off. The new reservation was isolated from almost everywhere and would remain virtually unpopulated by whites for years.[3] If the government sought to keep the Apaches away from the evil influences of white society, it could hardly have found a better place. The faraway location of the Tularosa agency, however, soon proved to be more trouble for the Americans than for the Indians, and ultimately it did not hinder illegal trading or liquor sales.

The weather at Tularosa concerned the Indians more than did its isolation. For all their toughness, the Chiricahuas were accustomed to a temperate climate. Before the Americans came and interrupted their natural nomadic flow, the Apaches gravitated seasonally toward moderate weather—higher mountains in the summer and warmer areas in the winter. Chief Loco's Warm Spring Apaches had the warm waters of Ojo Caliente year-round. Their forced removal to the Tularosa Valley disrupted these seasonal migrations and forced the Chiricahuas to tolerate some of

New Mexico's worst weather. The Tularosa agency sat at an elevation of 7,135 feet, about 1,875 feet higher than Ojo Caliente. The average temperature was almost nineteen degrees colder, often dropping into the single digits during the winter months. No one was surprised when the thermometer dipped below zero. Generally, winter precipitation fell in the form of freezing rain and what is euphemistically called a "wintry mix," but snows could range from two inches to four feet deep. Once snow or ice fell, the bone-cracking cold kept it on the ground for weeks.[4]

After struggling through the winter of 1872–73, Ben Thomas went into the business of taking care of himself, giving little thought to providing assistance to the Apaches. He started to prepare early for the coming winter of 1873–74. "During the month [of November] all hands have employed the time not necessarily devoted to the Indians in building new walls to the [agency] houses, building new chimneys and otherwise endeavoring to make the place habitable during the winter."[5]

Nasty weather struck in early January 1874. Thomas complained that "the weather has continued very bad indeed throughout the month . . . extremely cold for nearly two weeks, as low as five, seven, eight and ten degrees below zero. It has often been necessary during the winter for all hands to camp under a tent before a fireplace in the house, and sometimes it was necessary for one man to remain up the greater part of the night to carry water out of the house as it would run through the roof and fill the vessels set to catch it."[6]

It apparently never occurred to Thomas to assist the Apaches with construction of winter shelters. A year earlier, during an equally biting winter, he expressed surprise that the Apaches had not built log cabins to protect themselves from the elements. He attributed it to laziness: "They are unwilling to work—do not even build a protection for themselves against the inclemency of the weather, when there is an abundance of timber at hand, but exist miserably in 'Rancherias' made of old sacks and pieces of muslin and rawhide stretched over sticks stuck in the ground."[7] Although the Americans were educating the Apaches in everything from corn farming to Christianity, it seems that no one thought to teach them how to build houses. Nothing in the traditional Apache way required construction skills. Traditionally at this time of year, they would have long since gone to bask in Mexican sunshine. Despite the knowledge he had gained during his first winter, and despite dire warnings from the agency physicians, Thomas displayed an almost criminal neglect of the Indians as he braced himself and the agency staff for the coming cold. His belated order for winter clothing and blankets finally arrived in late November, but Thomas waited until December 8 to issue the supplies. A second, last-minute order allowed Thomas to dispense additional blankets and clothing on December 28. The government clothing consisted of Civil War surplus—low-grade, light wool trousers and shirts from the storehouses at Fort Craig. The Indians quickly wore them ragged with the hard use of reservation life. Cloth issued for women's dresses was worthless for cold-weather wear.[8]

Two months earlier, Henry Duane, the agency physician, had admonished Thomas that "the issue of blankets should be earlier in the season and of better quality. Last year they were not issued until the middle of December, and then the blankets were of a very inferior quality—six hundred weighing no more than eight hundred and fifty pounds."[9] To put this in a modern perspective, one of the blankets issued to the Indians weighed approximately the same as a queen-sized linen sheet. Victorio complained about the cheap clothing and blankets: "We don't like these kinds of blankets or these shirts. When we run, they all fall to pieces."[10]

Dr. Duane also expressed concern about the Apaches' shelter: "The Indians also need an issue of canvas as they are very poorly sheltered from the inclemency of the weather, having only a few pieces of canvas, which they have picked up from this post." Thomas never requisitioned canvas for the Indians' wickiups. He did, however, secure "all the canvas that could be had of the Quartermaster at Fort Tularosa" to protect the agency's supplies.[11]

Dr. James M. Lanig, who replaced Duane just in time to suffer the winter of 1874, noted that Indian housing on the reservation was unchanged from what Thomas had described a year earlier. "I found them . . . living in lodges made of boughs of trees fastened together at the tops, and covered with pieces of cotton, skins, Navajo blankets, and sometimes pieces of old canvas, which they might have been lucky enough to pick up."[12]

So while the Indian Office staff smoked cheroots and drank hot coffee before a roaring fireplace in their double-walled winter quarters, Loco's people shivered in partially covered brush wickiups, dressed in light wool army blouses and trousers or thin cloth dresses. In weather so cold that several of the Indians' horses froze to death, their only protection was flimsy, one-pound four-ounce blankets. By March, the weather-weary Apaches were ready to bolt the reservation and seek a more temperate refuge in Mexico.[13]

Angry tribal leaders complained bitterly. Sensing an incident if word of his failures reached Washington, Thomas reverted in his February 1874 report to a tried and true bureaucratic dodge—make light of the Indians' complaints and blame them for his malfeasance. "The chiefs have put in a long list of complaints. They want to leave the place, say they will never plant here; want pay for the two horses that have died [ultimately it was five or six]; did not cut hay last fall because they had no servants to do the work for them; want red pepper and onions added to their rations and want more sugar and coffee; they never get their beef issued to them on the hoof; heads of families are not allowed to draw rations for the whole family &c, &c, &c."[14]

As the weather warmed, tempers cooled, and most of the Apaches remained on the reservation. Apparently some Chihennes who had left Tularosa during the cold months began to return after wintering in Mexico or on the warmer Chiricahua reservation in southern Arizona. Thomas enthusiastically reported, "The new ones [returnees] say that a large number more are coming back as soon as the weather gets a little pleasenter [sic]."[15]

With spring approaching, the agency staff geared up for the gardening season. Loco's Chihennes had done a little small-acreage farming before the removal, but the Tularosa Valley was a sorry place for subsistence farming, especially of corn, which the government seemed to advocate and which the Apaches seemed to prefer. Captain Frederick Coleman, commanding Fort Tularosa, supported the Apaches' complaints "that the season here [Tularosa] is not good for corn. This is true, for my corn was severely frosted Sept. 11th last."[16]

Despite this, Thomas was persistent and managed to convince the Apaches to dig an irrigation ditch, put in about twenty acres of corn, and thus take the first steps on the road to self-sufficiency as corn farmers. Initially, everyone, Indians and agency staff alike, was enthusiastic, but the enterprise was a calamity, just as the Indians predicted. Thomas reported in June: "The Indians were for a time very much interested in planting corn and a few varieties of vegetables. They dug their irrigating ditch and planted about twenty acres, but when they discovered that the frost was killing the corn nearly as fast as it came up, they became discouraged and abandoned the whole thing."[17] By the end of their second planting season at Tularosa, the Apaches had given the Indian Office's corn-planting program their best shot. Two consecutive years of frozen corn sprouts convinced the Indians that they had been right all along. Dr. Lanig noted, "They were so much disheartened that I am afraid it will be difficult to get them to make another attempt."[18]

Good documentation exists that the Apaches' warnings about the isolation, weather, and difficulty of farming at Tularosa were correct. It seems unlikely, then, that they would have created a fairy tale about ghosts, but officials dismissed out of hand the Apaches' trepidation about evil spirits. Even today historians brush off the Apaches' dread of bad spirits at Tularosa with single-sentence references. Nevertheless, for nineteenth-century Apaches, specters were very real and had much to do with their misery on the new reservation.[19]

In the Indians' minds, ghosts were concrete, bona fide phenomena. They were real. They could make you sick, drive you crazy, or kill you. Although Victorio claimed before the removal that he had never been to the Tularosa Valley, other Apaches had, and there they had seen the remains of a large ancient tribe—ruins, pottery shards, an occasional skeleton, and a multitude of graves. Modern archaeologists have also found prehistoric ruins sitting squarely within the Tularosa reservation. Archaeologists call the ancient tribe the "Mogollon" and have determined that their culture began about 200 BCE. Then, some two hundred years before the Apaches arrived in the Southwest, the Mogollon people in the Tularosa Valley simply vanished. Archaeological theories abound about their disappearance. Although scientists are unsure of the cause, there was no uncertainty among the Apaches of the 1870s. They believed the entire settlement had been destroyed by a devastating plague, leaving behind thousands of spectral malefactors with unfinished business.[20]

In the search for the ghosts of Tularosa, modern scientists and Apaches agree on two points. A large population of prehistoric people lived on the site of the reservation, and they vanished suddenly. Archaeologists and Apaches part company when it comes to the existence of ghosts. Even today, many Apaches have never dismissed the notion that ghosts exist. For all nineteenth-century Chiricahuas, the proper place for the spirits of the dead was the underworld, "a place beneath the ground, where . . . there is no sickness, death, pain, or sorrow . . . but lots of good things to eat."[21] The Apaches believed owls were the earthly embodiments of evil spirits that never made it to the paradise below. These spirit-owls were the agents of disease, death, and malevolence of every kind. The Chiricahuas lived in fear of any contact with owls. One of anthropologist Morris Opler's Chiricahua informants discussed owls, spirits, and the afterlife: "The owl represents the spirit or ghost of a person who was bad during his life and continues to be vicious after death. He works by entering the body of an owl and exercises evil influence in this way. . . . Owls talk the Chiricahua language. . . . The call of the owl is very powerful. It can get into your body and cause trouble."[22]

As it turns out, the Tularosa Valley, home of the vanished prehistoric people, is also home to the largest known concentration of Mexican spotted owls in North America. Almost 56 percent of the North American population roosts on or near the site of the Tularosa reservation. Although declared an endangered species, almost 2,100 Mexican spotted owls were counted around the area in 1991. Their population in 1872 may have been three or four times that number. One of the larger owls in North America, the Mexican spotted is known for its distinctive call, which comes in multiples of three or four hoots in a row. One of Opler's informants pointed out the problem for the Indians at Tularosa: "If you hear an owl, you know a ghost is nearby, for the owl is connected with the ghost. The Chiricahua are afraid of the owl. . . . When it comes it is a sign that someone is going to die." The nocturnal cacophony of several thousand owls coming from every direction, each signaling a forthcoming death, no doubt terrified the Apaches.[23]

Many of the ghost-related problems at the Tularosa agency had to do with the San Francisco River. The river runs cold and clear along the length of the reservation site. The woodland along its banks is a cornucopia of foliage, including a lush medley of hardwood and evergreen trees. It is raptor heaven for the Mexican spotted owl.[24] The Indians believed the river flowed directly over the remains of the long-deceased Mogollons. With the river flowing over Mogollon bones and owls hooting from almost every tree along the bank, the Apaches thought it made good sense to avoid any contact with its waters. When Loco's following was moved to Tularosa, they essentially went into a dry camp.

Whether the specters were real or a figment, the Indians' fear of the San Francisco River led to hygiene and health problems. Everyone who knew them considered the Chiricahuas to be among the most hygienic Indians in the country. Children learned to swim at about the age of eight and subsequently were in the water often. Sweat-bathing followed by dips in a river was considered not only healthy but also a spiritual experience for Apache men. Men repeated their bathing ritual several times daily. Although women did not use sweat baths, they bathed often in the nearest river.[25] Two accounts written by Lieutenant Dr. Joseph Sladen in 1872 and one by Dr. James Lanig in 1874, illustrate the effect that moving the Apaches to Tularosa, with its haunted river, and away from their hot springs and the five rivers around Ojo Caliente had on the Indians' hygiene.

Sladen described two Apache camps, one a dry camp and one with access to abundant water. His description of the dry camp compares closely to Lanig's later description of the camps at Tularosa. Sladen wrote of the dry camp that "this band was very dirty, covered with smoke and grime. . . . Their dirty condition, we soon discovered, was due to the scarcity of water."[26]

Conditions in the camp with abundant water were strikingly different. "These wild Indians [who] had never been brought under the influences of civilization, had some characteristics that would have done credit to their white enemies," Sladen wrote. "They were a very cleanly people, strange as this may sound to those who are disposed to think of the Indians as a lazy, dirty, creature. . . . Where leisure and opportunity were amply afforded them, they were scrupulously clean, both sexes washing and bathing frequently. Not a day passed that the women and children did not spend hours in the stream near by, going in with all their clothes on, except their moccasins and leather wraps, frolicking and splashing, and shouting and having the greatest fun. Both men and women spent a great deal of time in dressing their own or one another's hair, and I frequently saw them using the marrow from bones as hair dressing. . . . These people were entirely free from vermin, and I neither found them myself, nor saw any evidence of them during the entire time I spent with them."[27]

Thus it seems certain that Loco's Chihennes, while living at Ojo Caliente, were well-scrubbed Indians. At Tularosa, however, James Lanig observed, "They are generally abominably filthy, their white manta soon assuming a full mud color and it is no uncommon thing to see them stretched on the ground about the agency on Thursday of each week, while waiting for the issue of rations, ridding each other of certain pests."[28] Aside from Lanig's confusing the Apache penchant for protracted hair grooming with a hunt for head lice, his observations of the Indians at Tularosa and Sladen's of Apaches living in a dry camp are remarkably similar. It appears that the Chihennes on the Tularosa reservation abandoned bathing in deference to their fear of the supernatural phantasms in the river. This created conditions ripe for the development of diseases. One might argue that the ghosts of Tularosa did kill Apaches, if only in a roundabout way.

Whooping cough proved to be the Apaches' worst disease-related nemesis at Tularosa. Agent Thomas reported: "During the month [of April 1873] several of the children have died from hooping [sic] cough." From January through August 1873, Dr. Duane treated seventy-eight cases of the disease, which meant it had struck 23 percent of all the Apaches on the reservation at the time. Whooping cough affects mainly children but can be fatal at any age. For the Apaches—especially Loco, whose affection for children is proverbial—it was a terrifying affliction. General Howard noted during his visit in 1872 that "every death became a cause of alarm, and the cause of a quick abandonment of camping grounds."[29]

Eye problems were also a continuing scourge for the Apaches at Tularosa. Both Duane and Lanig treated multiple cases of conjunctivitis. Conjunctivitis is a generic term for a range of eye diseases generally associated with people's having poor sanitation and limited access to water. Also, complicating the conjunctivitis problem, ill-protected Apaches hovered over campfires in smoky wickiups throughout the winter, which irritated both lungs and eyes. Lanig wrote, "Inflammations of the eyes are common, partly from their untidy habits, and partly from their habit of sitting round and stooping over wood fires, the smoke of which gets into their eyes."

Aside from whooping cough and conjunctivitis, exposure to the Tularosa Valley's icy winter brought on or aggravated a Pandora's box of other medical problems, including chronic rheumatism and seventeen cases of inflamed lungs and pleurisy.[30]

From a coldly analytical standpoint, virtually every one of the Apaches' miseries at Tularosa can be attributed not to ghosts but to inclement weather, stress, and pathogens. Still, to quote a modern superintendent of the Fort Apache agency: "If these Indians believe in ghosts, then you better consider the spooks when you are dealing with them."[31]

CHAPTER SEVEN

Gunfight at Victorio's

The Tularosa reservation's remoteness, bad weather, nonfeasant administration, and paranormal residents were not the only difficulties the Apaches faced. Idleness soon began to wear on the ordinarily active Indians. Dr. Lanig noted that the life of an Apache man was "one of absolute idleness varied by occasional squabbles under the influence of tiswin. . . . Being fed by rations issued once a week at the agency, they are incorrigibly idle, doing little or nothing for their own subsistence."[1]

Under the pressures of their situation and their pointless lifestyle at Tularosa, the Chihennes' tribal social fabric began to unravel. Concurrent with and possibly caused by conditions on the reservation, a plethora of social maladies plagued the Indians—high childhood mortality, wife beating, hunger, intratribal fights, thefts, and murders, and a continuation of off-reservation robbing and rustling.

Despite the best-laid government plans to remove the Apaches from temptation, drunkenness became a greater problem on the new reservation than it had been at Ojo Caliente. At least, Ben Thomas's monthly reports mentioned drinking more prominently than had Orlando Piper's earlier accounts from Ojo.[2]

Although Agent Thomas blamed home-brewed tiswin for the widespread drunkenness at Tularosa, hard liquor was probably the primary culprit. When Thomas arrived in the winter of 1872, he found illegal whisky sellers already poking about the reservation. He wrote, "The Mexicans living on the Rio Grande are in the habit of bringing whiskey onto the reservation clandestinely and trading it to the Indians." If the primary purpose of moving the Apaches was to isolate them from the evil sway of illegal booze vendors, the removal was a failure from the start.[3]

Along with increased drinking came an average of one or two murders a month—a previously unrecorded level of within-camp violence. Lanig noted that "wounds and injuries are by no means uncommon." Thomas kept score: "Seven have been killed in these fights and about twenty wounded . . . in the previous seven months."[4]

As time passed, the Apaches grew more rancorous. They began taking potshots at the agency staff. An arrow whizzed by Dr. Duane as he attended patients in the Indian camp. Another was launched at the agency interpreter, and still another at the beef contractor, all barely missing. Potshots were taken at the agent. By June 1873, Thomas had enough. He expressed a "settled determination on my part to put a stop to all these things if I could. They could not be tolerated year after year, and I had satisfied myself that talking would never make any improvement."[5] He requested help from Major William Price, commanding the troops operating in southern New Mexico.[6]

Major Price was on his way to Fort Wingate at the time but promised to return "in about three weeks with two additional companies of cavalry." Thomas's spirits soared: "We hope to accomplish good results among these Indians . . . showing them that it will be dangerous for them to continue threatening the lives of men at work for their good."[7]

All this led to a situation that started when Sanchez, an enthusiastic raider whom Thomas referred to as Sancho, returned to the reservation "from one of his thieving expeditions with three of his followers, one wounded." Sanchez had been on a horse-rustling spree south of Cañada Alamosa with five or six followers in mid-June 1873. The group was making for Tularosa with the new additions to its horse herd when it was overtaken by Captain George Chilson and a company of the Eighth Cavalry, who killed two of the raiders and wounded a third.[8]

Thomas concluded that "a few arrests, firmly and efficiently made at the agency, would have the desired effect both in putting a stop to the insolence on the reservation and their depredations and marauding over the country." He intended to make an example out of Sanchez and his fellow raiders.[9]

Without realizing that Sanchez and his cronies were Victorio's relatives, Thomas tried to enlist Victorio and Loco to assist with Sanchez's arrest and imprisonment. On Sanchez's first day at the agency after his fight with Chilson's troops, Thomas called Victorio and Loco into his office. It was July 23, 1873. The two leaders' response surprised the agent: "[I] told them privately what I wanted to do and what I wanted them to do. They replied that they were to be protected here and that they would not allow one of their number to be taken, and when I was disposed to press the matter, they went out and gave a signal at which the women and children all left the agency and the men got their arms and mounted."[10]

Thinking that the army was some distance away at Fort Tularosa, Victorio challenged Thomas. "Victoria [sic] then told me that if I wanted to fight, he was ready, or if the soldiers wanted to come there and to fight, he was ready." Circumstances called Victorio's bluff. Responding to a hasty note from the agent, Major Price rushed from Fort Tularosa with forty troopers and twenty Navajo scouts. Their arrival unnerved the Apaches. Price called for a parley, hoping to defuse the situation. It did not go well. Thomas reported, "All the warriors that were on the reservation (about 50) were present with their arms, and the talk was short and unsatisfactory and inclined to insolence on the part of the Indians. . . . They said their tiswin was ready; they would go and drink it, and when they were ready to talk tomorrow, that they would send word."[11]

The next morning, July 24, several "chiefs" gathered at the agency for talks. Victorio was conspicuously absent, apparently in the process of leading an escape. One Indian asked that he be allowed to take a note to Major Price to come to the agency to talk. This was a ruse to divert Price while the remainder of the Chiricahuas made for the mountains. The messenger did not return with the major but raced back to the agency, had "a little talk" with the assembled Apaches, and then announced that they had to return to their camps to welcome relatives returning from the Chiricahua reservation. When Price arrived at the agency, the Apaches came up with another diversion. "After awhile we rec'd word that all the Indians had left camp and that Victoria would talk in a canyon about two miles from the agency," reported Thomas. Price took about eighteen men and scouts to the canyon. Victorio did not show. On the way back to the agency, the troops found Loco's elderly, one-armed mother-in-law. She had tired quickly and decided the run was not worth the effort. Price pointed her toward the agency and sent her on her way.[12]

Two leaders named Bonito and Gavinda, with about thirty followers, came in next, revealing "that the women and children were hungry, and without water and wanted to go back to the agency." They, too, were left to return unaccompanied to the agency. Gavinda went out again on June 26 to encourage others to come in. On the twenty-seventh he returned, saying that he had "been unable to communicate with many of them the day before, as they were so much scattered, but that they now wanted to come in. He left out again, leaving the rest of the party with us." An hour later Loco came in briefly to assess the situation and quickly went to round up his following. "Pajarita and his cross-eyed brother with thirty women and children, among them Victoria's wife, grown son, and other children surrendered soon after." Loco with his band of forty rode into the agency accompanied by Major Price on July 28, saying that he expected Victoria to be in within the next few days. On the twenty-ninth, Gavinda returned to the agency alone, seeking the release of his people being held at the fort. Price wrote to Thomas: "He thought that Victoria and all the balance [of Indians] would be in the next day, that he [Victorio] was only remaining out to look after and get his people in."[13]

Victorio returned to the reservation on July 30 but did not make it to the agency as agreed until August 6. Instead, he went directly to Loco's camp, arriving sulky and out of sorts. Loco set about calming him down. Thomas described the arrival: "While I was absent from the agency on this duty, Victoria came in alone to Loco's camp at the agency. He was very distant and reserved, would have nothing to say to my foreman and would not dismount, until Loco offered him something to eat. He left before I returned from the post but Loco and Gavinda said that his [Victorio's] people were out gathering up the articles they had thrown away in their flight and they would all be in that night or the next morning."[14] So ended the outbreak.

The escape of 1873 was a puny affair that ordinarily would merit little attention. The Indians initially panicked when they thought Victorio had so riled officials that the army would retaliate against everyone indiscriminately. After they regained their composure, the Apaches' run was at best unenthusiastic. It lasted a total of five days. Nothing was stolen. Neither side fired a shot or spilled a drop of blood, except that the hungry runaways killed and ate a horse. Price easily caught up with the escapees, and they returned to their camps quietly within days.

Yet this undistinguished incident would prove to have far-reaching consequences. It ultimately affected the Apaches' conduct on the reservation, the overall peace with the Americans, leadership among the Chihennes, and Loco and Victorio's friendship. Significantly, Victorio's run of 1873 brought to light the reasons Loco's peace arrangements had begun to unravel in late 1871.

Loco arrived at the Tularosa agency early in the morning after Victorio visited his camp. Thomas related a conversation between the chief and Major Price: "The col. [sic] came to the agency about ten o'clock and had a long talk with Loco." His visit with Victorio the previous evening had left Loco worried that Victorio was still in a temper and unpredictable. During the meeting, Loco expressed concern that Victorio might again sabotage the fledgling peace with a reorganized and more destructive outbreak.[15]

In the course of the discussion with the chief, Price told Loco "that he had acted wisely in coming in with his people that he could now trust him as an Indian who told the truth and wanted peace . . . and asked him what he supposed Victoria wanted. Loco replied that he was no longer Principal Chief (Agt. Piper deposed him) and could not speak for Victoria nor form any idea as to what he would do since he had broken his word, as was his habit, but as for himself and his people that he commanded here—they were here, and here they wished to remain in peace and quit doing evil. Make him principal chief and return the Indians to the agency and he would be responsible for their good behavior."[16]

Loco's revelation that Agent Piper had removed him as the principal chief explains much about the developments at Ojo Caliente before the removal. When Loco came into Fort Craig seeking peace in May 1869, he was the only Apache leader whom Colonel Grover mentioned. Chief Loco was clearly calling the shots for the Apaches when Piper took over at the agency in the fall of 1870. Responding to Loco's successful peace efforts on October 19, 1870, Cochise, Victorio, Nana, Tomascito, and twenty-two other band leaders met with federal officials to talk about Loco's peace. They represented about 790 Apaches. Lieutenant Charles Drew had noted earlier that Loco appeared to be talking for most of the Indians. In everybody's mind—Indian agents, the military, modern historians, and most Apaches—Loco was the principal chief, keeping the Indians at peace and negotiating with the Americans on their behalf.[17]

Although it seems that Victorio attended a couple of meetings between Loco and the Americans, no records indicate that Victorio moved out of the mountains to join Loco until November 1869, six months after Loco's initial contact with the Americans. If anything, Victorio was indecisive about the peace negotiations. At some level he was interested in a peaceful arrangement with the Americans, but his primary desire was for a return to the glory days of old, not to start a corn farm on a reservation. Loco intended to end the fighting forever.[18]

Thus Victorio was a late joiner of Loco's peaceful group, of dubious commitment, suspicious and bellicose, and definitely more difficult to deal with than Loco. Members of his family often caused trouble on the reservation. He continued raiding throughout the Indians' stay at Ojo Caliente and their subsequent time at Tularosa, even after Piper appointed him the principal chief.[19]

What drove Agent Orlando Piper to remove amicable and cooperative Loco and replace him with the truculent Victorio? Unfortunately, nothing has been found in the historical record to explain Piper's thinking. Two possibilities come to mind. It is possible that Piper's strong religious beliefs included a disdain for drinking and heavy drinkers, and Loco often had a drop too much. Victorio did his share of tippling as well, but he was more discreet about it. Despite a touchy, ill-tempered personality and the fact that he was not at all committed to a total peace, Victorio would have been mostly sober when dealing with the sanctimonious Piper.

A second, more intriguing possibility has to do with Piper's coming on the job in late 1870, during the middle of the Apaches' successful resistance to being removed to Fort Stanton. Loco, clearly in charge at the time, was the spokesperson who took the Indians' case against removal to the government. Piper, therefore, might have offered Victorio the principal chief's job sometime around March 1872 as an incentive to sell out the tribe. At that point things were going poorly for the Americans in the Tularosa argument. The Apache leaders not only presented a united opposition to removal to Tularosa but also unanimously refused the repeatedly offered coercive trips to Washington. They remained firm in their opposition to the move until early March 1872. On March 17, 1872, Piper reported that Victorio had broken ranks with the other Chiricahua leaders and was the only chief to agree to a trip to Washington and subsequently a removal to Tularosa. Cochise and Loco declined the junket. Piper probably had installed Victorio as the new principal chief or promised the position to him if he cooperated with the American removal plans.

It was also around this time that Piper began referring to Victorio as the principal chief. Victorio stood alone for two weeks before the Apaches' open resistance to removal began to fade. Then, on March 28, 1872, Piper wrote to Nathaniel Pope that after "a long and satisfactory talk" with Victorio and Loco, they had said "they would go to Tularosa but not to Washington, [although] they would like to see their Great Father and that they are satisfied he is their friend."[20] The unified Indian resistance to the move was just beginning to have its effect when suddenly and inexplicably the two primary leaders on the reservation reversed course. I believe Piper bought off Victorio with the principal chief position and that Loco, now without government support and consequently wielding little influence among his tribesmen, was coerced into going along.

An appointed principal chief held extraordinary sway over the day-to-day existence of the average Indian on a reservation. A government-made principal man was the Indians' primary contact with the government agent. To a large extent he controlled the flow and distribution of rations and other necessaries.[21] For those who wanted to remain peacefully on the reservation, the principal chief's good will was essential for survival. His protection was also crucial for those who continued to raid and use the reservation as sanctuary. He could provide excuses for absences, cover for the raiders, and assist in avoiding or reducing jail time if they were caught. Above all, the principal chief could protect his own relatives from arrest or punishment by the agent, regardless of how deplorable their misconduct. The incident in which Victorio and Loco refused to aid Agent Thomas in arresting the survivors of Sanchez's raiding party was an example of Victorio's using his influence to keep his relatives out of jail.

Historian Dan Thrapp did not take into account the effect of "owning" the principal chief's job when he suggested that Victorio gained the position because he had matured into a wise counselor and great war leader.[22] Instead, Victorio's following increased specifically because he was appointed by Piper as the reservation's main man—the official dispenser of government rations and good will. This conclusion is supported by a brief look at Victorio's raiding activities from Ojo Caliente and the Tularosa reservation. About the time of his appointment as principal chief in 1872, he left with one hundred raiders for a massive foray in Sonora. After Loco resumed the position of principal chief, Agent Thomas reported in January 1874 that "Victoria left with eight or ten followers to go to Chiricahua Agency and into Sonora to steal some horses."[23]

The influence of the principal chief becomes more apparent in the events following the attempt to arrest Sanchez and the subsequent tribal breakaway. As Major Price rounded up the stray bands involved in the escape, he extracted a promise that they would report to the agency directly and then resettle in their old camps. Only Loco and Gavinda followed the agreement.

Upon his return to the agency and out of the presence of Victorio, Loco took the opportunity to lobby for the principal man position and to denounce Victorio. "Loco says that as the principal chief, Victoria has failed up to the present time to keep his promises and he [Loco] fears that he [Victorio] is acting deceitfully and does not intend to come in at all."[24]

For the next six days, Victorio shuffled between the different camps around the Tularosa agency in an apparent effort to find support among the local leaders for a more organized outbreak. Failing that, perhaps he was attempting to gauge a way to surrender at the agency, maintain his dignity, and avoid jail time. Major Price's impression was that Victorio "is so frightened that he does not know what course to pursue."[25]

On August 5, Nana, another leader, Raffaille, and their bands returned from a visit with relatives on Cochise's Chiricahua reservation. Upon learning of the chaos at Tularosa, they went immediately to the agency. Thomas wrote, "They all talked over the troubles here and Nana assured me that he would soon put things in order." Nana was the oldest of the Chihenne leaders at the time, and his suggestions were seldom ignored. Consequently, on August 6, Victorio and a "large number of his people reported to the agency," where he took an all-out tongue-lashing from Thomas. The agent concluded the scolding by firing Victorio from the principal chief's job. "I then told Victoria that he was not worthy to be principal chief any longer and put Loco in his place. Victorio said that he was very much ashamed of his conduct and would promise to do better but I told him that I would try Loco for awhile." Thomas was exuberant over his coup: "Great good has been accomplished in the last two weeks. . . . The lives of the employees at the agency will no longer be in constant danger."[26]

Following the Apache instinct to go with the winner, the best provider, the principal chief, all the Indians on the reservation except Victorio's immediate family switched allegiance back to Loco. Within three weeks of Loco's return to the principal chief's position, Thomas wrote, "Loco now has nearly all the people with him. Victoria having only about thirty in all."[27]

Meanwhile, Victorio, his immediate family, and a few friends were doing a slow burn in their ranchería. Loss of the principal chief's job was a hefty economic blow to Victorio's people, not to mention a humiliation for Victorio. The affair also stripped the group of the protection afforded by their leader's privileged position as the government's main man.[28]

Victorio's ranchería included Pajarita, Victorio's son-in-law, and Pajarita's three brothers, Pajarita Chiquito, Turevia, and one whose name is unknown. The Pajarita brothers were sons of the influential chief Cuchillo Negro, but they were all bad actors—seldom sober, bullies, and notoriously violent. Among other things, the Pajaritas were the culprits who shot arrows at the agency staff. That one of the brothers was cross-eyed might have accounted for the multiple near misses. During Victorio's stint as principal chief, the four siblings fell under his protection and had the run of the reservation. Agent Thomas was clearly afraid of the lot, but because they were shielded by Victorio, he showed little interest in arresting them until the breakout incident in July. They not only avoided punishment for their misdemeanors but also got away with murder. On June 12, 1873, "Pajarita, son-in-law of Victoria, the same that lately killed Snaggle Tooth Ponce and the squaw, came from his rancheria and commenced firing on the Indians at the outskirts of the crowd and fired four or five shots wounding one Indian. I suppose mortally and then, supported by his three brothers defied the whole tribe for half an hour . . . and soon after left the reservation, but the tribe was apprehensive of danger from them continually."[29]

This outburst pushed the reservation residents to their limits, but few were willing to deal with the troublemakers on their own. "The Indians were very anxious to have the soldiers kill the four desperados [the Pajarita brothers]," Thomas wrote to Price. Thomas denied the request, afraid that an arrest might trigger another outbreak. Thomas told Lieutenant George Walker, who commanded the agency guard, "to let the Indians manage the fight themselves as long as they confined it to themselves." Repeated requests from tribal members to rid the reservation of the "four pests" met with Thomas's reply that "there were men and arms enough in the tribe to manage four Indians and [that] the soldiers would have nothing to do with it. Finally the four went away. The whole tribe is greatly excited and demoralized and I do not know yet where the thing will end but I hope they will quiet down in a few days."[30]

Three weeks after Loco returned to his role as principal chief, the Pajarita brothers were at it again. Thomas recounted Loco's description of the incident: "Loco, the new chief, says the four Pajaritas wanted to go off on a stealing expedition and he opposed it strongly. Turevia, to vent his spite, shot a squaw but did not kill her, then Pajarita killed her outright." Taking Thomas's advice for the Indians to solve their own problems, Loco immediately recruited volunteers to clear up the Pajarita nuisance.[31]

To get a sense of the scene that followed, it is useful to know about the weapons involved. Almost all the Apache men owned the ever-present bow and arrow. Practiced warriors could let fly somewhere between eighteen and twenty arrows a minute.[32] Many carried black powder revolvers—six shots in a few seconds—and muzzle-loading percussion rifles—three shots a minute. A few probably owned breech-loading, single-shot cartridge rifles—up to eight or nine shots per minute. Loco and Nana carried bolt-action "needle guns." With a little experience, a good man with a needle gun could load, aim, and fire a shot about every six seconds—ten shots a minute.[33]

Agent Thomas described the scene when Loco's volunteers arrived at Victorio's camp:

On the 24th inst. they [the Apaches] had an ugly fight at Victoria's camp, about two miles from the agency. . . . Loco, feeling that they had had already too much of that sort of thing, found the Pajaritas and brought his needle gun to operate for their extermination. Nana also has a needle gun which he used freely for the same purpose. The fight became pretty general at very close range, the length of a lance. . . . Pajarita and Pajarita Chiquito and a squaw were killed. Turevia, another of the Pajarita brothers was shot through the body and it was supposed he would die the same night but I shall not be surprised to see him recover; the fourth Pajarita brother was slightly wounded in the arm. Victoria was shot in the face with an arrow. Rafaelle was shot in the leg, breaking it. A young man was terribly wounded in the elbow. A squaw was badly wounded in the side with an arrow. Jaralche's son was slightly wounded in the breast with an arrow— three killed and seven wounded. Loco and Nana seemed to make it their special business to rid the tribe of these four pests, and succeeded in killing two and wounding the other two— one only slightly but the other will hardly recover.[34]

The shootout took place in an area perhaps somewhat smaller than a basketball court. Many of the combatants blasted away at one another with large caliber guns in a space no larger than a modern living room. Thomas's measure of the distance between shooters—the length of an Apache lance—would have placed some of the combatants from eight to twelve feet apart, three to four paces. It is unclear exactly how many men were involved. Ten are mentioned, all of whom were wounded except Loco and Nana. Two or three times that many could easily have participated.

Loco had ended the Pajarita brothers' reign of terror and reestablished his leadership on the reservation in the agent's mind and, more importantly, among the Apaches. Further, he returned peace with the Americans to the front burner. The downside was that Victorio and his family were henceforth estranged from Victorio's lifelong cohort. A week after the shootout, Thomas reported that Loco had the support of most of the tribe and that "Victoria and his party feel very hostile on account of this loss but I do not think they will fight with their present force. Loco says that the [additional] Indians that are expected from Chiricahua [Cochise's reservation] are his own people." On September 3, Thomas noted that things had cooled a bit, but the tribe remained divided.[35]

It appears that Loco and Victorio might ultimately have mended fences enough to cooperate on a venture or two in the next few years before Victorio's death, but Loco was never really forgiven for the gunfight. Before his violent death, Pajarita had been married to Victorio's daughter. The Apaches of the 1800s thought of marriage less as a romantic undertaking than as an economic enterprise. A good son-in-law was a major financial asset, and as such, Pajarita contributed substantially to the fortunes of Victorio's family. Morris Opler discussed an Apache son-in-law's relationship: "So strong is the sense of economic obligation to the wife's parents that its dictates are heeded even when, for some reason, matrilocal residence [that is, with the wife's family] is not maintained." One of Opler's Chiricahua informants put it this way: "A son may help support the old people if he desires to, but the son-in-law has to support them. . . . If his father-in-law wants a son-in-law to do something he has to do it." When Loco shot Pajarita, he blasted a fifty-eight-caliber hole in the heart of Victorio's financial portfolio. Naturally, Victorio was left feeling "very hostile."[36]

With Loco back in control, the mood of the reservation changed almost overnight. Thomas wrote: "I appointed a new principal chief who exercises a good deal of wholesome authority over the tribe. . . . Three months ago the lives of the agent and employees were threatened almost every week, sometimes shot at with arrows and sometimes threatened with firearms. Now the Indians are pretty well convinced that such demonstrations are neither for their profit nor pleasure. Loco—the new principal chief—is quite an improvement on the old one [Victorio]. He commands more respect among the Indians than Victoria did—exercises more authority and uses his authority in keeping the Indians at home. If he continues to do so well, his promotion will have a general good effect."[37]

Under Loco's leadership things began to calm down at Tularosa, or at least they appeared to from the Americans' standpoint. That is not to say that the Apaches were any more satisfied with their location than before, or any more settled. A few were still raiding, mostly in Mexico, and Agent Thomas was continually in a tiff with one leader or another. Nevertheless, he repeatedly praised the Apaches. In November he noted, "The Indians have remained very tractable."[38] His December report read, "These Indians are more tractable now than I thought one year ago they could be made in three years."[39] Glowing reports continued to flow. In April 1874: "During the month the Indians have behaved remarkably well. . . . A large number of the Indians now seem willing to work for pay." In July: "The Indians are behaving well at the agency."[40]

A year after replacing Victorio with Loco as headman, Thomas summarized the accomplishments of the year: "The Southern Apaches have . . . acquired a new and tamer expression of countenance. . . . They have not offered on any occasion during the year to shoot the agent or any of the employees."[41]

Once again national economic woes intervened. In 1873, most of the country's principal financial firms again crashed. Another major panic followed. Government revenues dropped and remained down. Scrimping and saving became watchwords in government budget offices for a decade.[42] As a result, the idea of consolidating more Indians on fewer reservations emerged. Officials began efforts to consolidate all the Apache bands on two or three large reservations. The new superintendent of Indian affairs for New Mexico, Edwin Dudley, who had succeeded Nathaniel Pope, again tried to get Loco to agree to move in with Cochise or go over to Fort Stanton to join the Mescaleros, but to no avail. In May 1873 Dudley was forced to report that "it would be impossible to secure their removal by any means short of force."[43]

Government accountants soon recognized that if one sought to save money in Indian affairs in 1873, eliminating the Tularosa reservation was a good place to start. Hauling supplies over the mountains to the reservation was an extravagance, whereas the warehouses at Fort Craig lay only forty miles from Cañada Alamosa and could be reached by a relatively level, riverbottom road.[44] General Howard's comments of November 1872—that the Ojo Caliente area would make an excellent reservation, and a great deal of money could be saved by moving the Apaches there—rekindled Washington's interest in the area. Ben Thomas began promoting a return to Ojo Caliente among the Indians, apparently at Superintendent Dudley's request. On May 5, 1873, Thomas wrote Dudley, "I spoke to Victoria in regard to moving [back to Cañada Alamosa] and he said that Cañada was a good place but Cochise and his Indians were bad, and if they went there, he [Victorio] did not want to go."[45]

Despite the Chihennes' refusal to live at Ojo Caliente with the Chokonens, the commissioner of Indian affairs, Edward P. Smith, directed Dudley to visit Cochise and Agent Jeffords on the Chiricahua reservation to promote the plan and see what the Chiricahuas thought about the idea.[46] While calling on Cochise, Dudley also wanted to meet Loco, Nana, and Victorio's Apaches at Tularosa, but he fretted that if word leaked that he was scouting the Ojo Caliente area for a reservation, money-minded homesteaders would flood in. The government would then be forced to purchase the speculators' improvements at inflated prices. He wrote to the commissioner, "Of course that country will be filled with squatters as soon as it becomes known that there is a possibility of its being set apart as an Indian Reservation." To prevent that prospect, before he left, Dudley issued a directive reserving the area "until it can be decided whether or not the Indians will remove there."[47]

Dudley inspected Ojo Caliente, visited Forts Thorn and Bayard, and learned along the way that Cochise was not only behaving himself but was also protecting the road between Tucson and Fort Bowie from depredations by other Apaches. Seeing this, Dudley questioned the idea of moving the Chiricahuas from their location overlooking the road, but he indicated that he had decided that reestablishing the agency at Cañada Alamosa would "satisfy the citizens and Indians, induce a sedentary mode of life, and allow a successful concentration of the Chiricahuas at the same point." Commissioner Smith ordered further investigation.[48]

Dudley's trip proved to be unnecessary. Only days after he left to visit the area, President Grant issued an executive order on April 9, 1874, withdrawing a seven-hundred-square-mile area "from sale and reserved for the use and occupation of such Indians as the Secretary of the Interior may see fit to locate thereon."[49] It was approximately the same area proposed by Chief Loco in 1869. Government officials called it the Hot Springs Reserve.

Thomas continued to stew over the Chihennes' insistence that they were uninterested in sharing Warm Springs with Cochise and his people. "I cannot give you any definite idea of the feeling my Indians have in regard to the proposed change of location. Although they have hitherto lost no opportunity to declare one and all, that Cañada was the one place altogether desirable, they now seem to prefer remaining here. . . . [Because] the presence of Cochise is to be made the condition of their being allowed to go, they seem to have lost their zeal."[50] Whatever had occurred between the Chihennes and Cochise's people was not something easily forgotten, and both groups were clear that any mixing of the two bands was out of the question.[51]

Cochise died on June 8, without any help from his white antagonists. Superintendent Dudley expressed the opinion, "Cochise is now dead and I believe that fact will do away with all opposition among your [Thomas's] Indians to removal." The commissioner of Indian affairs notified Thomas that "your agency is to be removed immediately to the Hot Springs." Dudley wanted the new agency to be "ready for occupancy not later than July 15th."[52]

Three days later the Tularosa Apaches were still resisting the removal, but the Americans gave little regard for what the Indians thought. Thomas wrote Dudley on June 27, "I do not apprehend any trouble in removing the Indians. . . . I do not believe there will be much trouble in persuading them to go after we commence issuing rations at Hot Springs. The Indians are improving all the time and never gave so little trouble to the Agent or settlers as now."

Despite their concerns, once the decision was made, the Apaches enthusiastically headed for home. In early August 1874 the Chihennes returned to Warm Springs with Loco as the government-appointed headman. Thomas wrote of the milestone move: "The principal event of the month has been the removal of the Agency to Ojo Caliente and that work has taken almost the entire time and attention of all hands at the agency. . . . The Indians are anxious to be off for the new place, and they have already camped twenty miles out on the road so that they may have that much of the journey accomplished with their baggage and be all ready to move on to Ojo Caliente immediately after the next ration day—the last at this place [Tularosa]."[53]

In his end-of-the-year report Thomas declared, "The Indians are well pleased with their new location. . . . All the concerns of the Indians have been satisfactory and nothing in respect of them has transpired worthy of note."[54]

In June, two months before the removal, Thomas asked Loco if he was willing to make the move to Ojo Caliente. He replied, "Yes, but give us some place and let us remain there." Superintendent Dudley opined to the commissioner, "I believe that Tularosa has been a failure from the beginning."[55]

CHAPTER EIGHT

"We Are Good Indians"

John M. Shaw replaced Benjamin Thomas as agent for Loco's people on November 15, 1874, three months to the day after the Apaches returned to Warm Springs. Shaw was a close associate of Tom Jeffords, the Cochise Chiricahua agent from the inception of that reservation, and G. W. Cook, who had been an officer in the New Mexico Volunteers during the peace talks with the Chihennes in 1865. Through his associates, Shaw knew the ins and outs of the Indian business—and how to profit from it.[1]

Shaw wrote just after his arrival that the Warm Springs Indians were "now peaceful law-abiding Indians. . . . Should they never make any better Indians than they are now, the government is well rewarded for all it has cost. The change to us here seems almost unaccountable."[2]

When the Chihennes moved to Ojo Caliente from the Tularosa Valley, Ben Thomas was feeding about four hundred Indians. As soon as Shaw assumed control of the agency, the number of Indians on the reservation mysteriously grew by leaps and bounds. Nine months after he took office, Shaw reported that he was caring for 1,317 Apaches, an astounding 229 percent growth. Shaw's ration purchases skyrocketed, justified by the need to feed and clothe hundreds of imaginary new arrivals. He continually complained that supplies for the Indians were running low and put the Indians on half rations. Even as he reduced the Apaches' food supply, Shaw cooked the books to show that he was issuing more beef, flour, and other supplies than any previous agent and urgently requested authority to purchase even larger quantities. Unlike Orlando Piper, who had probably inflated the reservation population to give the Indians more food, Shaw was selling the supplies for personal profit.

The Apaches with Loco saw exactly what was going on. It is not surprising that illegal trading at Cañada Alamosa returned to where it had been before the Tularosa interlude. The Shaw-induced famine on the reservation worked well for illegal traders who encouraged the Apaches to raid for livestock that they could eat and swap for the necessities of life. Within six months of assuming his duties as the new agent, Shaw, ignoring his own complicity, complained that white ruffians were drifting onto the reservation, looking for easy profits. Lieutenant Colonel Edward Hatch, commander of the District of New Mexico, agreed that the reservation was attracting "a disreputable class of traders."[3]

Homesteaders in the area complained daily to Shaw about alleged thefts by the Indians. Shaw lamented, "I am doing my best to keep them quiet, but three parties were here yesterday and today reporting my Indians on the Rio Grande and that they are stealing stock."[4] Finally, "a party of citizens supposed to be, made a raid upon the reservation . . . and drove off a herd of horses belonging to the Apaches. The Indians are very much enraged and will no doubt retaliate. Some will no doubt join the Indians that are roaming and depredating on Sonora; strange Indians appear at the agency and suddenly disappear. Until those that remained in the mountains from the Chiricahua Reservation are driven in or brought in, they will cooperate together, and cause trouble. I counted nine strange Indians today."[5]

Under Shaw's starvation rations and agency mismanagement, the progress Loco's Chihennes were making toward a peaceful adjustment to the new order screeched to a halt. Civil disorder returned to the Apache camps, and old feuds erupted. In October 1876 Shaw reported, "They had a fight among themselves. . . . Killed three chiefs and wounded a large number yesterday. They had another fight, only one killed. This will cause a division among them and make my work still more difficult." Most of the nearby soldiers had been withdrawn by this point, leaving Shaw without any real protection.[6]

Despite the mounting problems, Loco continued to demonstrate his commitment to saving the peace. Although he knew that Shaw was defrauding his people, Loco shot and killed an Indian who balked at Shaw's starvation rations and threatened to end the agent's parsimony in the old Apache way. Shaw's version of the affair reflects his relief that Loco saved his skin: "Loco, my reliable chief, in trying to keep them in order was attacked by one and he was obliged to shoot him in self defense. This caused great excitement." Had the disgruntled man managed to kill any agency staff, the Chihennes would have been on the run again, facing the full brunt of American retribution. Loco had no other option.

To avoid a revenge feud between Loco's following and the band of the man Loco had killed, Shaw bailed out the chief with a deal brokered by Victorio. Shaw submitted a justification with a voucher to pay off the family of Loco's victim:

> I transmit voucher for $242.75 for merchandise purchased for the Southern Apache Indians and to explain the emergency and necessity for the same. The first purchase for Loco (principal Chief) was made by decision of the tribe in council, requiring him to pay the amount named to prevent an outbreak and quell a rebellion in the tribe against the constituted authority on account of his having killed an influential Indian of the tribe. Loco was endeavoring to maintain order at the agency on issue day when a serious disturbance threatened us by the over exacting demands of the Indians for a larger issue of rations than they were allowed. Loco, in order to maintain authority and protect the agent and employees from violence was compelled to shoot an Indian leader of the disturbance which if he had not done I am satisfied would have [been] followed by serious results. Although the relatives of the Indians demanded much more, Victorio . . . and myself settled it by paying the amount which I accordingly paid as mentioned. August 10, 1876.[7]

The need for food, coupled with the opportunity to trade their stolen stock and goods at the illegal emporium in Cañada Alamosa, pumped renewed vigor into the Apaches' old lifestyle and wore hard on Loco's ability to hold the reservation Indians in check. Finally, Colonel Hatch traveled from Santa Fe to Fort McRae in mid-April 1876 to evaluate the situation. He immediately saw that the Indians were suffering from food shortages and were "extremely defiant. . . . They declared openly that the Government had acted in bad faith, that no meat had been issued to them for four weeks, that many of their young men were away on raids for horses and mules and it was better for them all to go than to remain and starve."

Hatch also reported that under the conditions created by Shaw, "the chiefs Victorio, Loco, Sanchez, Rafael, Nana, declared their intention was to secure a peace with Sonora and then raid upon our Territory. Our territory was now rich and Sonora poor," they explained. "They declared they could do better by war on the United States than they could do at peace with this country and war with Sonora. They [Loco and Victorio] said all the other Apaches would join them, that the Indians had fully calculated upon this should open hostilities occur."

Hatch apparently calmed the reservation leaders but reported, "The leading chiefs stated openly that however much they might be inclined to keep the peace, it was impossible for them to hold their young men, who would raid for horses and mules, that the sale was a ready one among the Mexican towns, and through this means they were enabled to supply themselves with excellent arms and ammunition."[8]

Ignoring Shaw's excuses and disregarding the notion that the Indian Office might act with haste, the army made the Apaches technical prisoners of war. This allowed the military to legally assume the care and feeding of the Indians. Hatch observed that the military's actions saved the day.

The Chihennes' increased raiding was not the only reason the Military District of New Mexico focused its attention on the Ojo Caliente area. In June 1876 the Indian Office closed the Chiricahua reservation in Arizona but failed to remove all its residents to the San Carlos reservation as intended. Many escaped, and some of the escapees headed for the Southern Apache agency. The army, ever alert for Indian Office blunders, quickly dispatched additional troops to the Ojo Caliente area to await the expected arrival of Chiricahua refugees. Hatch believed that the timely arrival of troops prevented a combined Chihenne-Chiricahua war on the unarmed settlers in the area. The colonel's quick response to the food shortages probably did more to prevent an outbreak than did the army's rapid arrival.[9]

In the meantime, increasingly suspicious clerks in Washington delayed Shaw's request for additional rations. Shaw traveled to Santa Fe seeking political support in a bold effort to speed the delivery of supplies. The territorial delegate to Congress, Stephen Elkins, apparently bought Shaw's spiel and requested that the commissioner of Indian affairs look into the matter, something that was already in the works.[10]

The commissioner sent no-nonsense Indian Inspector John Kemble to assess the situation. Kemble arrived at the Southern Apache agency in early May 1876. Within two weeks he had seen enough. He sent back a scathing report on Shaw's activities. The agent was purchasing for as many as a thousand more Apaches than were actually on the reservation.

Agency records were in disarray. Shaw had kept neither head counts nor ration tickets (receipts). He had purchased three times more hay than was needed to feed agency livestock. Blankets, clothing, and cloth intended for the Indians could be found for sale in dry goods stores up and down the Rio Grande. Inspector Kemble accused Shaw and his suppliers of graft and urged his immediate removal from office.[11]

When Kemble exposed him, Shaw offered the ingenious excuse that he had calculated the number of Indians on the reservation on the basis of "the amount of beef issued, rather than the amount of issues from the number of Indians as fixed by actual count." Shaw was no fool. Without a census of the Apaches or receipts for the issues, it was impossible to prove that he was a crook. For Shaw, it was better to be counted as stupid than criminal—and counted stupid he was. The federal officials also liked the excuse. It was cheaper to chastise a fool than to prosecute a felon. Acting Commissioner S. A. Galpin wrote Shaw that his management of the agency "shows lack of judgment on your part, or an absence of business qualifications essential to the proper conduct of the affairs of an Indian Agency, and an extravagance in the issue of supplies, either willfully or ignorantly, not warranted by the most liberal construction of the rules governing the management of your duties as Indian Agent." Shaw resigned on June 19, 1877, upbraided but unrepentant—and a much wealthier man. With his ill-gotten profits he purchased a large ranch adjacent to the reservation. He was never indicted. His position was filled temporarily by Dr. Walter Whitney as acting agent.[12]

For all the troubles besetting the Chihennes at Ojo Caliente, in the end it was the circumstance surrounding footloose Chokonen refugees from the Chiricahua reservation that brought ruin to Loco and the Chihennes on the Southern Apache reservation. When the Indian Office shut down the Chiricahuas' reservation in the spring of 1876, a substantial number of Chiricahuas eluded the roundup and began rampaging through the territories or headed for Ojo Caliente to join relatives or friends there.

The man who had been chosen to roust the Chokonens from their reservation was the Indian agent at San Carlos, John P. Clum. Clum was a twenty-two-year-old college dropout when he arrived at the San Carlos agency on August 8, 1874. The young agent was also an incorrigible braggart, a shameless self-promoter with a personal agenda that always included self-aggrandizement. A tendency to fly off the handle led him to resign several times. Less than a month before his final resignation in 1877, Clum telegraphed the commissioner of Indian affairs and volunteered to handle the entire Apache problem if the government would increase his salary and provide him with two additional companies of Indian police. The editor of the *Prescott Miner* called Clum a "young bombast" whose "brass and impudence . . . is perfectly ridiculous." The editor recommended that Clum's head be "banded with iron hoops as a preventative to explosion. Where such an extraordinary amount of combined talents exist, mostly composed of gas, there is danger of explosion and death." That was pretty much everyone's opinion.[13]

Agent Clum attacked his work aggressively, with an arrogant self-confidence that offended many but impressed some. To his credit, he was remarkably competent and entirely honest. He pioneered innovative programs in reservation management and tribal government at San Carlos that are standard practice throughout the Bureau of Indian Affairs today.

Officials in the Indian Office were among those impressed with his work. In the spring of 1875 he superintended the removal of fifteen hundred Yavapais from the Date Creek reservation near Wickenburg, Arizona, and persuaded approximately thirteen hundred Coyotero Apaches on the White Mountain reservation into relocating to San Carlos. About a year later, in June 1876, Clum convinced 325 Chiricahuas under Cochise's sons, Taza and Naiche, to relocate to the San Carlos reservation from their Dragoon Mountains reserve. Every reservation he closed represented a substantial savings for the Office of Indian Affairs.[14]

Officials in Washington beamed at the alleged success of the Chiricahuas' peaceful removal, but at best only half the Chiricahuas went to San Carlos with Clum. The others spilled off the reservation and scattered throughout the Southwest, reverting to the old Apache ways. Many made their way to the Chihenne reservation at Ojo Caliente.[15]

The commissioner's annual report for 1876 noted that the agent for the Southern Apaches reported that 162 Chiricahuas "removed on their own account to the Hot Springs reservation in New Mexico, where they have friends and relatives." Agent Shaw wrote to the commissioner on June 23, 1876, that "others [Chiricahua escapees] are reported in the mountains near here and are expected in; I think there are more [hiding] on the [Warm Springs] reservation than have reported."[16] Shaw was in a quandary about how to handle the more volatile Chokonens: "Parties of Chiricahuas are arriving and I wish to know what action to take respecting them." Shaw reported that the arrival of the Chiricahuas caused "a good deal of excitement, and should I order them away, I fear some of these Indians [Chihennes] would go with them and take to the mountains and cause great trouble. . . . It is quite a critical time."[17]

After their reservation was closed on June 12, 1876, the indignant Chiricahuas began raiding almost immediately. By August 18, the roving bands had murdered at least twenty settlers and stolen more than a hundred animals. Fifteen other citizens had been killed in the Sonoita region alone. Even though angry Chiricahuas did most of the raiding, bad press focused attention on the Chihennes at Ojo Caliente. The Americans and Mexicans in the area were unable or unwilling to identify which band was doing the raiding. At first, Colonel August Kautz, the new departmental commander in Arizona, issued a lame defense of the Indians, blamed the attacks on Mexican hoodlums, and suggested that influential businessmen in the region exaggerated the violence to encourage the army to pump more troops and money into the area. He later acknowledged that the Chiricahuas were roaming in greater numbers than he at first realized, and the raiders probably included some Chihennes from the reservation. Lieutenant Austin Henely was sent to investigate. He soon turned up evidence that the Warm Springs Indians were joining the renegades. Not only that, but many of the Chokonen and Nednai raiders were using Ojo Caliente as a rendezvous for rest and rations. In February 1877, Lieutenant Louis Rucker tracked a band of raiders almost to the reservation boundary. The following month, Henely followed another raiding party directly to the agency.[18]

Any chance that Chief Loco might succeed in keeping his people at peace became increasingly doubtful. Loco, who saw the problem, was helpless to do much about it but complain. Nana joined Loco in trying to stop the influx of Chiricahuas, but Victorio thwarted their efforts. Most Chihennes, especially those with Nana's and Loco's groups, remained quietly on the reservation, but the army and the settlers believed the Chihennes were more deeply involved in the raids than they actually were.[19]

Balatchu, a Chihenne, told Morris Opler years later that Loco had caused no trouble, but both the Chokonens and other Chiricahuas persistently brought stolen horses onto the reservation, and Loco's people were blamed. He reported that Loco and Nana together told Victorio, "There are too many Chiricahuas and Tcokanans here. They are bringing horses. They will get us into trouble." Victorio dismissed the warning, commenting that "these people are not bothering us." He refused to take action. Ultimately, Apaches raided a Pima Indian village. The Pimas complained to their missionary, who wrote to officials in Washington. As a result, Balatchu told Opler, "they [Clum's police] came and took [some] men prisoners. They chained them and took them to San Carlos. Then they took the whole Tcihende [Chihenne] tribe there."[20]

Long-lasting resentments eventually developed between the peaceful Chihenne leaders and the raiders, such as Geronimo and Naiche, who brought in stolen stock and aroused hostility toward Loco's people.[21] As the tension mounted, Shaw ordered "all Indians belonging to other tribes and reservations to return to their own homes, or at least to leave this reservation."[22] The Chokonens ignored Shaw's ultimatum and continued to use the Ojo Caliente area as a base. Loco's young men continued to be drawn into the old raiding lifestyle.[23]

During the removal misadventure on the Chiricahua reservation, three previously unknown leaders, Geronimo, Juh, and Nolgee, readily agreed to relocate to the San Carlos reservation. Geronimo, however, persuaded John Clum to give them four-day safe passes, time supposedly needed to collect their people. The three took the passes and hightailed it to Mexico with approximately two hundred followers. Agent Clum was left holding the bag and nursing a badly bruised ego. He subsequently took up a life-long avocation of vilifying Geronimo. In his prolific publications following the removal, Clum blamed virtually every depredation in the Southwest on him. In 1876, Geronimo was little more than a garden-variety Apache with no remarkable abilities, virtually unknown. Clum's fiery articles decrying Geronimo's talents as a brutal raider elevated him to the status of a notorious and most-wanted outlaw, perhaps even a legend in his own time. He was in fact an intractable raider whose misdeeds and repeated appearances around Cañada Alamosa sabotaged Loco's peace efforts.

When Lieutenant Henely spotted the now notorious Apache leader on March 16, 1877, relaxing on the Warm Springs reservation, he fired off a telegram to Colonel Kautz saying he had located Geronimo and a large group of the runaway Chiricahuas. Geronimo had recently returned from a successful raid-and-rustle expedition with about 170 stolen horses. He called attention to himself when he made a scene after he was refused rations for the time when he was away from the reservation.[24]

News that Geronimo and more than a hundred renegades were in the army's sights near Ojo Caliente electrified the bureaucracy. Kautz quickly sent the word to Arizona Governor Anson Safford. The governor, in turn, telegraphed Edward Smith, the commissioner of Indian affairs: "I have good reasons to believe for some time past that the renegade Chiricahua Indians were making the Warm Springs agency a rendezvous where they go for rest and rations, to go forth on raids at their pleasure.... Those Indians should be removed and all concentrated at San Carlos." A second telegram specifically asked the commissioner, "Please order Agent Clum by telegraph to remove renegade Chiricahuas to San Carlos. Warm Springs agent [Shaw] should be removed at once."[25]

After his removal of the Chokonens from the Chiricahua reserve to San Carlos in 1876, his third such affair, Clum had become the Indian

Office's in-house expert on tribal removals, relocations, and concentration. When the opportunity to capture and remove about 135 Chiricahua escapees on the Ojo Caliente reservation arose in 1877, the Indian Office turned to Clum at San Carlos. The soon-to-resign agent leaped at the opportunity. It was a chance to even the score with his nemesis, Geronimo, bag an additional 135 of the recalcitrant Chiricahuas who had escaped removal the year before, and establish himself as the hero who subdued the wildest Indians on the continent.[26]

After receiving Safford's telegram, Commissioner Smith directed Clum that "if practicable," he should take his Indian police and arrest the renegade Chiricahuas at the Warm Springs agency. "Seize stolen horses in their possession . . . restore the property to rightful owners; remove renegades to San Carlos, and hold them in confinement for robbery and murder." At this point, apparently no one had given much thought to disturbing Loco's more or less peaceful Chihenne band at Ojo Caliente.[27]

Clum immediately notified Safford, "Am ordered to take Apache police and capture Geronimo at Ojo Caliente, New Mexico, will need my company of Apaches now in service of Arizona Territory. Request they be returned immediately to my jurisdiction." Safford agreed by telegram the next day. Clum then wired Clay Beauford, who commanded the on-loan scouts, to march at once to Silver City and await his arrival on about April 8.[28]

Eleven days after receiving the commissioner's telegram, Clum was on the move. "I start a company of Indian Police for New Mexico tomorrow. Another company will join me at Silver City. I have asked Gen. [sic] Kautz and Hatch to cooperate and will overtake the police at Silver City." Clum notified Kautz in Arizona of his plans and telegraphed a request to Hatch in New Mexico to move his troops into position to block possible escape routes, which would "enable us to dictate terms to the Indians and meet any resistance they may offer."[29]

Clum started for the Ojo Caliente reservation on April 1, 1877. He reached Silver City on April 14. There he met Martin Sweeney and his reservation police, who had come over the back trails from San Carlos. Clay Beauford and his Indian company made their appearance in Silver City right on cue. Clum's army now counted 103 men. His confidence was bolstered when Lieutenant Colonel Hatch notified him that eight companies of cavalry would be positioned around the reservation, including three with Major James Wade that were scheduled to link up with Clum's Apache police at the agency. For good measure, Hatch tossed in a company of infantry. The military units were to be in place around the Warm Springs reservation by April 20, 1877.[30]

Clum's contingent moved to Fort Bayard, where the men prepared to push on to Ojo Caliente. When they reached Fort Bayard on April 15, Clum learned from a "dependable scout" that Geronimo and his herd of stolen horses were still within three miles of the agency. More significantly, Clum calculated that there were fewer than five hundred men, women, and children of all bands on the reservation—considerably fewer than he had expected. If the spies' figures were correct, then the Apaches, both peaceful and hostile together, had fewer warriors than were included in Clum's two scout companies. By anybody's count, with the military backup, the American force outnumbered the entire reservation population and matched up against the Apache warriors at an overwhelming six to one.[31]

When Clum realized his numerical advantage, his expedition was quickly turned from a roundup of an estimated 135 runaway Chiricahuas into an ego-inflating plan to remove the entire Chihenne tribe along with the troublesome bunch accompanying Geronimo. Even though the Chihennes were and had been peaceful for the most part, removing them, too, would look impressive. It was an irresistible opportunity to polish off John Clum's career in the Indian business with one last spectacular stunt.

He wired Commissioner Smith immediately: "Hieronemo and nearly 200 stolen horses yet on the reservation. . . . My scouts inform me only six hundred Indians at Hot Springs, including renegades. I advise movement of all to San Carlos." He also noted that he would leave Fort Bayard that day with 103 Indian police and reach Ojo Caliente on April 19.[32]

It should be no surprise that the savings to be realized from closing another reservation played well with the Indian Office. The commissioner wired back on April 17, cautiously authorizing the agent to remove the Warm Springs Indians if he concluded that there was manpower enough to compel the removal. If not, he was at least to arrest and remove the 135 renegade Chiricahuas and disarm the Chihennes at Ojo Caliente before returning to San Carlos.[33]

Even before Smith's telegram reached Clum, he had crunched the numbers and made his decision, but he asked Walter Whitney, the acting agent who had just replaced John Shaw, to confirm "the exact number of men women and children . . . together with information as to the approximate location of the various bands and parties. I would also like your views as to the expedience of disarming the Indians of this reservation and would also be glad to know your opinion regarding the proposed removal of the Indians to the San Carlos Reservation."[34]

Whitney gave him an estimate of 625 persons and advised, "The Indians will naturally object strongly to being removed from their old home, but I do not think they will endeavor to resist by force, but no doubt many will try to escape.... If the policy of the Hon. Commissioner in regard to concentration of all Indians on a few reservations is to be carried into effect, no time more favorable than the present can be selected."[35]

Thus assured of little or no resistance, Clum and his "little army" reached the vicinity of the Warm Springs agency in the late afternoon of April 20, 1877, one day after he had planned. Because of the previous unrest on the reservation, most of Hatch's troops were in position by this time. Even so, the most important units for Clum, Major Wade's three companies of cavalry, were nowhere to be found. Acting Agent Whitney, apparently anticipating a shootout, was missing from the scene when Clum's force arrived. No one was left in authority at the agency, and to top it all off, Wade telegraphed that his troops would not reach the agency until April 22, two days later than expected. Clum decided to arrest the Indians with Geronimo the next day, lest the Apaches discover his plot.[36]

Once within striking distance of the reservation, Clum left Captain Beauford with eighty scouts and police concealed about ten miles out and moved openly to the agency with twenty-two scouts. During the predawn hours of April 21, 1877, Beauford's eighty quietly slipped onto the reservation and hid in a warehouse directly across the parade ground from the main agency building. Just after sunrise, at Clum's request, Geronimo and the other chiefs, apparently believing the twenty-two policemen they had watched arrive the evening before were no threat, came to the agency for a talk. After a brief I'm-more-macho-than-you exchange between Clum and Geronimo, Clum sprang his trap and called out his hidden reserves. Surprised at the sudden appearance of eighty additional rifles, Geronimo, Gordo, Ponce, Francisco, and thirteen other leaders surrendered without firing a shot.

Despite Clum's subsequent efforts to portray the capture as a hair-raising episode, in fact it was anticlimactic. Clum's sermonizing afterward to a captive audience of Apaches made it downright dull. The most exciting episode of the day occurred when a Chiricahua woman accosted Clay Beauford in a futile display of frustration.[37]

With the chiefs in custody, Clum fired off a wire to the Indian Office in Washington: "Arrived here last evening, this morning arrested Hieronemo and two other prominent renegades, this after[noon] counted all Indians here. Total present four hundred and thirty-four

[Clum included Loco's people]. My opinion at least fifty remain in camps, as many as forty now raiding in Sonora and Arizona." By luck, Clum's coup took place on the scheduled ration day at Ojo Caliente. According to Clum, when Loco's people arrived for the weekly grocery pickup, the Chihennes found Geronimo and his friends shackled.[38]

Clum's and Geronimo's versions of the subsequent capture of the Chihennes differ remarkably, and because both were well-established liars, it is impossible to pin down which is the true account. It makes no difference. Virtually all the Indians on the reservation, including Loco's band, were in Clum's clutches by April 23.[39]

Although things had been coming unglued on the Warm Springs reservation for some time, the Chihennes had been quiet for the most part since their return to Ojo Caliente. Even Clum acknowledged that the Chihennes had never been known as a troublesome bunch. Indeed, Loco, Nana, and at least some of the other Chihenne leaders would undoubtedly have been delighted to be rid of the Chiricahuas. So when those two and another leader named Eskinya (Skinya) approached Clum on ration day, they were pleasantly surprised to find seventeen renegade leaders trussed up in ankle irons. They walked into Clum's grasp, oblivious to the possibility that they, too, might become victims of the removal program, although according to Clum their expressions demanded an "immediate explanation."

Clum noted that when Victorio learned of the plan to remove the peaceful Indians along with the Chokonens and Bedonkohes, he protested, "You are unfair to me and my people. . . . We are good Indians. . . . We want to live in our mountains in peace, hunt the deer and wild turkey. We do not go on the warpath."

The Chihenne leaders then prepared to present a lengthy argument, but Clum cut them short: "You say you want to live at peace and improve your condition. Very good, I will give you a chance to live as the Apaches do at San Carlos."[40] Clum sent the Chihennes back to their camps with instructions to return the next day, one hour before sunset. That evening Loco, Nana, Victorio, and other Chihenne leaders held a meeting and discussed their dilemma.[41]

Major Wade arrived on April 22, two days late for his appointment to help arrest Geronimo's gang. Clum showed Wade his shackled trophies and bragged that "in addition to Geronimo's band, Victorio, I think, will bring in about four hundred of his folks this evening. I am going to march them all to San Carlos." The agent was overconfident. Only 175 Apaches turned up at the agency for his head count.[42] "I am informed . . . that

Loco, Skinya, and two other chiefs are camped about twenty miles east of the agency, and that they say they will be back tomorrow morning."[43]

According to Woodworth Clum, John Clum's son, Victorio met John Clum's deadline and came in unarmed on April 22, but Loco and Eskinya remained out of sight.[44] For Clum, the situation was reminiscent of the circumstances surrounding Geronimo's getaway during the 1876 Chiricahua removal. The aggravated agent told Major Wade that he did not think Loco and company were coming in, and he directed Wade to consider them "insubordinate and hostile" and to "punish them as hostile Indians." Loco, however, walked in with his band the next morning, before Wade's troops could mount a search.[45]

On April 24 Clum reported to Washington, "I had a short talk with the principal men and they readily consented to move to San Carlos. I hope to start with them on the 30th inst." Clum's claim that Loco, Victorio, and the other Chihenne leaders or any of Geronimo's following "readily consented" is patently absurd. Between Clum's scouts and the army, approximately 730 troopers, mostly cavalry, lurked on and around the reservation, poised to quash an outbreak. The Indians had no doubt scouted the area and decided that they could neither run nor fight, so they "readily consented." They would bide their time.[46]

On May 1, 1877, Clum notified the commissioner by telegram of the departure of 453 Indians from the Southern Apache reservation. Clum, supported by his contingent of Indian police, took charge of the most dangerous prisoners: "I go by road with [17] prisoners (shackled in wagons) and join [the bulk of the] Indians at Silver City. Military authorities concur with me that removal is completely made." One week later he reported that the Indians had reached Silver City, and "everything is working excellent. Will complete success. Chiefs are here as I write. Will move on tomorrow. . . . Expect to be at San Carlos with Indians on eighteenth."[47]

Although Clum claimed that both the Chiricahua and Warm Springs Apaches were dangerous, he acknowledged that the Warm Springs Indians were never very fractious. Indeed, he was certain he would have little or no trouble from Loco and Victorio's people and probably not much in a face-to-face fight with Geronimo. Acting Agent Whitney had assured Clum that although the Chihennes under Loco, Victorio, and Nana might run, they would not fight. So when Clum got word that two Chiricahuas, Pionsenay and Nolgee, were raiding in Sonora and Arizona, he was confident enough to send Beauford with seventy-five scouts back to Arizona by way of the Dos Cabezas Mountains to hunt the firebrands. This left the young agent and twenty-eight policemen to guard more than four hundred allegedly dangerous Indians. Although he was obviously unconcerned about an escape, Clum told Major Wade, "I may need some help to guard the outfit on the journey." Wade viewed Clum's catch of peaceful Indians with no foreboding and provided an escort of only twelve cavalrymen under Lieutenant William Hugo, "more out of a compliment than necessity."[48]

The deployment of Clum's forces for the move further emphasized that neither the agent nor the army believed the vast majority of his prisoners was hostile. Clum, with his twenty-eight Apache policemen, guarded the seventeen shackled troublemakers for the first part of the trip over wagon roads to Silver City. The twelve cavalrymen were left to guard a mix of 436 Chihennes and now docile Chokonens. From Silver City to San Carlos the Indian police mixed and chatted with the shuffling mass of Indians while the soldiers rode behind, apparently with the sole job of encouraging the slowpokes to keep up.[49]

The unseating of the more than three hundred peaceful Warm Springs Indians from their ancient homeland on May 1, 1877, effectively ended Loco's hope for an evenhanded peace with the American government. Clum's impulsive decision to move the Warm Springs band also undercut Loco's leadership among the Apaches, who always chose to ride with a winner. Loco's efforts to remain at peace were obviously not working. For no reason apparent to the Indians, the Americans had pulled the rug out from under the only Southern Apache leader who passionately believed in a policy of conciliation and consistently sought to come to terms with the undependable Americans. During Loco's eight-year effort, his people had endured near starvation in 1869 and 1874, had suffered privation, disease, and freezing temperatures at Tularosa, and now were headed for San Carlos, the netherworld of Apachería. Despite his penchant for drink, Loco had struggled with the effects of the illegal alcohol trade at Cañada Alamosa and Tularosa and had grappled with the troubles brought on by the Chokonens and Nednais. He killed at least three Apaches in his pursuit of amicable relations with the Americans. Although a core group of family, friends, and a few like-minded Apaches remained loyal to Chief Loco after the 1877 removal, his peace at Ojo Caliente appeared ever more distant. Just as government officials had finally come to understand that probably the only way to keep the Chihennes at peace was to leave them on the Ojo Caliente reservation, a twenty-six-year-old bureaucrat's egotistical whim destroyed it all. Clum's actions guaranteed that the conflict between the Americans and Apaches would continue for another nine years, resulting in the loss of hundreds of lives and costing between $4 million and $8 million dollars annually. It was a pricey enterprise to boost John Clum's ego.

CHAPTER NINE

A Run for Home

Although John Clum reported that the removal was going well, just an hour before the Indians' scheduled departure, one of them was found with a full-blown case of smallpox. Clum quickly arranged for a "pest wagon" to carry the sick and segregate them from the rest of the group. One of Clum's policemen, Cullah, an Aravaipa Apache, was conscripted to drive the makeshift ambulance. Cullah had previously survived a bout with smallpox and was immune. During the seventeen days it took for the 453 Apaches to reach San Carlos, eight Indians died of the disease. Untreated smallpox kills 30 percent of those infected with it, so it can be inferred that approximately twenty-four cases developed during the trek to San Carlos. Clum noted that "fortunately, the pest wagon was large and roomy . . . [but as] more smallpox developed, ambulance facilities were crowded at times beyond capacity."[1]

Although it was a depressing trip even for the healthy Indians, Clum characterized the affair as a "Western hegira to the promised land . . . a silent hopeful migration of weary and bewildered people to Utopia."[2] He was right about the Apaches' bewilderment, but no one except Clum has ever seen a utopia in the San Carlos reservation. Eugene Chihuahua, a Chiricahua, called San Carlos the "worst place in all the land claimed by the Apaches."[3] Jason Betzinez remembered that "the place was almost uninhabitable."[4] When Clum had first viewed San Carlos three years earlier, he exclaimed, "Of all the desolate, isolated human habitations!" Only in the wake of his controversial removal of the Apaches from Ojo Caliente did he assert that San Carlos was a paradise. He himself resigned from the Indian Office and left "Utopia" within sixty days, not to set foot in that promised land again for thirty-five years.[5]

The "undulating line of marchers," stretching out for over a mile, covered the four hundred miles to San Carlos at slightly better than twenty-three miles per day. They reached the reservation on May 17, 1877. When they arrived, they found the reservation completely devoid of people except for a few white employees. John Rope, a White Mountain Apache scout, recalled the reaction when the reservation Indians learned of the impending arrival of the pox-cumbered crowd: "Then they started to bring the Warm Springs people back to San Carlos. . . . On the way smallpox broke out among them. Our band heard about this, so all our people went off in the mountains and lived scattered in different places. When the smallpox was over, the subagent [Ezra Hoag] sent word and we came in again."[6]

The shackled Chiricahua leaders were deposited in the San Carlos jailhouse. Loco, Victorio, and Nana, who had traveled unfettered, pitched camp near the subagency in view of the Gila Mountains. The Indian Office had recently converted the abandoned buildings of an old military base, Camp Goodwin, into a subagency for San Carlos. Naiche and his band had been there since the Chiricahua removal. Clum claimed that he told Loco, Victorio, and Nana "to establish their permanent camps anywhere in the hundred little valleys within the spacious reservation." He implied that the Indians selected the location, but Clum likely promoted the Goodwin area as the best place for the Warm Springs people. The Chihennes probably found the immediate area attractive because it was curiously devoid of their traditional rivals, the San Carlos and White Mountain Apaches. Apparently, neither Loco nor Victorio ever questioned the fact that the local Indians adamantly avoided the Camp Goodwin neighborhood.[7]

At first glance Camp Goodwin looked good. Ezra Hoag had been the resident subagent there for the Chiricahuas since their removal in 1876. He was a pleasant alcoholic who liked and was liked by the Apaches. Good water gushed from a bold spring roughly five hundred yards from the subagency. Unfortunately, the bountiful flow created a bog, ideal for mosquitoes. A high casualty rate from malaria had caused the army to abandon Camp Goodwin in 1871. Too unhealthy for the military, it was turned over to the Department of the Interior for the Indians. Within a few weeks after the Chihennes set up camp in the Goodwin vicinity, cases of malaria began to pop up among the Indians. Just as the smallpox scourge was winding down, malaria evolved into its own full-blown epidemic.[8]

The Apaches faced other problems as well. Within two months of depositing the Warm Springs people at San Carlos, John Clum abruptly left his job. Clum had planned to resign sometime after the removal, but he used a snit over the army's inspection of his agency accounts as an excuse for an abrupt departure. His absence left Martin Sweeney and William Vandever in charge of the agency, with Ezra Hoag as subagent. Hoag had no independent authority and simply managed the subagency at the agent's direction. Sweeney was a faithful agency employee who had done well under Clum's oversight. Like Hoag, he habitually operated from an alcoholic haze, leaving the greenhorn Vandever to rely on his often good but rarely sober advice. Vandever, an Interior Department inspector, was a city slicker from Washington who detested the hardships of agency life. He had the misfortune of being at San Carlos when Clum resigned and was ordered to hold down the place as the interim agent. The inspector may have been a good accountant, but he had no experience in Indian agency administration, and he did not like the Apaches. First Lieutenant Lemuel Abbott, inspector for the army at San Carlos, watched Vandever's inept management through the summer of 1877. Finally, in August he complained that the acting agent was "gravely inefficient and negligent in the execution of his responsibilities at San Carlos" and was "wholly unworthy" of any confidence placed in him.[9]

Vandever and Sweeney's mismanagement rapidly put the Indians at Camp Goodwin in a swivet. Loco arrived at San Carlos in the midst of the annual fourth-quarter ration shortage, his fourth in eight years. Lieutenant Abbott noted that Vandever could have purchased supplies for the Indians on the open market but did not. The Apaches were forced to do without or to hunt and gather away from the reservation. Abbott reported that the hungry Indians who left the reservation, supposedly to hunt, often stole from neighboring settlers. Vandever and Sweeney neglected the problem until mid-July, when they were forced to accept fifty thousand pounds of inferior quality flour to have anything at all for the Indians to eat. That shipment was gone by the end of July, and it was late August before another 116,000 pounds of flour were delivered for the hungry reservation residents.

Vandever further riled the Chihennes when he began issuing inferior beef for rations. By late August 1877, half the cattle issued were substandard, well past the seven-year age limit allowed by the government contract. Most were sick, and all were emaciated.[10]

By far the largest problem for the Chihennes on the San Carlos reservation was that it was so completely filled with other Indians—Coyotero,

Tonto, Aravaipa, and miscellaneous San Carlos Apaches, large numbers of Yavapais, and even a smattering of Yumas and Mohaves. Although some of the Western Apache groups had occasionally joined with the Chihennes on raiding forays in the past, none of the tribes lost any love over the New Mexico Apaches. Some downright detested them. It was perfectly clear to the Warm Springs people that they were unwelcome at San Carlos, despite John Clum's claim to the contrary. Coming as they did, packaged with a smallpox epidemic, did not help their popularity.[11] Even Clum's replacement, the new agent, Henry L. Hart, quickly recognized that "these distinct organizations [tribes] . . . will not live together."[12]

Blatantly lying, Inspector Vandever reported that the Warm Springs Indians appeared "entirely contented." Contrary to his report, three months after arriving at San Carlos, the Warm Springs people were about as unhappy as they ever had been. They were surviving on short rations and living in a sickly spot on someone else's reservation, administered by a dilettante bumbler and two drunks. Dreadful diseases were widespread, and Loco's band was outnumbered thirty-three to one by unfriendly tribes. The largest band, the Coyoteros, outnumbered Loco's Chihennes almost seventeen to one. The Warm Springs people hated the place, disliked the tribes collected there, and thought the government men were fools. They wanted to go home. It was only a matter of time before trouble started.[13]

By the middle of August, most of the Chihennes were poised to escape at their first opportunity. Only Chief Loco opposed an outbreak, hoping to negotiate a return to Ojo Caliente. During the last ten days of the month, a series of unrelated events set the stage for a breakout. First, the enormous shipment of flour arrived at the agency with surplus enough to supply the Apaches on an extended journey. About this time Clum's replacement, Henry Hart, sent word that he would be arriving in Tucson and requested an escort to the agency. Leaving Sweeney in charge, Vandever went to Tucson to usher the new agent back to San Carlos. When Hart and Vandever returned on August 27, they found a note announcing that Sweeney had left on a scout after off-reservation Chiricahuas. In fact Sweeney's search for the missing Indians was taking place in a local grog shop in Globe. He was eventually found there, immersed in a prolonged binge. Vandever and Sweeney's absence left the agency leaderless during the critical period just before the outbreak. Meanwhile, under pressure from his people, Loco agreed to leave.[14]

Just as these star-crossed events came together during the last days of August 1877, Pionsenay, a Chokonen, began to skulk around the edges of the reservation. He was a true villain, an anathema to both Americans and Apaches, and a tireless troublemaker. Subagent Ezra Hoag said the Apaches feared him "worse than the devil." In 1876, his murder of two station keepers on the overland road provided the Indian Office with the excuse to close the Chiricahua reservation and remove the Chokonens to San Carlos. Just before the removal, Pionsenay led a shootout with Naiche and Taza, Cochise's sons, for control of the Chokonens, which ended with a permanent rift in that band. He refused to be removed to San Carlos, escaped, and launched a devastating series of raids in southern New Mexico. Much of the raiding that was blamed on the Warm Springs band at Ojo Caliente in 1876 and 1877 can be attributed to Pionsenay.[15]

In his hurried escape to avoid the Chiricahuas' deportation in 1876, Pionsenay left thirty-eight family members and friends behind. They were removed to Camp Goodwin with Taza and Naiche's people. Almost a year later, in mid-May 1877, Pionsenay showed up at Ojo Caliente looking for his relatives. Learning what had happened to them, he followed their exodus to Arizona. In late August 1877 the army reported that Pionsenay and his associates were headed north toward San Carlos. During the last days of August he began to prowl around Camp Goodwin, waiting for the chance to pluck his kin from the clutches of the Indian Office. On August 28 he made an insincere offer of peace to Ezra Hoag. Hoag refused the deal, but Pionsenay's visit to the subagency gave him a chance to scout out the place and notify his family that help was on the way. He also took the opportunity to make off with five government horses.[16]

On Saturday night, September 1, 1877, Pionsenay set things in motion when he slipped back onto the reservation, collected twenty-two women and children, stole six more horses from the Coyoteros, and took off toward Mexico. Agent Hart heard of Pionsenay's visit first thing Sunday morning, notified the army, and straightaway set loose a detachment of agency police to chase down the raiders. From the subagency, Hoag dispatched a second force of enthusiastic Coyotero volunteers. Pionsenay eluded them all and soon made it to Mexico. Ultimately, his success was short-lived. He was killed about four months later near Janos in Chihuahua, Mexico.[17]

The commissioner of Indian affairs later wrote in his annual report that after dark the next day, September 2, 1877, Loco, Victorio, Nana, and Francisco, with a "majority of the Hot Springs Indians and a portion of the Chiricahuas, numbering about 300 in all suddenly left the San Carlos reserve." Agent Hart calculated that the runaways numbered

310, accompanied by "twenty horses loaded with quantities of flour and other rations."[18]

Despite the Apaches' secrecy, the outbreak came as no surprise to anyone. A month before, in July, the commissioner had granted the San Carlos agent authority to hire additional police from among the local Indians to use as scouts in anticipation of a breakout.[19] Lieutenant Abbott warned the assistant adjutant general for the Department of Arizona in the third week of August that "the Indians were sulky and rebellious and that disastrous results would follow unless immediate steps were taken to keep them on the reservation and under control." Abbott's warning arrived in Prescott on August 27, six days before the blowup. Major James Martin, the departmental adjutant, relayed it to General Irvin McDowell in division headquarters in San Francisco. Abbott's warning was received in San Francisco on August 28. By return telegraph, McDowell immediately asked about the location of troops in Arizona who would be available to handle an outbreak and was assured that troops from Forts Thomas, Grant, and Apache had been warned and were ready for action on a moment's notice. Scouting parties were ordered out to watch for signs. Even old Colonel Kautz claimed he had "foreseen that the Warm Spring Indians would not stay even if well treated without a force that could compel them to stay."[20]

Throughout the day on September 2, Loco and Victorio watched the agency police and excited Coyotero volunteers dash off to the south after Pionsenay's Chiricahuas. They waited until the army joined the chase before departing from San Carlos en masse, headed in the opposite direction, toward Fort Wingate, taking with them about thirty Coyotero horses, stolen to haul old people, children, and supplies.[21]

The escapees had covered fewer than thirty miles before a mixed bag of San Carlos police, army scouts, and volunteer Coyoteros overtook them. Two fights followed, on September 3 and 4, at Ash Creek and below Nantanes Butte, respectively. By the end of the day on September 4, the pursuers had run out of ammunition. They broke off the fight and returned to San Carlos, taking with them thirty of Loco and Victorio's women and children and twenty-eight of their horses. Unfortunately for the escapees, the horses were loaded with Loco's entire food supply.[22]

After the government force withdrew, the Chihennes made a right-angle turn and headed southeast. What might have been a bloodless escape to Fort Wingate or Ojo Caliente turned ugly after the attacks of September 3 and 4. Now forced to replace their captured food supply and transportation, the Apaches descended on Henry Lesinsky's copper mine near Clifton, Arizona, picked the place clean of food stores, and stole thirty mules. From there they attacked a settlement on the upper Gila River near the New Mexico border, killed eight settlers, wounded two, and stole more stock. Continuing to the east, they raided Burro Springs, northwest of Silver City, killing eight additional people in the process and capturing a wagon train full of supplies.[23]

Victorio and Loco's luck ran out again on September 10 when scouts operating in advance of Captain Tillius C. Tupper's cavalry found the fugitives at the base of the Mogollon Mountains in western New Mexico. In the daylong fight that followed, one Chihenne man and eleven women and children were killed. Thirteen additional Apaches were taken prisoner, and six horses were recaptured.[24] One of the captured women told Tupper that the Warm Springs people were planning to return to their old reservation at Ojo Caliente. On the basis of this new intelligence, the army flooded the area between the Apaches and Ojo Caliente with troops. Major James Wade was "scouting actively with all his troops in the Mogollon Mountains." Two companies of the Ninth Cavalry were patrolling the Black Range to the east. The entire compliment of cavalry units from Fort Union and one troop from Fort Wingate were dispatched to the area around Ojo Caliente. The Chihennes' old reservation looked like a military camp.[25]

What the captured woman told Tupper seems to confirm statements that Apaches made later to Acting Agent Whitney at Ojo Caliente. They told Whitney that when they surrendered, they were headed "to the Navajo country, not daring to come here [Ojo Caliente] on account of the troops, etc. stationed at this point."[26]

During the last week of September the Apaches brought their slow-motion run to a halt fifteen miles north of their former reservation in the Tularosa Valley, near Escondido Mountain, about ninety miles due south of Fort Wingate. A small group of leaders went to Fort Wingate to arrange a safe surrender.[27] By the end of September, Kautz reported that two Warm Springs chiefs, probably Loco and Victorio, had met with officers at Wingate and that Loco "and 144 of the Warm Spring Indian renegades had offered to surrender." District commander Edward Hatch, who hurried to Ojo Caliente to be near the action, gave Agent Whitney a slightly different account on September 29. He reported that three chiefs, Loco, Victorio, and Chiva, had contacted officers at Fort Wingate and said they would bring their people in within four or five days. Actually, Chiva was still at San Carlos. Hatch probably confused Nana with Chiva.[28]

On September 29, after meeting with the chiefs, Captain Horace Jewett, commanding officer at Fort Wingate, dispatched Thomas Keams, Wingate's post interpreter, with five Navajos to accompany the Apache leaders back to their camps in the San Francisco mountains. Keams was married to a Navajo woman and spoke fluent Navajo, which was similar to the Apache language. He got on well with the Apaches.

Keams "arrived near their camp . . . finding them [the escapees] scattered over the mountains." He sent his Navajo runners out to notify the Indians of his arrival. By twelve noon, 179 men, women, and children had collected. He reported, "I then held a council with and informed them my purpose was to take them all to Fort Wingate. The Chiefs had told me some of them intended to [go] back into the mountains. These I requested to step aside and separate themselves from the others at once, as I would be responsible only for those who went with me and conducted themselves right, and would have troops sent after those that left. . . . The dissatisfied then came to me individually and said . . . that they would also go with me and remain with their chiefs."[29]

By October 8, 1877, Captain Jewett was able to report that "Loco, Victorio, with 187 Apache Indians, are now encamped at West Springs on this [Navajo] reservation. I still have them in charge of Mr. Keam." Fifty-five of the original escapees had been killed or captured. Sixty-eight refused to come in with Loco and Victorio and were still in the mountains.

Once the Apaches were settled in at Fort Wingate, Jewett met with the new arrivals. He concluded, "It is better to keep them in their present status [as military prisoners], and through them to influence some more to come in who are now wandering the mountains." After the meeting Jewett dispatched "two parties to bring in the sixty-eight Indians who had not surrendered themselves, one party in charge of Mariana, Navajo Chief, the other in charge of Juan Navajo. Each of these Navajos has two Apaches with them." Jewett thought his emissaries would return with another fifty-six Indians. They came back with fifty-one. Approximately 242 Chihennes from the San Carlos breakout were now camped near Fort Wingate on the Navajo reservation, about 150 miles from their home at Ojo Caliente. By the third week in October, the Warm Springs Apache outbreak of 1877 was in the history books.[30]

In an interview with a reporter named Willis that appeared in the Silver City newspaper on September 22, Ezra Hoag unwittingly revealed the political infighting that took place between Loco and Victorio before the outbreak: "Mr. Hoag, the subagent at San Carlos, told Willis that the

Indians who left the reservation had been persuaded by Victorio, who seemed disposed to support Pionsenay. That Loco opposed the move but was compelled to acquiesce as all his people were against him. Their complaint was that they had been removed from Ojo Caliente."[31]

Even though their original plan apparently called for a bloodless run to Ojo Caliente or Fort Wingate, Loco left thirteen (some accounts say eight) of his immediate family members at Camp Goodwin, apparently to avoid the arduous journey. Another 143 Chihennes, including 63 women, 29 boys, and 29 girls, mostly Loco's people, also waited at the agency for the outcome of the escape. Twenty-two warriors were left behind to watch after the women and children. Victorio and Nana apparently took all of their followings when they left.[32]

The 1877 outbreak had none of the characteristics of the traditional Apache uprising. It was not a run to escape a reservation for the freedom of the Mexican mountains. It was a carefully calculated dash from one reservation to another, Ojo Caliente. In all likelihood, the Apaches would have attacked no citizens during the entire episode if their supplies and horses had not been captured at Ash Creek and Nantanes Butte. From the first, it appears that Loco and Victorio intended to use the San Carlos supplies to make it to Fort Wingate and Ojo Caliente without the need to raid. It might be assumed from Ezra Hoag's interview with Willis that Loco discussed the outbreak with Hoag days before the Apaches left the reservation. Even if the military was unaware of where the Apaches were headed at the outset, halfway through their flight the army learned that the escapees "were trying to make their way to their old reservation or vicinity where they expected to live."[33] In anticipation of this, infantry units had been ordered to Ojo Caliente "to guard the Indians if they surrender" there, and a single company of infantry waited at Fort Wingate to "receive Indian prisoners" if they came in at that post.[34]

Although the fugitives sought to avoid capture until they were on home turf, as soon as they arrived in the vicinity of Ojo Caliente they surrendered straightaway. Although the army was in pursuit of them, they had not been chased down, and they were not defeated. Agent Whitney reported that the Indians divulged that they were "nearly all unarmed; that they had no intention of going on the war path; and were seeking a place of safety and went to the Navajo country, not daring to come here [Ojo Caliente] on account of the troops, etc. stationed at this point." The story rang true for Whitney because "no troops were nearer them than several days march . . . until they surrendered voluntarily at Wingate."[35]

Immediately after their surrender, the Chihennes emphasized that harassment by the San Carlos Indians was a leading reason for their leaving the reservation, and they declared their loathing for the place. They begged Thomas Keams to help them locate on a different reservation, preferably Ojo Caliente.[36] Loco later told a reporter from the Tucson newspaper, the *Arizona Star,* that they had made their escape because of their unfair removal from their own land, for which the Chihennes "had as much love as other nations." He further explained that the removal to San Carlos was unnecessarily cruel, a number of his band being ill with smallpox and other ailments. Indian Office officials at San Carlos had neglected them and reduced their rations, all of which led to widespread discontent among his people.[37]

Victorio's version held that the Chihennes left San Carlos "on account of continual fighting with the Coyotero Apaches." He complained that the fighting had become so prevalent that "they preferred living anywhere" except San Carlos.[38] Inspector Vandever reported that Loco and Victorio told him that the Apaches had been satisfied with the food and care they had received at San Carlos but that the climate was oppressive and the water bad, which combined to make their children sick. The skeptical might suppose that Vandever, who was the true source of the Chihennes' miseries, was lying, but he went on to say that Loco and Victorio's foremost complaint was the never-ending hostility from the White Mountain Indians.[39]

A finger-pointing argument developed over who was responsible for the outbreak. Ignoring the Apaches' explanation, Inspector Vandever claimed that Tom Jeffords had furnished whiskey to the Warm Springs Indians and "stirred them up to insubordination."[40] Lieutenant Abbott refuted Vandever's claim and asserted that Vandever had created the problems leading to the outbreak: "I am inclined to believe the report false and malicious. Vandever is very bitter against Jeffords and it is quite likely his prejudice has affected his judgment. Vandever is responsible for their not having been properly fed and kept well in hand and is probably more to blame . . . than any one else. . . . I am only surprised that today there is an Indian left on the reservation."[41]

Kautz indirectly laid the blame on John Clum and his removal of the Warm Springs people to San Carlos. He said he had predicted that "so many antagonistic bands thrown together will cause numbers to leave from fear of enemies among their own people."[42] Colonel Orlando Willcox, who replaced Kautz as commander of the Department of Arizona, also opined that Clum's removal brought on the problem: "It is believed by many that Victorio [and Loco] was unjustly dealt with in the first instance, by the abrupt removal of his people from Ojo Caliente, New Mexico to San Carlos; and that such removal, if not a breach of faith, was a harsh and cruel measure, from which the people of New Mexico have reaped bitter consequences."[43] Even General Pope, of the Division of the Missouri, who never liked Apaches, absolved them of any blame: "I do not know the reasons of the Interior Department for insisting upon the removal to San Carlos agency, but certainly they should be cogent to justify the great trouble and severe losses occasioned by the attempts to coerce the removal."[44]

The 1877 escape was not a rousing success for the Apaches. One hundred fifty-six relatives and friends were still at San Carlos, and fifty-five Chihennes had been killed or captured in the scattered clashes during their race for home. It was, however, a partial victory. A handful of officials in the government—perhaps not in the Indian Office, but a few in the army—began to see the value of leaving the Chihennes alone at Ojo Caliente. It seemed promising that the army would soon move the captives at least temporarily from Fort Wingate to their old reservation. The Apaches must have thought that surely the Americans would now understand that they were serious about remaining in their homeland. Nevertheless, having lost so many people, Loco could draw little satisfaction from the results.[45]

CHAPTER TEN

Final Removal from Ojo Caliente

Three months after Clum forced the Apaches out of Ojo Caliente, the Office of Indian Affairs submitted a draft directive to the White House regarding the then-vacant reservation. Subsequently, the president abolished the Hot Springs reservation and restored the land to the public domain. It was the week before Loco and Victorio made their run for home. By the time the two reached Fort Wingate in late September, plans were in the works to sell their old reservation in parcels.[1]

The sale was part of the continued government-wide campaign to cut corners in response to the successive recessions that bedeviled the national economy from 1872 to 1879.[2] The new secretary of the interior, Carl Schurz, believed that putting multiple Indian tribes on a few large reservations was the solution—good for the budget and not all that bad for the Indians. He wrote in 1877, "The government is desirous of reducing the cost of the Indian service to the lowest possible limit, consistent with the best interests of the Indians. This can be done by the sale of the lands, the funding of the surplus after the removal and settlement of the Indians, and the application of the accruing interest to the payment of the current expenses of the respective agencies, and that without affecting in the least degree the interests of citizens."[3]

Under the consolidation policy, there appeared to be no prospect of reopening the Hot Springs reservation. That being the case, what to do with the Chihennes at Fort Wingate became the subject of a heated argument between the army and the Interior Department.

Three days after the escapees arrived at Fort Wingate, Colonel Hatch decided that they could not stay on the Navajo reservation. By October 11, 1877, he had ordered that the prisoners be taken "under guard to Ojo Caliente." The commissioner of Indian affairs, Ezra Hayt, however, made it clear that although the army could do what it wanted, the Apaches would not be there for long. In his annual report he announced that the Apaches "have been taken to the old Hot Springs reservation, where their final disposition will be decided upon."[4]

War Department officials generally agreed with Hatch that the Chihennes were least likely to cause trouble if returned to Ojo Caliente and left there. Interior officials, on the other hand, doggedly sought some other boneyard in which to banish the Indians. Indian Territory was the Indian Office's preference. The commanding officer at Fort Sill, Oklahoma, thought it would be less trouble for everyone concerned, including the Indians, if the Chihennes were left at Warm Springs and their relatives who were still held at San Carlos were allowed to join them. William Sherman, commander-in-chief of the army, also disapproved of the Oklahoma option: "I doubt the wisdom of collecting at Fort Sill too many Indians of different and incongruous tribes. . . . It will cost a round sum of money, because they will have to be escorted nearly 1,000 miles."[5]

After reviewing the situation, Secretary of War George McCrary asked Sherman to refer the subject back to General John Pope, commanding the Department of the Missouri, who was quick to note, "I entirely concur in the opinion of the General of the Army that it will be highly injudicious to send these Indians to Fort Sill." Lieutenant General Phil Sheridan, Pope's superior, commanding the Division of the Missouri, agreed: "To send the Warm Spring Indians to the Indian Territory would in my opinion be the worst policy of which the Indian Bureau could be guilty."[6]

To overcome the military's objections, Commissioner Hayt directed Indian Inspector E. C. Watkins to look into the situation. Watkins not only enthusiastically endorsed removing the Warm Springs band to Indian Territory but also suggested that all the Indians in Arizona and New Mexico be sent there. Secretary Schurz wholeheartedly agreed: "There is a vast area of land in the Indian Territory not yet occupied. Into this should, and may, be gathered the major portion of the Indians of New Mexico, Colorado and Arizona." In early February 1878, Commissioner Hayt, bolstered by Watkins's recommendation and Schurz's comments, officially asked the Secretary of War to see that "the necessary orders be given for their [the Chihennes] removal to Fort Sill." The army balked at the request and thus thwarted a debacle.[7]

With the Fort Sill option off the table, the Navajo reservation was briefly bandied about as a possible site for relocation, but with little enthusiasm. Indian Office bureaucrats worried that the problem-prone Apaches would stir up the Navajos, and the Navajo reservation was soon removed from the list.

The Indian Office and the army clashed once again when the Indian bureau rekindled the failed 1870 notion of moving the Chihennes to the Mescalero Apache reservation. The agent at Mescalero was willing to receive the Chihennes, and at least some of the Chihennes were agreeable to moving there—if San Carlos was the only other option. But just as in 1870, few of them had much enthusiasm for living with the Mescaleros.[8] The army was also lukewarm to the idea. Recalling the Chihennes' stiff resistance to the attempted transfer seven years earlier, General Pope professed to be "not entirely sure, about the good policy of sending them to the Stanton reservation."[9]

The Mescalero plan died a quick death after Commissioner Hayt learned that it would cost $1,500 to transfer the 150 Chihennes left at San Carlos to the Fort Stanton reserve. Although this suggests that the Indian Office was concerned with the cost of resettling the Chihennes, the rejection of the Mescalero plan was followed by an illogical debate that refutes any pretense of concern about the economy. If money had been the sole consideration, the best deal was to leave the Apaches at Ojo Caliente and move those at San Carlos back to join them. This could have been arranged for the bargain price of about $1,200. The second least expensive option was to move the approximately 150 Apaches at San Carlos and the 250 at Ojo Caliente to Mescalero for about $2,000. On the other hand, it would cost, by the government's own reckoning, at least $3,000 to move the 250 Indians at Ojo Caliente back to San Carlos to join their relatives. Ironically, Commissioner Hayt preferred a plan to move all the Chihennes from both Ojo Caliente and San Carlos to Indian Territory at the upmarket cost of $6,000. Hayt forcefully noted that the cheapest option, Ojo Caliente, was not under consideration, because the land there was up for sale, and it would be "inconvenient" to alter such arrangements. It was the only reason ever offered by the Indian Office for not leaving the Apaches at Ojo Caliente.[10]

Thus, San Carlos loomed as the only choice for the Indian bureau. Inspector Vandever, the acting agent at San Carlos, pushed hard to return the Chihennes to the Arizona reservation. He turned up at Fort Wingate just before Hatch moved the prisoners to Ojo Caliente. Captain Jewett reported that "Vandever seems to think that their being taken back to Ojo Caliente, in the face of their being removed from there by the Government, displays a weakness on the part of the Government in yielding to the demands of the Indians, [and] that will establish a bad precedent in the management of Indian Affairs. San Carlos and the Indian Territory seem to be the two points, to one of which he thinks they should be sent."[11]

Vandever later met with Loco, Nana, and Victorio. After hearing the Indians' concerns, he reported that the Apaches complained of the hostility of the other tribes at San Carlos and that "they said further that the water was bad. . . . It made their people sick, and therefore they were determined to go somewhere else to live." They preferred to be returned to Ojo Caliente but told Vandever they would go anywhere except San Carlos. "My reply to them was, that they must learn to stay wherever the Government chooses to put them. . . . It was wholly out of the question to yield to their desire to return to Ojo Caliente."[12]

Ignoring protests from the Indian Office, the army moved the Apaches to Ojo Caliente on November 9, 1877. First Lieutenant Martin Hughes was charged with settling the Apaches when they arrived at their old agency. He reported on November 10, "I have this day dismounted and disarmed the band of [226] Apache Indians which arrived at this place from Ft. Wingate, N.M. on the 9th inst."

Hughes's inventory of impounded weapons confirms Loco's assertion that the Chihennes were poorly armed during the run from San Carlos: "The following is a list of the property taken, (36) Thirty-six horses, (3) Three mules, (2) burros, (1) colt, (6) six lances, (2) Two Remington revolvers, (1) horse pistol, (1) Sharps carbine, (1) Springfield rifle, (6) muzzle loading muskets, and eight bows, all of the animals taken, six horses and one mule were by directions of the Commanding Officer turned over to the seven principal men of the band, viz.; Loco, Victorio, Nana, Esquirre [Esquine], Mangas, and Tange (Thomaso) [probably Hiralchiddy]. The remaining animals were turned over to . . . Co. L, 9th Cavalry to be conducted to Fort Craig, N.M."[13]

The Apaches' former agent, Dr. Walter Whitney, was still serving as temporary agent, sans Indians, at the vacant Ojo Caliente agency when the returnees arrived. Whitney had been caretaking the buildings and looking forward to a new job at the Navajo agency. His transfer was put on hold, and he was retained as temporary agent at Warm Springs until the Apaches' final placement. He was unenthusiastic about the delay but gave the prisoners a reassuring reception, sought to clothe them properly,

and recommended that the Chihennes still at San Carlos be reunited
with their relatives at Ojo Caliente. He urged that they be allowed to
remain at Ojo Caliente.[14]

The Apaches, aware of the debate surrounding their relocation, immediately set about involving themselves in the deliberations. The Indian
Office generally discounted anything the Apaches had to say, but the
Indians entered the rhetorical dogfight just eleven days after their surrender at Fort Wingate. Loco, Nana, and Victorio met with Captain
Jewett to present their case for remaining at Ojo Caliente. All three
promised to remain at peace, and they asked for protection from outside
Apaches who continued to raid and whom the Chihennes blamed for
most of their misfortunes. Nana complained, "We do not want to suffer
any more on account of the bad Indians." Ironically, Victorio, contrary to
his earlier resistance to Loco and Nana, declared, "We do not want any
other Indians to interfere with us." Loco complained of being tired of
"bad Indians" who caused "all the trouble."

Both Nana and Victorio allowed that they would not mind remaining
on the Navajo reservation long enough to "take lessons from the Navajos
in order that we can do the same thing . . . [and] learn . . . how to work."
Loco was silent about staying on the Navajo reservation but agreed with
Victorio that "we want to stay at Ojo Caliente. . . . We want to die there.
There we have plenty of water, and plenty of rain and we want to go to
work." He wanted it "distinctly understood that his tribe does not wish
to be removed from Ojo Caliente."[15]

Although Loco was unwavering in his desire to remain at Warm
Springs, his first concern was with the well-being of his family—three
wives, three children, and two orphans he was raising. Thomas Keams
interpreted Loco's statement to Jewett:

> He asks all to do what they can for himself and family. A portion
> are at San Carlos with the Coyotero Indians and he does not
> want them to remain there. He wants them brought to him. Of
> his family there are eight [actually thirteen] there and a number
> of other Indians belonging to his band. We want all of them sent
> to us at Ojo Caliente. Those that are dead cannot be brought to
> life, but we ask earnestly for the living. We wish the General at
> Santa Fe to have sent to us all those of our families that are
> absent and still alive. Loco also says that he wants all done that
> can possibly be done to have some soldiers to go with him to
> where his family is so that he can take them back to the reserva-

tion [Ojo Caliente]. If he is allowed to go that way, he will go with a large heart and be contented, and if he finds some of his family, he will be thankful to all.

Loco's reference to the dead suggests that he might have lost a child or other family member during the September run for Fort Wingate.

After expressing his concern about his family to Captain Jewett, Loco complained that many Apaches who joined him under a flag of peace often forsook the reservation to raid and left his peaceful Chihennes to face the consequences: "He [says] he has done all in his power to rule his people [band] properly but on account of some bad men, he has had a great deal of trouble and work. It is ten years since he has done all in his power to live at peace and be contented, but on account of some bad Indians that came among us and have apparently thrown dirt in his face and caused all the trouble. What we want to do is plant, raise corn, vegetables, melons etc., so we can look on with pleasure while it is growing. These are all the words he can think of at present and 'can get out of my head.'"[16]

Finding the cost-conscious Indian Office unresponsive to their proposals, the Chihennes attempted to cut a deal with the army in August 1878. The new commanding officer at Ojo Caliente, Captain Charles Steelhammer, wrote: "The Indians wished me to say that they are happier than they ever have been were it not that they feared removal and that if the Government would permit them to remain where they now are they would gladly accept only one-half of their present ration, provided the Government would in the beginning furnish a few necessary tools and teach them how to till the ground."

Steelhammer also noted a change in the Apaches' demeanor since their return to Ojo under Loco's leadership: "I found everything in most excellent condition. . . . When I look back upon the condition of these Indians a year and a half ago and contrast it with their present, it seems almost incredible that such a long step in their civilization could have been taken in so short a time. Everything connected with the Indians at Ojo Caliente is done well." These were not Indians looking for a fight.[17] Even Inspector Watkins observed that despite living in the most unpleasant conditions at Ojo Caliente—kept under rigid military control and subjected to a daily head count—the Chihennes wanted to remain at the hot springs and continued to argue against a return to San Carlos. In October, General Pope reiterated, "The Indians have an invincible objection to returning to San Carlos Agency, preferring to go anywhere else."[18]

In spite of the Apaches' and the military's best efforts to convince them otherwise, Indian Office officials pressed forward with their plan to return the Chihennes to San Carlos. Finally the frustrated Apaches asked to speak directly to the new president, Rutherford B. Hayes. Hayes was a square-shooter whose Indian policy was based on the premise that "many, if not most of our Indian wars have had their origin in broken promises and acts of injustice on our part." On January 9, 1878, Agent Whitney sent the Chihennes' request to the commissioner of Indian affairs "that some of their chiefs and head men be allowed to go to Washington and have a 'talk' with the 'Great Father' relative to the future disposition to be made of them, etc." Whitney sympathized with the Indians and wrote a compelling justification for the trip: "When the hardships they have undergone for the past eight months are considered, it seems but natural that they should desire an opportunity to make known their grievances and receive some assurances." He asked that he be allowed to bring a five-man delegation to Washington. Commissioner Hayt, recognizing that President Hayes might sympathize with the Apaches, denied the request, squelching any chance for presidential intervention.[19]

Although Hayt remained adamant about removing the Indians from Ojo Caliente, the Apaches appeared to be gaining ground with several powerful generals and a few people in the Indian Office. Their agent, Dr. Whitney, asked his brother in Washington to talk with the commissioner about the situation. The tenor of his letter made it obvious that he wanted to know when he could move on to his new position at the Navajo agency, but he also expressed the opinion that "I do not think these Indians can be kept at San Carlos without much trouble; it only remains to let them stay here (at Ojo Caliente) or move them to Indian Territory."[20]

By this time the army was virtually unanimous that the Chihennes should stay at Ojo Caliente. General Pope thought "it would be well for the Secretary of the Interior to ascertain what were the engagements entered into and the promises made by the agents of that department from the time of General Howard's mission to this band of Apaches down to the late outbreak. It is probable that much would be developed by such investigation to extenuate, at least, the feelings, if not the conduct of the tribe."[21] General Sheridan puzzled over the Indian Office's bewildering rationale: "As the motives which control the Indian Bureau in their objection to these Indians remaining at the Warm Spring reservation are unknown to me, I can only say that . . . it would be best to let them remain at the Warm Springs and I so recommend."[22]

Still Secretary Schurz and Commissioner Hayt insisted on moving the Chihennes—somewhere, anywhere. The Indian Office's removal program was bolstered by assertions from its yes-men in the field, Inspectors Vandever and Watkins, that removal was a real money saver. The debate raged on throughout the winter and until June 24, 1878. Fed up at last, General Sheridan demanded action: "These Indians have been held as prisoners since last October and the Indian Department should have resumed control of them long since. Unless they are taken charge of soon by that Department I shall recommend that they be turned loose." That sped things up, and within a month General Sherman, commanding the army, ordered that the Apaches at Ojo Caliente "be turned over to authorized representative of the Indian Bureau, and a guard sufficient to ensure their safe transit to San Carlos be furnished." It was July 22, 1878.[23]

William Leeds, chief clerk of the Indian Office, telegraphed Agent Hart at San Carlos that the Apaches at Ojo Caliente were to be returned. He noted that the army would do the dirty work, if necessary, but it would look better if Hart could manage it with his Indian police. Nothing happened for two months. Tired of the bureau's foot-dragging, Colonel Hatch at Fort Wingate issued orders on September 18 to move the Indians with or without Indian Office involvement. "At the request of the Interior Department . . . the Warm Spring Indians, numbering 266 souls . . . will be returned to their proper agency at San Carlos." A company of cavalry and a squad of Navajo scouts were ordered to carry out the transfer.[24]

Captain Frank T. Bennett of the Ninth Cavalry drew the unpleasant chore of escorting the Apaches to San Carlos. He arrived at Ojo Caliente on October 10, 1878, and was shocked to learn that "the Indians had known [of their impending transfer] for ten (10) days or more," although "nobody knew how they got their information."[25]

Bennett called a meeting to announce the removal and to request the Apaches' cooperation. He was disappointed. A group of dour-faced Indians, headed by Loco and Hiralchiddy, turned up for the parley. The captain reported that he tried by "every argument I could, [to] make them as satisfied as possible to move," but he found them "very much opposed to going." Two other leaders, Victorio and Toggi, were on a brief trip to Fort Wingate and missed the October 10 meeting. Perhaps hoping that Toggi's and Victorio's irritable temperaments and solid reputations for trouble might lend weight to their arguments, Loco and Hiralchiddy refused to continue the discussions until they returned. A second session including Victorio was convened on October 12. The Indians again voiced their opposition to the removal: "They made very strong protest that they could not live at San Carlos, that the Indians there were unfriendly to them, were constantly abusing them and imposing on them, and had even killed some of them; that the water didn't agree with them; that their arms and horses were taken away and given to unfriendly Indians; that they were willing and wanted to do as the government wanted them to but asked and implored that they either be left at Ojo Caliente or given some other good place away from San Carlos."[26]

Bennett still made no headway with the Indians and called a third meeting for the next day, October 13, 1878. Once again the leaders ran through the Indians' objections. The officer explained that orders were orders. He had no room to negotiate. The Apaches would have to go.

When Loco saw that there was no alternative except to run and fight, he registered his protest but explained why he would agree to go with Bennett: "This is not just. There is no reason for this. We have been at peace. But I don't want to go on the warpath. I have raised many children and I love them. I don't want them to be killed out in the wilds. Therefore I will go for their sake."[27] When Loco agreed to go, Victorio also appeared to cave in. Bennett reported, "Victorio then told me that . . . he was opposed to going, but as he was obliged to go and could not change the decision of his Great Father in Washington, he was ready to go and only asked that they be escorted in safety." As it turned out, Victorio's apparent acquiescence was the classic Chiricahua double-cross—the same ploy Geronimo had used to trick John Clum during the Chiricahua removal in 1876.

On October 14, satisfied that he had convinced the chiefs to go without a fuss, the captain told the Indians to collect their things and gather at the agency. He was pleased that "they immediately commenced to move into the agency, and everything appeared to be running along smoothly. A great many had got in and were settled." Bennett's removal plans went awry that afternoon. "About three (3) o'clock in the afternoon, the chiefs brought a woman to me who said she was a Mescalero Apache and belonged near Fort Stanton, N.M., and wished to go there. She was well known by all to be as she represented, and I told her that as I was ordered to move only Warm Springs Apaches, if Victorio and Loco asked it, she could return to Fort Stanton."

Victorio and Toggi were nowhere to be seen during the discussions with the woman. Toggi's whereabouts came to light when one of Bennett's Navajo scouts dashed in with the news that Toggi and two or three other Indians were making tracks for the mountains. Bennett ordered Lieutenant

Henry Wright and sixteen men to chase down the escapees. Fearing that a widespread breakout was developing, Bennett also seized Loco and old Hiralchiddy. The woman took the arrests as a sign of Bennett's bad intentions. He wrote, "The Mescalero Apache woman . . . was mounted and started up the canyon toward the Indian camp, hallooing at the top of her voice that the soldiers were coming and going to kill them all, and for all to leave, and get out of the way, and save their lives. A stampede immediately followed from the Indian camp, and on surrounding and counting what were left, I found eighty (80) had gone. Of the eighty Indians that escaped forty were men and [the] balance women and children."[28]

Henry Wright and his men went breakneck after Toggi's bunch but managed to chase down only four runaways, a mother struggling along with three young children. Wright and Second Lieutenant Charles Merritt were dispatched again the next day on the same mission, but in different directions. Neither command showed any results after a week-long search. Victorio, Nana, Toggi, and Sanchez were once again on the run.

On October 20 Bennett was ordered to remove the remaining 186 Apaches despite their continued objections. He delayed the departure when one of the runaways, Sanchez, returned to Ojo Caliente on October 22 and reported that Victorio and a few relatives wanted to rejoin the fold. He thought they would return within a couple of days if Bennett would assure their safety. Bennett guaranteed Victorio's security and waited for three days. Victorio was a no-show, and Sanchez escaped again, this time "crawling out between the sentries," taking along seventeen relatives and friends.[29]

Finally, in what Captain Bennett called "an evil hour" on October 25, 1878, he gathered up the 169 Indians who were left with Loco and set out for San Carlos. A half-dozen wagons hauled the Apaches' worldly goods and as many Indians as could crowd aboard.[30]

When Commissioner Hayt learned that the army would be making the move without Indian Office involvement, he quickly authorized Agent Hart to hire additional policemen to welcome the incoming Indians. Hart was instructed to meet the army en route and take on the prisoners at any convenient point between Ojo Caliente and San Carlos. Three weeks passed before the agent received the instructions. By the time he launched his brigade of Indian police, the refugees were only thirty miles from the San Carlos agency. It was the first week in November 1878.[31]

Unlike John Clum eighteen months earlier, Captain Bennett opted to take the shorter but more difficult northern route, across the Black Range. The column would pass near Fort Apache before it reached the San

Carlos agency. The route was about fifty miles shorter than Clum's, but it was an unhappy choice. The steep climb over the mountains during the first part of the trip forced Bennett to stop and rest the column for a full day on October 28, just two days after setting out. Another delay occurred when four men came in to negotiate a surrender.

Foul weather set in shortly after the departure from Ojo Caliente—a wintry mix of cold rain, sleet, and snow. The bad weather turned the mountain roads to mush, bogged the wagon wheels, and slowed the column to a crawl. On November 6, after twelve grueling days, the convoy was within thirty miles of San Carlos when a four-day blizzard stopped it in its tracks. The ill-starred travelers were two and a half miles from Fort Apache when they were forced to make an icy camp in deep snow and bitter temperatures.

Bennett wrote, "The Indians suffered terribly, and the roads were so muddy and bad that it was impossible to travel." He desperately needed supplies, but telegraph lines had broken under the weight of ice. He sent runners to both Fort Thomas and Fort Apache for help. Unfortunately, pack trains could not leave without authority from the departmental headquarters in Prescott, forcing Bennett to wait another four days. On November 13, 1878, mule trains were dispatched with supplies from both Forts Apache and Thomas. As the captain waited for his relief, the San Carlos chief of police, Dan Ming, showed up with thirty-eight Indian policemen and a letter from Agent Hart requesting that Bennett hand over his prisoners to the Indian Office.[32]

The telegraph lines were still on the ground, and again Bennett could not contact headquarters for permission to transfer the prisoners. Once more he sent runners and waited. After six days, Bennett and Ming decided to move together toward San Carlos with the refugees in tow. The next day Bennett's runner caught up with the column and delivered the authorization for the transfer of 173 Indians to Indian Office custody. After the formalities, Captain Bennett turned his ponies to the northeast and set out on the shortest route back to Fort Wingate. Ming, his scouts, and the miserable Apaches continued to struggle through the snow and mud toward San Carlos.[33]

Loco's Apaches reached San Carlos on November 25, 1878. It had taken the column twelve days to get within thirty miles of San Carlos and an additional nineteen days to cover the last thirty miles. The overall excursion from Ojo Caliente to San Carlos took the army exactly two weeks longer than it had taken Clum to make a more roundabout trip in 1877. The prisoners were required to camp near the agency, where they could be shielded from any contact with Victorio, who was believed to have trailed the column from Ojo Caliente. He was expected to make an attempt to recover his relatives.[34]

As for Victorio, he spent a bad winter in the mountains of southern New Mexico, pummeled by unusually brutal weather. By February 1879 he had returned to the mostly vacant Warm Springs agency, but the Chihennes were long gone. He went over to Mescalero in late June, in an apparent effort to settle down someplace besides San Carlos. His stay was cut short during the third week in August when it appeared that civil authorities were planning to arrest him.[35]

Left without options, Victorio departed the reservation and launched an all-out war, killing somewhere between two hundred and five hundred civilians and a good number of soldiers and scouts. The Americans had not seen such widespread violence since Cochise sought to avenge the death of his relatives twenty years earlier. The *Arizona Star* proclaimed that "the hell-hounds are again at work in New Mexico." In the middle of Victorio's rampage, during the spring of 1880, Victorio's son, Washington, made a run for San Carlos to try to fetch relatives living with Loco. Captain Adna Chaffee, the temporary agent, learned of Washington's intentions, moved the Indians with Loco closer to the agency, and set a company of Indian police to guard them. The retrieval effort failed, but the failure did not slow the raiding.[36]

Ultimately, the American army made it too hot for Victorio's raiders north of the border, and he moved his reign of ruin into Mexico. There, at Tres Castillos, about 140 miles south of the border, Victorio led a mixed group of Indians—Chihennes, Chiricahuas, Mescaleros, and Comanches—directly into an assortment of 260 Mexicans—army regulars, citizen volunteers, and Tarahumara Indian scouts under the command of Colonel Joaquín Terrazas. Victorio was killed on October 15, 1880, two years from the day that he bolted from Ojo Caliente, along with seventy-eight other Apache men, women, and children. Terrazas also captured sixty-eight women and children, including Chief Loco's stepdaughter, Siki. He gave away or sold the captives as slaves and collected a bounty for scalps, for an estimated profit of $50,000.[37]

In a remarkable bit of irony, at the very time of Victorio's outbreak from Mescalero, the army and the Indian Office were in the process of moving his relatives from San Carlos to Mescalero. The Indian Office had reluctantly decided that leaving the Chihennes at Ojo Caliente might, after all, be less problematic. During the late winter of 1879, another plan was floated to permanently return the Warm Springs Apaches to their old reservation.

Inexplicably, the Interior Department officials had been at a loss to understand the Chihennes' discontent with San Carlos. Perhaps in hindsight, with Victorio terrorizing the countryside, moving the Apaches from Ojo began to look like a blunder of prodigious proportions. Ultimately the department agreed in principle to returning all the Chihennes to Ojo Caliente, but not before the Indian Office refigured precisely which land was occupied by squatters, how much it would cost to buy them out, and the price of refitting the agency.

Colonel Hatch enthusiastically agreed with the scheme. He noted that the deserted agency was still in good shape, and the land proposed for the reservation was not yet overrun by squatters. Contradicting Vincent Colyer, other advisors, and earlier agents, Hatch observed that there was "agricultural land sufficient to sustain 1,000 Indians, and [ample] grazing [to feed] 200,000 head of sheep and 25,000 head of cattle in the vicinity."[38]

The Interior Department's process, however, became so wearisome in the last days of 1880 that Hatch proposed that the army take on the job, return the Chihennes to Ojo Caliente, and assume the responsibility for their care. This set the Indian Office officials astir. The acting commissioner sent orders to Captain Chaffee at San Carlos to return all the Warm Springs Apaches at San Carlos to Ojo Caliente.

Chaffee was shocked when he delivered the good news to the Indians. The Warm Springs Apaches said they were no longer interested in another move, even back to Warm Springs. When the Apaches were returned to San Carlos, they were compelled to live near the agency, under close guard. The arrangement was intended to keep Loco's band on a very short leash and was expected to nettle the Indians. As it turned out, the Indian Office had unwittingly eliminated the Chihennes' two most serious complaints about the reservation. The new campsite near the agency was dryer and healthier than their previous location at Camp Goodwin. There were less swamp sickness and malaria. More importantly, close surveillance by the agency staff and police inadvertently protected the Chihennes from harassment by the annoying Coyoteros and other Indians on the reservation. It was also unlikely that the habitual Chiricahua firebrands would move in with the Chihennes while they were living next to the agency and being closely guarded.[39]

If Captain Chaffee ever learned the Chihennes' reasons for refusing to return to Ojo Caliente, he did not set them to paper. Nevertheless, on March 12, 1880, Chaffee recommended to the commissioner that the Warm Springs Apaches not be required to return to Ojo Caliente. This prompted a comical reversal of positions. General Pope now urged that the Apaches be forced to move back to the place they were forced from in the first place, regardless of what the Indians thought about the idea. Chaffee argued that a third removal against their wishes would be an injustice to them. His arguments carried the day.[40]

Chaffee's support of the Chihennes' request to stay at San Carlos might also have surprised the Indians. The Apaches had played the same game before they were returned to Ojo Caliente from the Tularosa Valley but then were enthusiastic and delighted with that move. Eventually the plan to reestablish a Chihenne reservation was reduced to an obscure file in the Office of Indian Affairs, never to be reopened. The Chihennes became San Carlos Indians, at least for a while. They would never again return to Ojo Caliente as a tribe.

Chief Loco at San Carlos with six-year-old son John and two unidentified boys, probably other sons or grandsons, 1883. "I have raised many children and I love them. I don't want them to be killed out in the wilds," Loco said. Courtesy National Anthropological Archives, Smithsonian Institution (INV. 020889800).

Chief Loco, 1883, at age sixty. This is among the first photographs taken of him. Courtesy Fort Sill National Historic Landmark and Museum.

Chief Loco in 1883, eleven years after the fight at Victorio's camp. Courtesy Frisco Native American Museum (Raymond, Norman, and Moses Loco Collections).

Chief Nana supported Loco's efforts to make peace. He joined Loco in the gunfight at Victorio's camp. Date unknown. Courtesy National Archives and Records Administration.

John P. Clum, agent for the San Carlos reservation, about six months after he forcibly evicted Loco's band from their Ojo Caliente reservation in May 1876. Courtesy Frisco Native American Museum (Raymond, Norman, and Moses Loco Collections).

Geronimo at Fort Sill, Oklahoma, about 1905. Loco and Geronimo were lifelong adversaries. Courtesy Fort Sill National Historic Landmark and Museum.

Chief Mariana, seated, right, with 1874 Navajo delegation in Washington, D.C. Mariana assisted Loco in his effort to avoid the 1882 kidnapping by Chiricahuas with Geronimo. Courtesy National Archives and Records Administration.

Chiz–pah–odlee, Loco's first and oldest wife, 1886, at age sixty-three. She was fifty-nine when she escaped Geronimo's abduction of Loco's band. Courtesy National Archives and Records Administration.

Captain Tillius Tupper, about 1883. Tupper commanded the combined force of cavalry and Apache scouts that illegally crossed the Mexican border and attacked the Apaches at Sierra Enmedio, Chihuahua. Courtesy National Archives and Records Administration.

Chiz-odle-netln, Loco's second wife, in 1886, at about age fifty-seven. She was about fifty-three when she escaped from the Chiricahuas in Mexico. Courtesy National Archives and Records Administration.

General Nelson Miles, shown here in about 1895, promoted the removal of all Apaches, including Loco's peaceful people, from Arizona to Florida. Courtesy National Archives and Records Administration.

Chief Loco in Washington, D.C., with the 1886 Apache delegation, representing the Warm Springs band. On his necklace is a good-luck star and a pair of homemade whisker pullers. Courtesy National Archives and Records Administration.

Chatto in Washington, D.C., with the 1886 Apache delegation, representing the Chiricahua portion of the delegation. Courtesy National Archives and Records Administration.

CHAPTER ELEVEN

Loco's Dilemma

Hard times hounded Loco's people after they settled in at San Carlos. The Chihennes suffered through the terrible winter of 1878, short on blankets and clothing. The infamous winter of 1879–80 was even worse, a record-breaker for nasty weather. Once again winter attire for the Indians failed to arrive, this time until January 1880. When the supplies had not arrived at the reservation by Christmas 1879, Clinton Fisk, chairman of the Board of Indian Commissioners, warned the Indian Office that if the Apaches were not supplied with winter wear straightaway, they would soon be on the warpath. Upon investigation, it was found that the contract teamsters hauling clothing for the Indians had pulled up in Socorro after learning that Victorio was ravaging the area. They halted their wagons in early November and refused to leave the city limits without a cavalry escort. Once the problem was discovered, the shipment was again on its way, four months late, but apparently with the military attending.[1]

Ration shortages also continued to be a problem throughout 1878 and well into 1880. Bone-cracking cold and intense ice storms in January and February 1880 brought food shipments to a standstill. Captain Chaffee was forced to reduce rations.[2] The food predicament reached crisis proportions by the late spring, but the emergency was over by the middle of the summer when the new agent, Joseph C. Tiffany, arrived at the agency on July 1, 1880, with an increased budget.[3]

Despite the period of tight rations, Loco's people were not starving, especially after Tiffany's arrival. Even Jason Betzinez acknowledged that "the government did feed us after a fashion."[4] Undoubtedly a dearth of government groceries led to meager menus, but to unfairly cast the Apaches in the role of helpless welfare recipients is to believe they would sit idly starving when other sources of food were available. San Carlos, among the largest reservations in the country, had been closed to white hunters since January 1870. Game, although skimpy, was still ample enough to supplement government rations. During severe ration shortages, agents also issued passes allowing the Indians to hunt and gather away from the reservation. During the administration of Agent Henry Hart, four hundred Apaches were permitted off the reservation to look for food. When rations were replenished in the new fiscal year, Hart sent word for the Indians to return to the reservation. The editor of the *Globe (Arizona) Silver Belt* gave front-page attention to the fact that "about one hundred, homeward bound [Apaches] passed through Globe one day. Their ponies were laden with acorns and grass seed, and the squaws also carried well-filled sacks, baskets and children." Rumor had it that Agent Chaffee followed Hart's lead and gave off-reservation passes to as many as twelve hundred Apaches, some for as long as forty days, during the food crisis. Although Chaffee denied such a large-scale issue of off-reservation permits, he soon established a policy of regularly issuing passes, although fewer at one time than Agent Hart. When Joseph Tiffany took over the agency from Chaffee, he made off-reservation hunting and gathering permits reasonably easy to come by for small groups of Chihennes wanting to hunt and gather.[5]

At first glance, Betzinez seems to have disagreed: "We were issued rations once a week and as we were not allowed to wander away to hunt game, we were entirely dependent on this issue." This was only partially true. He might have been referring to the period just after Chaffee replaced Hart as agent. Chaffee maintained tight control over the Warm Springs Apaches' movements when he first assumed the agent's job. Things loosened up after he found he had inherited a food shortage and discovered that Loco wanted to settle down. He continued issuing permits throughout his tenure as agent.[6]

The Indians could also purchase additional food or other necessaries with money made from work around the agency. Chaffee had opened a variety of wage work prospects by mid-1880. Tiffany expanded on Chaffee's program and arranged for some Apaches to work away from the reservation on white-owned ranches and businesses in Globe. A few Indians were drawing small weekly wages for picking up the agency's mail and telegrams and running errands in Globe. Farming and cattle ranching on the reservation also provided both jobs and additional food.[7]

Agent Tiffany had powerful political connections in Washington, including Clinton Fisk. Under Tiffany's administration, San Carlos received an unusually large budget. Tiffany used the money to launch an expansive building and jobs program on the reservation. Apaches were hired to make and lay adobe bricks for the construction of new agency buildings. In September 1880, Indians were employed to string a telegraph line from the reservation to Globe. Some went to work unloading and storing supplies as they arrived at the agency. Others labored as teamsters and as cowboys tending the tribal cattle herd.

The agency police force employed thirty-nine Apaches. In mid-1880, during Victorio's rampage, Tiffany took on 150 extra police to protect the reservation and to accompany the troops bird-dogging the insurgents. Meanwhile, the army employed four companies of scouts, about two hundred men, in October and November 1880. By the start of 1881, almost four hundred Apaches, about 40 percent of all men from every band on the reservation, were drawing government paychecks as scouts or police.[8]

Betzinez again seems to contradict all this. He complained that "the great disadvantage of this kind of life [on the reservation] was that we had nothing to do." While the Chihennes may have had "nothing to do" just after the band returned to San Carlos, undeniably work was available for some Chihennes by July 1880, and much more after Tiffany arrived. By 1882, virtually every Chihenne on the reservation who wanted a paying job had one. The Chihennes were eating well and living without fear of attack—or so they thought.[9]

Loco's Chihennes would hardly have considered their location in the shadow of the San Carlos agency an ideal place to live. It was unpleasantly cold in the winter and hot enough to melt Hades in the summer, but it was healthier and more secure than the Camp Goodwin area. In addition, their proximity to the agency offered the Chihennes the opportunity to adjust to the peculiarities of white society.[10] Sam Kenoi, a Chihenne and an informant of Morris Opler's, discussed the differences between agency Apaches and Indians living farther out: "From the way they talked in the old days, it seems that the Indians didn't say much about the white people except what good they were doing, giving them plenty of blankets and rations. . . . It was the people who lived around the agency, who saw white people all the time, who were controlled. The people out away from the agency were wild. That's why some thought the white men had queer ways and hated them. After they got to know the white man's way, they liked it. The white men gave them new things, new food for instance."[11]

By mid-1881, Loco's ideas were showing promise for the Chihennes. They were developing amicable relations not only with whites on the reservation but also with those in the surrounding area. They were safe, protected by the San Carlos police and the army, and working at a profusion of wage jobs. Their farming operations blossomed, and their cattle herd was growing. The rationing system, although scanty and undependable, was close to adequate most of the time. It appeared as if the Chihennes were becoming thoroughly modern Indians, adjusting well to white civilization and leaving the traditional Apache lifestyle.[12]

Just as things were looking up for Loco, Nana, with about fifteen warriors, boiled out of Mexico near El Paso and went on a month-long rampage through New Mexico. The venerable chief's men shot up and scorched more than a thousand miles of New Mexico, with the Ninth Cavalry in hot pursuit.[13] At the same time, up north things were going badly for the White Mountain Apaches. In the spring of 1881, the Indians at White Mountain were intensely discontent, mostly because they were hungry. They began holding dance-and-drink ceremonials that were supposed to lead to a grand war of white extermination. On August 30, 1881, the situation erupted into a firefight at Cibecue Creek between a force of 124 scouts and troops under Colonel Eugene Carr and several hundred White Mountain Apaches. The fight ended with eight troopers and eighteen Apaches killed, including Noch-ay-del-klinne, the uprising's instigator. Carr's command retreated to Fort Apache. The Indians regrouped, made a half-hearted lunge at the fort, and then scattered.[14] There is no record that either the Chiricahuas with Geronimo, Naiche, and Juh at Camp Goodwin or Loco's Warm Springs people had much to do with the Cibecue Creek affair. But whether they participated or not, the conflict created a raft of trouble for Loco.[15]

After Nana's raid, and in the wake of the Cibecue affair, the southwestern territories braced for widespread Apache trouble. Departmental commander Colonel Orlando Willcox packed the territory with twenty-three additional companies, which joined the military units already patrolling around Fort Apache and San Carlos. Hundreds of new troops roamed the area, putting the Indians on edge, especially the skittish Chiricahuas at Camp Goodwin. They were primed to bolt by the fall of 1881. On September 30, when soldiers arrived at the Chiricahua camp to arrest a leader named Bonito for his part in activities that followed the Cibecue incident, Geronimo, Naiche, and Juh, with about 326 followers, broke for Mexico. After a running fight with First Cavalry troops under

Captain Reuben Bernard, the Chiricahuas slipped to safety across the international boundary.[16]

Almost as soon as they arrived in Juh's Mexican Sierra Madre hideout, Geronimo and Juh's Apaches began to talk about fetching the remaining Chiricahuas at San Carlos and forcing Loco's Chihennes to join them for a revival of the old Apache way. No adequate explanation has ever been offered for this scheme. It appears that different factions had different reasons for participating in the venture. Most of the raiders probably wanted to retrieve relatives from the reservation. When Juh and Geronimo made their escape in 1881, they left twenty-six women and children at Camp Goodwin under the care of Chiva and four men.[17] In addition, when Victorio and Toggi escaped from Ojo Caliente in 1878, they left between twenty and sixty women and children under Loco's care. In 1882 these people were living in Loco's village at San Carlos. Other relatives of Victorio's who survived the Tres Castillos massacre were in Juh's camp with Nana. They were eager to reunite with their kin.[18]

Also living with Loco's people at San Carlos was Zele with his band of eighty to ninety souls. Although Jason Betzinez believed Zele to be a "member of our Chihenne band," he was probably a Bedonkohe Apache. He had been taken to San Carlos from Ojo Caliente with Geronimo in the John Clum removal of 1877. He stayed at Camp Goodwin with Geronimo and Naiche when Loco and Victorio made their run to Fort Wingate that year, but he joined Loco's Warm Springs Apaches in late 1878 or early 1879. Some of Loco's descendants thought Zele served as a spy for Geronimo. Whoever or whatever else he was, he was Geronimo's boon companion, and Geronimo apparently thought a rescue of Zele's people was in order.[19]

Thus, at least some of the Indians in Mexico wanted to retrieve and reunite with friends and relatives. A number of volunteers were also undoubtedly involved for no reason other than the excitement of the adventure. It was to be the Apaches' largest raiding party in years. It harked back to the glory days of Cochise and Mangas Coloradas—the old Apache way revisited. Besides, Loco's Apaches were peaceful, unarmed Indians with plenty of livestock, and Apaches or not, they were a raider's dream target. No self-respecting young warrior would want to miss this one.

Why the Apaches from Mexico did not simply fetch their relatives and steal Loco's livestock is the question. If the raiders collected only their relatives, about 180 people would have made the return trip. With Loco's crowd included, the flight back to Mexico would involve almost four hundred fugitives, most of whom would be uncooperative. They would move slowly, lay down a trail more than a hundred yards wide, and raise a plume of dust visible for twenty-five miles. Including the reluctant Warm Springs people in the plot seems to have made no sense.[20]

Chief Loco's descendants believe that the true incentive for the raid—or at least the kidnapping of Loco's people—lay with Geronimo, probably egged on by Naiche. Betzinez agrees that Geronimo was in charge of the kidnapping operation: "It now began to be clear to me that Geronimo was pretty much the main leader although . . . there were several Apaches with [the raiders] . . . who were recognized chiefs."[21]

Loco and Geronimo had a long-standing enmity. Loco and most other Chihennes believed Geronimo was untrustworthy, dangerous, and quite unhinged. Loco had tried repeatedly to prevent Geronimo from bringing stolen livestock onto the Warm Springs reservation, but with Victorio's encouragement, Geronimo continued to import hijacked herds. It was one of the excuses the government used to justify the 1877 removal of the Indians from Ojo Caliente. Consequently, Loco blamed Geronimo for the loss of that reservation and the removal to San Carlos.[22]

From Geronimo's standpoint, Loco's dogged efforts to remain at peace reflected a faint heart. When he found himself and his fellow Chiricahuas back on hard times in Mexico, he resented Loco's prosperity on the reservation. When the subject of returning to San Carlos to retrieve women and children came under discussion around the campfire, Geronimo saw the opportunity to vent his rancor against an old antagonist.[23]

Twenty-five years after the fact, Geronimo offered another explanation for kidnapping Loco's people. He told his biographer, S. M. Barrett, "We returned to Arizona to get other Apaches to come with us into Mexico. The [numbers of] Mexicans . . . were so much greater than ours that we could not hope to fight them successfully." Thus, Geronimo justified the debacle on the basis that the Apaches in Mexico needed reinforcements.[24]

His explanation is nonsense. Three weeks after Geronimo, Naiche, and Juh left San Carlos, Agent Tiffany took a census of Chiricahua men remaining on the reservation. Tiffany found no Chokonens, but thirty-two Warm Springs Apache men were still in camp with Loco. Loco's people had been on one reservation or another for thirteen years, since 1869. They had moved on, left the old ways, and become reservation Indians and aspiring farmers. They had been virtually unarmed since 1878. Among Loco's men were young "warriors" who had never shot a rifle in anger and others who had never owned a firearm. The idea of bringing thirty-two farmers to save the Apache nation in Mexico had nothing to do with the reasons for the 1882 kidnapping. Geronimo's excuse also ignores the fact that along with the Chihenne men were more than three hundred women and children. Aside from slowing the raiders' escape, they would require an awesome effort to feed and would contribute next to nothing in a shootout.[25]

Eve Ball, who interviewed older Chiricahua Apaches living at Mescalero in the 1950s and 1960s, suggested that Geronimo conceived of the raid out of his concern for the welfare of Loco's Chihennes at San Carlos—his fear that the bad water, mosquitoes, and heat there would do them all in. This line of reasoning overlooks the fact that the animosity between Geronimo and Loco makes it unlikely that Geronimo cared what happened to Loco's Chihennes, and it implies that Loco was unable to save his people from heat, disease, and starvation. It also ignores the fact that any of the three hundred Indians with Loco could and would have left him if they thought a better deal awaited them. They had done just that ten years earlier, when the entire band abandoned Loco after Orlando Piper ordained Victorio as principal chief. Leon Perico, a Chihenne, spoke to the issue with anthropologist Sol Tax: "If the tribe is dissatisfied with their chief, if they are sick of him and don't like him, they may just move away and camp elsewhere and get another chief."[26] Although the Chihennes' new location near the San Carlos agency was not a place they would ordinarily have chosen, they were satisfied that it was the best they could get, and the band was prospering there. The idea that Geronimo's concern for Loco sparked the 1882 kidnapping—a kind of crisis intervention Apache style—can be written off as a nonsensical excuse for an unwarranted attack on three hundred peaceful Apaches by other Apaches.[27]

The raid, or perhaps the scope of the raid, was the subject of lengthy discussions among the Indians. Some of the Apaches may have had misgivings about the suicidal nature of the operation or about the attack on Loco. Nana purportedly supported the idea of retrieving the willing relatives, especially Victorio's, but declined to participate in the kidnapping, possibly because of his close relationship with Loco. After weeks of hearing the wrangling over the proposed raid, Kaahteney's wife, a bad-tempered woman who was never seen in public without a pistol strapped to her hip, grew tired of the grousing. She interrupted one of the campfire conferences with a shout: "Here we are, hungry and chased by the army while Loco is sitting on the reservation, fat and comfortable." A woman's wrath can set men in motion, and within days her audience was on its way north. Ultimately, sixty-three warriors signed up for Geronimo's chancy scheme.[28]

Strategically deployed between the raiders and Loco's camp at San Carlos, 2,630 seasoned troops waited, forewarned and looking for a fight. Determined to dislodge Loco from the comforts of San Carlos, the raiders were undeterred by the forty-to-one odds. The Apaches inching their way up from the south were hardcore ravagers, very good at what they did. They were either unaware of or unimpressed by the Americans' numbers and confident that they could dodge the soldiers, extract all the Chiricahuas and Loco's Warm Springs band, and make it back to Mexico untouched. Eight experienced leaders—Geronimo, Naiche, Chatto, Kaahteney, Mangas, Sanchez, Bonito, and Chihuahua—would lead the marauders through the gauntlet.[29]

Complicating the job for the raiders, the forthcoming "Loco outbreak" was given more advance notice than any previous raid in Apache history. Geronimo and Naiche sent word of their intentions to Loco in late December 1881. Loco reported the threat to Agent Tiffany, and by New Year's Day 1882 the army was bracing for Geronimo and Naiche's arrival. Colonel George Forsyth wrote, "Word has come to us that the renegade Apaches in Mexico were known to be contemplating a movement that might, and probably would eventuate in their trying to enter the Apache reservation at San Carlos, Arizona and compel the reservation Indians to break out and go back to Mexico with them." A general alert went out to field commanders in southern New Mexico and Arizona regarding rampant "rumors of hostile Indians attempting to return to Arizona."[30]

Sometime about the middle of January, a second group of messengers arrived in Loco's camp and threatened the chief with the impending forced removal. Loco again reported to Tiffany that the Chiricahua henchmen had urged him to join them in Mexico or else a war party would soon arrive to force his people to go.[31] Lieutenant Charles Morton summarized the events surrounding one threat: "About January 20, 1882, a Yuma Indian near the San Carlos agency had some ponies stolen which he trailed to the camp of Loco's band. A Chiricahua squaw reported that the ponies were stolen by four renegade Chiricahuas who had been in Loco's camp several days and had then said they would return in forty days and bring along sufficient force to carry the whole band back with them and any who refused to go would be killed. This was reported 4:00 P.M. on Monday [January 23] and the following Friday [January 27], Loco's camp was moved near the agency, where the conduct of the band could be closely observed and the [Indians] kept under surveillance."[32]

A third gang of six Chiricahuas slipped into San Carlos a few weeks later, in February, to repeat the threat. This time Loco reported the visit to Indian Inspector Charles Howard. Loco informed Howard that he had been notified that Juh and Naiche would come north in forty days, in late March or early April, and take his Chihennes out of San Carlos to the Sierra Madre. Howard reported that the six visitors were "emissaries" bearing serious threats from the Chiricahua leaders in Mexico. He passed the word to Major David Perry, commanding military operations in Arizona, who in turn passed it along to department headquarters, with the unnecessary admonition that "it is important to keep the border scouted." Everyone was now forewarned and waiting.[33]

Tension reached its peak in February 1882. Army units from Fort Thomas moved into the San Carlos area. The Warm Springs people were moved to within a mile of the agency. Tiffany put his Indian police on high alert, although he had too few men to do much if Geronimo showed up with any force at all. The agency police force had been reduced to about twenty-eight active officers, and about half of them were running errands away from the area. Guarding the rickety San Carlos jail required ten or eleven men in three shifts. That left three lawmen to protect Loco's village. Tiffany set these men out as pickets on the southern end of the reservation to watch for the expected arrival of the raiders. The tension in Loco's camp was palpable, but the forty-day deadline came and went. When nothing happened by the end of February, the anxiety waned. The army moved back to Fort Thomas. The Indian police relaxed, but Tiffany left the three pickets in place—a thready first line of defense for Loco's village. Overlooked was the thought that the Apaches in Mexico were operating on Indian time. Nothing would happen until late in April. The scare however, prompted Tiffany to request additional police. The Indian Office eventually agreed, and by the middle of April the agent had recruited an additional twelve or so lawmen, bringing the total police contingent to between forty and fifty.[34]

The ever-cautious Colonel Willcox, the departmental commander, was less certain that things could be kept under control. As a precaution, he ordered increased patrols along the international border, alerted all military units in Arizona, and notified post commanders in New Mexico to keep their eyes peeled for trouble. By late March 1882, a defensive line stretched across the expected path of the hostiles from Fort Yuma on the Arizona-California border to old Fort Fillmore, south of Mesilla, New Mexico.[35]

Just days before the outbreak, Captain Alexander MacGowan, now commanding Fort Apache, notified Willcox that rumors around his post had it that Juh and Geronimo had sent a fourth set of messengers to recruit other "renegades" on the reservation to join the Loco abduction. Eight days before the outbreak the *Grant County Herald* in Silver City, New Mexico, reported that "the subordinates of Agent Tiffany, especially Mr. Hoag, apprehended trouble from the Indians at San Carlos. Renegades have been coming in from Juh's band and have held talks with disaffected chiefs."[36]

Ironically, at the same time the Indian Office and the army were straining to prevent a forced removal of Loco's band from the reservation to Mexico by other Apaches, bureaucrats were holding discussions about removing the Chihennes from San Carlos to almost anywhere. After Nana's raid, the fight at Cibecue Creek, and the Chiricahuas' escape to Mexico, citizens throughout the territory were screaming for the government to remove the Apaches from Arizona and thus end the threat of depredations forever. A grand jury in Gila County declared the policy of "taming, christianizing and civilizing the Apache" to be a failure and demanded that the Apaches be removed from the territory. Secretary of the Interior Samuel J. Kirkwood revitalized discussions of removing all the Apaches in Arizona and New Mexico to a more remote location. He asked Secretary of War Robert Lincoln to find a suitable, out-of-the-way place to put the Apaches. Kirkwood dredged up an old Interior Department chestnut, Indian Territory, as a possibility. At this point, Interior officials were also pondering the possibility of cleaning out both the Mescalero and San Carlos reservations and relocating the Indians to anywhere remote and unfamiliar. Kirkwood asked Inspector Howard to check with the Apaches at Mescalero and San Carlos to see how they felt about a removal. He found that the Indians on both reservations loathed the idea, with one exception—Loco.

Chief Loco received the news of Geronimo's plan just at the time Charles Howard was asking the Apaches about a possible relocation. It was more than a coincidence that Loco was especially interested in a possible move to the Navajo reservation. Mariana, a Navajo leader, was married to an Apache, the aunt of Loco's two oldest wives, Chiz-pah-odlee and Chiz-odle-netln. So when word arrived that Chiricahuas in Mexico planned to kidnap the Chihennes just as Inspector Howard was inquiring about moving them to the Navajo reservation, Loco arranged for a pass to visit relatives in Navajo country.[37]

Mariana was agreeable to Loco's plan to have the Chihennes move in with his clan. Together they presented the proposal to Colonel Luther Bradley of the Thirteenth Infantry at Fort Wingate. Bradley thought the plan had some merit but suggested that Mariana consult with his people. Loco went back to San Carlos and discussed events with the Chihennes. Both Loco's Warm Springs people and Mariana's Navajos unanimously approved the move.[38]

A small Warm Springs delegation was selected to visit Mariana and Colonel Bradley to cement the deal. Inspector Howard was surprised to find that Loco's Warm Springs people were delighted with the idea of a move. Bradley wrote to Secretary of the Interior Kirkwood on March 25, 1882, twenty-five days before Geronimo's attack:

> Only one tribe has any disposition favoring a removal, namely those known as the Warm Spring Indians. They are related some-what to the Chiricahuas, the old band of Victorio, and they have some relatives among the Navajos. The latter have signified a willingness to have them come to live on their Reservation in New Mexico. The clandestine occasional return of small parties of Chiricahuas from Mexico is a disturbing element to them. This would be more difficult if they were with the Navajos, whose territory the Chiricahuas have never lived in and is much remote from here. . . . The tribe here seem to be quite unanimous in their desire to go to the Navajos.[39]

Howard, too, liked the idea and recommended a removal under the super-vision of Indian scouts, not soldiers, because "they seem quite anxious to join the Navajos on their reservation."[40]

Things began to look up for Loco, at least for a while. Both Howard and Bradley recommended the proposal to Colonel Ranald S. Mackenzie, district commander. Mackenzie also believed it was an idea worthy of serious consideration and recommended it to General Pope, sending along Howard's comments. Even Agent Tiffany agreed the program was a good idea. General Pope, however, rejected the recommendation out of hand. He did not believe a move from San Carlos to the Navajo reservation would be of any benefit to the Apaches. Other military men concurred. Departmental commander Willcox thought Loco's efforts to avoid an outbreak were in fact a plot to instigate an uprising among the Navajos. Misinterpreting Loco's visits to Mariana, he noted, "It is also rumored that they [the Chihennes] have sent to the Navajos advising them to break out." In early April 1882, just days before the outbreak, General Sherman stopped by San Carlos on a trip through Arizona. He, too, was against the idea of another Chihenne removal, but he apparently did not bother to talk with the Indians. "I do not believe you can ever prevail on them to move again," he wrote, "nor is there any place in the territories where they are less in the way of the railroad and the requirements of white settlers than here [San Carlos]."[41]

In the end, it was Galen Eastman, the Navajo Indian agent, who finally pulled the plug on the whole scheme. Eastman had been the agent for the Navajos since 1877, and a most unpopular one. He was within months of resigning under death threats from the Navajos, assertions of fraud from the army, doubts about his abilities within the Indian bureau, and the out-and-out disgust of his staff. One of his employees wrote, "Mr. Eastman has no friends here, he is hated by everyone." John Bourke thought Eastman was a "psalm-singing hypocrite whom the Navajos despised and detested and whom they tried to kill." Nevertheless, in 1882 Eastman was running the show at Navajo, and he believed the proposed removal was a bad idea.[42]

Eastman wrote a five-page letter to the commissioner of Indian affairs to administer the coup-de-grace to Loco's plan to avoid the raid. He accused Colonel Bradley of supporting the plan, if not dreaming it up himself, as part of a plot to stir up the Navajos in order to provide the army with a pretext to massacre them. He asserted that the reason the Navajos were willing to accept Loco's plan was that "some of the Navajos residing in the vicinity of Fort Wingate who have acquired a love for alcohol did advocate the locating of Loco's band in that vicinity because the Apaches promised to make tiswin for them."[43]

With a move to the safety of the Navajo reservation denied, Loco found himself, within days of the threatened attack, with nowhere to hide, no way to run, and no weapons with which to fight. If he remained at peace on the reservation, he would be set upon by Geronimo's associates and forced into the fugitive life he had tried to avoid for thirteen years. If he bolted from the reservation with his 150 followers to avoid the threat, he would step into a hostile landscape packed with army units intent on killing any off-reservation Apaches they came across. All that aside, the government might remove the Warm Springs people to some isolated place no matter what they did. The Chihennes were now sitting ducks, relying on three San Carlos Indian policemen for protection. Regardless of what happened, Loco was in a bind.

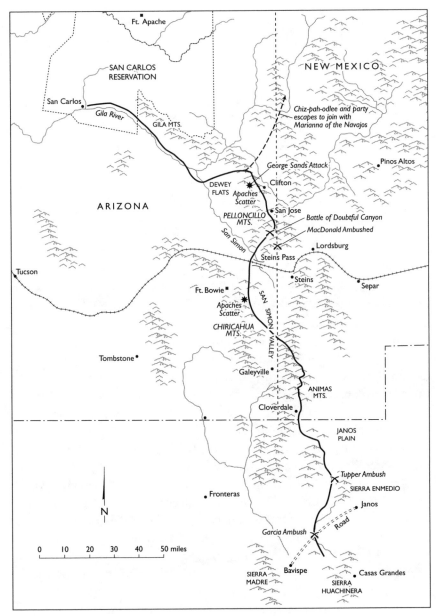

Apaches' escape route, 1882

CHAPTER TWELVE

The "Loco Outbreak"

Early in April 1882, sixty-three of the "most savage and brutal" Apaches ever to cut a throat left the fastness of their Sierra Madre campgrounds in Mexico and headed for the San Carlos reservation. Once in Arizona, the group headed for George Stevens's ranch on Ash Flats, about twenty miles north of Safford. Fortunately for Stevens, he had won the recent election for Graham County sheriff and was policing Safford at the time. During his absence, Stevens left a dozen Mexicans and a few White Mountain Apaches under Chief Bylas to run the ranch.[1]

The Apaches found the Stevens crew at an outlying work camp near the ranch on the afternoon of April 17, 1882. Geronimo and his accomplices straightaway killed all the Mexicans except the foreman's nine-year-old son, Stanislaus Mestas, who was saved after a Coyotero woman "begged hard" for his life. To keep the surviving Indians from warning the army of their arrival, the raiders forced Bylas and his men to tag along with the war party and assigned two men to keep the women at the ranch until things broke open on the reservation.[2]

Around twilight the following evening, the raiders slipped by the subagency at Camp Goodwin and collected Chiva's band of thirty Chiricahuas who had been left behind when Geronimo and Juh ran for Mexico the year before.[3] As the raiders continued toward San Carlos, they cut the telegraph line from the subagency. They reached the banks of the Gila River across from Loco's camp just after midnight on April 19, concealed themselves along the river, and waited for first light. During the wait, a Nednai messenger slipped into Loco's village to notify Zele to make ready to move the next morning. Chief Loco's descendants believe the Nednais' visit before the attack is proof that Zele was a spy for Geronimo.[4]

The kidnap party launched its attack just before six on the morning of April 19, 1882. Jason Betzinez, awakened by the commotion, remembered seeing "a line of Apache warriors spread out along the west side of the camp and coming our way with guns in their hands. Others were swimming horses across the river or pushing floating logs ahead of themselves." The raiders surrounded Loco's village and began a noisy assault on the drowsy Chihennes.[5]

Pandemonium prevailed as the attackers pulled over wickiups and clomped their horses through the crowd, but no shots were fired at first. Loco's camp lay about a mile from the agency, and the raiders wanted to avoid attracting the Indian police with gunfire. One of the leaders, believed to be Geronimo, repeatedly bellowed above the din, "Take them all! No one is to be left in the camp. Shoot down anyone who refuses to go with us! Some of you men lead them out." Loco's entire band was rounded up, surrounded by the raiders.[6]

Loco tried to negotiate, but he got nowhere. He persisted with his arguments. Finally, one of the men with Geronimo, Chatto, leveled his rifle at the chief and threatened to kill him. Still Loco refused to leave. The incident later led Loco's daughter to tell a scout for Colonel George Forsyth that Chatto and Naiche were leaders of the kidnapping. At the end of it all, several raiders who were said to "hesitate no more at taking a human life . . . than killing a rabbit" held Loco's unarmed men at gunpoint while others started viciously beating the women with pieces of firewood and roughing up the children. It was not the Chiricahuas' finest hour, but it was a persuasive argument. Loco gave in and agreed to leave with the raiders. Betzinez remembered, "We weren't allowed to snatch up anything but a handful of clothing and other belongings. There was no chance to eat breakfast."[7]

According to John Rope, the White Mountain Apache scout, as soon as the last of the escaping Indians left the village, the raiders deliberately fired two shots. Albert Sterling, the chief of police at San Carlos, heard the shots and went to investigate. He was accompanied by Sogotal, also known as the chief of police by the Indians. Other accounts have it that Ed Pierson, the telegraph operator at Camp Goodwin, having repaired the line, wired a warning to the agency that the Chiricahuas were coming. The result was the same in either case. After hearing the shots, or on receipt of Pierson's warning, Sterling rushed toward Loco's camp with

Sogotal and was shot dead as soon as he arrived on the scene. Sogotal was killed a few minutes later when he persisted in following the Apaches despite being warned not to—that they did not want to shoot him. It is apparent that the raiders did not originally intend to kill any Indians during the affair. They intentionally left Bylas's Coyoteros alive and tried to spare Sogotal.[8]

Some historians believe the Warm Springs Indians, possibly even Loco himself, had a hand in Sterling's murder. Police Chief Sterling was a tough customer with no qualms about tossing Indians in jail for minor offenses. Peaches, later one of Crook's scouts, who was married to two women from Loco's band, recalled that the Chihennes helped Geronimo kill Sterling because Sterling had locked up a number of them for making tiswin. Only four months before the outbreak, on Christmas Day 1881, Sterling had arrested Loco and one of his wives, presumably for consuming and producing tiswin. The chief went to jail for ten days for imbibing, and his wife was confined for twenty days for doing the brew work. Although it is possible that Loco or some in his band were involved with Sterling's murder, Geronimo had earlier declared his intention to kill as many whites at the agency as possible. Because the raiders had disarmed the Chihennes, it is more likely that Geronimo's bunch did the shooting.[9]

When the ruction broke out, a white man named Tom Horn was camped about two miles north of Loco's camp with a small ranchería of Chief Pedro's Coyoteros. Horn had been adopted by old Pedro, spoke fluent Apache, and had just hired on to live with the White Mountain group as the resident government man. Twenty-one years later, Horn wrote a fanciful account of the events of April 19–29 as he sat in a jail cell waiting to be hanged for murder. Much of his story has been shown to have come from his whimsical imagination, but parts of the tale agree with oral accounts and documented versions. If carefully parsed and taken with a grain of salt, his narrative provides some colorful insights into the episode. He probably was not a scout, as he intimated, but it seems certain from the details in his account that he was involved in the affair. Toward the conclusion of the episode, he was probably working as a mule skinner for Captain Tillius Tupper's cavalry.[10]

After hearing the shots that killed Sterling, Horn and a few of his Coyotero comrades scrambled up the easily defensible rock formation known as the Triplets and watched the slow-moving column of Apaches as it inched toward the subagency at Camp Goodwin. His panoramic description of the escaping column is remarkably similar to Clum's depiction of the procession from Ojo Caliente to San Carlos in 1877:

"Just as the sun came up, here they came. Great droves of horses and mules were strung out for about a mile and a half. . . . Squaws and Indian children everywhere, driving the stock. Of course they had their camp outfits. The squaws were all yelling at the children, and the children yelling at the loose stock. A small bunch of perhaps 20 warriors was in front, and behind was the main band of warriors."[11]

It was the largest array of Apaches traveling together since the Americans had arrived in Apachería—63 raiders, 30 Chiricahuas from Chiva's bunch, Zele's crew of about 90, and Loco's Chihennes, around 180 strong. In all, almost 400 Apaches were off the reservation and on the move. Strung out for over a mile, they looked like twice that many. General George Crook estimated the escaping Indians to number about 700 and set the warrior strength at 176. Scout Al Sieber thought there might be as many as 300 warriors. Actually there were about 99 men of fighting age in the group, but Loco's 32 men were unarmed and remained that way throughout the entire affair. Army officials assumed that any Apache on the loose was armed to the teeth. In truth, nobody was sure exactly how many warriors they were facing—just that there were a lot of them.[12]

Word of the outbreak spread instantly, and the army's response came about as fast as the army did things in those days. The hero of the moment was the telegraph operator at Camp Goodwin, Ed Pierson, who left the safety of the subagency, crawled through the Apache-filled night, repaired the telegraph lines, and was dashing off telegrams warning of the outbreak less than an hour after the raiders first struck Loco's camp. Pierson's wire read, "Sheever's [Chiva's] band at Sub Agency, four men and about thirty women and children, skipped last night. This morning Chief of Police Sterling went to see if Warm Springs Indians near Agency were all right. Sterling was killed and all of Loco's band left after killing him. Chiricahuas threaten to kill everyone at Sub Agency and here today or tonight. Suggest troops be sent at once."[13]

Within the first few hours after their departure, the Indians were being bird-dogged in a bizarre chase by the San Carlos post trader, leading the agency police force; cavalry units from Fort Thomas, Fort Apache, and Camp Grant; auxiliary scouts and trackers; and a few tag-along civilians. A mob of angry White Mountain Coyoteros was at the forefront. The raiders had commandeered a Coyotero horse herd with a promise to return the horses. The Coyoteros doubted the promise, presumed they had just been robbed, and set off after the thieves.[14]

Approximately eight miles from the agency, about where the Fort Apache to San Carlos road intersects with the river road, lies an open plain called Dewey Flats. There, just before noon, the escaping Apaches came across three wagons operated by a contract freighter, Mr. Gilson, his son, and one employee. At first glimpse of the oncoming Indians, the three men abandoned their slow-moving wagons and escaped with an impressive display of footwork.[15]

The Chiricahua raiders swooped down on the wagons looking for supplies to feed their unwieldy crowd of dependants. Instead they discovered that Gilson was hauling a load of calico and "lots of barrels" of commercial-grade whiskey. A freight wagon in 1882 could haul six 50-gallon hogsheads of liquor weighing about 600 pounds each. In his three wagons Gilson may have been hauling as many as 900 gallons of potables in 18 barrels, with room for a profitable load of calico. Even if only one wagon was loaded to capacity with firewater, the freighter was hauling 300 gallons.[16]

The debauch that followed soon attracted most of the raiders, but all the kidnap victims and a few of their captors continued their trek toward the mountains. Around Gilson's wagons the bottle-bash went into full swing. The Apaches seldom had access to unlimited quantities of hard liquor, and at Dewey Flats they intended to make the most of it. By the time the first of the White Mountain pursuers caught up with the Chiricahuas, they were thoroughly inebriated.[17]

When the Coyoteros discovered the outlaws in a roaring soaker, they dropped the idea of recapturing their horses, convinced the Chiricahuas to share, and joined the merrymaking. Even in their cups the raiders realized it would be politic to move along when the first Coyoteros arrived. After tossing down a few with their pursuers, the fugitives packed in a quantity of whiskey and resumed their escape. Shortly afterward, a larger group of White Mountain pursuers also quit the chase and joined the all-Coyotero binge. At least two of the White Mountain revelers died of alcohol poisoning before daybreak.[18]

There is no record that any of the Chiricahua raiders lost their lives to alcohol, but there were some very sick Indians riding toward the Gila Mountains that evening. The Chiricahua revelers, carrying enough of Gilson's liquor to continue the party all the way to Mexico, joined the main column just as it reached the hills. It was well after dark.[19]

Throughout the documented portion of his life, Chief Loco was renowned as a resolute drinker. Ordinarily he was not one to miss a good bacchanalia. The Chiricahuas, however, were troubled by the possibility of a Warm Springs escape, and Betzinez suggests that they kept Loco's group on a tight leash as they moved toward the Gilas, preventing them from joining the festivities on Dewey Flats. With many of his captors drunk, a cold-sober Loco waited until the drinkers fell into a stuporous sleep. He then slipped his oldest wife, fifty-nine-year-old Chiz-pah-odlee, and twenty-six other relatives away from camp and pointed them northward toward Chief Mariana's camp on the Navajo reservation. It would be more than two years before the chief would see Chiz-pah-odlee and the others again. Seventy-seven years later, Jason Betzinez believed Loco's wife and her group escaped four days after their kidnapping, but Chiz-pah-odlee told Colonel Bradley at Fort Wingate that she gave her captors the slip on the night they were forced from the reservation, April 19.[20]

The intrepid Chiz-pah-odlee made it unseen to Mariana's place but was "immediately arrested" even though army officials recognized that the group consisted of "several families not wishing to go on the war path with their band."[21] She and her refugees were next heard from three weeks later when Colonel Bradley reported on May 11 that twenty-seven prisoners had surrendered—two men and twenty-five women and children. "One man and nine women and children belong to the Navahos, one man and 16 women and children belong to Loco's band of Warm Spring Apaches. . . . They committed no depredations before they surrendered. These people wish to return to their respective bands on the San Carlos and Navajo reservations."[22] The man from Loco's band, forty-five-year-old Ast-te-wah-lah, was on his last legs with an advanced case of tuberculosis when he reached Fort Wingate. He died shortly afterward. One of the women with Chiz-pah-odlee escaped some weeks later and made her way back to San Carlos alone, reducing the prisoners to twenty-five.[23]

It was decided to hold the captives at Fort Union, New Mexico, as hostages until Loco surrendered. Captain Tom Smith, commanding Fort Union, requested "authority (on account of the small number of men for guard duty) to shackle some of the party and keep them in the guard house proper."[24] Bradley responded that it was hardly worth the effort, noting that the Indians were mostly nonviolent women and children and that "of the two men, one is Navajo, and the other, an Apache man who is so far gone with consumption that he is unable to do any mischief." Loco's wife and part of his family spent the duration at Fort Union until their release in June 1884.[25]

By late afternoon of April 19, the scouts from Fort Thomas spotted the Apaches' dust cloud. Even though the cavalry was gaining, the Apaches made a brief rest stop at a spring in the mountains. Although certain the army would make camp at nightfall, the Indians quickly resumed their run in an effort to distance themselves from the troops.[26]

It was in the dark early hours of April 20 that the runaways finally took a break at Eagle Creek, Arizona. Everyone needed a rest. The drinkers were suffering woefully from hangovers and needed recovery time. Loco's band had not been in the wild for thirteen years and was out of shape and worn out. Even though almost three thousand troops and hundreds of Indian scouts were after them, the escaping Apaches decided to take the day off.[27]

Just after the exhausted fugitives settled down, Al Sieber, chief of scouts, with two others, located the Apaches' camp. In the pitch black of a new moon, the three miraculously came across Lieutenant George Sands with fifty-three troopers only twenty miles from the Indians. At first light Sands's troop attacked. Although the Indians suffered the only death and had another warrior wounded, they got the best of the brief firefight that followed. Hoping for reinforcements, Sands allowed the Apaches to withdraw, followed them at a discrete distance for about three miles, and then bivouacked for the night.[28]

Lieutenant Colonel George W. Schofield, commanding units of the Sixth Cavalry, later claimed his units had chased the Apaches until the cavalry "made them scatter in all directions." It was almost true. While Sands's men rested, scouts continued tracking the Indians, expecting Sands to catch up when reinforcements arrived. The next morning, however, Sieber "found that the Indians had broken up into small bands." George Sands's hoped-for reinforcements never came. When his scouts reported that the Apaches had scattered and gone, Sands "unaccountably ran out of ammunition and food and returned to Ft. Thomas."[29]

After the skirmish with Sands, the Apaches broke into small parties and dashed off in every direction. No record exists of the sizes of the different groups. Descendants of Chief Loco suggest that there were a surprising number of small parties, "maybe up to thirty." If the Loco family estimate is correct, then most of the groups ranged from six to fifteen people, although some probably included as many as thirty. Loco's remaining family was probably among one of the larger factions. It was a popular strategy for Apaches on the run to scatter in different directions and meet at some distant location. The groups were left to their own devices to find their way to the rendevous.[30] Citizens reported violent incidents for fifty miles on both sides of the Arizona–New Mexico border as the groups foraged for supplies on their way down to the Mexico line.[31]

Units from Fort Apache, Fort Thomas, and Camp Grant pressed the Indians from the rear while others from Fort Craig to the northeast moved out to deal with the Indians if they came toward their old stomping grounds around Ojo Caliente. Simultaneously, Colonel Forsyth built a phalanx of troops along the Southern Pacific Railroad line composed of nine companies of cavalry, including a large force of scouts—altogether about five hundred men. Infantry units from Texas and cavalry from the Department of the Platte added another 1,085 officers and men to Forsyth's numbers. Forsyth led the defense in a special train that ran between his base at Separ, New Mexico, and San Simon, Arizona. He believed the Apaches were most likely to cross the tracks along that line. Four troops of horse soldiers and one infantry company rode the rails with the colonel.[32]

Meanwhile, several of the Apache groups moved independently along a trail commonly used by war parties toward Doubtful Canyon, a labyrinth of rocky canyons in the Stein's Peak Range, an easy place to lose a pursuer or to ambush one. Somewhere in the canyon area, several splinter groups met and combined into a larger band of approximately one hundred, about one-fourth of the group that had left San Carlos. Loco's descendants believed he and his remaining family were with the large group assembled in the canyon.[33]

Unfortunately for the Indians gathering in Doubtful Canyon, soldiers discovered the tracks of two small parties moving toward the area from the south. They were probably two of the splinter groups from Eagle Creek taking roundabout routes to the canyon rendezvous. Just at sunrise on April 23, Forsyth dispatched Lieutenant David McDonald with six Indian scouts and two enlisted men to survey the area south of Doubtful Canyon. The scouts quickly came across tracks of ten Apaches moving north toward the canyon. McDonald sent the news to the colonel. About an hour later, Forsyth received a second message from the lieutenant reporting that "fifteen more Indians had come in on the trail having with them one mule and two horses and were still tending northward." Forsyth "at once determined in [his] own mind that this was a party of renegades from Mexico going up to help their comrades back to Mexico." He was not especially excited about McDonald's discovery, because the Indians were moving in the wrong direction, but he sent the lieutenant's messenger back with two additional troopers. He ordered McDonald to keep after the twenty-five warriors.

McDonald, with his enlarged compliment, soon stumbled into an ambush at the mouth of East Doubtful Canyon. Four of his scouts were shot dead instantly. The lieutenant and the survivors hastily built shallow rifle pits, but not before McDonald put a Mojave scout, Quah-day-lay-thay-go, on the fastest horse in the Fourth Cavalry, Jumping Jack, and sent him bounding for help from Forsyth.[34]

Meanwhile, sixteen miles distant, near the little town of Richmond, now Virden, Colonel Forsyth was pointing his troops north toward the Indians' abandoned camp at Eagle Creek. He continued to believe that the footprints McDonald had found must be those of Indians moving north from Mexico. Before the troops were under way, a shout arose from the rear ranks. Hurtling across the desert came Quah-day-lay-thay-go on Jumping Jack.[35]

McDonald's scout reported the ambush, mounted a fresh horse, and led four companies of cavalry in a sixteen-mile race to save McDonald. The dash to the rescue took place under terrible conditions. Forsyth noted, "It was an intensely hot day, and the sun beat fiercely down, while the plain was baked to a thin crust everywhere. . . . The sand of the plain . . . was crusted for an inch or so, and the stride of the horses broke it to bits as we swept over it." Clouds of talc-like dust rose from two hundred galloping horses as they thundered toward McDonald's position. In an effort to find clean air, the four companies rode in echelon, side by side, for the entire distance.[36] The mad dash concerned his officers, who warned the colonel, "Our horses can never live at this pace." To which Forsyth replied, "They must live till we reach McDonald."[37]

The cavalry arrived just in time, saved McDonald, and sent the Apache bushwhackers in full retreat back to the larger body of escapees in the canyon. The Indians took up fortified positions on the south side and in the toe end of Horseshoe Canyon, a large U-shaped notch in the Doubtful labyrinth. Forsyth described the Indians' defenses as "impregnable positions which were from six to eighteen hundred feet high." For some reason he failed to station any troops behind the Indians' position, south of the canyon. It was an obvious escape route for the Apaches.[38]

Horseshoe Canyon is a rugged place. Forsyth said it was the "worst I ever saw." The jagged rocks covering the canyon's slopes twisted ankles and forced the soldiers to struggle for balance. The walls of the canyon rise steeply. A dry wash, fifteen feet deep in places, clefts its way through the center of the canyon, ending at a small spring that was described on April 23, 1882, as a muddy pool.[39]

Following the trail left by McDonald's ambushers, Forsyth entered the canyon with two hundred near-dead horses and four troops of cavalry carrying bone-dry canteens. Not an Indian was in sight. They were out of view, concealed on the rocky canyon walls. Sergeant Neil Erickson, riding with Troop E of the Fourth Cavalry, was among the first to enter the box canyon. "We rode into the Horse Shoe Canyon and all made a leap for a mud hole where the first water we had seen in hours was standing. Every man had his cup out and was getting a good drink when the Indians cut loose at us from the surrounding crags. We were ambushed and in the middle of a fine scrape."[40]

The first shots were fired around one o'clock in the afternoon. Forsyth's troops relentlessly pushed up the sides of the canyon but were unable to dislodge the Apaches. Firing was fierce in both directions. Sergeant Erickson wrote, "Firing volleys that forced the Indians to keep their heads down, we outflanked their position, crawling around boulders, sneaking up crevices until our clothes were in tatters. It was tough going with lead spitting from every elevation and Indians hard to locate." The Indians were twice flanked. Each time they withdrew to higher elevations where they continued to fire down on the troopers. In the end, however, it was the lack of water that ended the fight. Forsyth began to withdraw his men sometime between three-thirty and five in the afternoon. He explained, "I found it impossible to dislodge them without great loss. I gave up further operations at five in the afternoon and started again for Richmond. . . . I am compelled to go to the Gila River at Richmond for water for the animals."[41]

Forsyth's corps made it to the Lordsburg road before dark but was unable to find water and made dry camp there for the night. Early the next morning he sent his wounded to Lordsburg for treatment and back-tracked to Horseshoe Canyon, where the tiny spring yielded enough liquid for morning coffee and one canteen full for each soldier, which the men shared with their horses.[42]

Curiously, Forsyth persisted in his belief that the afternoon's fracas was with Apaches moving north to help Geronimo, noting that "we had not at any time caught a glimpse of Loco's women and children." This contradicts Betzinez and Loco's descendants, who remember being told that many of the women, especially the young women, bravely stood in plain view at the top of the canyon walls, above the fighting, to watch the fight and cheer their men on.[43]

Forsyth's casualties consisted of seven killed, including the four scouts caught in the McDonald ambush. The colonel believed he had killed two Apaches, and several of Loco's family thought that a number of the exposed female observers were killed. The colonel reported that he captured thirteen of the Indians' horses, which were given to the walking scouts, and "those we did not need for the use of our scouts, we killed." The most disturbing equine loss of the day was that of Jumping Jack, the Fourth Cavalry's fastest mount—dead from "exhaustion and heart failure."[44]

After the cavalry left Doubtful Canyon, the Apaches remained in place until around seven-thirty that evening. They then carefully withdrew en masse over the south side of the canyon, made their way into the San Simon Valley, and raced for the Chiricahua Mountains, about thirty miles to the southwest. They reached the security of the mountains early the next morning, April 24, where they rested along the banks of a small creek, a favorite stopover for Apache travelers.[45]

The one hundred or so Indians in the Horseshoe Canyon fight made no effort to cover their tracks as they hastened toward the Chiricahua Mountains. After he was finally convinced to give up the idea of moving to Eagle Creek, Forsyth headed his men after the Indians across the San Simon Valley and through the Chiricahua foothills. When the Apaches spotted the cavalry's dust, they abruptly moved eastward and reentered the San Simon Valley farther south. Again the Apaches had stymied Forsyth: "At daylight we resumed the trail, which led down the mountain and out into the valley for some miles, where it suddenly disappeared. A careful search showed that the Indians here scattered in every direction, and probably arranged to work back to the foothills individually to throw any pursuing party off their trail."[46]

Once more Forsyth made a poor assessment, seemingly determined to focus his search in places the Indians had abandoned. While he doubled back to search for the long-gone Apaches in the mountains, they continued their escape to the southeast, recrossed the San Simon Valley, and converged at their primary rendezvous, Black Point Mountain, a sixty-five-hundred-foot peak in the southwestern corner of New Mexico. It was in sight of Cloverdale, a tiny agricultural community about five miles from the international boundary.[47]

Meanwhile, Sieber's scouts continued to tail one of the splinter groups until it reached the vicinity of Black Point Mountain early on the morning of April 25. Tom Horn recalled: "Daylight found us on a hill overlooking Cloverdale, and the whole place seemed alive with Indians. . . . We stayed close to the Indians to see all that there was to be seen, for that was all we could do. Sieber estimated that there were five hundred of them. . . . Along about three o'clock in the evening we saw they were getting ready to go."[48]

On April 26, most of the 360 Apaches who had left San Carlos a week earlier left their rendezvous at the base of Black Point Mountain, eased across the Mexican border, and heaved a collective sigh of relief. They knew it was illegal for the American army to cross the border. Once in Mexico, they were confident the Americans would not follow.[49]

North of the border, the Apaches left a path of destruction littered with casualties. An army board of inquiry surveyed the effects of the raid on the territorial population. In the eight days from April 19 to April 26, 1882, seven soldiers and scouts had been killed and five wounded in combat. Forty-two civilian settlers were murdered in cold blood and five were wounded. The Chiricahuas had stolen, burned, vandalized, drunk, ate, or otherwise despoiled $30,250 of livestock and private property in a hundred-mile-wide corridor from Clifton to Cloverdale. At this point, Geronimo could have counted his venture a success.[50]

CHAPTER THIRTEEN

Ambushed at Sierra Enmedio

By the time the Apaches reached the San Luis pass in the Animas Mountains, they had merged into a single group about the size of the one that had left San Carlos. At the pass, they abruptly turned south and crossed into Mexico. Scouts watched as "at sundown [April 26] . . . everything in sight was in Mexico, and all headed, so we calculated, towards the Sierra Media in Mexico."[1]

Meanwhile, Captain Tillius Tupper was tracking a splinter group that had struck Galeyville in southern Arizona, about five miles from the New Mexico line. There, Tupper linked up with Captain William Rafferty, whose troop had followed the band from Horseshoe Canyon on the night of April 24. Rafferty's scouts counted "possibly 30 or 40 Indians" on foot and "about 70 or 80 animals," each probably carrying at least one Indian.

Like many other cavalry outfits of the era, Tupper's and Rafferty's units were at about half strength. The combined command consisted of 107 troopers and scouts—Tupper's Company B and Rafferty's Company M of the Sixth Cavalry with two scout companies, B and D, under Lieutenants Francis Darr and Stephen Mills and chief scout Pat Keogh. Tupper had received his captain's bars eight months before Rafferty, so he assumed command.[2]

Tupper and Rafferty rested their troops in Galeyville during the day of April 25, to avoid alarming the Indians with the cavalry's dust cloud. They resumed the chase at nightfall. Tupper decided to "make as long a night march as possible. [It is] the only show I can see, but think it impossible we can overtake them before they get into Mexico unless they loiter in camp." The command reached Cloverdale about six o'clock that evening and made camp for another layover while Tupper decided what to do next.[3]

Under cover of darkness, Sieber and his scouts returned to the vicinity of Cloverdale, where they discovered Tupper and the troops. "At Cloverdale we struck some new soldiers," remembered Tom Horn, "and they had a pack train and some grub and grain with them. . . . Tupper was glad to see us. . . . He wanted to get a lick at the Indians. . . . While the men got us up a really good meal, he made a good many inquiries about the country to the south, Mexico."[4]

When Tupper learned that Sieber was familiar with the terrain and believed he knew where the Apaches were headed, the two quickly hatched a plan to go after them. With instructions "to locate the Indian camp if possible," Sieber and ten Indian scouts left to ferret out the Apaches. The ace scout quickly pinpointed the camp and sent a runner back with directions. The Indians were camped about seventeen miles below the border at the base of Middle Mountain, the Sierra Enmedio. They were about twenty miles from Tupper's position.

Horn reported that "Tupper was 'tickled' to get a chance to get at them, as he said, 'he wanted anyhow to have a scrap of some kind and to capture a pony for his little girl.'" So in direct disobedience of his military orders not to cross into Mexico, Tupper gave the order to "get-a-going . . . at three o'clock in the morning on April 27."[5]

Meanwhile, farther to the west, Colonel Forsyth was still searching for nonexistent Indians in the Chiricahua Mountains when he got word that Tupper and Rafferty had found the Apaches. He immediately headed for Cloverdale to join the pursuit. The chase now assumed a surreal quality. The Apaches were making no effort to cover their trail as they moseyed their way toward the Sierra Enmedio, unaware that they were being stalked by Al Sieber and a small coterie of scouts. Roughly a mile and a half behind Sieber's advance team, Darr and Mills followed with the remainder of the scouts. Tupper, Rafferty, and the cavalry came next, plodding at a slow walk, three miles behind the scouts. Tupper deliberately "held back to avoid routing the hostiles by the clatter of hoofs, or other noise made by horses." Twelve hours behind Tupper, George Forsyth with 450 men slapped leather to catch up.[6]

When Sieber and his scouts got within five miles of the Apache camp, they spotted several fires in the distance. It was an unusual sight. Apaches on the run seldom built fires in the open. The Indians obviously believed they were free from further pursuit.

Leaving their scouts in place, Darr and Mills moved in closer to better view the spectacle while Sieber and his three best men bellied in closer yet for a tactical appraisal. Pat Keogh stayed with the main body of scouts to delay Captain Tupper until Sieber returned. Darr reported that "Sieber and four Indians [actually Sieber and three scouts] . . . returned within an hour, reported that there seemed to be about 115 warriors, and that the enemy camp was 'making medicine.'"[7]

What Sieber had seen was an abbreviated Chiricahua victory bash, celebrating a successful raid with minimum casualties. Such affairs included high-spirited dancing, loud singing, and feasting. An old Chiricahua described a victory celebration for Morris Opler: "There is a big fire, and they dance all night and for four days and nights. Some hardly sleep."[8]

These celebrations were usually reserved for the final return to the raiders' home camp, but this was special. Everyone, including the Loco faction, was in the mood for a party. None of the merrymakers had the slightest notion that more than one hundred well-armed intruders were watching their celebration from the surrounding darkness.

If one were to have an insane urge to hold an outing on any part of the Janos Plain, the best place would be where the Apaches put up on April 27. They located their camp at the edge of the Sierra Enmedio in a small basin bounded on one side by a bold spring and a shallow arroyo that was carved by runoff from the wellhead. One hundred fifty yards from the spring, two rock-covered hillocks, seventy-five feet high, mushroomed from the flat basin floor. On the opposite side of the basin, to the south, about two hundred yards from the two hills, a hundred-foot-high rocky ridge ran nearly the entire length of the basin.

The Apaches had built a large bonfire near the spring for the celebration. Beyond that, dozens of cooking fires flickered around the basin. Most of the celebrants were around the big fire near the water. The Indians' horses and mules grazed in a narrow flat between the arroyo and the two hills. The wash was shallow, but deep enough to keep the stock from straying back into the Janos Plain under ordinary circumstances. Four herders kept them from wandering away or onto the dance ground.[9]

Four thousand yards away, Captain Tupper set his plan into motion at four-thirty in the morning, an hour and a half after the quarter moon blinked out below the horizon. The celebration was in full swing, at its noisy best. The sound of the soldiers' movements concealed by the party, Tupper's entire command quietly eased forward into their jump-off positions, about a thousand yards out, a two-minute gallop to the Indians' camp. Leading the different units were five West Pointers—Rafferty, Darr, Blake, Mills, and Timothy Touey.[10] Darr and Mills, with forty-seven scouts, were sent wide around to set up positions on the ridge to the south and east. From there, a rifleman would have a commanding view of the entire campsite, an unrestricted field of fire, and almost perfect protection in stone pockets formed by wagon-sized boulders. Lieutenant Tim Touey took Tupper's Troop B, about thirty men, in a similar roundabout in the other direction, to block the Indians' escape route to the south and west. Once in position, they would have the Indians in a crossfire, with the scouts blazing away from the ridge and Touey's men shooting from positions on a third knoll about four hundred yards away.

The two oldest officers, Tupper and Rafferty, planned to lead the thirty men of Rafferty's Troop M in a frontal assault, charging out of the north headlong at the Apaches from the thousand-yard marker. As a military courtesy, Tupper allowed Rafferty to command his own men for the charge. Al Sieber would stay with Tupper and Rafferty. One of Tupper's scouts was purportedly assigned to gather up a few ponies for the captain. The plan looked like a winner. The Indians would be surrounded, trapped in the exposed basin, and taking fire from three directions. Theoretically, the cavalry would charge into the basin moments after the first signal shots were fired and annihilate or capture the confused Indians milling about in the open.

The trickiest part of the operation was to get the scouts into position, unnoticed on the ridge across the basin. To assure that they could move unheard, Darr and Mills doffed their boots and crept along in their army-issue socks. It was a bold act, because almost everything in those parts comes with either a sticker or a stinger. Things that do not are biters. The scouts, on the other hand, sensibly concluded that their moccasins would work just fine.

With their movements covered by the noise from the celebration, the two lieutenants avoided detection. Darr's company was situated and ready for action well before dawn. Mills was still working his way toward his position on the far end of the ridge when things went haywire. As Darr's in-place scouts waited for Mills to fire the first shot, four of the celebrators walked up on one of the redoubts occupied by two scouts, Sherman Curley and another White Mountain Apache. The four, three women and one man, Chief Loco's twenty-year-old son, were killed on the spot. Darr reported that he conclusively recognized Loco's son in the group and that all four were killed in the premature blast.

Rafferty, in his report to Major David Perry, noted that "Loco's son was certainly killed in the first volley in the Darr fight." Several scouts and troopers later identified him.[11]

Loco's son had been under stress for some months before his death. An old woman in Loco's camp at San Carlos had long been considered a witch, a caster of hexes and spells. She and the young man apparently had words, and the woman put a curse on the boy that sent him into the doldrums for weeks. According to Apache tradition, the one sure way to remove such a jinx was to kill the witch who conjured it. Newspapers in two territories reported the young man's effort to combine American law with traditional Apache justice: "Son of Loco, formerly war chief under Victorio . . . applied for permission to kill a squaw charged with bewitching him." The agent denied permission, the alleged witch continued with her spells, and the boy died an untimely death.[12]

While the Americans' Apache scouts were generally loyal and fierce fighters in a scrap, they were often a little shaky in their discipline. The maverick shooter was acting in the accepted Apache tradition of revenge for personal losses. Scout Curley explained, "When it was pretty near dawn, [the] four . . . came out on a little bluff right in front of where I was hidden in the rocks. They were going to a little pit where they were roasting mescal stalk. One of them was a girl, as she wore a lot of beads around her neck. This girl was walking in front. [Bert Nesbit's father] was with me. He was a sergeant also. The women were getting pretty close now, and I said not to shoot the girl, that we would catch her alive. But this sergeant with me shot her anyway, and killed her. I think he did this because his brother, who was Chief of Police [Sogotal] got killed there along with Sterling while in the Chihenne camp at San Carlos."[13]

So it was the murder of Sogotal, the San Carlos policeman, nine days earlier that came back to haunt the fugitives. Unfortunately, the four young people were from Loco's band, victims of the Chiricahua kidnapping themselves, and probably had nothing to do with killing Sogotal. As it was, however, the vengeful scout's lack of discipline prevented a massacre. It was still dark when the four mescal cooks were shot. Touey was caught by surprise and not yet in place, and his angle of fire was bad. Tupper and Rafferty were too far out, had the two knolls between them and the dancers, and could not make out any targets. Mills's scouts were out of position and exposed, thus limiting any effective marksmanship from that quarter. Darr's men, already settled in their firing positions, were only slightly better off, because they had only the light from the campfires by which to see their marks. Nevertheless, the first shots were

followed by a firestorm of lead directed toward the dancers. It was estimated that eight hundred shots were fired into the dance ground in the
first four minutes.

The first shots not only killed the four young people but also doomed
Tupper's cavalry charge to failure before it began. When the starting gun
cracked prematurely that morning, Tupper, Rafferty, and their men were
waiting for first light, and it took several minutes to launch the charge.
Because it was still pitch dark, the hazards of the desert were invisible, so
the charge began at a trot rather than a full gallop.

On Rafferty's command, "Forward, you men of Company M!" the
cavalry lurched forward to about a quarter mile of the Indians' camp,
where they spotted wholesale movement in the darkness to their front.
Thinking the Indians had been driven from the basin back into the dark
plain, the captain dismounted his men and attacked the formless crowd
on foot. After a brief shooting spree, Rafferty discovered that his troops
were facing a herd of horses accompanied by an unarmed old man
and three women who were trying to catch the panicked animals. The
four wranglers and fifteen horses were killed in the misdirected attack.
Recouping his dignity, Rafferty remounted his troops and resumed his
charge toward the real fight.[14]

By the time Rafferty's men reached the knoll, the Apaches had changed
from dancing and singing revelers in the exposed basin to fierce fighters
in fortified positions atop the rocky knoll. Perhaps still believing that
their cavalry would overrun the Indians, Tupper and Rafferty sent their
men charging up to the base of the hill, putting their troopers directly
under the Indians' rifles. The Apaches immediately tended to the threat
by moving most of their marksmen around the hillock to face Rafferty.
This move put their fortress-knoll between themselves and the scouts
on the ridge and limited Touey's available targets. The warriors were now
about seventy-five feet above the dismounted troopers, shooting down
at them. For once the Indians had more than enough ammunition, and
they poured a relentless fire on the men at the bottom of the hill. Sieber
later commented that "if the hostiles had kept cool, there would have been
no chance at all, and every man would have been shot down. As it was,
they fired too high, and the bullets passed over our heads every time."[15]

The Apaches soon realized that they outnumbered Rafferty's company, but initially they thought it was a trick to draw them out. When
they discovered that Rafferty was using everything he had, they launched
an attack against the pinned-down troopers. It failed in the face of heated
fire from the soldiers, but the Indians soon reorganized for a second run.

Sieber said, "There was but one thing left for every one to do and that was for each man to get out the best way he could."[16]

Company M was forced to withdraw about one hundred yards to the protection of the shallow gully. Tupper ordered the dangerous withdrawal. "The troops withdrew slowly and continued firing into the rocks where the Indians were hidden, a few at a time under the covering fire of the others." The shallow wash was neither long nor deep enough to protect many men at one time. "So we concluded to get out and . . . the safest way [was for] one man [to] get up and run about twenty or thirty yards and drop on the ground for a few seconds. In about five minutes another man would do the same thing. Bullets hailed about every man." From the ridge, Sherman Curley thought he saw two men killed. One, Private Goodrich, was indeed killed in the withdrawal, but the other, Private Miller, fell with only a wound in the side.[17]

During the sniping that followed, the Indians spotted Miller when he crumpled to the ground, and one warrior sought to finish him off. Scout Curley watched the entire episode from his position on the ridge about 250 yards away. He did not see Miller and believed the would-be executioner was running inexplicably "towards the horses, and back again to the rocks. He did this three times. The third time he got shot through the thigh." Lieutenant Darr seems to have seen only the last sprint and thought the warrior had been killed. "He got within forty yards of where the cavalry man lay, and all the time exposed to the fire of the scouts and soldiers. Finding bullets coming too thick he started back, but fell dead within fifteen feet of the former shelter." The warrior did not die there but had an extremely serious leg wound.[18]

Just as the last of his troops were withdrawing, Tupper ordered about fifteen men under Lieutenant John (Bo) Blake to capture what remained of the Indians' horse herd between the hillock and the wash. In a daring charge along the flat between the hill and the wash, less than one hundred yards from the Indians' guns, Blake and his squad raced "at a bounding gallop along the hostile front, receiving their close range fire at every step." They swept up seventy-four of the Indians' horses and herded them "off down a valley and onto the plain below."[19] Tupper purportedly kept several ponies for himself. The balance of the captured horses and mules were distributed as booty to the men and scouts who wanted them, a common practice in those days. Blake's charge had set most of the escaping Apaches afoot. Some of the Indians' livestock eluded the army, and Betzinez noted, "About night, just as we were starting off, some of the warriors came in with a few horses which they had been able to recapture."[20]

When the first shots sounded, the gala on the dance ground turned into pandemonium. Horn described the chaos: "Well, there were 'things doin' all right just then Indians were yelling and squaws were yelling . . . dogs barking, and horses running every which way. . . . The Indians were firing terribly fast at us." Betzinez recalled that "several women and children were hit while we were running toward the hills [the two hillocks]." Loco's people, unlike Geronimo's, were virtually unarmed. A few of the men had traditional bows, but these were useless at the distances involved. So while the firestorm raged around them, the chief's 180 men, women, and children could do little but crouch behind the boulders and wait for the shooting to end. Misshapen chunks of lead that splattered against the rocks around them can still be found on the hill. Loco's unarmed Apaches made two efforts to convince the scouts to turn on their cavalry companions or at least stop the shooting. Both failed. As soon as the firing slowed, Loco shouted across the basin, asking the scouts why were they killing their own people and declaring that most of those with him had been forced off the reservation. The scouts responded with a barrage of cat calls and insults and a fusillade toward his position. One sharpshooter found his mark. Betzinez wrote that "Old Man Loco was wounded slightly in the leg while leaning against a rock right beside me."[21]

The second effort to call off the scouts proved to be a fatal one. "About noon an old Apache woman climbed up to the highest point of the hillock where she stood in plain sight, calling out to her son, Toclanny, who was an Indian Scout. She thought mistakenly that he was with these particular troops. In vain she called to him telling him that we had been run off against our will by the hostiles from Mexico. But her son wasn't there and she was shot and killed."[22]

By midday the army's position was eroding. At eleven-thirty that morning, Tupper and Rafferty concluded that "we could not get the savages out of the rocks and that no good could result from further firing, which would reduce our supply of ammunition." A tedious withdrawal began that lasted for three or four hours. Darr reported, "Both sides now kept up a continuous fire until a quarter of three o'clock p.m. At that hour, having been twenty-one hours without rations or water, and having but three rounds of ammunition to each man . . . it became absolutely necessary to withdraw." Adding urgency to the scouts' withdrawal, Curley reported that a few Indians "had worked around behind where we had been in the rocks, and we only just got out in time." Betzinez confirms Curley's account: "Early in the afternoon four young warriors slipped through to the southeast and circled around behind the Indian scouts. They attacked the scouts from the rear, driving them out into the plain where they joined the troops."[23]

Tupper left the field to the Apaches just before sundown and withdrew nine miles, to just beyond the place where the attack had begun that morning. His men set up camp around eight o'clock. The soldiers had been on the hunt or in the fight for twenty-nine hours. They had one badly wounded man on their hands and another slightly wounded. They left the dead trooper on the field, although the captain sent a squad to tend his body the following day.

As soon as things settled down, Tupper sent a runner north to the telegraph office at Fort Bowie to file his after-action report with General McDowell. Realizing that his neck was on the block for crossing the international boundary, Tupper reported that the shootout took place east of Cloverdale, not south of it in Mexico. McDowell forwarded the report to Washington:

> Tupper 6th Cav in command of troops reports from camp on east side of Animas, April 28 as follows: "Jumped a large force of Indians at daybreak this morning about 35 miles east of Cloverdale, killed 12 or 15, among them Loco's son; captured 70 head of stock. Engagement lasted until 12 noon but we were unable to dislodge them from a very strong natural position. During the fight Loco endeavored to induce our scouts to turn against us. Lost one man killed, two wounded, two [army] horses killed."[24]

It had been a bad day for the Apaches. Most of the Indians had been packed on the tiny hill, about one-half the size of a football field, for twelve hours. Most found partial protection hunkering behind giant boulders atop the hill. Others built semicircular stone sanctuaries with small piles of cantaloupe-sized rocks stacked two or three high. These one-man redoubts were scattered around the sides of the hill facing the army's positions. By day's end the army had fired between five thousand and eight thousand rounds into the Indian position. Tupper reported, "I suppose every man fired from 50 to 80 shots, some more. I used about 40 cartridges, shooting very deliberately at intervals." The Indians left seventeen warriors and women dead where they fell. The exact number of wounded was uncounted, but it was in the dozens. Some died later from their wounds.[25]

Just after sundown the Apache survivors abandoned Sierra Enmedio and beat a panicked retreat to the south. In their haste to escape, they left "a trail that even at night could be followed as easy as [one] can Capitol Avenue in Cheyenne" across the Janos Plain toward Casas Grandes and the Sierra Huachinera.[26]

As the Indians moved south, nine miles north of the battlefield Tupper and Rafferty's exhausted troops, now reduced to 105 men, ate for the first time in a day. They were settling in for some well-deserved rest when Forsyth and his troop of 450 pounded into the camp. Forsyth's men had been in the saddle since before light that day, pushing "over the range on one of the worst trails I have ever seen or heard of," and were worn out themselves, though not nearly as badly as Tupper's troops. Captain Charles Hatfield, who arrived with Forsyth, observed that Tupper's bunch "had been badly used, without making much impression on the Apaches."[27] When Forsyth suggested that the pursuit continue that night, Tupper declined, explaining that his men could not possibly go further without rest. With Tupper out of business for the night, Forsyth's enthusiasm waned.[28]

The chase resumed at first light the next morning, April 29. Scouts found the scene of the previous day's pandemonium to be "still as a graveyard." Sieber and Pat Keogh poked around the battlefield and found three dead but estimated that seventeen Apaches had been killed. Not far behind, Forsyth, Tupper, and Rafferty rode at the front of 550 troopers and scouts. As the soldiers passed the battlefield, they "found the sergeant [sic] of the 6th Cavalry killed the day before. He was rolled in his blankets and buried where he fell on the flats."[29]

Only a couple of miles into the pursuit, the scouts began to find other casualties from the fight, dead Apaches and wounded ones who could not keep up with the escaping Indians. One scout, Slim Jim, found and shot "a scout who had deserted from our forces in the Horseshoe Canyon fight. . . . This deserter had been wounded the day before in the brush with Tupper's men and had concealed himself cunningly in the sand, leaving only his nose above the sand so he could breathe."[30]

Jason Betzinez gave a sad account of how a second victim of the fight was reluctantly abandoned by the Apaches. "One wounded woman who had been shot in the ankle was carried for a way on a stretcher made of reeds, then on a recaptured horse. The animal bucked her off, so she asked her relatives to leave her there. They finally had to abandon her. I understand she was later picked up by the troops."[31]

Forsyth's scouts discovered the woman only a few miles past the partially buried fellow. He wrote that "we found a poor old wounded squaw on the trail. . . . She was very much frightened, expecting to be killed." Her foot had been nearly amputated by a shot through her ankle. The colonel now faced a dilemma. The command was not supported by wagons or ambulances. If left sitting on the Janos Plain, the woman would be finished after a couple of agonizing days, dead of thirst, hunger, or complications from the wound. If they tried to haul her by travois, she would most likely die before she finished the jolting trip back to Fort Bowie.[32]

Forsyth reported that he ordered his doctor make the matron as comfortable as possible and then, "giving her some water and bread, we left her on the trail." Apparently Forsyth's account was incomplete. Sergeant Erickson, a trooper in Forsyth's command, added that "Forsyth sent one of his doctors to see what he could do for her. He found her badly wounded, she wanted water and was unable to travel, so the doctor gave her a drink all right, one that left her sleeping there forever. She couldn't be taken with us and this was an act of mercy." If Erickson was telling the truth, the doctor probably overdosed the woman with laudanum, a popular opium-based painkiller often used for painless suicides in those days.[33]

Taking up the trail again, Forsyth, Tupper, and Rafferty pressed southward in the general direction of Casas Grandes, passing five miles west of Janos. They were approaching the Janos River when they came across the corpse of the warrior who had been shot in the thigh while trying to finish off Private Miller. Forsyth wrote that he "had died of his wounds, the wicker stretcher that lay by his side showing that he was of sufficient importance in rank for his companions to try and get off [carry away], notwithstanding they were so sorely pressed by their pursuers."[34]

Had Forsyth been aware of Apache tradition, he might have realized that the fatally wounded man had been carried for almost seventeen miles by exhausted friends and distraught relatives. Scout Curley's keen eye for detail caught the fact that "his hair was all combed out, his face was painted red, he had on a black coat, and on his feet were some beaded moccasins." The family had meticulously prepared the warrior for burial but was forced to abandon the effort when they saw the Americans approaching.

On closer inspection, the scouts recognized the dead man's "moccasins as being the ones the chief of police [Sogotal] was wearing when he was killed along with Sterling, at the camp at San Carlos. [The dead man] had pulled the moccasins off the dead policeman, and put them on his own feet. Now we took the moccasins off him, stripped him, and threw his body in a hole."[35]

It had been two long days for the soldiers. "Pretty soon we came to a little creek with some red willows growing along its banks. The soldiers and their mounts were all completely worn out, and Forsyth ordered camp." The troopers gratefully settled down for a meal and a night's rest on Alisos Creek, headwater of the Janos River. They had traveled about twenty-five miles from the scene of the previous day's battle and made at least three stops to attend to wounded or dead Indians, but they had gained steadily on their equally exhausted quarry. Colonel Forsyth wrote, "I felt confident that we would overtake the hostiles the next day, and so did all my officers."[36]

CHAPTER FOURTEEN

Ghastly Scenes at Alisos Creek

The Apaches were spent by the time they started their run from Sierra Enmedio. No one had slept on the nights of the twenty-sixth and twenty-seventh. The survivors from the Horseshoe Canyon skirmish, about one-fourth of the crowd, had managed only one night's sleep since the fight there, five days before. The band had made camp at the foot of the Sierra Enmedio by midmorning on April 27 and rested during the day, but then the people had held their all-night dance. Sleeping was out of the question on April 28, during the ten-hour gunfight with Tupper. Afterward, the Apaches were in for another sleepless night while they put distance between themselves and the Americans. The Indians were now mostly on foot, "hampered with many wounded." Jason Betzinez recalled that the exhausted survivors were forced to creep along "very slowly." The leaders decided they "had to stop to rest because many of our band were completely worn out." After "an hour or so," they resumed their slow trudge southward.[1]

Now aware that the Americans were in hot pursuit, the Apaches arranged their column to deal with the threat to their rear. A small vanguard of warriors ranged about a mile ahead of the main body, scouting for but not expecting danger to the front. Most of Loco's men, with the women and children, walked slightly less than a mile behind the advance guard. Most of the Chiricahua warriors stayed well behind the main body to delay the Americans should they catch up. Betzinez recalled that the rear guard was about two miles behind the women and children.[2] By the time the Indians approached Alisos Creek, everyone was exhausted and in serious need of sleep. Unnerved by the bad day at Sierra Enmedio, lack of sleep, and the present unhappy circumstance, the Chiricahua men began to bicker among themselves. It was a critical distraction.[3]

Unknown to the Indians, two of Geronimo's raiders headed for San Carlos had been captured by Mexican troops about two weeks earlier. The two had paused long enough near San Simon to steal four horses from a small ranch, but they were caught. The American military had warned Mexican officials that a large band of Chiricahuas was moving south from San Carlos and was expected to pass just north of Janos. To get specifics, Mexican officers interrogated the two horse thieves and offered to release them unharmed if they provided details of the Indians' plans. They threatened to kill them if they lied. Without hesitation the two told the Mexicans everything they wanted to know—the raiding party's numbers, their likely route, and their expected times of arrival. John Rope reported, "The two Chiricahuas said it would take them [Geronimo's raiders] about four days to get up to San Carlos and that they would probably be back in about twelve days." Some fifteen miles southwest of Janos, the Apaches' route would take them along Alisos Creek, a feeder stream for the Janos River when there was rain enough to make it flow. On April 29, Lieutenant Rafferty noted puddles of "water here and there." When the Apaches got to Alisos Creek, they would have five flatland miles to travel before they reached safety in the five-thousand-foot Sierra Hauchinera.[4]

Acting on the information provided by the prisoners, Sonoran National Guard and federal troops under General Bernardo Reyes moved quickly toward the Alisos area. A second column of troops commanded by Major Louis Ceroso was soon ordered to join the expedition. Colonel Lorenzo García was left in charge of the entire operation when General Reyes fell ill and was taken to Casas Grandes for medical treatment. Ceroso teamed up with García at Alisos Creek and waited. They commanded approximately 140 infantry troops and about 60 cavalrymen, who were sent to roam the countryside in search of the Apaches.[5]

Nothing happened for several days. Apparently, in their haste to intercept the Apaches, the Mexicans packed too few rations for an extended campaign. By April 29 García's men had gone without a decent meal for two days.[6] García was about to pull up stakes when his scouts reported that a crowd of Indians was headed his way from the north. His troops were just finishing their morning coffee when the news arrived. García strung his men out for a half mile along the Indians' path, concealed in a shallow ravine along the southern bank of the creek.[7]

Just before the Apache column reached García's trap, a handful of unusual things happened. At the last moment, some of the Indians detected the faint aroma of campfire smoke and coffee hanging in the air, leftovers from the Sixth Infantry's breakfast. If the Indians had been atop their game, the smell would have sent everyone scurrying for cover, but on this day, most of the sleep-deprived Indians ignored it. A few of the Warm Springs people, however, paused when they got a whiff of the coffee to see what was up. It saved their lives.[8]

At about the same time, part of the vanguard, including Chatto, Naiche, and Kaahteney, stopped to smoke a few hand-rolled cigarettes and allowed the Warm Springs people to plod past them. Loco and the unarmed Chihennes "kept right on going, strung out in a long, irregular column." The remainder of the advance guard recklessly raced forward, past García's hidden troops, riding "right on to the foothills." García let the vanguard pass and then "struck the rear of the Indians' column . . . consisting principally of [Loco's] squaws and children."[9] Once beyond the Mexicans' clutches, the advance riders apparently looked around and spotted the soldiers lying in ambush. Inexplicably, they did not sound the alarm. Betzinez said they later told the survivors that "they saw Mexican soldiers but were afraid to go back and let us know." After the fight Betzinez bitterly complained, "We found about fifteen Apache warriors . . . who had ridden ahead that morning and had failed to warn us of the danger they saw. Thus, they were partly to blame for our Warm Springs Indians being slaughtered."[10]

Thus in the early morning of April 29, about 250 heavy-eyed and leg-weary Warm Springs men, women, and children shuffled to within fifty yards of 140 Mexican rifles. The troops fired point-blank into the crowd, killing and wounding dozens on the spot. As soon as the fusillade was fired, the Mexicans plunged into the panicked crowd with fixed bayonets.[11]

Betzinez described the frenzied scene: "Almost immediately Mexicans were right among us all, shooting down women and children right and left. Here and there, a few Indian warriors [Loco's men] were trying to protect us while the rest of the band was running in all directions. . . . Whole families were slaughtered on the spot . . . unable to defend them-selves. These were people who had never before been off the reservation, had never given any trouble and were from the most peace-loving band of the Apaches—the Warm Springs band."[12]

After viewing the field the next day, "Rafferty and Blake said they never saw such shambles and ghastly scenes in their lives."[13] Colonel García explained the lopsided death rate—about six women and children to every man killed—by complaining that the warriors were mixed in among the women and children. He asserted that the excessive numbers of dead women and children "could not have been avoided, as they took cover with the warriors." However, the first thing Sergeant Neil Erickson saw when he went over the battlefield on April 30 indicates that much of the ruthless attack was focused specifically on the women and children: "The first body we saw was that of a squaw. Her head had been crushed above the eyebrows and her brains were mashed to a jelly. Her clothing had been burned by a shot fired close to her and she had a bayonet wound in her abdomen. In fact the bayonet had been left sticking in her. It was a terrible sight."[14] Undoubtedly the woman was not a collateral casualty, accidentally killed in a shootout between the men.[15]

Betzinez noted that Geronimo, as leader of the raiders, was able to muster thirty-two men from the rear guard to save the women and children. At a full gallop it would have taken them five to ten minutes to reach the scene of the slaughter.[16] Loco and most of the surviving men were already fighting hand to hand with the Mexicans when the rear guard arrived, but they were poorly armed. Betzinez said that none of the Warm Springs men was armed, but a few apparently had bows and arrows. One account of the fight indicated that Loco's men responded immediately to the Mexican attack with a sheaf of arrows.[17]

In the end, approximately fifty Apache warriors—thirty-two Chiricahuas and whatever was left of Loco's men—faced off with about four times as many Mexican soldiers. Despite being badly outnumbered, the Apaches quickly drove the Mexicans from the creek bed and back to their original positions. Their surprising success was in large part due to the hardware used by both sides.

García's Sonoran National Guard was packing Remington Rolling Block rifles. The Rolling Block was purportedly the "the finest rifle in the world," but it was a single-shot weapon and nearly six feet long with its nineteen-inch bayonet attached. It was a slow shooter and unwieldy in close quarters.[18] On the other hand, most of the Chiricahuas were toting Winchesters and Marlins—short, light, and holding sixteen shots when fully loaded. The repeaters gave the Apaches a substantial advantage in the close-quarter fighting taking place in the creek bed.[19]

After the better-armed Apache rear guard joined the fight, the Mexicans withdrew to their original positions. García then launched his troops in a series of unsuccessful frontal attacks in an effort to overrun the Indians. He abandoned the costly assaults by midmorning, and the battle settled into a drawn-out shooting match between the two groups.[20]

Sometime after midday, the guns of García's Mexican Sixth fell silent. The soldiers vanished. Not a trooper could be seen. The Chiricahuas were immediately suspicious. After a long silence, a young Indian girl, probably a captured teenager from Loco's band, shinnied up a mesquite tree in full view of the Apaches and shouted that the soldiers were gone. None of the Apaches recognized her voice. The Chiricahuas mulled this over briefly, decided it was a bit of Mexican trickery, and discussed shooting the girl out of the tree but decided against it. They sat tight in their stronghold, and García resumed the contest.[21]

Around noon, an additional problem arose for the Indians. Although the Apaches were fending off the Mexicans' repeated charges with their rapid-fire repeaters, the weapons had a gluttonous appetite for ammunition. By early afternoon the Indians were running short of cartridges. As it happened, someone had dropped a sack of five hundred bullets when the shooting began. The cloth bag was lying on an open flat in clear view of both the Mexicans and the Apaches. Any effort to recover it would draw unwanted attention. Even though the situation was critical, no one volunteered to dash out for the bullets. Finally, Loco, approaching sixty years of age and with a leg wound from the previous day, lurched from the creek bed and hobbled toward the ammunition pouch. With a hailstorm of bullets sizzling around him, the old man made it halfway to the cartridge bag. Suddenly he crumpled and fell face-first into the sand, apparently dead. He remained unmoving as the fighting continued. After a prolonged stretch, Loco resurrected himself and limped through a second barrage back to the protection of the creek bank. Finally, in utter desperation, "right in the thick of the fighting, one old Apache woman" volunteered to go and successfully returned with the bag.[22]

Just before dark someone set fire to the red willow and grass along the creek bank. Betzinez later claimed that the Mexicans tried to burn the Apaches out. Geronimo maintained that the Apaches set the fire as cover for their escape. As the Indians began to move out, Betzinez reported, some of "the warriors asked the consent of the few women who were there to let them choke the small children so that they wouldn't give away their movements by crying." Betzinez, an admirer of Geronimo, failed to note that it was Geronimo who proposed killing the babies. Historian Angie Debo observed that he had done something similar three times before. The Warm Springs warriors, already infuriated at Geronimo, would have none of it. Fun, one of Loco's men, pointedly told Geronimo that if he showed the slightest inclination toward hurting any of the children, the Chihennes would kill him on the spot. Geronimo purportedly slinked off, made good his own escape, and left the poorly armed Warm Springs men to escort their families away from danger.

As the Indians withdrew, someone threw a buckskin over Loco's six-year-old son, John, to protect him from the fire as he crawled away. Years later, John's most vivid memory of the fight was peeking from under his cover and seeing the sand around him "boiling like a pot of gravy" as Mexican bullets burrowed into the dirt. Betzinez noted that before the evening was finally over, "they all crawled through the fire and got away without being seen."[23]

American soldiers who arrived with Colonel Forsyth on the following day commented on the gory sights left on the field of action. The accounts of what they saw attest to the violence of the previous day. The Americans found bodies scattered for approximately two miles along the riverbed and for some distance south of it. Tupper reported, "The killed were, of course, scattered over a large area of the country." Rafferty reported, "Along the sandy creek were evidences of a hard fight. I counted twenty-one dead bodies—about half of them squaws, I should judge, strewn along the creek bottom. Also, many dead Mexicans in full uniform unburied."[24]

A little more than a mile south of the ambush site, Forsyth and Rafferty found another large pile of bodies. Betzinez noted that when the attack began, "a few warriors [Loco's men] were trying to protect us while . . . the confused crowds of women and children headed rapidly for the mountains." To reach the mountains and safety, however, the panicked dependents had to pass through a narrow arroyo. García's men apparently anticipated this route and stationed a squad of men at its entrance. Rafferty noted the results: "We then left the creek and rode about a mile toward the point [where] the Indians [were] evidently trying to enter the foothills of the mountains. At its entrance in a little gully washed out of the prairie by the rains, I saw more dead Indians."[25] Betzinez remembered that some women stayed with the men and "dug a big hole in the dry creek bed" as a central redoubt. "The women also dug holes for other warriors in the bank of the little arroyo, around the center strong point. This made a good defensive position from which the men began shooting."[26]

While looking over the battlefield, the Americans found several of these foxholes, all piled high with dead Apaches. A Mexican lieutenant toured the field with Captain Hatfield, who described two of the rifle pits: "We were on the edge of the battleground and a few Mexican lieutenants were proud to show us the result of the fight. [One] showed us a washout pocket seven feet deep, filled with dead Apaches, and climbing down, fired his revolver into the breast of one still breathing. He then took us up a sloping bench 300 yards away, where another pit was filled with dead Indians."[27] Captain Tupper also reported, "I saw nine [dead] in one place, a small party the most if not all bucks, two dead Mexicans within ten yards of them."[28]

The Mexicans suffered their share of losses. Three officers and twenty men were killed, and two officers and fifteen men wounded. American doctors "said that several of their wounded would die." If Hatfield's and Erickson's stories are accurate, two Apaches had accounted for 56 percent of the Mexican dead. Hatfield wrote, "He [the Mexican lieutenant] showed us the body of an old grey head Apache, who, from behind a soap weed, had killed 8 Mexicans before losing his own life." Sergeant Erickson and the scout Slim Jim made their tour with an enlisted man as their guide and found "an Indian's body riddled by bullets. The guide explained that this Indian had been a sniper and that he had cost the Mexican force so many losses that the entire regiment had concentrated its fire to wipe him out. Pointing to the bodies of five dead Mexicans, our guide showed us what a sniper this Indian had been. Every Mexican in this group of five had been shot through the head." The two Apache dead-shots had killed thirteen of the twenty-three dead Mexicans.[29]

Captured Apache women and children were among the remnants the Americans found on the battlefield. Scout Sherman Curley noticed a cluster of women prisoners: "A little way apart on the ridge, the Mexicans were holding a bunch of women whom they had captured. There were guards around them. We went over to these women, and the Mexicans told us to get back, but we went and talked with them anyway." Among the prisoners was Chief Loco's fifteen-year-old daughter. Her Apache name is uncertain, but a list of many prisoners captured by the Mexicans shows a fifteen-year-old girl listed with a forty-five-year-old woman, Loco Viejo. Davis thought Loco Viejo was "probably Loco's wife," but she was likely his sister or a more distant relative. According to Davis, the girl listed with her was called 'It'eedee. The was a fairly common Apache name, meaning "young girl" or "young woman." 'It'eedee was the pride of the Loco family, purportedly gorgeous with a captivating personality. Virtually every American who wrote about the Alisos incident, from Colonel Forsyth to Sergeant Erickson, took note of her breathtaking beauty.[30]

'It'eedee believed that her family had been annihilated. Rafferty wrote, "Loco's daughter . . . said that she lost her father, mother, brother and uncle. . . . Whether she is to be believed or positively knew is a question." Erickson thought that "the Chief [Loco] and his family, except for this beautiful young woman, were all dead." 'It'eedee had seen her father fall when he went after the bag of bullets but was then swept away in the chaos and failed to see his return to safety. Separated from her family in the commotion, she thought her uncle and mother, Clee-hn, had also been killed. 'It'eedee's brother who had died the day before at Sierra Enmedio was apparently listed in her count. Curiously, one of the American packers claimed that he knew Loco and confidently reported that he had seen his body. Reports of Loco's death were subsequently carried in *The New Southwest and Grant County Herald,* the newspaper published in Silver City, New Mexico. Clee-hn, the youngest of Loco's wives, in fact survived and lived until 1909.[31]

When 'It'eedee saw the Americans, she hoped they would save the women. Sergeant Erickson was quite taken with the good-looking teenager and remembered her vividly: "One young girl, dressed in a Mother Hubbard said she was Chief Loco's daughter, and begged the Americans to take her back as their prisoner, but the Mexican officers wouldn't surrender her. The Americans tried to persuade the Mexicans to permit them to take the girl back. This could not be done." Apparently other women had the same idea. Curley recalled that "the women wanted us to give the Mexicans some money to ransom them, as they wanted to go back with us. They were afraid to be taken off by the Mexicans as captives. We did not have any money so could not do anything."[32] Erickson was convinced that the Mexicans killed all the prisoners, with the possible exception of Loco's daughter. He noted, "The whole band of fugitives, except for the young woman was lined up at sundown and shot by the Mexicans."[33]

Once the Americans left Alisos Canyon, García's men set about the morbid task of cleaning up the battlefield. They dug twenty-three graves and buried three officers and twenty soldiers. Afterward, they undoubtedly spent the rest of the morning in the grisly but profitable business of harvesting seventy-eight Apache scalps. If García was able to exchange his scalp collection for the same price that Colonel Joaquín Terrazas did after the Tres Castillos fight in 1880, $225 apiece, he would have collected about $17,550. The Mexicans left the Indians' bodies lying where they fell.[34]

Both Sergeant Erickson's assumption and subsequent newspaper accounts about the execution of the women were wrong. Most of the thirty-three prisoners turned up on lists prepared by Lieutenant Britton Davis, Third Cavalry, in 1884 and 1885, when the Americans sought a return of the captives. Davis reported that sixteen of the youngest prisoners were given to the mayor of Bavispe by the now-recovered General Reyes, to be doled out to Mexican families for adoption or as slaves.[35]

The remaining prisoners, all women, were taken to Guaymas, Mexico, for sale in the thriving slave market there. García's women captives represented another windfall for the colonel. In 1882 the cost of Indian slaves in Sonora hovered between $100 and $300, but especially good-looking women and comely teenagers such as 'It'eedee could bring in $500 or more. Two years earlier, Terrazas had sold sixty-eight Apache women and children captured during his fight with Victorio for $10,200—an average price of $150 each in Chihuahua. So it is little wonder that García had no interest in releasing his prisoners to the Americans. After donating the captured children to Bavispe's mayor, the colonel was left with approximately seventeen women prisoners to sell. At the going rate, he could expect to make about $2,550, and probably more because eight of the women were teenagers or preteens. All totaled, the sale of scalps and prisoners taken from the Alisos Creek ambush benefited García to the tune of about $20,000.[36]

As the sun rose on the morning of April 30, 'It'eedee and thirty-two of her friends and relatives faced the disheartening prospect of a lifetime as Mexican slaves. Indian women taken as captives by the Mexicans faced several possible fates. A few escaped, but escapes were notably rare and usually took years to pull off. Many women captives were consigned to the fields and spent the rest of their lives in stoop labor. Others worked in haciendas as housekeepers, au pairs for children, or kitchen help.[37] The most dreaded destiny for women prisoners was life as public prostitutes. Jacob Dunn, a lawyer and an Indian rights activist in the 1880s, wrote that "the Apache women were noted for their chastity. In this respect they were far superior to the Mexicans, and equal, if not superior, to any Indians on the continent. The fate to which their captive wives and daughters were doomed often caused poignant sorrow among them."[38] Those who were purchased by brothel owners or pimps had it the worst. They lived miserable lives and died early. The good-looking women may have done a little better as courtesans, servicing only men of rank and wealth. An especially beautiful captive was often reserved as the mistress of her captor or of a wealthy man. A mistress might acquire a higher status than that of slave and paramour. Such women were often given separate haciendas and were supported by the man in a kind of second family arrangement, including children—all the amenities of marriage except the paperwork.[39] Whatever their destinies, the bottom line was that none of the Alisos women and children captives were ever returned to their families.[40]

About seven months after the fight, on November 9, 1882, Colonel Lorenzo García was the guest of honor in a dazzling ceremony held on the central plaza of Hermosillo, Mexico. In commemoration of his victory at Alisos Creek, García was awarded an exquisite sword of Damascus steel, inlaid with silver and gold and encased in a gold-plated presentation box. García, the steely colonel who had blasted sixty-six women and children into early graves, taken sixteen young children from their parents and given them to strangers, and sold a throng of innocent women into lifelong bondage, was so "overcome with emotion" that he choked back tears as he in turn presented the sword to his battalion.[41]

All the American officers in the Sierra Enmedio fight except Timothy Touey, who died an early death in 1887, received promotions for "gallant service in action against Indians." George Forsyth was overlooked for any commendation or promotion and remained a lieutenant colonel until he retired in 1890. Scout Al Sieber left government work in 1891 and was killed in a road construction accident along Tonto Creek in 1907.[42]

For the Chiricahuas with Geronimo, the whole business had been little more than a good idea gone bad, a nothing-ventured, nothing-gained affair with no major losses for the Chiricahuas but plenty of good war stories. Geronimo got his revenge on Loco but admitted that he "had gained no recruits."[43] He was universally blamed for the Apaches' disasters of April 1882. The Warm Springs people had little use for him for the rest of his life. Years later at Fort Sill, Geronimo in his old age bemoaned, "I am without friends for my people have turned from me."[44]

Loco and his band of peaceful Warm Springs Indians were the clear losers in the ten-day debacle. Depending on whose count one uses, from one to nine persons were killed at Horseshoe Canyon, and seventeen dead seems to be the accepted figure for Sierra Enmedio. As many as one hundred may have died at Alisos Creek, although seventy-eight appears to be the most likely number. An uncounted number of the wounded died in the days that followed. John Bourke reckoned that "in all their [three] engagements with Mexican and American troops, they lost 109 men, women and children [killed]."[45]

As far as the Apaches were concerned, the thirty-three women and children who were taken prisoner by the Mexicans were as good as dead and lost forever. After the fight, of the 360 Indians forced from San Carlos eleven days earlier, more than one-third were dead or gone, and according to Loco's descendants, most of those left were nursing wounds. In a small band like Loco's, everyone outside the immediate family was an aunt, uncle, or cousin, by either blood or affinity. Two years later, John Bourke commented that "it was noticeable that nearly all of the Warm Springs had cut off their hair . . . as a result of the García fight." It was the Apaches' deepest expression of grief. Ordinarily an Apache mourner's hair was allowed to grow out again after the first cutting, but after Alisos Creek, Loco never again wore his hair long.[46]

What became of 'It'eedee? Loco's descendants do not know. No records have been found of her after April 30, 1882. She believed her entire family had been killed, and perhaps that made her new life in Mexico more acceptable. With any luck she might have been adopted or become a well-cared-for mistress. No one knows. The list of the captives being held in 1885 shows that one girl who was captured at Alisos Canyon was living in Hermosillo with the Lorenzo García family. Her Apache name was not given. The family called her Guadalupe, but her Apache name might well have been 'It'eedee.[47]

Six months later John Bourke noted that he had been told "that Loco has only fourteen [out of an original thirty-two] bucks left." Besides those killed at Sierra Enmedio and Alisos Creek, some of Loco's younger men may have drifted away from his leadership into the more warlike fraternity of Geronimo or one of the other Chiricahuas. Either way, with half his Chihennes dead or captured and most of the others wounded, there was little left of Loco's Warm Springs band. Ironically, although the Indian Office, the military, and the newspaper reporters knew that Loco had been forced from the reservation and wanted no part in what followed, the episode became known as the "Loco Outbreak."[48]

CHAPTER FIFTEEN

Chiz-odle-netln's Escape

When the surviving Apaches who evaded capture finally broke away from the Mexicans after dark on April 29, 1882, they made their way individually and in small groups to a low mountain less than five miles due south of the scene of the fight. It was probably their intended destination from the day before. There they regrouped, patched their wounds, and waited for stragglers.[1]

On the following morning the Indians watched from their mountain perch as the American and Mexican troops examined the battlefield together. Neither army seemed especially interested in continuing the chase. Forsyth claimed he wanted to press on, but García was more concerned about the Americans' unauthorized intrusion into Mexico than he was about another round with the Apaches. His men were badly shot up, but he had prevailed. The colonel told Forsyth, "If your sole object [of being in Mexico] is the punishment of this band of marauders, it is already accomplished. . . . My command fought, routed, and scattered them yesterday." Thus foiled, the Americans did an about face and moved north.[2]

The night of their escape was a bad one for the Indians. Jason Betzinez remembered, "All during the night in our camp on the cold mountainside we could hear people mourning and wailing for their relatives who had been killed or captured. There was no help for the wounded, no food, no chance of getting reinforcements." Adding to their misery, after the fight at Sierra Enmedio the Indians had discarded their few possessions, including blankets, in their rush to escape the Americans. Twenty-year-old Betzinez lamented, "When we were forced to leave the agency, we did have a few blankets and utensils. Now we had nothing except our bare hands and the clothes on our backs."[3]

Early the next morning the survivors with Loco moved eastward over the mountain. On the opposite side they unexpectedly stumbled into Geronimo, most of his warriors, and another batch of survivors. An excited exchange took place between the two groups, some people reuniting with relatives and others asking after the fate of missing family members. Geronimo boasted of the bold defense he and his men had raised and "the great fight they had put up to protect the families." The Chihennes, who had just been dragged into one of the deadliest defeats in Apache history, viewed Geronimo's bragging with contempt.[4]

It was about a fifty-mile trip from the ambush site at Alisos Creek to the Indians' destination, one of Juh's mountain hideaways. Ordinarily, if everyone had been healthy, the trip might have taken a day, perhaps two. Betzinez remembered that "on account of the many wounded who had to be helped or carried, we had to move slowly, painfully crossing successive ranges of hills." The short jaunt took about two weeks. Several of the wounded Warm Springs people died during the trip, further delaying the Indians' progress as they stopped to bury the dead.[5]

The refugees limped into Juh's Nednai hideaway about the middle of May 1882. Juh's people were waiting for them when they arrived. In an earlier era the Nednais had lived and operated mostly in Mexico. Lately the Mexican military had pushed them northward, toward the border, where they had more frequent contact with the Warm Springs Indians. Although a few Chihennes had relatives by marriage among the Nednais, for the most part Loco's band never had much to do with them. The Warm Springs people looked on the Nednais as uncivilized lowbrows, "true wild men . . . devoted entirely to warfare and raiding." Betzinez noted that "when they couldn't find anyone else to mistreat they fought among themselves. They were hard to deal with on friendly terms."[6]

Although Juh's camp was an unlikely sanctuary for Loco's people, who had been reservation bound for thirteen years, it was Geronimo's choice. Geronimo claimed that he was a Bedonkohe, but he was a close cohort of Juh's. With the addition of Loco's rank and file, several hundred people were assembled in one camp—possibly as many as six hundred. It was the largest assembly of Apaches in years. Except for Loco's bunch, they were armed to the teeth. Seventy-five of them were considered to be seasoned fighters.[7]

After a few days, Juh decided to move the camp southeast toward the San Miguel River, south of Casas Grandes. There things settled down for a while as the wounded recovered. "There was nothing to do all day long but play games and gamble," said Betzinez.[8] The lull weighed heavily on Geronimo. His love of alcohol was legendary, and it had been a month since his raiders had emptied Gilson's whiskey barrels at Dewey Flats. He and Juh, also a heavy drinker, decided to make the short trek to Casas Grandes for a drinking party. Juh's Nednai raiders had plenty of loot from a recent raid to trade for mescal. About a third of all the Indians in the camp, roughly two hundred people, traveled twenty-seven miles and set up camp about three miles outside the walled town.[9]

A Spanish-speaking woman was sent to make arrangements with the town officials. Accordingly, a committee led by the mayor traveled the three miles to meet with the Indians. "They assured the [Apache] leaders that it would be safe for all Indians to come into town to trade and to get acquainted. The town was wide open to them."[10]

Juh and Geronimo apparently accepted the mayor's hospitality at face value. Juh had often gone unhindered into Casas Grandes to drink and to sell stolen goods. Geronimo, after his recent military debacles, was eager to make peace in Mexico. With the deal struck, the Indians flooded into town, and the binge began.

The Apaches drank high-powered liquor nonstop for two days and two nights. Then, early in the predawn hours of the third day, Thursday, May 25, 1882, twenty-six days after the Alisos disaster, five hundred Chihuahuan troops pounced on them as they slept off the aftereffects and set about killing them. That any of the revelers survived the ambush can be attributed to premature shots fired by overeager troopers.[11] Nevertheless, the Mexicans killed about a dozen Apaches and captured between twenty-five and thirty-five. The losses were remarkably low only because most of the Apaches had made it back to the Indian camp before the attack. Those who had been unable to stagger the distance had stopped for the night just outside the city walls and became victims.[12]

It is unclear how many of Loco's Warm Springs people were at Casas Grandes on the day of the massacre, but some went. One might speculate that Loco, too, was in attendance, for he seldom missed an opportunity to moisten his day. On the other hand, his band had just been shattered by Mexicans. He was wounded and grieving the losses of a son, a daughter, and other relatives less than a month before. Further, he was, in theory at least, being restrained by his kidnappers. In the aftermath of Alisos Creek he had continually "blamed his troubles upon the others who had forced him to leave the reservation," specifically Geronimo and Naiche. It is unlikely that he wanted to drink with them, and he probably did not attend the party.[13] After the Casas Grandes attack, the survivors regrouped and slipped deeper into the Sierra Madre, toward the Yaqui River. The combined band, now reduced to fewer than six hundred, rested for some length in a stronghold selected by Juh. The leaders began to argue over what to do next. Juh, always jittery about remaining in one place too long, decided to move back to his main sanctuary, perhaps one hundred miles south of Casas Grandes.[14]

Although everyone apparently thought Juh's plan to retreat into the Sierra Madre was the "sensible" thing to do, Geronimo, Chihuahua, and Kaahteney were tired of sitting around and wanted to return to the raiding circuit. Consequently, taking about eighty companions with them, the three launched a devastating series of raids in Sonora. Juh, along with Naiche, Chatto, and Loco, headed for the mountains in the southeast. Before departing, Geronimo's men left their families with Juh's group, but by the spring of 1883 the raiders' dependents had moved in with Loco's Warm Springs people.[15]

Loco tarried briefly with Juh, but the two groups separated soon after Geronimo headed west in early January 1883, just before a series of misfortunes befell Juh. Several months later press reports noted that "Loco's band has split up and cut loose from Juh's and they want to come in, but Juh says he will never surrender." Loco settled in the mountains southeast of Casas Grandes.[16]

Without Juh's band for company, and with Geronimo's raiders rampaging through Sonora, Loco found his band alone about 170 miles south of the border. It appeared to be a good time for the Warm Springs people to make a run for the American line, but Loco stayed in place. Several accounts report that his band had only fourteen adult warriors remaining of the thirty-two who had left San Carlos the previous April. A census taken after Loco's band returned to San Carlos in 1884 showed thirty-one heads of household with the chief, but seventeen of those were in their twenties or younger, and seven were teenagers, all too young to be considered family heads in the traditional Apache sense. In the same 1884 census, the average age of heads of household in Nana's Warm Springs band, which missed the Alisos Creek calamity, was fifty-one. The young ages of family heads with Loco indicate that his band suffered the brunt of the losses in the García attack at Alisos Creek.[17] If Loco tried to escape back to San Carlos, he would have had only a few experienced warriors to defend against a certain pursuit by Geronimo.

Loco's chances to escape were further reduced when Victorio's people, the survivors of the Tres Castillos debacle in 1880, moved in with the

Warm Springs Indians and added to the dependents in his care. The women and children in Loco's camp numbered perhaps four hundred. One report summarized the situation: "Loco is in a stronghold four days march southeast of Casa Grande with fourteen men, remnants of Victorio's band, and all the women of the bands now out." Dodging the Mexican army and racing the war-ready Chiricahua warriors to the border with four hundred women and children was not the solution. Even if Loco and his group made it to the reservation, it would be only a matter of time before the April 19 abduction was replayed, probably with a fight this time. A prisoner told Lieutenant Bourke, "Loco's band dare not come now on account of the other Indians would kill them if they tried to return."[18] Other prisoners told Bourke that "some of the Chiricahua [Loco's people] would like to come in but they can't. The country down there is full of Mexican troops. When they reach the border, American troops are there and now they have Apache scouts with them."[19]

Beyond this, the chief's decision to wait for a better time to run was almost surely based on his obsession with keeping the band's children out of harm's way. At this point it made good sense to avoid another confrontation. He sat tight and waited for a better opportunity.[20]

Meanwhile, Juh was having a bad time. In late January 1883, a posse of citizens from Temosachic in western Chihuahua caught the chief drunk and surrounded his camp. They killed a dozen of his people, wounded many more, took thirty-three prisoners, including Chatto's family, and made away with more than eighty pack horses and mules. As a result, Juh's entire following abandoned him in the Batuco Mountains, leaving him with only "one middle-aged man, 2 great big boys and 5 women," probably all close relatives. After deserting their leader, most of the Nednais joined the other Chiricahuas, looking much the way the Warm Springs band had after the Alisos ambush nine months earlier. Betzinez reported, "One day Juh's band arrived at the canyon edge where we were camped. Our hearts filled with sorrow over their plight."[21]

About a month after the arrival of the Nednais in early March, Chatto, Bonito, Chihuahua, and Geronimo organized a raiding party of more than a hundred warriors. They quickly split into two groups. Geronimo and Chihuahua, with about eighty men, launched off across Sonora, where, according to Betzinez, they "attacked every village [they] came to." Chatto, with more modest ambitions, headed for the United States with Bonito and about twenty-five warriors to collect additional American-made weapons and ammunition to feed their sixteen-shooters. As it turned out, his journey would have unimaginably damaging repercussions for Loco and the Chihennes for the next thirty years.[22]

After crossing the border, Chatto's and Bonito's groups split once again into small parties and set off on a six-day rampage upon ranches, isolated mining camps, and travelers from Tombstone to Silver City. On March 28, 1883, south of Silver City on the Lordsburg Road, the raiders with Chatto and Bonito attacked former federal judge Hamilton C. McComas, his wife, Jennie, and their six-year-old son, Charley. On their way from Silver City to Lordsburg, the family had stopped for a leisurely picnic in Thompson Canyon. The judge was killed immediately, shot at least five times. Jennie was killed trying to protect Charley, her skull staved in by a powerful blow from a rifle butt above the right ear. Little Charley, terrified but unharmed, was purportedly tied to Bonito's saddle and carried away by the Indians. The raiders made off with $125 and the judge's ammunition belt, Winchester rifle, Colt revolver, and engraved gold pocket watch. They also took Mrs. McComas's undamaged dress, two gold bracelets, and a diamond ring.[23]

From Chatto's perspective, it had been a successful six days. His raiders had amassed almost one hundred rifles and pistols, a supply of ammunition, a sizable herd of cattle, and some jewelry. They had lost only one warrior killed and had one desertion—Peaches, a White Mountain man who lost two Chihenne wives and a child at Alisos Creek. In the process they had killed twenty-five white men and one woman, Mrs. McComas. Significantly, they also kidnapped the most politically connected six-year-old in New Mexico.[24]

Charley McComas's uncle was Judge Charles C. McComas, Judge H. C.'s brother. He was a prominent Albuquerque attorney and a member of the New Mexico territorial legislature. A man of appreciable clout, he made it clear that something would be done about the loss of his brother and the abduction of his nephew.[25]

Jennie McComas had been well connected in her own right. Little Charley was named after her youngest brother, Charles Ware, a prominent Kansas attorney and successful businessman. Her older brother, Eugene Fisk Ware, was also an attorney and sometime newspaper editor. He was in his second term as a Kansas state senator. As a sideline, Eugene wrote and published poetry under the pen name "Ironquill." He became the poet laureate of Kansas, and his book of poems, *The Rhymes of Ironquill,* was a best-seller, endearing him to Americans nationwide. The Ware family of Kansas was popular and had powerful national connections. Eugene Ware also declared that something would be done to avenge his sister's death and recover Charley.[26]

The H. C. McComas family, then, was no ordinary household whose deaths on a dusty New Mexico road might have gone unnoticed. Chatto's raiders had assassinated American gentry and nabbed a scion from America's upper crust. The country was outraged. The Chiricahuas were catapulted to the top of the country's most-despised-Indians list. Stories of the family's gruesome deaths ran in newspapers nationwide and blasted liberal sentiment for the fair treatment of the Apaches into backpedaling silence. Eugene Ware, who went to New Mexico to recover the bodies and to push the search for Charley, observed, "A feeling that seems to be universal is that the entire Apache tribe, [both] quiet and hostile, should be exterminated."[27]

Charley McComas was never found, but the public's obsession with the incident and his destiny lasted for years. Seventy-six years after the event, Jason Betzinez published an account of the boy's fate. Charley was in Bonito's camp when it was attacked by General George Crook's scouts in 1883. Nine Apaches in the ranchería were killed, including one old woman who was attempting to surrender, the mother of a warrior called Speedy. When Speedy saw his mother gunned down, he sought revenge in the old Chiricahua way, by killing someone else. In this case, the nearest easy target was Charley. Speedy beat him about the head with a large stone, threw him into the bushes, and fled. Women from the camp found Charley the next day, unconscious but still alive. There was a brief discussion about trying to save him, but the women feared they would be blamed, so they left him where they found him. He undoubtedly died soon thereafter. For years, other Apaches covered for Speedy and claimed that Charley must have run off during the fight. While they were classmates at the Carlisle Indian Industrial School in Pennsylvania, Ramona, Chief Chihuahua's daughter, who saw the incident, told Betzinez about it. Almost eight decades later, Betzinez told the story in his 1959 book.[28]

Chatto's raiders regarded the McComas incident as no more than a few minutes of easy pickings—a bit of serendipity in a successful but not unusual six-day raid. The consequences for the Chiricahua and Warm Springs Indians, however, would be enormous. The McComas and Ware families continued to press for punishment of the perpetrators for years. Ultimately, their efforts contributed to the removal of the Chiricahuas to the East Coast. From Loco's standpoint, in the short run the results were beneficial. The attack brought the American cavalry to the rescue, freed his Warm Springs people from the Chiricahua stranglehold, and returned them to the reservation.

George Crook, who had returned to Arizona six months previously, had plans well under way for an offensive into the Mexican Sierra Madre when the McComas family was killed. The McComas incident gave Crook the excuse he needed to capitalize on the "hot pursuit" policy stipulated in a recent treaty with Mexico. The policy allowed American troops to cross the border if they were in hot pursuit of an Apache raiding party. At the same time, Peaches's escape from Chatto provided Crook with a guide who knew exactly where the Apaches were. Peaches was looking for payback for the Chiri cahuas' kidnapping of Loco's people and the deaths of his family at Alisos Creek.[29]

By the time the McComas and Ware families put pressure on the army to find little Charley, Crook was already on the move. From his headquarters in Whipple Barracks, near Prescott, Arizona, he dispatched hundreds of troops to take up key locations and scout along the Mexican border. Unrelenting news accounts riveted the public with details of the efforts to find the boy. The front-page newspaper coverage led the public to believe that the primary purpose of Crook's expedition was to rescue Charley. Crook's pack master, Henry W. Daly, wrote that the campaign was launched "with the expectation of rescuing Charley McComas." Although Crook encouraged the public impression that he was out to save the child, he had a bigger agenda. It would be a pleasant bonus to find Charley alive, but he wanted all the Apaches.[30]

Less than a month after Chatto and his men attacked the McComas family, most of the Apaches in Mexico assembled at a remote point "whose name is unknown" in Moctezuma district in central Sonora, Mexico. It was a varied bunch—Chiricahuas, the Nednai ex-followers of Juh, Loco's Warm Springs people, and Geronimo's mixed bag of raiders. Betzinez suggests that even Juh and his family showed up. The assembly might have taken place for a victory dance to celebrate Geronimo's return from his successful sweep through Sonora with a herd of one hundred stolen cattle. An opportunity to socialize and a generous serving of beef invariably attracted a good crowd.[31]

Initially, the Apaches gathered at a popular sanctuary on the edge of the Huachinera Mountains. It was described as a placid place with "a fine pine forest on the eastern edge of a high and steep mountain in a thick grove of young oaks and tall grass, now dry and brown." The *Arizona Star* reported that it apparently had been an Apache safe haven for years, "judging from the number of animal skeletons scattered about the generations of brush huts."[32]

The tranquil scene was disrupted when a roaring fire with flames "thirty or forty feet high" broke out in the high dry grass near the camp. Driven by high winds, the blaze raced through the bivouac, killed several tethered horses, and sent up an enormous plume of smoke, visible for "a hundred miles in all directions." Always concerned about attracting notice, the Apaches moved their celebration to an area southwest of a Mexican village called Huachinera.[33]

A few men backtracked to see whether the smoke had attracted any attention. When the scouts returned, they reported seeing a large body of Mexican soldiers pressing hard and headed their way, following the tracks left by Geronimo's herd of cattle. The Indians quickly pulled up stakes and moved about twenty miles farther south into the Madeira Mountains.

Unknown to the Apaches, Colonel Lorenzo García, the commanding officer at Alisos Creek, and Colonel Lorenzo Torres were leading the chase. Torres had apparently been searching for Indians for twenty days when he ran across García with eighty-six soldiers and a handful of scouts. The two officers joined forces and quickly struck a fresh trail—Geronimo's group with its stolen cattle, headed for home. García and Torres doggedly tracked the Indians with forced marches for five days and five nights.[34]

Keeping a close eye on their pursuers, the Apache men set up for business on the rim of an immense gorge described as "a dangerous, rocky, almost unaccessible place, having plenty of wood, water and grass, but no food except what was stolen from the Mexicans."[35] The Mexican minister of war and marine, Bonifacio Topete, called the Apaches' "long unknown stronghold . . . impregnable." When the Indians arrived at the site, a place they called Pah-gotzin-kay, most of them set up a temporary camp approximately two miles beyond the rim of the gorge. Some of the warriors remained at the gorge to watch for the arrival of the army and arrange an ambush. When the Mexicans were seen descending the opposite side of the canyon, the sentinels raced back to warn the camp, and the main body of warriors rushed forward to meet the threat. Over the years, the Apaches had established a justifiable reputation as masters in the art of ambush. The bushwhacking at Pah-gotzin-kay was one of their best. The site picked for the ambuscade was "the worst mountain in the whole country."[36]

The Indian defenders arranged themselves in positions along the ridge and on two outcrops at the top of the gorge, putting most of the trail up the canyon wall in a crossfire. Some of the more experienced warriors were concealed in the rocks along the trail. The pièce de résistance came when a few men moved large boulders in place to roll down on the retreating Mexicans and create landslides to bury them.[37]

The Mexican pursuers were tired and hot when they arrived. They had endured forced marches with little rest for the last five days and nights. Climbing down and then up the steep canyon walls was exhausting. Climbers on the narrow path to the top were easy targets for the waiting Apaches. By the time they reached the crest, the Apaches were ready and waiting. The first shots of the battle were fired when the heads of two sweaty troopers popped over the edge of the canyon. Both men died immediately. It was two o'clock in the afternoon of April 24, 1883, exactly five days short of a year after Colonel García sprang his ambush at Alisos Creek. On this occasion at Pah-gotzin-kay mountain, the tables were turned.[38]

Once the Indians "were located," as Colonel García phrased it, "the most savage fight ever made with the Apaches" began in earnest. The Apaches were "well armed with plenty of ammunition." The Mexicans reported that they fired 2,876 rounds of .50 caliber Remington cartridges. The din lasted from three to four hours. Afterward, both sides claimed victory.[39]

While the fighting raged on the edge of the gorge, two miles back in the Indians' camp Chiz-odle-netln, Loco's second oldest wife, found herself and twenty relatives isolated from the others. The group included four men in their twenties and thirties, two teenage boys, eight women, and five girls and one boy under fourteen. Those in Loco's immediate family were Chiz-odle-netln, another daughter of Loco's, a son, a son-in-law, and four or five grandchildren.[40]

Seizing the opportunity, with Chiz-odle-netln in charge, the group slipped off and went into hiding, away from the immediate vicinity of the battle. While waiting for things to cool, one of the men slipped back into the main Apache camp and tried to convince Loco to come along. He declined, claiming he was too old for that kind of travel, but he gave his blessing to the enterprise and told the group to leave without him. He sent his would-be rescuer back with his youngest son (probably John) and the few weapons he could collect, "3 worthless guns and a revolver and a few rounds of ammunition." Loco no doubt realized that if he went missing, the Chiricahua kidnappers would go after the group, but a few absent Warm Springs folk would hardly be worth the trouble.[41]

Chiz-odle-netln's group lay low for three days to be certain that both the Apaches and the Mexicans had left the area. The escapees then headed north on April 27, with four horses and two mules, enough transportation to carry half the group at a time if they rode double. They reached the San Carlos area on May 28, in bad shape. Fifty-four-year-old Chiz-odle-netln may have been trying to reach her older sister, Chiz-pah-odlee, whom she believed to be in Mariana's camp near Fort Wingate, but she diverted to San Carlos because the group was in desperate straights by the time it reached the border. The San Carlos reservation was a hundred miles closer.

When Second Lieutenant Parker West received word that "two Chiricahua squaws had come into one of the camps up the river" and that others were hanging back in the nearby mountains, he immediately requested that the commander at Fort Thomas send a detachment behind the group to block a retreat. He then set out to find the women. He met the two about seven miles from the agency and was pleased to discover that one of them was Loco's wife and "in charge of a party of Indians."

Chiz-odle-netln told West that she and her companion had come in "to try and make peace" and that her group was in the mountains opposite a place called Paymaster's Tanks. "Finding that most of the party was squaws and children, I sent Loco's wife and some Indian scouts in charge of the Interpreter Antonia to communicate with them with instructions to inform them that if they gave themselves up to me, I would hold them as prisoners until I could hear from General Crook; and that I did not know what he would do with them. They gave themselves up under these conditions this morning near Green's Hill on the Apache road. The party consisted of six bucks and 15 women and children."

When Chiz-odle-netln's group arrived, West noted, "They have little or no clothes and claim to be almost starved having had very little to eat for months." The "months" part may have been a bad translation. Chiz-odle-netln probably intended to say they had eaten little since escaping the fight at Mount Pah-gotzin-kay about a month before.[42]

Lieutenant West reported that he had "informed Agent [P. P.] Wilcox that I had them at my camp and he declined to either receive or ration them and requested me to hold them as prisoners which I have done. . . . If to hold them as such, I would ask for permission to ration them as they are in a destitute condition." West received orders to "hold the Indians as prisoners and issue them rations." It was a strange turn of events and foretold of problems for Loco.[43]

CHAPTER SIXTEEN

Returned to San Carlos

On April 30, 1883, General George Crook suggested that his scouts might want to organize a good war dance after sundown. They danced all evening, and on the morning of May 1, in a howling sandstorm, 193 scouts, 51 officers and troopers, and 76 mule drivers crossed the international boundary into Mexico. So began Crook's much vaunted Sierra Madre campaign to end the "Chiricahua troubles" forever. He left four companies of cavalry scattered along Arizona's and New Mexico's southern borders to intercept any Chiricahua raiding parties heading north.[1]

Fifteen days into what proved to be a forty-one-day trek, a single skirmish took place when Crook's scouts found and attacked Bonito and Chatto's crew, just returned from their rampage through the American territories. In the ensuing clash, the scouts killed nine and captured four children, including Bonito's teenage daughter. This was the fight in which Charley McComas became a collateral casualty.[2]

Bonito's daughter told John Bourke "that her people had been astounded and dismayed when they saw the long line of Apache scouts rushing in upon them; they would be still more disconcerted when they learned that our guide was Peaches, as familiar as themselves with every nook in strongholds so long regarded as inaccessible." The girl was "positive that the Chiricahuas would give up without further fighting since the Americans had secured all the advantages of position." She knew that "Loco and Chihuahua would be glad to live peaceably upon the reservation, if justly treated." She was less sure about Geronimo and Chatto.

She was certain that Juh would never surrender, but by this time he had only a few followers left.[3]

Most of the Chiricahuas had already decided that the hardscrabble life in the wild was not all it once had been. Perhaps old Loco was on the right track after all. While on his recent raids in Arizona and New Mexico, Chatto had sent two men, Dutchy and Goody, to San Carlos to consult with Merejildo Grijalva, a former Apache captive turned scout and interpreter, to determine what terms they might expect if they surrendered. Their directions had been to "find out all you can about the agency and how the Indians there feel. . . . Perhaps it may be difficult for us to surrender, but go to Merejildo and learn all from him." Grijalva advised the two envoys that a surrender was in their best interests.[4]

With the girl's information, Crook set loose Bonito's young daughter on May 16 with food enough for two days and told her to spread the word that he was accepting no-fault surrenders. The results were immediate. The day after she left, Rogers Toclanny's two sisters came in shouting "with full voice" and wanting to talk terms. On the second day, six more women, including Chihuahua's sister, came in furiously waving large white rags. After that, Nana observed that "Chiricahuas were coming in by every trail." Within twelve days, 384 Indians were under Crook's protection. A few others later joined the column as it proceeded northward.[5]

There is confusion about when Loco came into Crook's camp. Apparently, "an old woman who was sent after Loco returned with him" on May 23 or 24. Other reports have him coming in on May 25 and 26. On May 30, Bourke noted in his diary that "Loco returned early in the night [May 29] with another small detachment of his people and had supper." Loco apparently went out several times and brought in more people each time.[6]

On one such return, Loco and Chatto came in together. Loco's first order of business with Crook was to report that "Geronimo had sent them back to say that the Chiricahuas were very much scattered since the fight [with the scouts], and that he had not been as successful as he anticipated in getting them united and in corralling their herds of ponies. . . . He could not get them to answer his signals, as they imagined them to be made by Apache scouts trying to ensnare them." Loco was a curious choice to bear the message, but one might suspect that the chief was happy to report that Geronimo had deceived General Crook just as he had John Clum in 1876 and had vanished into the mountains. Britton Davis knew that Geronimo had played this gambit before and was not fooled. "About two-hundred, including most of the fighting men, had remained in Mexico, ostensibly to gather up the remnants of their people, but in reality to raid Mexican ranches for horses to trade to the Indians of the reservation."[7]

In his meeting with General Crook, Loco also went to great lengths to detail his band's kidnapping from San Carlos. He explained their innocence and expounded in detail about his long-standing desire for peace. Loco had a tendency to ramble in such conversations, but Bourke summarized his statement: "Loco for his part, expressed himself as anxious for peace. He had never wished to leave San Carlos. He wanted to go back there and obtain a little farm, and own cattle and horses, as he once did." Both General Crook and Captain Bourke were impressed with Loco's sincerity. Bourke noted that "Loco has by all odds the best face of all the Chiricahuas." Crook wrote to the assistant adjutant general of the Pacific Division that Loco "was not at heart hostile to us, but was induced by Juh and Geronimo to leave the reservation. . . . I am satisfied that if allowed to come back he will never return to the war path."[8]

It was a difficult, 350-mile trek back to San Carlos. Crook strived to avoid meeting any Mexican troops, for fear a sighting would scatter the Indians. Instead of taking the direct route back to San Carlos through Sonora, he circled east through Chihuahua, staying in the high mountains for most of the trip. The caravan traveled in the Sierra Hauchinera until it bypassed Casas Grandes, then turned to the northwest and dropped down into the Janos River valley. Temperatures dropped below freezing as the column reached the eight-thousand-foot main divide of the Sierra Madre—"the nights bitter cold, with ice forming in pails and kettles on the 2d and 3d of June." In the lower, warmer regions, rattlesnakes plagued the travelers, both on the trail and in their camps. Occasional rain showers drenched the caravan, but they were welcomed because they kept down the dust. Bourke noted that the travelers were "nearly all wearing garlands of cottonwood foliage to screen them from the sun. . . . All the old Chiricahuas were piled on mules, donkeys, and ponies; so were the weak little children and feeble women. . . . Old women and feeble men got along as best they could, now riding, now walking."[9] Crook brought the column to a halt at the edge of the Alisos Creek battleground on June 4. It was a scheduled stop to replenish the travelers' water supply. A year earlier, George Forsyth had reported pools of water standing in the creek bed. This time Alisos Creek was dry as a bucket of dust.

Much to the alarm of the Indians, the camp was only a half mile from where the first shots of the Mexican ambush had been fired. In addition to the twenty-three crude wooden crosses over the graves of the Mexican soldiers, the remains of seventy-eight Apaches lay where they had died—now only bleached bones picked clean by vultures and scattered by coyotes. Bloodstained pieces of dresses, bracelets, baskets, "and lots of beads [were] scattered on the ground."[10]

The old ambush site was now considered to be haunted by the ghosts of those killed in the battle, and every one of the Apaches with Crook, both prisoners and scouts, was vulnerable. Worse yet, the ghosts of the Mexican soldiers killed at the creek were more dangerous—they had hated the Apaches even before they joined the world of specters. Nevertheless, curiosity was too much for some. Betzinez viewed the scene: "Their skeletons were still visible, the bodies having been eaten by buzzards." John Rope, who was scouting for the expedition, later reported, "We shouldn't have gone to look at this place, but we did anyway." There is no indication that any of the Apaches were tainted with "ghost sickness" in the immediate aftermath, but the tribe did have more than its share of bad luck later.[11]

The expedition crossed onto American soil on the morning of June 10, 1883, and linked up with Major James Biddle's Sixth Cavalry at Silver Springs, near present-day Douglas, Arizona. After resting for a few days they moved northward toward San Carlos. The travelers stopped again and camped for a day near Crook's temporary headquarters at Willcox while the general arranged for military wagons to haul the "women and children and our camp gear."[12] As the party halted on the outskirts of town, an enterprising peddler drove out to the Indians' camp with a wagon piled high with used clothing for sale. The trader did a booming business as the Apaches refitted for a spectacular return to the reservation.[13]

On June 23, 1883, the people of San Carlos were treated to an immense parade, the likes of which had never been seen before nor since. Hundreds of excited residents turned out to watch the grand entrance. John Rope remembered, "All the people at San Carlos knew we were coming that day and waited for us." Lieutenant Britton Davis rode out two miles from the agency to welcome the arrivals. Leading the procession, the scouts came to a halt atop a low hill named Copper Reef to regroup for an impressive close-order march into the reservation. John Rope recalled, "From here [Copper Reef] we could see lots of looking glasses flashing signals to us from San Carlos." As the spectacle entered the reservation, "there was a crowd of Indians on both sides, watching us."[14]

A procession of about seven hundred souls stretched out for a mile or more as it moved toward the reservation. Al Sieber rode at the head of the column, followed by about one hundred scouts in full face paint. They were trailed, in turn, by Chief Loco and Mangas leading the Warm Springs and Chiricahua contingents of 324 prisoners, their faces also painted, men with red stripes across their faces and women with red circles on their cheeks and foreheads. A few days earlier, Bourke had described the column as "a confused assemblage of ponies, horses, and mules, with bundles or without, but in every case freighted with humanity." By the time the caravan reached San Carlos, the mix included a dozen or so army wagons filled with women, children, and the elderly. The second platoon of scouts, about ninety strong, fell in behind the returnees. They were followed by four troops of cavalry, perhaps about two hundred troopers, headed by Captain Emmet Crawford, which had been drawn from Crook's reserve at the border. Seventy-six mule skinners and about 260 mules brought up the rear.[15] The grand arrival had a sense of carnival. Both men and women sported new clothes. The women wore sand-cast silver bracelets and turquoise rings and were festooned with mounds of beads in which lay nestled wooden crosses and small pictures of Catholic saints, apparently acquired from dead Mexicans.[16]

The column made its way to the San Carlos agency schoolhouse, where the scouts set up camp on one side of the old school. The Indian prisoners settled down across the schoolyard. Their pack train and the wagons were brought to rest on the playground between the two camps. Scout John Rope remembered that "all our relations came to see us." No historical records indicate that the Warm Springs people celebrated their return or were welcomed by anyone.[17]

The agency soon relocated Loco's band and Mangas, with the Chiricahua women and children, in camps along the bottomland of the San Carlos River, under the close watch of Davis, Crawford, Sieber, and a contingent of scouts. Until this time the returnees had been cooperative, amiable, even docile, but no one wanted to take chances.[18]

Unfortunately, the distinction between the peaceful Warm Springs Indians and the trouble-making Chiricahuas became blurred, even among the Western Apaches on the reservation. Despite their non-violent lifestyle, Loco's Warm Springs people could not overcome the Chiricahuas' reputation as troublemakers. The confusion had intensified when Geronimo forced the Warm Springs band from San Carlos in 1882. The collective runaways all became known as "Chiricahuas" in the minds of the American public. Reports emanating from Crook's Sierra Madre campaign referred to both groups, kidnappers and victims alike, as "Chiricahuas." Agent Wilcox did not distinguish between the two bands. He considered all those returning from Mexico a single bad lot, Chiricahua "criminals." By June 1883, the Chiricahuas—or any group labeled Chiricahuas, peaceful or otherwise—were personas non grata on the San Carlos reservation.[19]

Even before Loco and his band arrived there, a controversy arose between the Indian Office and the army over where to put the Indians and under whose charge. When Crook telegraphed the San Carlos agent from Willcox in May 1883 that he would arrive in a few days with about four hundred prisoners, he was dismayed at the response. Agent Wilcox immediately telegraphed the secretary of the interior, "I cannot consent to receive these prisoners at San Carlos."[20]

San Carlos tribal leaders also protested any return of the Chiricahuas (and Warm Springs Apaches), probably at the instigation of Wilcox. They complained, legitimately, that if "Crook's Chiricahuas" made another outbreak, white citizens would blame them. The Western Apaches agreed to allow the "Chiricahua" women and children to move in, but they wanted the leaders hung and their men sent some faraway place. As General Crook noted, that simply was not going to happen without a "war to the death."[21]

Wilcox's friend Henry Teller, secretary of the interior, however, concurred with the agent's proposal to arrest and remove the Chiricahuas and offered to open the Department of the Interior's Indian schools to the Chiricahua children. He forwarded the agent's message to Secretary of War Robert Lincoln with his personal assessment: "I trust that you will give General Crook orders not to take them to San Carlos. I have instructed the agent not to receive them."[22]

Ironically, for the most part the Chiricahuas and Warm Springs people were the same Indians whom the Indian Office had twice gone to great effort and expense to move forcibly to San Carlos. Crook fired off a series of telegrams protesting the Interior Department's contradictory positions and attempted to discern exactly where the Indian Office would like to have these Indians live.[23]

Crook went to Washington to present the army's arguments in midsummer. By July 7, 1883, a compromise had been reached allowing the Chiricahuas to remain under the army's control on the Fort Apache portion of the reservation, away from but sandwiched between the San Carlos Indians and the Coyoteros. It would be almost a year before the accord was implemented, but Loco's group was cautiously satisfied. Betzinez noted that "from then on we had no further dealings with Indian agents from the Department of the Interior. This pleased us, because it was one of the latter [John Clum] who had been responsible for moving us from our old Warm Springs reservation in the first place."[24] Despite the Indian Office's complaints and Wilcox's irritation, the prisoners were ensconced near the agency, where they would remain for almost nine months while everyone waited for Geronimo to arrive from Mexico.[25]

In the meantime Crook, his reputation on the line, waited anxiously for the Chiricahuas in Mexico to turn themselves in. The Americans' delight with Crook's success waned when they learned that he had returned from his highly touted campaign with only Loco's pacifists and the hostiles' dependents. He had left the bulk of the raiders footloose in Mexico to continue their business as usual. Stories began to circulate that Geronimo had effectively fast-talked Crook into caring for his dependents and the cumbersome Loco band while he and his allies set off on an unimpeded raiding spree. Citizens' attitudes shifted from relief to anger.[26]

Tensions grew as journalists nipped at Crook. Weeks turned into months, and in early October 1883, Crook sent Britton Davis down to the Mexican line with a company of scouts, hoping to encourage the fugitives to return. Davis noted that his "scouts [were] now almost all Chiricahua and Warm Springs." These were Chiricahuas who did not much care for Geronimo and Warm Springs men who were looking for payback for the 1882 debacle. As the pressure mounted, Davis sent scouts into Mexico to see if they could hurry the truant Indians along. They could not find them.

Finally the hostiles began to trickle in. By mid-November 1883, Naiche, Chihuahua, and Kaahteney had come in with about twenty-five followers, including nine warriors. Zele reported in a few days before Christmas. Chatto brought his group in on February 7, 1884. Geronimo finally rode in toward the end of February with about ninety people and 350 recently acquired cattle, which confirmed the suspicion that he had spent more of his ten-month hiatus raiding than searching for relatives. The last of the missing Chiricahuas showed up on the reservation in mid-May 1884, a year after they agreed to surrender.[27]

Two days after the last arrivals appeared, on May 17, General Crook wrote, "The Indians all agree that there are now [no] Indians of either of these bands [the Chiricahuas and the Warm Springs] or from the White Mountain reservation in Mexico, and I believe their statements are true." Juh, however, never came in. He died while drunk in September 1883 when he jumped his horse over a cliff on the Casas Grandes River. By the middle of May 1884, 512 Chiricahua and Warm Springs Apaches were peacefully situated on the reservation. Crook noted, "I am convinced that they are all satisfied and perfectly contented and will give no further trouble if treated with common fairness."[28]

As soon as the late-arriving outcasts reached the reservation, the army began searching for a place to settle them. Crook allowed the Indians to select their own village sites. On March 23, 1884, Loco and Mangas left "with Archie Sunday [McIntosh] to look over country in the vicinity of Ash Creek and Natans mountains." Ultimately Loco selected his band's campsite on Turkey Creek, a few thousand feet higher and seventeen miles southwest of Fort Apache, not far from John Daisy Peak. Once again things were looking up for the chief. On June 30, 1883, the *Army and Navy Journal* reported that "Loco said he was anxious to get settled once more."

Davis, who was assigned to look after the Chiricahuas in the new location, was delighted with Loco's choice: "Turkey Creek was a beauty spot and a game paradise. On the crest of a spur of the White Mountains, the climate in summer was ideal. My camp was pitched in a little glade on the stream of crystal-clear water. Surrounding the camp were giant pines, with low hills rising to the south and north. As we entered their domain, wild turkeys fled before us. The Indians reported deer and bears within an hour's ride. In shallow pools giant frogs croaked a welcome, oblivious of the doom I mentally promised them, a promise soon made good. The Indians scattered among the trees and began erecting their simple homes of brush covered with cotton cloth, old shirts, pieces of blankets, or any other available material."[29]

Jason Betzinez also reported that the Apaches liked the location: "In the spring of 1884, we heard that we were to be moved north to the Fort Apache reservation. That area, having a higher elevation than San Carlos, and consisting of pine-covered mountains and upland meadows traversed by clear, cold streams was much more healthful and pleasant than the hot, desert wastes of San Carlos." Besides that, "we were thankful too at the opportunity to get away from the unfriendly San Carlos Indians who had never invited us to share in their privileges or take part in tribal councils and business affairs. At the new reservation [Turkey Creek] we would be with the somewhat friendlier White Mountain Apaches."[30]

Geronimo, however, was not especially happy with Loco's selection. He preferred a site on Eagle Creek, about fifty miles east of Turkey Creek. Geronimo argued that the Turkey Creek area was overcrowded with White Mountain Indians. Besides, there was no mescal to bake, and the place was not as healthy as Eagle Creek. Unfortunately for Geronimo, his selection on Eagle Creek was not on reservation land. When informed of the problem, he argued that it should be purchased for his Apaches. His request was denied. In the end, the Chiricahuas settled along Turkey Creek and on the White River, but still some distance from Loco.[31]

The Chiricahuas' new proximity to the White Mountain Apaches inadvertently brought "individuals and families face to face with the progress made by more peaceable Apaches, and at the same time to enable trusted members of the latter bands to maintain a more perfect surveillance over every action of the Chiricahuas." Despite everything, the Americans still had no confidence in Loco's peaceful intentions.[32]

Coyoteros and other White Mountain Indians began to join the Chiricahuas along Turkey Creek. The new additions soon brought the number of Indians under Davis's watch to more than 550. By 1885, Robert Frazer, from the Indian Rights Association, reported that about 135 White Mountain Indians had moved in with Loco's band.[33]

Lieutenant Davis was assigned to manage the affairs of the Indians accumulated along the stream. He set up for business about fourteen miles east of Loco's camp and seventeen miles from Fort Apache in a small army "A" tent with a dirt floor. Mickey Free and Ramón Montoya served as interpreters, and Sam Bowman did the cooking. Davis reported that "Company B [scouts] was still with me"—twenty-two Chiricahua scouts. After July 1, 1884, Company B was "again reorganized and now consisted entirely of [50] Chiricahua and Warm Springs selected from the recently hostile bands."[34]

At this point, about four months after Loco's return to the reservation, it appeared that his "good peace" was taking hold. A huge dance was scheduled for "the first snappy day of fall." The traditional fete was to properly launch the Indians' annual move to a warmer climate as winter approached. Word was spread for miles around, and some news articles claimed that a thousand Apaches attended.[35]

Not long after the celebration, the first snow of winter fell. It was the cue to begin the move. Under the circumstances, the warmest spot the Apaches could manage was in the lower elevations near Fort Apache, just above Davis's camp, about three miles from the post. Although it was somewhat milder than their Turkey Creek location, the Fort Apache area was still bitter cold in the winter. Snow around Fort Apache is inevitable. In a bad winter, accumulations can reach waist high or more, and the winter of 1884 looked to be a bad one. The Indians were first to recognize the signs and began requesting additional blankets and clothing by the middle of September.[36] They had acquired no additional clothing or blankets since they bought clothes at Willcox five months earlier. In late October, Agent Wilcox reluctantly doled out one blanket for each family. He delayed any further issues of clothes or blankets until his replacement, Charles Ford, arrived on the reservation in November 1884. Unfortunately, the feud with the army continued after Ford's arrival, and the supplies remained in the San Carlos warehouse while the Chiricahua and Warm Springs internees at Fort Apache shivered.[37]

When it became obvious that his officers were getting nowhere with agency officials, General Crook wrote to the adjutant general in November: "These Indians are absolutely destitute and it is not probable that they will be able to get anything from the Indian Department." He also asked General Pope to request permission to issue surplus uniforms to the Indians. Pope wrote that "the need of clothing for . . . the Chiricahuas is very urgent they get nothing from the Interior Department and there is absolutely no way in their power to obtain anything to cover their nakedness. They have no money and it is now impossible to get skins." Nevertheless, it was not until January 11, 1884, that the War Department finally authorized the Division of the Pacific to issue "such limited amounts of clothing of obsolete pattern as will afford one garment to each of the destitute Chiricahuas."[38]

Vintage Civil War uniforms, manufactured by the lowest bidder in hard times, arrived on the reservation from the military depot in San Francisco in late January. Davis noted that they were barely adequate for a Fort Apache winter: "If you have ever tackled a blizzard in the mountains with four feet of snow under foot, and no protection other than ordinary army clothing worn in Arizona, you have a thrill ahead of you—that is providing you like those thrills that make you guess whether or not your obituary will appear in the home papers next spring." Once the clothes arrived from San Francisco, Davis reported that "no incidence of importance" occurred for the rest of the winter.[39]

In spite of the usual problems of reservation life, the Warm Springs people on Turkey Creek enjoyed an overabundance of food for the first time since they began relying on government issues. Not only were they regularly receiving full beef-based rations, but game in the area was also plentiful. In August 1884 Davis allowed his wards to travel off the reservation to the Eagle Creek area to hunt and collect nuts and other edibles. With the arrival of spring, the Apaches started farming. Bourke noted that all the Apaches "cultivated little open glades and planted corn and vegetables. . . . Cantaloupes, watermelons, muskmelons, beans, and pumpkins are raised by them to a considerable extent." Jason Betzinez opined that "those of us who settled along the head of Turkey

Creek did real well with our crops. The first year, 1884, we raised corn and potatoes." In addition to their small-plot farming, by the end of May 1884 the Indians had cleared and planted between sixty and seventy-five acres on the east fork of the White River. Crawford reported that year that the Apache farmers raised 45,000 pounds of corn, 3,000 pounds of potatoes, and other vegetables, along with respectable quantities of hay, oats, and barley. They sold much of their crop to the army or in Globe. Crook's "prospects for remunerative results" were becoming a reality.[40]

Kaitah, a peaceful Chiricahua scout living at Turkey Creek, described this period: "I live peaceably. Nobody bothers me. I sleep well; I get plenty to eat. I go wherever I want, talk to good people. I go to bed whenever I want and get all my sleep. I have nobody to fear. I have my little patch of corn. I'm trying to do what the white people want me to do." All things considered, things were going well for Loco's people along Turkey Creek.[41]

The Chiricahuas, however, were seething about almost everything. They claimed that the agent and his staff were "down on them." Geronimo and Naiche felt surrounded by soldiers and feared a massacre. They disdained farming, were intolerant of the ration shortages, and deplored the thought of wearing surplus army gear. They generally disliked reservation living and especially resented Crook's orders against drinking, making tiswin, and beating their wives. Even before the clothing crisis arose, Aaron Hackney, editor of the *Globe Silver Belt,* warned the Indian Office in October 1884 that the Chiricahuas were disgruntled and were plotting an outbreak.[42]

CHAPTER SEVENTEEN

Loco Saves the Chihennes

The Warm Springs people and most of the Chiricahuas lived peacefully in the Turkey Creek–Fort Apache area for about twenty-eight months, from late spring 1884 until the end of August 1886. The Apaches' farms exceeded everyone's expectations. They had contracts with the army to deliver corn, hay, barley, and firewood. Their vegetable gardens were abundant, and a cattle herd was in the works. Several tribal members had wage jobs, and most of the Warm Springs men enlisted as scouts for the army.

For Loco personally, the times were very good. By the spring of 1885 he and his three wives were reunited for the first time in three years. Clee-hn, Loco's youngest wife, had faithfully remained with him throughout the hard times after the 1882 calamity. Loco's middle wife, Chiz-odle-netln, who escaped from the Chiricahuas during the fight at Pah-gotzin-kay gorge, reached San Carlos about a month before Loco in 1883. Then in September 1884 Loco traveled to Mariana's camp on the Navajo reservation looking for Chiz-pah-odlee, his first and oldest wife, and their daughter Bey-ih-tsun. At Mariana's camp, Loco learned that mother and daughter, along with other relatives and friends, had been held as prisoners of war at Fort Union since 1882. Loco returned to Fort Apache to work on his family's repatriation. Lieutenant Davis reported: "Loco returned yesterday and brought twelve of his people with him. . . . Loco heard that some more of his people had been taken to Ft. Union, NM for safe keeping as military prisoners. The Indians here are all anxious to have these captives returned to them. They number some nine or ten in all, and are women and children. If there are no reasons to the contrary I would recommend that their request be granted."[1]

Loco's petition to recover his wife and other relatives at Fort Union took six months to wend its way through the bureaucracy because the July 7, 1883, agreement between the War and Interior Departments required that the Indian Office approve the chief's request. Commissioner of Indian Affairs William Price finally wrote to the secretary of the interior in March 1885 to recommend that the war department "issue the necessary orders to the Commanding officer at Fort Union for the release and immediate return to their kindred at San Carlos of the Chiricahuas now confined at that post."[2]

In the late spring of 1885, Chiz-pah-odlee and eight others from Loco's band rode the five hundred miles from Fort Union to Fort Apache in an army wagon. Two were still missing from the Loco family—'It'eedee, who was captured at Alisos Creek, and Seykonne, or Siki, as she was commonly called. Siki was Loco's stepdaughter, Clee-hn's daughter by her first husband, who had been killed in some long-forgotten skirmish. Unfortunately for Siki, she was on the run with Victorio's band when it was decimated at Tres Castillos. She was among the sixty-eight women and children captured during the fight and sold into slavery. She ended up working for five years as a field hand on a large hacienda about forty miles east of the city of Chihuahua. She was released with several other women in June 1885, thanks to General Crook's diplomatic efforts to free Apache captives held in Mexico. The women said they were "given some money when they started" but received no help or transportation for their return. They managed to buy and beg "food along the road until they were near the border." The former slaves finally reached Cañada Alamosa on Independence Day, 1885. They had traveled about 350 miles to where their families had been living when Siki ran off with Victorio in 1878.[3]

The women were dressed to the nines when they walked in on Captain Boyd's Eighth Cavalry as it celebrated the Fourth of July. Their arrival was recorded in the *Albuquerque Journal* on July 7, 1885: "Seven squaws came in from the mountains [to Cañada Alamosa] to buy provisions. They stated that they came up from old Mexico afoot, but as their moccasins were but little worn this story was discredited. They had plenty of money, their fingers were loaded with fine rings, and they also had pocket books and jewelry evidently of American make. All signs indicated that they were Apache squaws, and that their money and jewelry were part of the booty taken from the settlers murdered by their bucks."[4]

Their money, nice clothing, and accessories might well have come from a cache of goods probably taken from murdered settlers during Victorio's 1880 uprising. As slaves, the women had left Mexico wearing clothes for field work. By the time they neared Cañada Alamosa, the rigors of travel had reduced their dresses to tatters. In order to spruce up for the expected return to their relatives, they apparently did a bit of shopping at one of Victorio's old caches.[5]

Captain Boyd reported that they claimed to be Warm Springs Indians and asked, "Where shall I send them?" He was ordered to pass them on to Lieutenant Charles B. Gatewood, in charge of the Indians at Fort Apache. Gatewood got wind of rumors that "Chiricahua squaws" were being sent to Fort Apache. Asking around, he reported that Loco said that "they probably belong to his people," and he noted that "they do not like to talk of their captivity, but Loco thinks more may be learned hereafter when he has had a chance to talk with them, especially with his daughter." As in the case of Chiz–pah–odlee six months before, the army provided transportation by wagon for Siki and her friends. They were back with their families by September 1885.[6]

Before their kin returned to the fold, Loco and Chiz-odle-netln had talked of the prospect of a white man's education for the Loco children. Joe Tiffany's ambitious school project crashed after the 1881 Cibecue uproar, and the multibuilding complex fell into disrepair. As early as September 1882, Commissioner Price urged the new agent, Wilcox, to reopen the school as soon as possible. The indolent Wilcox refused to comply. He cited the cost of restoring the buildings and claimed that Tiffany's school had been a snake pit of promiscuity, resulting in the spread of prostitution and syphilis, and that the children had drawn bawdy pictures on the walls. As a result, there was no school at San Carlos or Fort Apache. In January 1884, with the encouragement of Captain Emmet Crawford, Loco and Chiz-odle-netln sent their oldest son, twenty-year-old Dexter, across the country to the Carlisle Indian Industrial School in Carlisle, Pennsylvania, along with fifty-two other reservation youngsters.[7]

By the spring of 1885 the Warm Springs people were making significant strides toward a modern American lifestyle. The reservation was as peaceful as it had ever been since they were first forced to San Carlos in 1877. Their farming techniques were improving. Crops were larger and showing a profit, and the cattle herd was multiplying. The army was supplying full rations regularly.

At the same time, Geronimo, Naiche, and some of the other Chiricahuas grew surlier by the day. As it turned out, Wilcox and the Western

Apache headmen had been correct about the negative effects of returning the Chiricahuas to the reservation. The more traditionally minded Chiricahuas appeared to be ready to break out at the first provocation. Everyone expected trouble. Sam Kenoi remembered that the Geronimo Chiricahuas "would rather be on the war-path than anything else." Betzinez thought that the Chiricahuas "hadn't been mistreated at Fort Apache but weren't ready to settle down."[8] Thus Loco's Warm Springs folk found themselves in a bind. They were as worried about the warlike Chiricahuas as were the other reservation Indians, but the Western Apaches lumped them with the more mischief-prone Chiricahuas and seemed to detest both bands with equal vigor.

Ironically, the Apaches' success at farming led to unexpected problems. As soon as their cornfields began to sprout, tiswin parties became all the rage. Crook tried to stop the practice with bans on making tiswin, holding marathon drinking parties, and the unfailing byproduct, wife beating. The ban riled even the most moderate Apaches. Tiswin was an essential social medium for the Apaches. The Indians had no intention of halting their tiswin drinking.[9]

The Americans were convinced that the Chiricahua drinking parties would lead directly to outbreaks and widespread violence. By early May 1885, official concern grew in the face of an upswing in bacchanals and the related wife abuse.[10]

Two notable tiswin extravaganzas took place in 1885. Loco attended both. In each case the old chief made attempts to diminish the consequences. Britton Davis noted the upswing in unruly behavior and decided a crackdown was necessary, but evidence was difficult to come by. Although the festivities were frequent and sometimes raucous, they were generally held away from prying eyes or were tacitly ignored if nothing violent happened. In early May 1885, Davis wrote, "Reports of brutal beating of women came to me, but the women refused to complain." Finally, one Chiricahua woman had enough after her drunken husband bludgeoned her with a chunk of firewood. Davis described the damage: "A young woman came to me with her left arm broken in two places, her hair matted with blood and her shoulders a mass of welts and bruises. Her husband had disciplined her with a stick of wood. I arrested him and locked him up in the jail at Fort Apache."[11]

Several leaders complained to Davis about the arrest, but the wife beater remained in the lockup. As a result of the arrest, and to prove a point, the Apaches held a second monumental tiswin party on the night of May 14. Everyone who was anyone turned out—Geronimo, Chihuahua,

Naiche, Mangas, Nana, Benito, Loco, and Zele, along with most of their followers. Early the following morning the still-beery leaders were waiting for Davis when he opened the flap of his tent. In the meeting that followed, Loco tried to open a dialogue, undoubtedly in an effort to present the Indians' complaints diplomatically. Chihuahua, however, jumped to his feet and shouted him down. He then told Davis, "What I have to say can be said in a few words. Then Loco can take all the rest of the day to talk if he wishes to do so." He proceeded with an irrefutable argument that the Apaches "were not children to be taught how to live with their women and all their lives had eaten and drunk what seemed good to them. The white men drank wine and whiskey, even the officers and soldiers of the posts. The treatment of their wives was their own business." The Apache women "were not ill treated when they behaved," and "when they would not behave the husband had a right to punish her."

Davis had no good rebuttal. He told the Indians he would refer the matter to General Crook. Three days later, on May 17, 1885, with no response from Crook, Geronimo and possibly Mangas panicked and hatched a plot to frighten other leaders into an outbreak. They told the other Indians that they had killed Lieutenant Davis and a few of his scouts, and that the rest of the scouts had become frightened, deserted, and left the reservation. In fact, they said, everybody was leaving. None of it was true. Naiche, Nana, and Chihuahua, however, bought Geronimo's story and raced off with him, bound for Mexico with 43 warriors and 101 women and children. Loco, Bonito, and Chatto, with two-thirds of the Apaches, sat tight, glad to see them go. Nevertheless, Loco was worried about a recurrence of the 1882 kidnapping and asked the army to provide his men with better weapons. A suspicious military declined.[12]

The drinking parties continued even after Geronimo's escape. On July 8, only twenty-two days later, Loco reported that a tiswin bender had taken place the night before, and Bonito's wife had killed another woman while drunk. First Lieutenant George Roach reported, "The drunk was general throughout the camp." It probably would not have come to Roach's attention except for Chief Loco, who apparently was attempting to stop a second outbreak and came in to reveal there were problems afoot. "Loco who was also drunk came in and reported that Bonito's band was about to leave. He afterwards modified this to the statement that Bonito and his squaw had left." Roach sent in scouts to watch the camp from a distance. As it turned out, Bonito had second thoughts about an escape and remained to plead his wife's case for justifiable homicide—extreme provocation on the part of the deceased.

Roach jailed her anyhow. Roach worried, "I very much fear trouble, and believe that unless a display of force is made here, the outbreak of the balance of these Indians is only a question of time."[13]

Geronimo's outbreak in May confirmed the San Carlos Indians' worst fears. The Chiricahuas were too wild to remain on their reservation, and all the Apaches would be blamed for the troubles that were certain to follow any outbreak. Geronimo's 1885 escape brought renewed calls from the press for action against the Chiricahuas. Journalists began pressuring politicians and the army to do something about all the Apaches.[14]

All along, Indian Agent Wilcox had been at the forefront of the effort to rid the territory of the Chiricahua scourge. "The renegades constitute a standing menace not only to the reservation Apaches but to every white man in Arizona," he wrote to the secretary of the interior. He made repeated efforts to arrange the arrest and civil trial of the Apaches for depredations committed during the 1882 outbreak. Crawford reported that the Indians complained bitterly that the agent, his staff, and all the white people outside the reservation were "down on them."[15]

The white public had not forgotten the McComas murders. Once the last of the Chiricahuas returned to the reservation without six-year-old Charley McComas, it was obvious that the missing youngster was dead. Finally certain that Charley's captors could not retaliate against him, Judge McComas's brother-in-law, Eugene Ware, stepped up the pressure to put on trial every Apache who had taken part in the murders. The politically well-connected Ware raised the call for action to a national level. Newspapers around the country picked up the cry for civil punishment of all the Indians who had taken part in killing the McComas family.[16]

The Western Apaches at San Carlos joined the white diatribe about the Chiricahuas and openly called for their removal from the reservation. Indian Office Inspector Frank C. Armstrong was quick to notice the Apaches' attitude. He wrote to the secretary of interior: "The San Carlos agency Indians and the White Mountain Apaches are bitterly opposed to the Chiricahuas remaining near them. The entire Chiricahua band, about 450, should be moved from Ft. Apache to some place east and be made to go to work." Armstrong thought Fort Leavenworth, Kansas, would be a good place.[17]

Even before Geronimo's outbreak, Betzinez lamented, "the San Carlos Indians showed us no friendliness nor even courtesy. We felt that we were not welcome here, that they wanted us to be removed from their reservation." Davis observed that the Chiricahuas were "feared and hated by the other Indians of the reservation." In the aftermath of the May

1885 outbreak, White Mountain and San Carlos men rushed to volunteer for scouting duty with the army. None of the men from Loco's band joined the 1885 breakout with Geronimo.[18] Practically every member of Chatto's and Loco's bands also enlisted as scouts in the campaign to end the Geronimo problem once and for all. Not only did they feel a pressing need to revenge the 1882 catastrophe, but they also wanted forever to end any association with the troublemakers.

Meanwhile, the Chiricahua escapees were wreaking havoc in Mexico. Geronimo later remarked, "On our return through Old Mexico we attacked every Mexican found, even if for no other reason than to kill." Tiring of that, in the fall of 1885 Geronimo and four other men set out to recover family members who had been left behind at Turkey Creek in their hurried exodus from the reservation. Geronimo was especially looking for one of his wives, She-ga, and their three-year-old daughter. In the early hours of September 22, 1885, the five slipped onto the reservation and stole a few horses for the trip back to Mexico. They had trouble locating the camp where She-ga was waiting. After the May outbreak, Lieutenant Gatewood had moved all the remaining Chiricahuas, both Loco's band and Geronimo's relatives, closer to Fort Apache to prevent further escapes. Eventually, the raiders kidnapped a young Coyotero woman and forced her to lead them to their kinfolk. The White Mountain woman was carried off with She-ga and her daughter. Geronimo's foray apparently had no other effect on the reservation except to scare the White Mountain Apaches and incense the clan from which the woman was taken. Geronimo did not retrieve all the relatives he sought, and he acquired no new recruits, but he did further arouse the White Mountain Indians.[19]

After Geronimo's incursion into the Fort Apache area, Gatewood met with the Chiricahuas and Warm Springs Indians near their new location around Fort Apache. None admitted having seen Geronimo's party. The White Mountain Indians, however, claimed several sightings. Curiously, they did not report the invasion, but they were frightened enough to gather in armed groups to fend off further murders and abductions by the gang. By the time Geronimo's raiders left, the entire reservation was on a short fuse.

Two months after the big tiswin party on May 14 and Geronimo's subsequent departure, Captain Francis E. Pierce, the military Indian agent at San Carlos, was ordered "to investigate causes of Chiricahua Outbreak." He questioned a number of Indians about the incident, including Chief Loco. Loco made it clear that neither he nor his people were involved, and he spoke to the state of affairs between the Warm Springs people and the Chiricahuas:

> Loco says that he and Zele were living on Turkey Creek some distance from those who went out—that he never had much to do with those who left—was always friendly with them and they never did him any harm but he was never intimate with them and knew nothing of their plans. That the morning of the day they started, he went up to the Creek to work on his farm, and was there all day and none of them came near him and towards night went home and after being there for a little while some of his people came and told him they had started, and that was the first he knew of it; that he knows of no reason for their going. That General Crook did everything he promised and that he is well satisfied to stay and work, and do the best he can. That Mariano (Navajo), was here about a year ago and advised him to settle down and get some sheep and live like Navajos; that he saw seven Navajos at Turkey Creek last spring just before the outbreak and that six of them belonged to Mariano's band.[20]

The last straw came two months later, on November 22 and 23, 1885, when Chihuahua's brother, Ulzanna (also known as Josannie), and ten friends slipped onto the reservation, also looking for missing relatives and for an opportunity to kill a few of the men who had been scouting for the army. Finding that Loco's group and the other Chiricahuas were being watched more closely than ever, the Ulzanna party directed its wrath at the White Mountain Indians, specifically Sanchez's clan. They killed eleven women, four children, and five men. Before leaving the reservation, they also murdered two agency employees as they tended the tribal cattle herd. None of the Chiricahuas or Warm Springs Indians budged from the reservation, and ultimately Ulzanna was unable to locate his family, which was being held at Fort Bowie. His raiders did manage to kidnap several White Mountain women. Eluding a desperate pursuit by scores of army units and relatives of the captive women, Ulzanna's Chiricahuas escaped into Mexico on December 31, 1885. They had traveled an impressive twelve hundred miles and left behind thirty-eight dead, a reservation full of enraged White Mountain Apaches, and two territories of angry citizens who were fed up and prepared to do anything to be rid of Chiricahuas.[21]

Under the leadership of Sanchez, whose band had lost the most members in the Ulzanna attack, the Coyoteros at Fort Apache devised a plan to avenge Geronimo's intrusion and Ulzanna's murder and kid-napping spree. With the help of Alchesay, a long-time army scout, Sanchez's Coyoteros set about to rid the reservation of all the Chiricahuas, including Loco's peaceful Warm Springs band. The Coyoteros were well armed and outnumbered "Crook's Chiricahuas" by approximately four to one. Once the Fort Apache Indians got things started, they could count on the other Apaches at San Carlos and perhaps even a few outside whites to help cleanse the place of the undesirable Indians. They were united in their disgust for the Chiricahuas, including the Warm Springs people, and they now had a cause célèbre.[22]

Gatewood got wind of the plot when Sanchez and Alchesay asked for extra ammunition for the scouts. Curious about the need for extra bullets, Gatewood probed for details. The two Coyoteros became nervous and evasive. Gatewood, in turn, became suspicious and probed for a better answer. The two chiefs protested that "their hearts were made sore" that the lieutenant might think they would do anything unauthorized by the government. Still Gatewood was unconvinced, but despite his deter-mined efforts to uncover the Coyoteros' true agenda, "no bribes, threats, nor persuasion could get one man, woman or child to even hint at what would be the result."

After the Coyoteros left the meeting, Chief Loco secretly slipped into Gatewood's office and asked to move his people into the fort for protec-tion. When the captain asked why, Loco replied that the White Mountain Indians were setting up for a wholesale massacre of the Chiricahuas and Warm Springs Indians. Gatewood wasted no time moving Loco's flock into the confines of the fort and sent runners to the other Chiricahua villages to warn them to move closer to the post for protection.

As soon as the White Mountain Apaches realized that the Chiricahuas had moved out of their grasp, they hurried to Gatewood in frustration. The lieutenant told the assembly that he knew they were up to no good and ordered them to go home and forget all thoughts of revenge. Sanchez was quick to give Gatewood a lesson on Western Apache law and cus-toms: "Our homes have been invaded, and our women and children outraged and massacred. Where can we get revenge? Those who com-mitted these crimes are by this time far away in Mexico, and we can't reach them there. By our laws, their kindred here are proper victims, but you have placed them beyond our reach."[23]

Ironically, just as Sanchez was lecturing Gatewood, a clamor outside disrupted the meeting. Before anyone could move a muscle, a Chiri-cahua youth bolted headlong into the crowded office. Hot on his heels came a group of White Mountain warriors, waving guns and knives at the terrified teenager, now cowering behind Gatewood. A crowd of angry Coyoteros began to gather outside, apparently hoping to watch the boy's final moment. They became unruly in no time and began to chant, "Chiricahua, Kill him. Chiricahua, Kill him." Gatewood quickly whistled up his scouts, who arrested the leading troublemakers and cooled the situation.

When the commotion settled down, Gatewood negotiated a compromise. The deal mollified both Loco and Sanchez but satisfied neither. The lieutenant designated a portion of the reservation as a safe sector for the Chiricahuas. The Coyoteros were free to kill any Chiricahuas they found outside the protected zone but must leave them alone if they remained inside. It was a temporary solution. Coyoteros were soon complaining that they were tired of waiting for the Chiricahuas to leave their safe haven. The Chiricahuas, on the other hand, complained about the tighter restrictions. To say things were tense would be to understate the case.[24]

Chief Loco had undoubtedly saved the entire Warm Springs and Chiricahua bands from annihilation. Although a large-scale massacre was thwarted, Loco's band was trapped in a setting much like a prison camp, controlled by the army and surrounded by enemies poised to kill every one of them. Nevertheless, it is evident that had Loco not acted when he did, the modern Fort Sill Chiricahua–Warm Springs Apache Tribe would not exist, or at the very least would be a lot smaller.

So it was that by the spring of 1886, through no fault of their own, the Warm Springs Apaches had not a friend in the world. All the other Apaches on the San Carlos reservation hated and feared them. Because of Geronimo's actions, the Mescaleros were also angry with them and were supplying scouts in the search for the renegades. White settlers in Arizona and New Mexico were ready to do them in or ship them out, and Mexicans believed the only option was to exterminate them. This left the federal government with the delicate problem of where to put such an unwanted crowd. General Phil Sheridan summarized the dilemma: "Their removal from Arizona would undoubtedly be a relief to the people in that section but would unquestionably be equally distasteful to the inhabitants of any section east of New Mexico where they might be sent, and [they] would probably make every effort to prevent its accomplishment."[25]

CHAPTER EIGHTEEN

Exiled to the East

It took eight months, but in the middle of January 1886 General Crook's forces ran Geronimo and Naiche to ground in Mexico. A proper surrender was scheduled to be held in Cañon de los Embudos, Mexico, between March 25 and 27. Geronimo left nineteen of his followers as good-faith hostages. Three, however, escaped en route to Fort Bowie.

The March canyon conference came off without a hitch. Everyone agreed that Geronimo, Chihuahua, Naiche, Nana, and their followers would surrender. There would be no civil trial for any of the Apaches, and none would be hanged, but they would be exiled in the East for two years. Crook left the prisoners in the care of Lieutenant Marion Maus and headed for Fort Bowie to wire the news to General Sheridan. With Crook gone, Geronimo spent the evening with friends drinking thirty dollars' worth of mescal supplied by a bootlegger, Bob Tribolett. By morning, all agreements were off the table. Geronimo and Naiche, with about twenty men and nineteen dependents, were on the lam once again.[1]

Chihuahua, Nana, and Ulzanna, with fifty-eight followers, stayed behind and returned to Arizona with the Americans. They reached Fort Bowie in two groups, one on April 2 and the other on April 7, and there they joined the sixteen hostages. Even if Geronimo and Naiche did not keep the Embudos agreement, the government did. On April 17, 1886, the fifteen men, thirty-three women, and twenty-nine children were on a train to Fort Marion in St. Augustine, Florida, accompanied by Lieutenant James Richards and a company of infantry.[2]

The uneventful transfer of Chihuahua's group to Florida was concurrent with discussions about removing all the Chiricahua and Warm Springs Indians. General Nelson Miles, who replaced General Crook as commander of the Department of Arizona on April 12, 1886, began work on a total removal soon after he took charge. In early 1886, Miles and Lucius Lamar Jr., Interior Secretary Lamar's son and assistant, traveled to Fort Apache to find a justification for a mass removal of the Indians. The general asserted that the Warm Springs Apaches "had been in communication with the hostiles, and some of them had been plotting an extensive outbreak." It was untrue, but Miles had a reputation inside the military for bending the truth to suit his purposes. General Sheridan was later quoted in a Chicago newspaper saying, "General Miles cannot tell the truth; he will lie." In this case, that is exactly what he did.[3]

Miles wired Sheridan on July 4, 1886: "I respectfully request authority to send a few of the tribe to Washington, under charge of two officers, and to locate them on such land as the Government may be willing to grant them. Mr. Lamar, who is here from the Interior Department, concurs with me as to the advisability of the measure." A second telegram reported that ten leaders had agreed to the trip "to make a permanent arrangement for their future."[4]

For years there had been talk of moving the Chiricahuas somewhere, almost anywhere except in Arizona or New Mexico. When asked where he thought the Chiricahuas should be relocated, Al Sieber recommended that the government send them "to Missouri, or to hell, or some such place." Oklahoma, however, was the most frequently suggested destination. It was favored by General Miles, who wanted to put them on a reservation adjacent to Fort Sill.[5]

Sheridan disagreed with a removal. He believed it would be in the best interest of neither the government nor the Apaches. On July 7 he wrote to the secretary of war that the history of Indian wars in the United States was traceable to the government's forcing the tribes to move from their traditional territories. He cited the forced removal of the Warm Springs people from Ojo Caliente as an example, pointing out that they "protested that though they would go, they would be bad Indians, and bad Indians they have been nearly ever since."[6] General Crook, too, objected to the removal plan: "The glibness with which people generally speak of moving them would indicate that all we have to do is to take them from their camps, as you would chickens from a roost."[7]

General Miles ignored Crook's and Sheridan's objections and forged ahead with arrangements for both the Washington trip and a widespread removal. He believed that the Apache leaders would be overwhelmed when they glimpsed the capital city and would agree to a mass relocation. On the other hand, the Apaches viewed the trip as an opportunity to go directly to President Grover Cleveland with requests to avoid another removal and for help retrieving their captured families from the Mexicans.[8]

Ultimately, ten men and three women were selected to make the trip. The chief delegates were Loco, speaking for the Warm Springs band, and Chatto, for the Chiricahuas. Other delegates included Kaahteney and Patricio, Chatto's brother. Two of the three women were Loco's wives, the sisters Chiz-pah-odlee and Chiz-odle-netln, and the third, the youngest delegate, was Loco's granddaughter Kenaididlg. All were enlisted and paid as scouts for the trip, possibly making the Loco women the only women scouts in the army at the time. Clee-hn remained at San Carlos to attend to the family—a half dozen or so children, some in-laws, and a generous collection of other kin, perhaps as many as forty. On Miles's assurance that they would be returned to their families in Arizona, the delegation left Willcox, Arizona, for the eight-day ride to the capital. They were accompanied by a toady for General Miles, Captain Joseph Dorst, and four interpreters, Mickey Free, Concepción Esquerra, Victor Gómez, and Sam Bowman.[9]

The delegation reached Washington on Saturday evening, July 17, 1886, and was taken directly to the timeworn Beveridge Hotel, only eight blocks from the White House. Once an elegant home, the Beveridge had been converted into a cut-rate hotel, a rundown, musty place. Bourke, now a captain stationed in Washington, called it a "squalid rookery." Victor Gómez and Concepción Esquerra complained that the "house was untidy, the beds very poor, the food worse—broken plates and no napkins." Bourke was angry that the government had missed an opportunity to impress the Indians with the "comforts of civilization."[10]

On July 19, federal officials set about persuading the Apaches to accept a removal to a reservation in the East. When the delegation arrived in Interior Secretary Lamar's office, Chief Loco acted as spokesman for the group.[11] The *Washington Evening Star* described the meeting:

> Some thirteen Indians from the San Carlos Reservation in Arizona representing that part of the Chiricahua Apache Tribe of Indians which have not been engaged in the recent raids [of Geronimo] had an interview with the Secretary of the Interior this morning. One old Chief [Loco, who] was rather gaily dressed and made a better appearance than his companions who were clad in rather

nondescript garments, half American and half Indian, was the spokesman for the rest. . . . The old chief and the Secretary through this double medium [interpreters] had quite a lengthy conference during which it was developed that the Indians wanted to remain where they were as they said that they were getting along very well. . . . The Secretary . . . told them that he would consider what had been said and at a future meeting tell them what would be done. He also said that he would introduce them to their Great Father. The Indians then filed past the Secretary and shook hands.[12]

On the following day the group went to the Bureau of American Ethnology, where they posed for portraits in their western outfits. That done, they took carriages to Saks and Company to buy formal wear for their meeting with the president. With Captain Dorst supervising, they selected ten-dollar suits, which Bourke described as "shabby and a very cheap kind . . . [along with] fairly good straw hats . . . and heavy leather shoes." The women bought gingham and calico, which Mrs. Beveridge, the hotel's owner, sewed into dresses and jackets for the upcoming meeting.[13]

Meanwhile, the Apaches' presence in Washington did not go unnoticed by Eugene Ware in Kansas. Still seeking retribution for the McComas family's murders three years earlier, he enlisted the help of a congressman and the local newspapers to demand the arrest of "the entire delegation, especially Chatto." The newspaper articles created a controversy that quickly reached the secretary of the interior's office. Lamar held firm against the pressure. His response was printed in the *Evening Star:*

They have come here, he said, at the invitation of the government. They are here as both guests and wards of the government. While they are here, they will offend nobody and the government will see that they are not molested. We brought them to Washington for a conference to see if they would consent to be transferred from Arizona to some other place . . . but they are now entirely opposed to the proposition and in a few days we shall send them back to the reservation.

Lamar also had an answer to the *Washington Post*'s charge that Chatto was fifty times a murderer and the killer of the McComas family: "If that is so, and if the others who accompany him are all murderers, the facts are not known to the Department. . . . They were at war with us but now they are prisoners of war under a treaty. By the terms of that treaty we are prohibited from delivering them up for destruction; we are bound to protect them."[14]

Despite the controversy, Loco and the other delegates continued their sightseeing while waiting to meet the secretary of war and the president. Bourke spent his off-duty time escorting the Indians around the city. On the evening of July 22 he took the delegation to see a performance by the "Mexican Orchestra," featuring vocalist Florissa Forbes, at the Harris Bijou Theater. The Apaches clapped their hands and stomped their feet with gusto after each rendition. They were especially amused by Forbes's singing. "That a squaw should come out and sing and above all trill and quaver, which was more than they could understand, diverted them highly and kept them hilarious for a long time." After the performance, Bourke treated the Apaches to ice cream and soda pop. He noted that they could eat only a little of the cream because it "burnt their mouths with its coldness," but they "guzzled" the soft drinks.[15]

The following night, Friday, July 23, as he was returning from a dinner party, Bourke was diverted to the home of Secretary of War William Endicott by a former West Point classmate, Captain Daniel Taylor. Endicott requested that Bourke attend a meeting scheduled with the Apaches the following Monday.

Chatto, Kaahteney, and Charlie were the only members of the delegation to attend the two o'clock meeting. Endicott specifically requested that Chatto attend to receive some good news. The Mexican government had finally located his missing wife and children, who had been captured in the January 1883 assault on Juh's camp. General Crook had sent a photograph of the chief's family to Endicott for Chatto. Endicott announced that Chatto's family would most likely be returned to him, but it might take a while because of red tape. Chatto never saw his family again.[16]

Chatto's plea to the secretary of war paralleled that made by Loco six days earlier to the secretary of the interior: "He says he wants to ask you about his country, his land; and he does not want to ask too much; and that after that he will speak of other things. He came here to ask for his country; to ask for his land, where he lives now; to ask, that is why he has traveled so far. At Camp Apache what he plants grows up very well; the water that runs there is very good; that is why he wants to have that land."

Endicott's reply was evasive and entirely avoided the possibility of removal: "I will consider what he says in regard to wagons, tools, plows and other things that he wants, and if possible, will see that they are supplied. I am very pleased with what he has said, and with the good feeling and good intentions he has expressed.... If he wishes I will present him to the President." Endicott closed the meeting with instructions on proper etiquette for a presidential visit: "Shake hands with the President and it will not be necessary to go through this talk." The appointment was set for noon on the following Wednesday, July 28.[17]

The delegates arrived at the White House just before noon on the appointed day. The *Washington Evening Star* recorded their entrance: "The delegation of Apaches who are in the city visited the President at noon today, in charge of Captains Bourke and Dorsey [*sic*]. As they ascended the main stairway the creaking of their new shoes sounded as if the White House was invaded by a regiment. While waiting in the Cabinet Room, for the President, their attention was attracted by the beautiful view from the south windows and they expressed their admiration.... They were soon ushered into the library and were introduced by Captain Bourke to the President who shook hands with each one."[18]

The meeting went pleasantly enough. President Cleveland told the Apaches that all they had said to Lamar and Endicott had been written down and would be given to him, and he promised that he would "give the matter very careful attention." Cleveland then gave Chatto a silver peace medal bearing the likeness of former president Chester Arthur. The other Apaches had to settle for gold-embossed commemoration certificates. Cleveland closed the meeting with another round of handshakes.[19]

After meeting the Great Father, the delegates went on a second government-sponsored shopping spree at the Lansburg and Brothers Store on Seventh Street. Most of their purchases appear to have been gifts for the women back on the reservation—144 yards of calico, 48 yards of sateen, 15 fans, miscellaneous items of jewelry, and 13 valises to carry their booty.[20]

Three days after the White House visit, Cleveland called a confidential meeting with Secretaries Endicott and Lamar, Lamar Jr., and Captains Dorst and Bourke. He wasted no time raising the main order of business: "Would it be proper and expedient to seize the Chiricahuas now at Fort Apache and send them to Florida, and in the meantime retain Chatto, Kawtenne [*sic*] and the others now in the east at Carlisle or other suitable point?"

Bourke spoke strongly against the plan, arguing that the delegation and those it represented at Fort Apache had been at peace since 1883, and many of them had chased hostile Apaches as army scouts. Dorst, speaking for General Miles, adamantly opposed Bourke and vigorously endorsed a total removal. Bourke was outraged at the proceeding and noted that the only remarkable thing about the three-hundred-pound Cleveland was that "he had a very small head," an "enormous neck," and "adipocerean" dimensions. Bourke concluded that the president was "self-opinionated, stubborn, and not too tenacious of the truth. It made very little difference what any of us said; he knew it all already."[21]

To be fair, Grover Cleveland had a very full plate in 1886. Although what became of the Apaches was an emotional issue in southern Arizona and New Mexico, relative to the other national problems facing the president, it was a minor nuisance. He had no patience for negotiating with five hundred insignificant Indians who had not a vote among them. A complete removal of the entire tribe—good, bad, or indifferent—was a quick, clean solution to the Apache troubles. It would also look good in the upcoming election.[22]

On the very afternoon following the July 31 meeting between Endicott, Lamar, and Cleveland, General Sheridan wired Miles in Arizona: "The President wishes me to ask you what you think of the proposition to forcibly arrest all on the reservation and send them to Fort Marion, Florida, where they can be joined by the party now here."[23] Miles, of course, had no problem with it. He preferred Indian Territory as a destination but recommended holding the leaders at the Indian school in Carlisle, Pennsylvania, until their fates could be decided. Consequently, while the bureaucrats formulated a plan, the delegation was taken by rail to Carlisle, about 180 miles from Washington. Carlisle was probably selected as the holding pen because some of the delegates, including Loco, had sent children there two and a half years earlier. Loco and Chiz-odle-netln were reunited with Dexter for the first time since 1884. While the delegates remained in Carlisle for five days, the plan to send all the Chiricahuas to Florida was set into motion. Dorst was to keep the delegation at Carlisle for about a week or until he received further instructions. Unfortunately, the telegraph equipment from Washington failed just when needed, and the delegates left Carlisle on August 9. They were in Emporia, Kansas, before Dorst received word to hold up on August 12. He immediately returned with the delegation to Fort Leavenworth, where they would be detained until he received additional instructions.

Their suspicions aroused by Dorst's U-turn, Loco and the delegation became increasingly surly. Dorst requested instructions from General Miles, who was in Albuquerque at the time. Miles ordered Dorst to leave the Indian delegates under guard and report to him. The general armed the lieutenant with a fabricated tale to calm the delegates-turned-prisoners for long enough to get them to Florida. Upon his return to Leavenworth, Dorst informed the Apaches that they were now prisoners of war who must abide by whatever disposition the government deemed best—but he insisted that this was a good thing. The citizens of Arizona would arrest and hang them if they returned. Dorst told them that General Miles had proposed a sixty-square-mile Chiricahua-only reservation away from Arizona and New Mexico for their safety. Each family would receive livestock and $600 worth of farm equipment, and the headmen would be paid about $20 to $50 a month as long as they remained peaceful. Thus, on the promise of a large reservation, lifelong paychecks, and a few incidentals, the leaders made their marks on an agreement to relocate the entire Chiricahua and Warm Spring tribes. With the agreement in hand, Major General Alfred Terry, commanding the Division of the Missouri, wired the adjutant general on September 15, 1886: "Captain Dorst with Apache Indians left for St. Augustine last evening."[24]

While the government was making arrangements for the delegation, Lieutenant Colonel James Wade, commanding Fort Apache, received orders to transfer the remaining Apaches to Florida. On August 29 he sent word to the Apache camps that a roll call would accompany the usual issue of rations, a process that required everyone's presence. When the Indians turned out for the count, they were surrounded and disarmed. The soldiers held them under close guard for five days until transportation could be arranged for the trip. In order to avoid trouble until the Apaches were aboard the train, they were told that they were going to join their leaders in Washington, where they would meet the Great Father.[25]

On September 4, a caravan two miles long stretched along the road from Fort Apache to Holbrook, Arizona. The procession included 8 officers, 84 soldiers and scouts, 383 Apaches, 140 horses, a small herd of cattle to butcher for rations on the trek to Holbrook, and what one of the officers thought to be "thousands of dogs."[26]

The column reached Holbrook eight days later and camped in the dry bed of the Little Colorado River. The tracks of the Atlantic and Pacific Railroad ran beside the riverbed. The Apaches' train stood on a side track. Most of Holbrook turned out that evening to see the Apaches, but the soldiers kept them at a distance. Lieutenant William Strover, one of the officers scheduled to accompany the Indians to Florida, described the scene: "Several hundred small fires were glowing among the low brush and around each one of them was a group of Indians, dancing and singing in celebration of their coming journey to see the Great Father. Drums were sounding incessantly, the monotonous chant of the . . . Indians pervading the night air, and the mournful howling of the thousands of dogs. . . . They seemed to scent a coming catastrophe."[27]

It was a twelve-car train, the first and last cars for the guards, two cars for baggage, and eight cars for the Indians. As the train rumbled out of Holbrook on September 13, "there was tremendous excitement, everybody standing up and yelling. When nothing happened, the excitement subsided gradually and all sat down in their seats."[28]

When the train pulled out of the Holbrook station, it left behind the tribe's livestock, dogs, two Chiricahua men with five women and children who escaped during the trip from Fort Apache, and several piles of household goods that could not be fitted into the two baggage cars. Souvenir hunters moved in and picked over the leavings. The camp dogs, which had loyally followed the tribe from Fort Apache, "began a terrific racket, and when the train started, thousands of now homeless dogs tried frantically to keep up, at the same time yelping with all their might." Some reportedly ran with the train for almost twenty miles. Afterward, most of the dogs returned to Holbrook, where they roamed the streets for days. A long-time Holbrook resident later told Strover, "Oh man! We had to turn out and shoot them, and believe me it kept us busy. The cowpunchers helped us and had a great sport shooting them from the saddle." The last of the Indians' possessions, their 140 horses and mules, were rounded up and later sold at Fort Union for $2,599. Chief Loco's share for his stock, three horses, was $31.80.[29]

The train's coaches had been specially modified to prevent any possibility of escape. On the positive side, the accommodations were reasonably spacious, and each car could hold fifty to sixty passengers comfortably.[30] With about forty-seven Apaches in each, the cars in the Indians' train were not overloaded, as some historians have suggested. Clee-hn, Loco's children, and other relatives would have filled one coach.

In its efforts to make the passenger cars escape-proof, however, the army made the ventilation even worse than it normally was aboard a train at the time. Coaches like the ones that carried the Apaches had 19 to 20 large windows and 17 to 20 clerestory transoms on each side of the car. A clerestory was a raised section built into the central portion of the roof with small transoms for light and air. The most common ways to ventilate a railroad coach in those days were to open the windows or rely on the clerestory during foul weather. From the army's perspective, the windows and clerestory transoms loomed as escape exits for the

Indians and were nailed shut. If it could be avoided, there would be no escape during the trip to Florida. Nor would there be a single breath of fresh air for the Apaches.[31]

The Master Car Builders Association admitted that railroad cars, even with open windows, were then the most poorly ventilated of all public gathering places. Studies during the period showed that carbon dioxide levels in railroad passenger cars were nearly double those of theaters and other poorly ventilated public places. As a result, travelers on long railway trips frequently showed symptoms of carbon dioxide poisoning—lassitude, delirium, headaches, nausea, vomiting, dizziness, and occasionally convulsions—all symptoms that the Indian travelers later reported.[32]

With the windows and clerestories sealed, there remained but one potential getaway route to block. Railroad coaches in 1886 included one, sometimes two, "salons," closetlike rooms approximately three feet square in which passengers might relieve themselves in private. Each salon was equipped with a wooden box in which a round hole had been cut for a seat, similar to the arrangement in an outhouse except that the railroad "hoppers" dropped the excreta directly onto the tracks through an opening in the floor.[33]

Army personnel concluded that the train's salon hoppers offered direct exits from the train, so they boarded up the toilet tops and replaced them with buckets to serve as chamber pots. Chamber pots had been used briefly on earlier trains but fell into disuse because of the stench that wafted through the cars. Some accounts suggest that during the Apaches' trip, the buckets overflowed and sewage sloshed in the aisles of the cars. These are undoubtedly exaggerations. A one-inch door jam separated the salon from the aisle. Further, virtually all steam engine trains were required to stop every hundred miles or so to take on water for the boilers. The "honey buckets" were probably emptied at most stops, or at a minimum during the stops for meals. Nevertheless, the smell was not limited to the salons but drifted through the enclosed cars. For the Apaches, who were accustomed to relieving themselves at great distances from their camps for privacy and sanitation, using the chamber pots was not only disgusting but humiliating.[34]

Fortunately, the Apaches were not confined to these conditions for the entire trip. During regular stops to take on water for the boilers, the prisoners were generally able to leave the train to stretch and eat. The train would "halt at some lonely water tank. There the Indians were let out and fed. Six of the bucks had been designated, each as 'captain' and had been placed over a group of his people, and to this captain was turned over the amount of grub for the group. At every halt, in some lonely place, rations were put in six piles and the interpreter would call for the six 'capitanos' who each would divide the food among his particular crowd." On at least one occasion in St. Louis, the entire group was allowed off the train to eat at a depot restaurant. A St. Louis reporter noted that "crowds gathered at the station to see the captive Indians were rewarded by seeing them breakfast at a modern restaurant which they were evidently not accustomed to doing." He counted 385 Chiricahua and Warm Springs Indians. After their meal the Indians were transferred to a Louisville and Nashville train in nearby Mount Vernon, Illinois. Four transfers were made during the trip—one each in Mount Vernon and Waycross, Georgia, and two at Jacksonville, Florida. Although the trains were all similarly prepared to prevent escape, each transfer offered a clean start.[35]

Still, as the prisoners' train chugged its way across the country, carbon dioxide, body odor, and the stench from the salons filled the sweltering, airless coaches. Smoke from the coal-fired engine added to the bouquet. Officers returning to Arizona after the trip called the conditions "simply brutal."[36]

Strover wrote of the conditions found in the coaches: "At the first halt, after the Indians had been let out [to eat], the division superintendent of the road, who was on the train, wanted to go inside one of the cars, but he did not get further than inside the door. 'Holy Moses!' he exclaimed. 'That's awful! I guess all we can do with this equipment is to burn it when we get to our destination.'" Strover experienced the conditions first hand: "That night I had to go to the rear car of the train as there were no stops, I was compelled to make my way thru the whole train. Heavens! When I think of that trip, even at this time, I get seasick."

After Strover's experience, "when the train stopped for the morning feed, the superintendent had each car washed out with a hose and a powerful stream of water. Of course, it was not a pleasure to go into one of these cars after this cleaning, but it was the only way to make it possible for any human being, other than an Indian, to enter them at all."[37]

Newspapers across the country followed the train's progress as it slowly wound its way through Albuquerque and Kansas City to St. Louis, Missouri, and then on to Atlanta. Forewarned crowds of hundreds greeted the train at every depot to catch a glimpse of the wild Apaches. The largest crowds gathered at the stations where the Apaches changed trains. At the Indians' first transfer point, in Mount Vernon, Illinois, about one hundred miles from St. Louis, an estimated fifteen hundred onlookers turned out. A reporter noted that during the transfer, "the crowd was given an opportunity to mingle with the Apaches and buy beads, trinkets and other Apache items." It was reported that "the noble red man reaped a harvest."[38]

At Waycross, Georgia, gawkers began to gather a week before the train's scheduled arrival, some making the seventy-five-mile trip from Jacksonville, Florida. By six-thirty in the evening of the designated day, the crowd had grown to almost two thousand, but about half left upon rumors of a delayed arrival. Twelve Louisville and Nashville coaches chugged to a halt at about seven o'clock. An hour before the train's appearance, the Waycross police chief, Captain Murphy, turned up with the entire Waycross police force, twenty-two deputies, and some personal friends to maintain order. They cordoned off the area to allow the unhampered transfer of the prisoners to ferryboats that would carry them across the Satilla River, where they boarded their third train. It would take them as far as Jacksonville.

From the government's perspective, the trip so far had been uneventful, except for the escape of Massai, a Warm Springs Apache who slipped from the escape-proof train early in the junket. No one was ever sure how or where Massai made his escape. Some said he got away in Kansas; Betzinez declared it was near Saint Louis. Lieutenant Strover remembered that his absence was discovered during the train's first stop, in Las Vegas, New Mexico. "How he was able to get away was a mystery." A good guess is that he pried the lid off the salon's hopper and had friends replace the lid once he slithered through the opening.[39] Massai made his way back to the Mescalero reservation, where he kidnapped a young woman for company and lived the rest of his life in the mountains.[40]

After a brief train ride from Waycross, the Indians were met on the outskirts of North Jacksonville by enthusiastic crowds, eager to see the infamous Apaches transfer to yet another train across the St. Johns River, destined for South Jacksonville. A crush of sightseers wanting a close look at the Indians engulfed the train as they disembarked in the North Jacksonville depot. Troops guarding the Apaches were forced to let the prisoners fend for themselves while they kept order among the crowd.

At South Jacksonville, the *Florida Times Union* reported, "there were at least 600 people gathered to see the Indians arrive. The transfer from the ferry boat to the train was made quietly in a short space of time, after which the train, in two sections, left for the Ancient City." In recording his impressions, a newsman, obviously unaware of the hardships the

Apaches had faced during the trip, unsympathetically described the travelers' arrival:

> A more dirty, disgusting, strong scented mass of humanity never
> before alighted from a train in Jacksonville. The stench that came
> from the cars as they stood on the side track was worse than ever
> came from a nest of ten year polecats. It would be utterly useless
> to attempt a description of the scene as they came from the cars
> but those who were there to witness their arrival and who could
> see, can bear witness to the amount of filth displayed.
>
> Barely clothed, their hair matted, and small children, naked and
> clinging to the backs of their mothers, the squaws carrying loads
> of bedding and cooking utensils, and the braves carrying a shirt
> and a pair of leggings, gave the crowd an idea of the Indian make
> up and the slovenly and scanty manner in which the Redskins
> dress. It is said however, that this tribe is very cleanly, bathing frequently and taking Indian pride in their dress, but we feel sure
> "Indian Pride" can not be appreciated in this part of the world.[41]

On September 25, the *Army and Navy Journal* reported that both the
Washington delegation and the tribe had arrived at St. Augustine:

> Capt. Dorst arrived at Ft. Marion Sept. 18 from Leavenworth with
> ten bucks, three squaws, and three interpreters, including Chato [*sic*],
> a Chiricahua, Loco the head man of the Warm Spring Indians, and
> Bowman, a Cherokee half-breed. This party is under pay as Indian
> scouts, and form the delegation that recently went to Washington
> to petition the President that they should not be removed from
> their reservation. They appear resigned to their fate, but do not
> relish the change at all, and are adverse to mingling with the other
> Apaches previously at Ft. Marion [Chihuahua's band]. Lieutenant
> Colonel Wade . . . arrived at Marion Sept. 20 with 381 Indians, and
> turned them over to Colonel Langdon.[42]

The men in Geronimo's group never made it to Fort Marion. On
October 25 they arrived at Fort Pickens, across the bay from Pensacola,
Florida, and about two hundred miles short of Fort Marion. The eleven
women and six children with him had been put on a different train in
San Antonio, Texas, and shipped to Fort Marion. Mangas and his sole
surviving warrior, Goso, arrived at Fort Pickens on November 6, 1886.

Their women and children, too, went on to Fort Marion. For all practical purposes, by mid-November 1886 the Southwest was devoid of Chiricahua and Warm Spring Apaches. The Apache wars were over, although Massai and the seven Chiricahua escapees carried on for a while.[43]

Modern photograph of Fort Marion, St. Augustine, Florida, the Apaches' prison during their stay in Florida. The fort's proximity to the town is about the same as it was during the Apaches' stay. Collection of the St. Augustine Historical Society.

Loomis L. Langdon, about 1865. As acting commandant of Fort Marion, Langdon set a lenient standard for treatment of the prisoners that prevailed throughout their imprisonment. Courtesy National Archives and Records Administration.

The third group of youngsters taken from Fort Marion in April 1887 as they arrived at the Carlisle Indian Industrial School in Pennsylvania. Older youngsters, including some younger married couples, were taken in this group. Courtesy Frisco Native American Museum (Raymond, Norman, and Moses Loco Collections).

Herbert Welsh, about 1910. Welsh was an Indian rights activist who fought for better conditions for the Apache prisoners and for their ultimate release. The Apaches voted unanimously to give Welsh an allotment of land for his "valuable services for many years." Courtesy Frisco Native American Museum.

The first village at Mount Vernon, Alabama, and the first houses ever for the Apaches, about 1890. The village was abandoned in April 1891. Courtesy Alabama Department of Archives and History, Montgomery, Alabama.

Marion Juan Loco, Chief Loco's daughter-in-law and John's wife, in 1910. Apache women prisoners acquired their sense of style from their wealthy friends in St. Augustine. They aspired to remain fashionable throughout their stay at Mount Vernon and Fort Sill. Marion was purportedly the tribe's best dressed woman. Courtesy Frisco Native American Museum (Raymond, Norman, and Moses Loco Collections).

Left to right: Chihuahua, Naiche, Loco, Nana, and Geronimo standing outside the wall surrounding the main post at Mount Vernon, about 1889. Chihuahua is in the clothing that the Apaches criticized him for wearing just after his wife died. Courtesy Alabama Department of Archives and History, Montgomery, Alabama.

239

Geronimo, 1904. During the prison years the Apaches relied on the sales of traditional arts and crafts for money to purchase food and clothing. Geronimo is shown here with two unfinished bows and an arrow. Among other items, he also crafted and sold hand-carved walking sticks and dance rattles, as well as signed photographs of himself. Courtesy Frisco Native American Museum (Raymond, Norman, and Moses Loco Collections).

William Wallace Wotherspoon just after he was promoted to captain, about 1894. Wotherspoon was in charge of the Apache prisoners during most of their stay in Alabama. Courtesy U.S. Army Military History Institute.

Members of Company I, Twelfth Infantry, pose at Mount Vernon, about 1892. Kneeling, left to right: Naiche, Perico, Chatto, probably Kaahteney, and an unidentified man. Standing at far left is Rogers Toclanny, and at far right, Yanoza. Courtesy National Archives and Records Administration.

Apaches learned the fundamentals of baseball from white children in Florida, developed a love for the game, and honed their skills on poorly equipped pickup teams in Alabama such as the one pictured, about 1890. Later, at Fort Sill, Apaches played on fully equipped and uniformed all-Indian teams representing Indian military units at Fort Sill. Bud Shapard personal collection.

Loco in citizen's clothing and a farmer's hat at Mount Vernon, about 1892. By the time the Apaches reached Mount Vernon, dressing in the non-Indian style was commonplace. Courtesy U.S. Army Military History Institute.

Second village, Mount Vernon, about 1892. Unidentified women and children sitting in front of a house on one of the village streets. Courtesy U.S. Army Military History Institute.

Gambling circle in the first village at Mount Vernon, about 1892. At the rear of the group, Major Sinclair (left) and Lieutenant Wotherspoon (right) watch the sport. Gambling was later forbidden. Courtesy Alabama Department of Archives and History, Montgomery, Alabama.

Notables pose in the first village at Mount Vernon, about 1890. Seated, left to right: Chatto, Loco, George Wratten (interpreter), Nana, Fun, and unidentified man. Standing, left to right: Coonie, Binday, Fawn, Chicil, Naiche, Geronimo, Chiricahua Jim, Perico, and Yanoza. This picture of Fun was taken just days before his suicide. Courtesy Museum of the Great Plains, Lawton, Oklahoma.

Loco's son John and his wife, Marion, at home in 1912, still prisoners of war, dressed for church. Courtesy Frisco Native American Museum (Raymond, Norman, and Moses Loco Collections).

Chiricahua survivors. Their numbers reduced from approximately 1,200 in 1870, the 274 surviving members of the Chiricahua, Bedonkohe, and Warm Springs bands pose just before their release as prisoners of war on April 2, 1913. Loco's son John is standing eighth from left, and Marion, his wife, is standing fourth from right. Courtesy Fort Sill National Historic Landmark and Museum.

CHAPTER NINETEEN

Fort Marion, Florida, 1886—1887

If one were looking for a place to warehouse five hundred southwestern Apaches in 1886, Fort Marion, Florida, in the city of St. Augustine, would not immediately come to mind. First, it was small. The fort itself embraced just over three acres. Chatto wryly commented, "Captain Dorst said that they were going to give us sixty square miles of land, but we were taken here and this don't look like sixty miles of land."[1] If history was any indication, confining the Apaches inside its walls was not an impossibility and was perhaps even a reasonable option. In its prime, when Fort Marion, begun by Spaniards in 1672, was called Castillo de San Marcos, the fort's garrison averaged about 450. On one occasion in 1740, the fort's entire garrison of almost one thousand soldiers and sailors squeezed inside for two months during a British siege. It might have been tight, but keeping five hundred Apaches there did not seem problematic. Besides, precedent existed for using Fort Marion as an Indian prison. Some two hundred Seminoles had been locked up there in 1837, and seventy-two Plains Indians spent hard time inside its walls in 1875.[2]

Not only was Fort Marion small, but it was old and run down. The entire structure was built of coquina, a porous stone composed of lime deposits and seashells, impossible to keep sanitary. When Castillo de San Marcos was completed in 1695, it was a showpiece, but the place was allowed to deteriorate after the United States acquired it in 1821. When the Apaches arrived in 1886, troops stationed at nearby St. Francis Barracks were focused on keeping up the St. Augustine National Cemetery adjacent to the barracks. Neither money nor effort was spent on preserving Fort

Marion. By 1886 the crumbling structure had become, by default, more a tourist attraction than a military post. It was in a shabby state. The terreplein was dilapidated and cracked. The casemates below, which might have housed the prisoners, were dank and moldy and leaked badly. The fort's glacis was eroded. The once pristine parade ground was scarred with a sandlot baseball diamond. A large advertising billboard jutted up prominently from center field, and two private, above-ground sewer pipes stretched across the former parade ground from town to Matanzas Bay.[3]

Colonel Romeyn Ayres was commanding Fort Marion when the first Apache prisoners arrived. He tried to air out the old rooms on the fort's lower level. When that failed, he ordered his men to keep bonfires burning day and night inside the casemates. The cavernous chambers remained dank and uninhabitable.

Aside from the inadequate prison accommodations, the government's decision to place five hundred of the country's most dangerous Indians inside the city limits of the nation's top tourist destination appeared to newsmen of the day to be sheer buffoonery. In 1886, a direct rail line from New York turned St. Augustine into a winter resort for very rich and famous northerners. The Rockefellers, Vanderbilts, and Morgans built splendid winter homes there. Henry Flagler, a founder of Standard Oil, not only built a mansion but also was developing two ultra-posh hotels catering to the nation's wealthiest.

A few local citizens complained about putting the warlike Apaches in with such a cosmopolitan crowd, and the press did its best to provoke controversy.[4] For much of the year, however, most of the residents of St. Augustine were upper-crust sophisticates, mostly liberals who would brook no abuse of Noble Redmen trapped in such indelicate circumstances. The news stories slacked off after the editors realized that the citizens of St. Augustine rather liked having the Apaches around.

Indeed, some of St. Augustine's wealthiest citizens were probably responsible for bringing the Apaches to Fort Marion. Florida's big cities at the time, Jacksonville, St. Augustine, and Pensacola, all competed to host the Indian prisoners. It was thought that an exotic collection of wild Indians—under the appropriate restraint, of course—would do wonders for the local tourist and railroad industry. A year after the first Apaches arrived, the army and political officials decided to move them to better circumstances. Reflecting on the political maneuvering that had brought the Indians to town in the first place, Roger Jones, inspector general for the army, warned Washington officials that "it would be well to keep [the move] secret as possible, because all the railroad interests of Eastern Florida and the influential men of that region will make the most strenuous endeavors to prevent it by besieging the War Dept. with petitions and remonstrances against the change which will divert a great deal of travel from that country and cause a loss to the railroads and hotels in that side of the state."[5]

Although Jacksonville and Pensacola fought vigorously to acquire the Apaches, Jacksonville was out of the contest almost immediately—it was too big and lacked facilities. Pensacola probably would have been the best bet, with Fort Pickens, a fort much larger than Marion, sitting on a forty-mile-long island just across the bay from town.

In the end, however, with the likes of the Rockefellers, Vanderbilts, Flaglers, Astors, and Morgans running interference, the government opted to keep the Apaches in St. Augustine. All the infamous Apaches were scheduled to be sent there, if they were not there already, not just as prisoners of war but as the nation's top tourist attraction.[6] However, a glitch arose before the entire tribe could arrive. In September 1886, President Cleveland stopped the train carrying Naiche and Geronimo's thirty-seven holdouts at San Antonio, Texas, to find out exactly what General Miles had promised the Indians. It took until October 20 to determine that Miles had lied to Secretary of War Endicott and the president about the conditions of Geronimo's surrender. During the delay, the citizens of Pensacola swung into action. Geronimo, his celebrity firmly established in newspapers and dime novels, became a prized catch. Petitions and letters from Pensacola bombarded the president, the secretary of war, and Congress, suggesting that it was "all very well to send minor chiefs to . . . old rooms in Fort Marion, but really, Geronimo is the man we want here."[7]

While Geronimo's group was detained in San Antonio, Congressman Robert Davidson used his connections in the Democratic party to sway Cleveland and Endicott. "A move has been set on foot to have some of these red devils sent down to this place and incarcerated at Fort Pickens. Congressman Davidson has been consulted and he has sent a strong recommendation in favor of the scheme to the proper authorities in Washington. If Bob succeeds in this, he can point with pride as having been instrumental in giving Pensacola an attraction which will bring here a great many visitors." Davidson did succeed, and the "Geronimo Indians" were directed to the Pensacola area. Thus, in October 1886, Geronimo and a few men with him became Pensacola's leading players in the competition for Florida's tourist dollars.[8]

Chihuahua, Nana, and their people arrived at St. Augustine in early April 1886. When Colonel Romeyn Ayres's efforts to make the ancient fortress livable failed, he decided that keeping the Indians inside the fort's walls was impractical. He made a camp for the first seventy-seven Apache prisoners on the banks of the North River, about three miles north of the old fort. The North River was a narrow saltwater estuary surrounded by a large tidal swamp. By the middle of June 1886, the *Army and Navy Journal* reported that the Apaches were "now in camp on North Beach, about three miles from town, and seem thoroughly contented and happy. In addition to their tents, they have brush 'wicky-ups' which give the camp very much the same aspect as one should find on the trail." It may have been healthier than living inside the casemates, but not by much.[9]

Colonel Loomis Langdon assumed command of the prison camp on June 16, when Ayres left for an extended sick leave. Langdon immediately recognized that the Apaches could not live inside the fort, but he was equally certain that the arrangement at North Beach was a bad idea. The area was infested with mosquitoes, and the campground was "liable to overflow every fall and winter," creating "the danger of getting drowned." Furthermore, the prisoners would "have to face the diseases peculiar to the low grounds of such localities." Malaria, yellow fever, and cholera had been a problem along the Florida coast for years.[10]

Only three days after he took command, Langdon moved Chihuahua and Nana's people to eighteen army tents atop Fort Marion's terreplein. Just as these seventy-seven first arrivals settled in, the acting secretary of war asked Langdon if he could manage another four hundred or five hundred prisoners. Langdon thought he might be able to fit in twenty more tents for another seventy-five or eighty people, "but the sanitary conditions will be bad." He pointed out that the leaky casemate problem and the size and general condition of the fort rendered the place uninhabitable for so many. He also noted that since the town surrounded the fort, any idea of quartering the Apaches outside the walls was unworkable. General Sheridan's endorsement on Langdon's letter in reply to the secretary, however, indicates that the decision was already a done deal: "The conditions stated by Col. Langdon need not interfere with sending the remainder of the Chiricahua and Warm Springs Indians to Fort Marion." Because of his endorsement, Sheridan was generally accused by the press of selecting Fort Marion, but the political history seems to indicate that President Cleveland made the final decision.[11]

Consequently, when Loco and the delegation arrived on September 18, 128 Sibley tents with wooden floors had been pitched on top of the ancient fortress to house the prisoners. The tents were equipped with standard accessories, framed canvas walls, and "rain caps" to cover the

smoke holes. During the winter months, Sibley stoves, designed specifically for the tents, sat in the center, with four-inch stovepipes extending
to the tops of the tepee-like tents. The prisoners did not sleep on "hard
concrete," coquina, or brick floors, as has been asserted. Sleeping on the
conglomerate or on bricks might have been briefly necessary for the
seventy-seven early arrivals, but by the time Loco and the main body
arrived, the tents sat on raised wooden floors.[12]

The Sibley is a large tent. The army usually slept twelve men to a
tent, but in a pinch it could hold twenty. As a field tent without walls, it
looked like a tepee. For longer stays or to shelter more occupants, canvas
walls were attached. Fort Marion's terreplein could hold 128 Sibleys
with walls if they were arranged atop the terreplein and four bastions in
two offset rows, sixteen to each row. That would leave an uncomfortably
narrow pathway through the "camp." Although the walled version of the
tent gave the Indians more room inside, it required guy lines that stretched
across the passageway. Negotiating the walkway over, under, or around the
lines provoked frequent complaints from visitors. A local doctor, Horace
Caruthers, wrote to the interior secretary in January 1887: "There are
450 men, women, children crowded in the old fort. Their cotton tipis
cover parapets so thickly that it is difficult to thread one's way without
being tripped up by ropes of the tents."[13] After an inspection in March
1887, Herbert Welsh, an Indian rights activist from Philadelphia, complained, "The ramparts are closely crowded with tents, so that but a narrow
space is left for a passageway."[14]

Welsh erroneously charged that "most of the tents are crowded with
occupants." Some of the tents may have had more occupants than others,
but if some appeared crowded, it was by the Apaches' choice, not the
army's. Langdon allowed the Indians to make their own housing arrangements and kept no records of who or how many were in each tent. If the
Indians were evenly distributed, no more than four or five would have
occupied each tent, well under the army's guideline for troop comfort
and health. After the children left for the Carlisle School, only two or three
residents remained in each tent. Although the Indians' tents were tightly
clustered, they were not "crowded with occupants."[15]

Five days after the largest group of prisoners arrived from Fort Apache,
the *Army and Navy Journal* reported that "the Indians are comfortably
lodged in tents, floored and framed, and pitched on the terreplain." In
spite of this, they were living more closely together than Apaches would
choose to if left on their own, and the porous coquina on which the
tents rested could hardly be kept as germfree as a traditional camp in the

mountains. John Bourke observed that the natural coquina conglomerate absorbed filth like a sponge. Consequently, just as Colonel Langdon predicted, the sanitary conditions were bad. When Bourke and Welsh inspected the place in March, Bourke wrote that the "police [cleanup], drainage, and ventilation" were all substandard.[16]

When the Apaches came from Arizona, they brought several serious aliments with them. Malaria was the first to appear, cases turning up only two days after Chihuahua's group arrived in April. The post physician treated about fifteen cases within the first two weeks of the main group's arrival in September. The next batch of new cases was likely caused by local mosquitoes from the North River marshes.

Dysentery was another medical problem for the prisoners. Bacteria in drinking water are usually the primary cause. An artesian well providing fresh clear water was completed just as the Apaches were arriving. Part of the water from the aquifer was diverted and flowed constantly through pipes in order to flush the residue from the fort's single toilet directly into the bay. The well probably lay too close to the latrine and may have caused the Apaches' bowel problems.[17]

Respiratory diseases, colds, influenza, and bronchitis also hammered the Indians throughout their stay in Florida. Their greatest scourge, however—tuberculosis—came to Florida with them. The tuberculosis curse had beset the Chiricahuas for generations, probably from earliest contact with non-Indians. As prisoners, most of the tribe had been crowded on an unventilated train for seven days for the ride east. Then the entire group was clustered into the three-acre fort with daily face-to-face contact. A tuberculosis epidemic was inevitable, but it would not strike with full force until the Indians left St. Augustine.[18]

The military officers who worked directly with the Apache prisoners did everything in their power to keep them as healthy as circumstances would permit. Langdon reported that despite the "excessively crowded" conditions, the camp was kept scrupulously clean. He might have overstated the case. According to Welsh and Bourke, camp sanitation was poor and probably contributed to the prisoners' health problems. Although men were organized into cleaning crews and required to police the fort, Welsh "noticed scraps of bread or meat lying about," and Bourke complained that he saw rats dragging garbage into cubbies, "where much of it rots and ferments into a factor dangerous to health and comfort."[19]

Colonel Langdon employed a local physician, Dr. DeWitt Webb, to watch after the health of the prisoners. Webb required a hospital steward to drench the Indian camp area with "copious amounts" of carbolic acid daily.

Carbolic acid is toxic, however, and heavy exposure causes wheezing, diarrhea, and skin rashes. Langdon and Webb's well-intentioned passion for sanitizing the camp might have aggravated the health problems they were trying to eliminate.[20]

Langdon also had two large, above-ground bathing pools constructed from oak boards sealed with tar. Although he called them bathtubs, they were large enough for a host of children to splash about in at once. The colonel reported that the prisoners "had much improved their cleanliness by the frequent use of the . . . bathtubs," which were "in constant use."[21]

Langdon's commonsense approach to the care and feeding of the Apaches was undermined by directives from Washington. Only two days after the largest group of Indians arrived from Fort Apache, Brigadier General Robert Macfeely, commanding the army's Subsistence Department in Washington, ordered that the Apaches' food rations be reduced by one-half, because the prisoners were not required to do a soldier's work and therefore should not need a full ration. Colonel Langdon objected: "The rations issued the Indians are of good quality, [and] while the attending surgeon reports the quantity sufficient, I desire to express the opinion that the rations should be larger." Sam Bowman, one of the interpreters still with the Indians, opined that the rations at Fort Marion were less than those issued at San Carlos. Langdon continued complaining about the shortage in his monthly reports. His insistence paid off, and by the first week in January 1887 he reported that although the prisoners "really suffered at first owing to the smallness of the ration," by the end of the year they were being adequately supplied.[22]

Herbert Welsh, however, concluded in March that still "the rations are insufficient." The Apache hunger problem was due in part to their refusal to eat pork products. When the Indians refused pork, the army tried offering fresh ocean fish as an alternative, but the Apaches, who had never been keen on fish, declined after seeing the creatures washed up on the Florida beach. From the Indians' perspective, not only were the rations reduced, but part of the issues was inedible. Eventually the army issued beef rations.[23]

Further, the army's menu for the prisoners included no fruits or fresh vegetables, a necessity for the prevention of scurvy. A lieutenant in the quartermaster's office took it upon himself to swap some of the unwanted pork for potatoes and onions.[24] Sympathetic citizens from town soon spotted the food problem and began giving boxes of vegetables and other groceries to Indian families. By early January 1887 the prisoners themselves were able to supplement their army rations with groceries purchased with money they made selling handicrafts to tourists. Consequently, with a little help from their friends and by their own enterprise, the Indians ate reasonably well, at least for the last half of their stay in Florida.[25]

Further adding to the prisoners' problems, no thought was given to clothing for them before cool weather set in. The Apaches came to Florida clad in their Arizona summer wear. Their outfits were inadequate for even a moderate Florida winter, but the winter of 1886–87 in St. Augustine came with record-breaking cold. Finally Dr. Caruthers convinced Senator Henry Dawes, chairman of the Subcommittee on Indian Affairs, to move the War Department to action. Some clothing for the men arrived in December, but ensembles for the women and children did not make it to Fort Marion until March. Even at that, the entire shipment did not reach the prisoners until after they left Florida. By the time Welsh and Bourke visited the Apaches in the latter part of March, temperatures had eased somewhat. Nevertheless, Welsh reflected on the winter past: "The clothing of the Indians during the winter has been totally insufficient and unsuitable. During cold days when, even in St. Augustine, great coats were necessary, the Indian children were obliged to keep within their tents [by the Sibley stoves] for protection. Many of them had nothing to cover their nakedness but a calico slip."[26]

In the meantime, local citizens again came to the rescue. They donated clothing, and several local sewing circles stitched furiously to provide relief. One sewing club made and donated red flannel shirts to each male prisoner. Several days after the gift shirts were distributed, the women returned to bring additional items. They were dismayed to find some of the prisoners wearing as many as six shirts, one over the other, while other men went without. The women protested vigorously to Langdon about the army's unfair distribution. A subsequent investigation discovered that the sewing circle's handiwork had been won and lost in the prisoners' unending card games. After that, under the watchful eyes of the St. Augustine Ladies Sewing Society, no Apache ever again lost his shirt in a card game while at Fort Marion.[27]

During the Apaches' stay in St. Augustine, many townspeople made efforts to befriend the naturally reticent Indians. Most citizens genuinely enjoyed having the new arrivals in town. St. Augustine's mayor expressed the widespread view that the Apaches were a "great addition to the charms of the place."[28] The citizens' sympathetic interest in the prisoners' welfare quickly created friendships that would have been impossible had the Apaches actually been treated as prisoners of war. Everyone was surprised to see the Apaches adjust so quickly to the wealthy white world of St. Augustine and actually flourish there.

CHAPTER TWENTY

Life at Fort Marion

Initially the army kept the Indians carefully guarded and inside the confines of the old fortress. Colonel Langdon, however, soon realized that he was watching over 365 noncombatant women and children and 65 government scouts who had actively served "during the whole or a portion of the time that Geronimo was out." Loco and the entire Washington delegation were on the federal payroll when they were arrested. Chihuahua and Nana and their thirteen or fourteen men could have been classed officially as outlaws, but actually they had been farmers, tricked off the reservation by Geronimo and in the process of surrendering when they were captured. When Langdon concluded that his prisoners were "resigned to their fate" and had no inclination to escape, he became possibly history's most lenient prison camp commandant.[1]

Early on, Langdon wrote that the Indians "have the run of the place" and "are allowed full liberty within the walls." After observing that no escape attempts took place, he further reduced the restrictions: "They are frequently, almost daily, taken out to exercise on the outskirts of the town." Shortly after that the colonel reported that he "was giving the Indians permission to leave the fort so they could exercise properly." Langdon reported that the added freedom "caused no problems since the Apache appeared to be more afraid of the whites than the whites were of them."[2]

Betzinez was surprised at their independence: "You might think that the prisoners of war were confined in the old dungeons at the fort. Actually we were kept in only at night when the great gate was shut. During the day

259

we were allowed to wander around at will, go down town, or any place we chose, without getting permission from the caretaker sergeant. He only required that we be in by dark."³

Freedom proved to be a problem for the Indians more than for anyone else. Before he left for his sick leave, Colonel Ayres complained that the Apaches strolling outside the walls were "swarmed about by the curious and idle . . . disinclining them often to fresh air and exercise." It was discovered that there was less disruption when the men traveled about in groups of fifteen or twenty, accompanied by a single interpreter. The interpreter was along to protect the Indians from "evilly disposed white men," whom Langdon feared would sell them liquor, create some unfortunate incident, or cheat them in their purchases. Groups of formerly fierce warriors were often seen around town, shopping in boutiques for good deals on small items. Because St. Augustine had been a colony of Spain, most local residents spoke Spanish as a second language. Although a number of the Apache men, such as Loco, could muddle through with a little "bad Spanish," and some could speak a bit of pidgin English, they preferred not to talk with non-Indians in town unless an army official was present. Consequently, they did most of their shopping through the interpreter.⁴

Apache women, on the other hand, were seldom bothered by "the curious and idle," probably because of Victorian notions about women. Accordingly, they showed great enthusiasm for mingling with the locals. Women and girls from the fort went to town frequently, generally unaccompanied, to sell their handicrafts and buy food and incidentals.⁵

Once the women of St. Augustine's high society discovered that the Apaches could get along in English or Spanish, it became chic to entertain women prisoners in their homes. Before long, Apache women from Fort Marion topped the guest lists in the best places. Carriage drivers were often seen at the gates of the fort, picking up honored guests and delivering them across town for a tea party or some other affair. Siki, Loco's stepdaughter, and Huerra, Mangas's wife, were especially popular with St. Augustine's high society because of the fluent Spanish they had acquired while they were Mexican captives.⁶

At first Colonel Ayres issued a pass to any tourist or local citizen who wanted a close look at the Indians. The tent city atop the fort was continually crowded with sightseers who piled in to see the "worst Indians in the country." This not only became an administrative nightmare for the military, but the visitors also annoyed the Indians. Orders were soon issued to end indiscriminate visiting "for the gratification of idle curiosity." Only clergymen, physicians, and those "who might be of benefit to the Apaches" were allowed inside the walls to visit the Indian camp. Unaware of the curb on rubbernecking, tourists from out of the area continued to arrive at the commandant's office requesting passes to enter the fort and see the "savages." Langdon, now in charge, denied them, and soon Secretary Endicott began receiving complaints from the tourists' political representatives in Washington. Langdon held firm, and in early September, only five days after the largest group of Apaches arrived, he began placing notices in newspapers to solve the problem. The *Army and Navy Journal* reported, "Colonel Langdon does not believe these Indians were sent there for an exhibition, however willing some tourists may be to make them one, and has therefore directed that no more passes be granted to visit the Indians. As many people come from a distance for this purpose, to save them from disappointment hereafter an official notice has been published in the Florida papers that permits must not be expected by people visiting St. Augustine for that purpose."[7]

Despite the notice that no more passes would be granted, it appears that the policy was loosely interpreted, especially after Ayres returned to duty in October 1886. Betzinez remembered, "We had many visitors at the fort." Nevertheless, the ban on visitors created a stir, mostly in the press. Jacksonville newspapers, still smarting from the loss of the Apache tourist trade, printed a vitriolic article entitled "Remove the Apaches." It complained about the inconvenience to the tourists: "Hundreds of people who visit the ancient city of St. Augustine do so to explore the venerable fort [but] while it harbors its present occupants, visitors are refused admission."[8]

The army made no effort to force the Apaches to work. Women and children gathered firewood, and the women did the cooking, watched after the children, and attended to their men—no change from their camp chores on the reservation. They also picked up the family's daily rations every morning at nine o'clock from Sergeant George Brown.[9]

The most oppressive burden for the men was enforced idleness. Herbert Welsh, the Indian rights activist, complained, "They are employed occasionally in the light and insufficient labor of keeping the fort clean, and in a few odd jobs from time to time. Beyond this, so far as physical work is concerned their time is passed in idleness." Betzinez complained that the former warriors did little but loaf: "The majority of the men had no occupation and didn't learn a trade. The most any of them accomplished was to whittle a few bows and arrows or serve on a detail to clean up around the fort."[10]

The bows and arrows Betzinez mentioned were part of a respectable arts and crafts industry created by the Indians. The bows and arrows became a high-demand item for youngsters in St. Augustine and were among the best sellers in the Apaches' inventory. The Apache women bought glass beads in town and, with their children, collected seashells along the beach. They turned the shells into animal shapes or crosses and strung them together with the beads in elaborate necklaces, bracelets, and other handmade items. Once they located proper substitutes for materials used in the Southwest, weaving baskets became a popular and profitable pastime. Betzinez remembered, "Our women sold bead-work and other handicraft to the sightseers, while the men and boys sold souvenir bows and arrows which they had made." In fact everyone, men and women, made "Indian objects" to sell to the tourists. The artistically inclined bought crayons, watercolors, pencils, and paper and produced quality art that was a fast seller. Betzinez was one who profited from his skills as an artist: "For my own part I had a flair for drawing and painting. So in the evening I made pictures of various wild animals and other scenes from the west, which I sold to the tourists and other visitors."[11]

Virtually anything the Apaches could whittle, stitch, craft, or draw sold quickly. Souvenir shop owners snapped up items the Indians did not sell directly to tourists. Even the wealthy Herbert Welsh reported that the Indians had turned a "tidy profit" from their arts and crafts operation. Estimates of the Apaches' earnings over their seven-month stay in St. Augustine ran as high as $10,000—about $200,000 in modern dollars. In addition, local citizens hired a few of the prisoners, men and women, to do odd jobs. Together, it was enough to indulge their whims in the local emporiums and, more importantly, to supplement the army's short rations and put a little away for lean times to come.[12]

Doing odd jobs and making crafts for sale left the Indians with great blocks of idle time, but Langdon's lenient policies toward prisoner care and a sympathetic local citizenry combined to provide a full calendar of activities to fill the hours. Virtually all the prisoners took advantage of the opportunity to walk unsupervised along North Beach. Weather per-mitting, women and children often strolled the beaches daily, gathering shells and other seashore treasures. Window shopping in town was also popular. Langdon organized sightseeing junkets, not only to relieve the boredom but also to impress the Apaches with the sights of the "civi-lized" world.[13] Betzinez remembered that "on Saturdays and Sundays there were organized for us numerous excursions to near and distant cities and other points of interest."[14]

The prisoners spent many of the empty hours in traditional social activities. *Frank Leslie's Illustrated Newspaper* reported, "It is said that they

sit about at Fort Marion and while the time away singing, in their peculiar monotone, sad and familiar songs."[15] There were no restrictions
against holding traditional dances in the fort's courtyard or on the old
parade ground. Betzinez noted that "on several occasions the Indians
were given permission to hold a dance."[16] John Bourke felt lucky to be
able to view a four-day ceremonial, apparently to ward off the bad luck
the Apaches had been having. Mountain Spirit dances were organized as
girls came of age. The Indians also convinced their jailers to allow social
dances, but without the usual quantities of alcohol consumed during
reservation parties. Langdon was an ardent prohibitionist and ferreted out
bootleggers with bulldoggish tenacity. He caught several visitors attempting
to smuggle bottles into the camp. Nevertheless, just as in Arizona and
New Mexico, "a certain class of white men," spurred on by high profits,
seemed able to surmount the most daunting obstacles. Inevitably, a few
bottles slipped past the embargo. Because the Apache men were free to
roam around town, a small amount of liquor unavoidably found its way
into camp through that route. Herbert Welsh acknowledged the problem
and expressed his wrath at the townsfolk who profited by selling whiskey
to the prisoners. He suggested that the illegal dealers should spend some
time as prisoners themselves in the nearby federal prison.[17]

The Apaches filled hundreds of hours with lengthy card games, often
involving extraordinarily large bets. After the shirt incident, Langdon
attempted to limit the ante, but wagers continued to include almost anything. Other, more physical games had been popular on the reservation,
but they required open space outside the fort and invariably attracted
crowds of spectators. The self-conscious adults seldom gave them a try.[18]

The younger boys of the tribe had no such inhibitions and mixed
freely with white youngsters on the green, just beyond the moat. The boys
from town taught their Apache counterparts the art of constructing paper
pinwheels, which the Indian children would hold between their teeth
while racing about the fort's green, watching cross-eyed as their creations
spun before their noses. The Apaches were introduced to baseball for the
first time. The Indian boys who learned the game in Florida became the
foundation for an all-Apache team, "The Apaches," that achieved distinction years later at Fort Sill. The Indian boys in turn taught the white
youngsters bow making and archery.

Young girls had fewer opportunities and played mostly among themselves. Handmade dolls and small cradleboards were popular. Several games
similar to jacks were prevalent, and the girls were geniuses at creating cats'
cradles and unusual string figures. Many of the girls and younger children

spent time along the beach collecting shells or playing in the sand. No records could be found that the "young ladies" from town spent any time playing with the Apache girls.[19] Sewing was one of the most frequently seen activities among the Apache women. A local sewing circle from town organized informal classes and visited the fort regularly to teach the American style of stitchery, making garments for their Apache students and their families. The local sewing clubs provided materials without charge until the military appropriated funds for thimbles, thread, and cloth.[20]

Volunteers also organized classes for men. Mr. Warden, a local building contractor, furnished tools, lumber, and a woodworking instructor at his own expense to teach the Apache men the art of carpentry. After the program's initial success, Betzinez reported, "the War Department bought lumber and carpenters' tools. They appointed instructors to teach us the trade of carpenter, at least all who wanted to learn."[21]

The army, Indian Rights organizations, and local white citizens became concerned about educating the child prisoners soon after they arrived. Locals formed the "Society for the Preservation of Education Among Indians Now Quartered at St. Augustine," which campaigned for the government to establish an Indian industrial school in town, similar to the one at Carlisle, Pennsylvania. While that effort was under way, Mrs. Horace Caruthers and Sara Ann Mather, who had operated Miss Mather's Female Seminary in St. Augustine before the Civil War, held classes for the Indian youngsters in one of the fort's casemates. Just a month before the prisoners were transferred from Fort Marion to Alabama, the Sisters of St. Joseph, from a nearby convent, received a contract from the Indian Office to educate the Apaches for $7.50 quarterly per student. The Indian bureau chipped in with a school outfit for each student.[22]

The army began to consider sending the prisoners' children to the Carlisle Indian Industrial School at about the time Chihuahua and Nana's people arrived at Fort Marion in April 1886. Once the main body of Indians arrived in September, the idea of reducing the numbers inside the fort by sending all the children elsewhere became an attractive proposition. Mather and Caruthers's program operated for only two hours a day, and the Sisters of St. Joseph held daily classes for about an hour and a half. Although the two private programs were probably satisfactory, officials believed a full-time education program would more quickly "civilize" the children and would be seen as a benevolent gesture on the part of the administration. The press strongly supported the idea of a full-time program. The Jacksonville *Florida Times-Union* thought it was easy to see the young prisoners' "brightness and general intelligence," and it would be a pity if they "grew up in ignorance."[23]

Colonel Langdon was among the first to recommend that as many students as possible be sent to Carlisle as a way to make more room in the fort, but he urged that they not be sent unless they were accompanied by their families. Captain Richard Pratt, founder and superintendent of the Carlisle School, rejected that proposition, but everyone was afraid of a repeat of the 1884 fiasco. In that episode, Loco and a few others had allowed their children to go to Carlisle from the reservation, but most of the Chiricahuas rejected the idea. Under their present circumstances, and given the Apaches' reluctance to be separated from their young, there was no doubt that sending the children off to boarding school was out of the question as far as the Indians were concerned. In the end, the War Department, the Indian Office, and Captain Pratt, with President Cleveland's approval, hit upon a plan to abduct the children even as their parents watched.

On the appointed day in early November 1886, most of the children were playing on the parade ground when soldiers suddenly blocked the fort's entrance, surrounded the children, and marched them off to a waiting train. Potential students still inside the fort were carried out individually, kicking and screaming, past their distraught parents. Before the train left for Pennsylvania, the youngsters were screened for health problems, and four were rejected as too sick, probably with tuberculosis.

Loco's family fared better than many in the first Carlisle snatch. Clee-hn sensed that something was wrong when she saw the number of soldiers increasing and called to her eleven-year-old son John from over the edge of the parapet. John managed to dash back into the fort and to the terreplein before the trap was sprung. Clee-hn pushed the boy into Loco's tent and buried him beneath a pile of bedding and clothing. She then lounged atop the pile, apparently unconcerned as troops scoured the camp for additional children. Several accounts exist of children hiding under long skirts or in barrels and boxes stashed around the fort. A few escaped by running along the beach.[24]

Stephen Mills, the lieutenant who had been on the ridge behind Loco's camp at Sierra Enmedio five years earlier, was in charge of the prisoners' affairs at Fort Marion. He later said that separating the children from their parents was the most distasteful thing he had ever done during his thirty-year career. The Apaches' descendants still consider the "stealing of the children" the cruelest action ever taken by the government against the Chiricahuas. Nevertheless, a second sweep through the camp a month later took an additional forty-four for the Carlisle experience.[25]

The army changed tactics for a third roundup on April 18, 1887. This time Captain Pratt himself came along, bringing one of the Apache boys seized earlier. The Carlisle student was brought to extol "the value to the Indians in attending this school" and to enlist volunteers. Not a single youngster stepped forward. A third sweep was then conducted, after which Betzinez reported, "They lined us all up in front of Captain Pratt, who went down the line choosing forty-nine boys and girls to return with him to Carlisle. He also selected thirteen young men including me. The other twelve were married and some of them had children, but it was explained that families could accompany the married students." Up until this point, all the young people taken to Carlisle had been between the ages of twelve and twenty-two. Betzinez was twenty-five.[26]

Although John Loco managed to evade all three snatches, the Loco family otherwise did not fare as well in the April sweep. Talbot Goody, Chief Loco's grandson, was among those Pratt selected. Another of Loco's grandchildren, fourteen-year-old Nahdoyah, was caught running bare-footed on North Beach. She apparently dropped one shoe as she was escorted from the beach and selected from Pratt's lineup. Family stories say she wore one shoe all the way to Carlisle, but more likely she traveled to school unshod. She survived Carlisle, married Benedict Jozhe Sr., and became the mother of Benedict Jr., who was later a long-serving tribal chairman for the tribe in Oklahoma. She is remembered as Mabel Jozhe. The annual report of the commissioner of Indian affairs for 1887 lists 156 Apache students at Carlisle. About fifty youngsters under the age of twelve remained for the Sisters of St. Joseph to educate. Mrs. Caruthers and Miss . Mather reorganized and also opened a class for twenty-five men.[27]

After the removal of the children, about 350 prisoners remained in Fort Marion. Three ill-starred decisions that came out of Washington— the selection of Fort Marion as the location for the prison camp, the reduction of rations, and the late shipment of winter wear—inevitably combined to wear down the Apaches' resistance to contagious diseases. Illnesses and deaths among the prisoners began to mount. More than 170 cases of malaria, or "remittent fever," were treated among the prisoners. Because of the Indians' weakened condition, the recurring attacks became life threatening. A bronchitis epidemic circulated through the camp, killing five or six children. Diarrhea often developed into dysentery, increasing the fatalities. An unrecorded number of Apaches died of tuberculosis, possibly as many as fifteen. Before they died, they unwittingly spread the disease to as many as half the tribe.

The unwholesome conditions in the Indian camp brought out legions of civil rights activists, vociferously complaining to federal authorities. Dr. Horace Caruthers was one of the more steadfast advocates of humane treatment of the Apaches. Although Herbert Welsh and the Indian Rights Association received more credit nationally for their work on behalf of the Apaches, Caruthers's less flamboyant endeavors were no less effective.[28]

Led by Caruthers's efforts, a barrage of letters requesting better conditions for the Apaches poured into congressional offices. Interested people and organizations throughout the East began to take up the prisoners' cause. The Women's Indian Rights Association pressured the secretary of war for a more charitable handling of the prisoners. Caruthers, a man of some influence in Washington, convinced Henry Teller, former secretary of the interior and now a recently elected senator, to inspect the prisoners' condition during the spring of 1887. Afterward, Teller wrote to Secretary of War Endicott with his conclusion: "I desire, however, to call your attention to the necessity of providing more room and better accommodations for these Indians. It is not possible to accommodate them in a humane manner at Fort Marion."[29]

Caruthers also alerted the Indian Rights Association to conditions in Fort Marion in early January 1887. Corresponding Secretary Herbert Welsh made an informal and unannounced visit there later that month. He returned to Washington insisting on a formal investigation. John Bourke, who remained on duty in Washington, had continued to follow the Apaches' descending course and had linked up with Welsh in May 1886. He began feeding Welsh restricted information about the prisoners from within the War Department. Welsh then specifically requested that Bourke assist the Indian Rights Association with the investigation. There was some delay while Secretary Endicott tried to avoid any investigation at all, especially one headed by the two Apache advocates. Finally, after intervention by the politically potent Boston Indian Citizenship Committee, Welsh and Bourke left for Florida on March 8, 1887. The Indian Rights Association went public with its report in late April. It was a barn burner. Welsh damned the incarceration of peaceful Indians along with guilty ones, slammed the crowded conditions, cursed the food shortages, bemoaned the lack of adequate clothing, and railed over the absence of productive activity for the prisoners.[30]

Apparently hoping for information to counter Welsh's expected allegations, General Sheridan ordered a sub-rosa War Department inquiry during the same month that Welsh and Bourke toured Fort Marion. Colonel Ayres supervised the army's secret investigation and reported the worst—that most of the prisoners had at one time or another been scouts working for the government, and almost 80 percent of the women and children were families of scouts. When he reported his findings to Sheridan, Ayres confided that "care has been taken, in collecting these points, that they be not public."[31]

The association's report leaked out in late March, almost before the ink was dry and well before it was printed for distribution. Suddenly, everybody in the administration was distressed over the Apaches' situation. Newspaper accounts of the report claimed that its publication "had given the President much anxiety." Secretary Endicott told Bourke that the president was concerned over the Florida situation and claimed that the prisoner Apaches "had been under discussion by the Cabinet at various times for several weeks."[32]

The *Philadelphia Record* reported, "The agitation set on foot by Senator Dawes and Mr. Herbert Welsh relative to the imprisonment of the Apache Indians who are at Fort Marion, Florida has had its effect upon the President [Cleveland] who brought the matter up in a cabinet meeting on April 5, and has caused the Secretary of War to prepare an order for the removal of the Indians to a more secluded reservation."[33]

As soon as the Welsh report was out, every Indian rights organization in the country organized a petition calling for improvement in the prisoners' conditions and demanded to know why so many innocents were imprisoned. All the organizations had direct connections with the press, and within days, virtually every large newspaper east of the Mississippi had printed lurid articles about conditions at Fort Marion. The prestigious *Frank Leslie's Illustrated Newspaper* printed a compelling editorial titled "Fair Play for the Apaches." Average citizens wrote in criticizing General Miles, President Cleveland, General Sheridan, and sundry other bureaucrats in the Interior and War Departments for the Apaches' maltreatment and demanding better.[34]

The administration went into damage control. Endicott suggested that the Welsh report was slanted and unfair. Two weeks after the Indian Rights Association's report went public, Welsh met with the president, who made an undistinguished effort to put the best spin on the situation. Cleveland said, "in regard to the Apache Prisoners that there was not time to separate the guilty from the innocent ones before taking them down there. There was an urgency about it [the situation in Arizona] that did not admit of delay." Under continuing public scrutiny, Cleveland said that "he did not think there was such a crowded condition as to endanger health," but he promised to move the Apaches to a healthier location. He noted, however, that the army "was having difficulty finding the proper place to locate them."[35]

At first the administration tried to have the Apaches at Fort Marion join the Geronimo group at Fort Pickens. Both Langdon, now supervising the Apaches at Pickens, and Ayres at Fort Marion thought it was a good idea. The Indians would be away from town, in a healthier situation with more room. General Howard, now commanding the Division of the Atlantic, was enthusiastic, pointing out that because Fort Pickens was on an island, visiting by sightseers would be easier to control. Congressman Davidson may have been behind the idea. Pensacola's tourist industry salivated at the prospect of the entire Chiricahua nation camped across the bay from town.[36]

On the other hand, Caruthers vehemently protested the idea, pointing out that Santa Rosa Island was just as humid and no healthier than St. Augustine. Typhoid, cholera, and yellow fever epidemics were annual events along the Florida panhandle. Much of the coastal population in that area retreated inland every year to avoid the seasonal medley of diseases. Malaria was so common that it was treated as a nuisance, and to top it off, hundreds of tubercular patients had moved to the area erroneously believing that the warm, humid climate would help their affliction.

Bourke picked up word of the planned removal to Fort Pickens from his contacts inside the War Department and forewarned Welsh. Welsh quickly fired up the Boston Indian Citizenship Committee, the Indian Rights Association, and the Women's National Indian Association. The Fort Pickens move was off the table within four days.[37]

Herbert Welsh focused the Indian Rights Association's efforts on relocating the Apaches to a more rural site. The administration was also looking for somewhere rural, east of the Mississippi but well out of the public's view. The *Mobile Register* printed a government announcement that "it has been decided at the War Department to remove the Apache Indians now at Fort Marion to a more northerly location. . . . It is thought best that they should not be held in a place so much frequented by visitors as Fort Marion now is and they will benefit by a change. . . . The change is understood to be the result of a consideration of the entire matter at a Cabinet meeting during the past week."[38]

As far as the army was concerned, Mount Vernon Barracks, Alabama, fit the bill. Thirty miles north of Mobile, Mount Vernon was isolated deep in a forbidding forest. Besides, it was on a rail line, making it only a short trip from St. Augustine and easy to supply. On orders from Secretary Endicott, Captain John Bourke inspected Mount Vernon Barracks and pronounced it to be "one of the prettiest posts in the army."[39]

On April 16, 1887, Bourke gave a positive report to Secretary Endicott and was taken directly to President Cleveland, to whom he repeated his findings. Eleven days later the Apaches departed Fort Marion for Alabama. They left St. Augustine in the dark of night to avoid protests from local citizens.

On the morning of April 27 Colonel Ayres wired Washington: "I have sent under charge of 2nd Lieutenant John Conklin, Jr., 2nd Artillery, and a proper guard, 30 to Fort Pickens, Florida, these are the wives and children of the Indians now confined at Fort Pickens, and all the rest, 354, to Mount Vernon Barracks, Alabama."[40]

On the same day, the Jacksonville *Florida Times-Union* gleefully reported that as of one o'clock that morning, the "Ancient City is now rid of one of its greatest attractions—the Indian." Fourteen soldiers and 354 Indian prisoners boarded a special train to Jacksonville. There they transferred to eight passenger coaches of the Savannah, Florida, and Western Railroad. The sympathetic reporter wrote, "The people [of St. Augustine] readily pitied their position and misfortunes."[41]

At St. Augustine, Loco's people perhaps saw a different side of the Americans. Many had even come to like the place and the people. When the move was announced, a few Apaches applied to stay with families in St. Augustine, but none apparently remained except twenty-two or twenty-three who were left in sandy graves along North Beach. The Chiricahuas had been careful to bury their dead in desolate places, always at night, to conceal the bodies from the ever-present souvenir hunters. In spite of their precautions, grave robbers found one of the burials a year after the Indians left St. Augustine and stripped it clean of artifacts.[42]

There can be no question that the Apaches missed their free and easy life in the West and despised their confinement. Nevertheless, it would be a stretch to imagine them as prisoners of war in the sense the term is usually understood. No skeletal prisoners stared pitifully through barbed wire with sunken eyes. "Kill zones," "dead lines," torture, beatings, and executions were nonexistent. The Apaches were apparently free to move about the area during daylight hours. Some developed strong friendships with local people. Their arts and crafts business made remarkable profits. They held dances and social events, played games, went on long walks in town and along the beach, and took adult education courses, and the children went to school with St. Augustine children. Some Apaches worked at jobs in St. Augustine. The government sponsored weekend tours to nearby cities.

Bad decisions made in Washington were their bane. The food shortage was brought on by a malfeasant decision made by one bureaucrat. Yet the Indians suffered from hunger only briefly at St. Augustine. The ration deficiency was resolved by their own enterprise and by food donated by local citizens. The clothing shortage came from ignorance and was ameliorated by local sewing circles. The crowded conditions resulted from a political decision that ultimately brought on the tuberculosis plague that decimated the tribe, but the death rate at St. Augustine was probably about what it would have been in Arizona. Doctors treated the sick responsibly with the most modern techniques available at the time. Separating the children from their parents to be sent to Carlisle was a despicable act. That the people of St. Augustine were already in the process of establishing an education program only compounded the error.

Romeyn Ayres, commanding Fort Marion when the Apaches arrived, took sick leave less than two months after Chihuahua and Nana arrived. He returned in October 1886, about a month after Loco's and Chatto's people came, still a sick man. He died eight months after the Apaches left Fort Marion. Loomis Langdon assumed command and administered the prisoners' affairs during Ayres's absence, from the middle of June 1886 until late October that year. He was then transferred to Fort Pickens to watch over Geronimo's people until they left for Alabama. Ayres's physical condition might have been responsible for his apathy toward the Apaches. When he returned to duty, he continued Langdon's lenient administration of the Chiricahuas. Langdon had set a precedent for the next twenty-six years of the Apaches' confinement in Alabama and Oklahoma.

CHAPTER TWENTY-ONE

Mount Vernon, Alabama, 1887–1894

In 1887, Mount Vernon, Alabama, was a one-dirt-road town nestled at the southern end of a six-million-acre pine forest that stretched from Mobile to Tuscaloosa. Downtown consisted of a post office, two general stores, and a cotton gin. Several bars near town provided an assortment of liquor refreshments. After the Apaches arrived, a small railroad depot was added because of a dazzling increase in tourist traffic. Although the town lay on the main line of the Mobile and Birmingham railroad and only thirty miles north of the growing seaport metropolis of Mobile, Mount Vernon, by any standard, was remote.[1]

The 2,262-acre military post, Mount Vernon Barracks, sat atop a grassy slope two miles distant from and 224 feet above the town. A twelve-foot brick wall encircled the post, giving it an imposing appearance when viewed from downtown Mount Vernon.[2]

The humidity in that part of Alabama remains at a constant 70 to 80 percent on most days. Rainfall is rarely less than four inches a month. For five months a year, the average temperature ranges between the high eighties and the mid-nineties. Doctor Horace Caruthers in St. Augustine had thought Mount Vernon's location might be a bit healthier than Fort Marion's, but "only slightly." Interpreter Sam Bowman had no doubts when he wrote to Herbert Welsh, "There is hardly any improvement in their [living] condition. . . . They will never improve at this place. . . . The inhabitants tell me that no one but the colored race who are born here can stand it, being swampy and malarious. . . . They prophesy an early death to the Indians."[3]

Nevertheless, most people in Alabama considered the "salubrious pine woods" around Mount Vernon to be a sanctuary from the hot-weather maladies that ravaged Gulf Coast residents during the summer. There was no doubt in most minds, including those of the Apaches when they arrived, that living at Mount Vernon would be healthier than living at Fort Marion. There was also no doubt in the local citizens' minds that with the nation's most popular tourist attraction in town, the local economy would also be much healthier.[4]

On April 28, 1887, the day after they left St. Augustine, 354 Apaches arrived at Mount Vernon. The forty-six dependents from Geronimo's band had been dropped off at Fort Pickens on the ride over from Fort Marion and did not arrive at Mount Vernon until thirteen months later, on May 13, 1888. One hundred fifty-six children remained at Carlisle.[5]

From the very first the Apaches were free to select campsites anywhere in the dense woods on the two-thousand-acre military post. Using the Sibley tents brought from Fort Marion, the Indians scattered into several camps that, except for the lack of wickiups, might have been mistaken for a large traditional ranchería in the Southwest.[6]

Tent living at Mount Vernon was temporary. The matter of putting the Indians in their first houses, ever, began in September 1887, when the Apaches started clearing an area north of the post's main gate, cutting logs and erecting cabins. By January 1888, thirty-five log cabins with hand-hewn wood shingle roofs and pine plank flooring were mostly finished. Construction on another twenty-seven was completed by February. More were built when Geronimo's group arrived in May. The tiny cottages each consisted of two ten-square-foot rooms connected by a ten-foot covered breezeway. One small window in each room served for ventilation. A Sibley stove provided heat. The Indians did their cooking outside except during foul weather, when they cooked under the breezeway.

Some later accounts note that the cabins had dirt floors and that the Indians had no furniture and slept on the ground. This may have happened before the houses were completed, because the army wanted the Apaches out of the winter weather as soon as possible. A few of the abodes might have been left with "swept dirt" floors, but several accounts describe "two floored rooms" in all the cabins. As for furniture, Zele commented, "They gave me a house to live in—I live in it; a chair to sit on—I sit on it; a bed to sleep in—I sleep in it; they told me to take good care of them, and I do it." Zele did not mention his table, but he had one.[7]

A few Sibley tents were left standing among the log cabins. For the most part, however, in less than a year after their arrival in Alabama, the prisoners were living in floored bungalows, complete with furniture made by the Indians and a couple of professional carpenters.[8]

A *New York Times* reporter described the Apache village: "It would be difficult to find anything more picturesque and interesting than the camp of the Chiricahua Apache Indians now held prisoners of war at Mount Vernon Barracks, Alabama. It consists of a hundred or more cabins [actually about seventy cabins after Geronimo's arrival] and a few wigwams, which the older women have been unable to abandon."[9] A reporter from Mobile found that "the Indians . . . lived in houses and were as comfortable as mortals ever got to be. . . . They slept on cots and under mosquito bars."[10]

Major William Sinclair, commanding Mount Vernon Barracks when the Indians arrived, was aware that the Apaches had made no attempt to escape during their time in Florida. After a brief period of keeping one sentry in each of the different camps, he discontinued that practice. He then removed the requirement that the prisoners be in their camps after dark. George Wratten, who had been the interpreter at Fort Pickens and moved to Mount Vernon with Geronimo's group, remarked, "These Indian prisoners of war are virtually on parole. They are not confined or guarded (as one would expect) and are allowed to come and go when and where they please, provided only that their conduct is proper." One northern reporter noted that the prisoners "are daily met coming and going between their village and the trading stores at Mount Vernon, where they are both sellers and buyers."[11] Other visitors who came to Mount Vernon to see the Indians were also surprised by the prisoners' unrestricted freedom. Less than two weeks after the Apaches were moved to Alabama, one reporter noted, "It seems that the Indians are not kept as prisoners, but are allowed freedom of movement. There were a number at the depot when the train arrived."[12]

It was not long before the Apaches were allowed to travel unattended by train to Mobile. To get there they mastered the art of commuting—the etiquette of it all—fares, schedules, and depot decorum. The $1.50 round-trip ticket was no problem.[13] They could travel from Mount Vernon to Mobile in the morning and return in the evening. The *Mobile Register* observed that the Apaches "were becoming civilized fast. They curse the railroad when the trains are behind time."[14]

When the Indians arrived at Mount Vernon Barracks on April 28, 1887, they were still a ragged-looking lot. Two reporters, one from New York and one from Mobile, described the Indians' outfits. "Their clothes consisted chiefly of two shirts and cotton drawers. . . . Only one man was seen wearing civilized clothes. He had on jeans trousers and a hickory shirt. Most women wore Mother Hubbards."[15]

The last of the clothes ordered while the Indians were in Florida arrived shortly after the Apaches reached Mount Vernon in April. It was a disappointing assortment of twenty-year-old surplus Civil War uniforms and "civilian" suits cut from discarded tents and mattress covers. Both the uniforms and the canvas suits were uncomfortable in the Alabama humidity and were quickly discarded, although pictures of the prisoners indicate that some of the men continued to wear the outfits for a while.[16]

While in Florida, the Apaches had acquired a taste for stylish clothes, probably from the swells in St. Augustine. When they became more financially independent, they began to shop for their own clothing at the local general stores in Mount Vernon or in downtown Mobile. This prompted the army's inspector general to recommend that purchases of government clothing for the prisoners be abandoned. By June 1888, anyone who had peeked inside the Apaches' cabins might have noticed two or three Sunday dresses and bandboxes apparently containing "the latest style of hats" for the women. One woman wrote to her son at Carlisle, "We live very well here. We work and get nice things, coats and dresses and everything we want."[17]

Among the older set, Chief Chihuahua had developed a penchant for fashion and was undoubtedly the best dressed of the lot. Sophie Shepard, a teacher in the school established for the Indian children in 1889, noted that he shocked his fellow Apaches by appearing in public only two days after one of his wives died, wearing a stovepipe hat, a ruffled shirt front, and cuffs. His detractors deplored the fact that the old war leader had become a "dude," and his popularity faded because of his vanity and constant primping.[18]

Among the teenagers, John Loco, Loco's son, was the acknowledged leader in the younger generation's quest for sartorial splendor. Sophie Shepard, who was sensitive to such achievements, described John and his new suit in detail:

> Several of them [students] have work by which they earn three, four, and five dollars a month. For instance, Johnnie Loco, son of Chief Loco receives three dollars a month for taking care of the horse of one of the sergeants. . . . To our great amazement, and, I need not add, pleasure, Johnnie Loco saved his small wages until he had accumulated fifteen dollars, in order to buy himself

an extra suit of clothes to wear to his "parties," and also a rain coat, because he necessarily has to go out in the rain, not only to his work, but to school, as we hold the sessions regardless of weather. . . . So John's coat is a wise provision, though he by no means limits its use to rainy days. He came to see us the evening after he returned from Mobile with his precious cargo. The stars were shining radiantly, and a young crescent was hanging in the west, but there stood John at the door, covered from head to foot with rubber. His beautiful new suit was, of course, under it, and peeping out from the long sleeves was a pair of kid gloves. He also wore a new felt hat—and very pretty and soft it was— which he took off, and in the most insinuating, confidential manner asked me to smell it. I did so. It was . . . delicately perfumed. He is evidently acquiring aesthetic tastes. . . . No one seemed in the least jealous of John's magnificence.[19]

Initially, clothing was not the most pressing issue for the Apaches after they arrived in Alabama. General Macfeely's policy of providing half rations remained in effect after their transfer. Fortunately, when the prisoners left St. Augustine, they took with them a sizable amount of cash saved from their crafts venture and substantial gifts of money given to them by their wealthy white friends just before their departure. Additionally, a little money from the sale of the livestock confiscated when they left Holbrook finally reached them just before they were to leave Florida. The prisoners used their savings to supplement their scanty rations during the first few weeks at Mount Vernon.[20]

Their personal funds quickly ran short. Only a month after their arrival, Major Sinclair reported his concern: "As the government does not furnish them with sufficient beef, they have been buying cattle, sheep, etc., with the money they brought from St. Augustine, but it is believed that their money is almost exhausted, and as they have no market here for their bows, arrows, and trinkets, they have no prospects for earning more. The inedible nature of a large portion of the meat further reduced the prisoners' food ration. . . . The contractor who is now furnishing the Indians with beef under regular contract for the post, until a contract can be made for them, having heard of their fondness for head, heart, liver, etc. has attempted to send those parts in lieu of good beef. The Indians do not eat head, liver, etc., and do not want the heart."[21]

Macfeely in Washington did not respond to the initial complaint, and in July 1887 Sinclair again asked that the prisoners' rations be restored.

"The Indians still complain of hunger and weakness from want of sufficient food. My recommendation of last month that the rations of the
Indians be increased is respectfully but urgently repeated." Again, no action
came from the tightfisted Macfeely. When a score of children died of
malnutrition, the Apaches became sullen and balky. In September 1887
Sinclair warned the adjutant general, "They have sold or pawned about
all of their private effects; they have sold the greater part of the blankets
issued to them at St. Augustine, Florida by the Quartermaster Department. They have tried to sell and pawn their crosses and other religious
articles. All of this has been done to buy food. When they came here,
they did not beg, their want has reduced them to that, but there are but
a few people here to beg from and they are mostly poor and have but little
to give. It will be readily understood that not getting sufficient food, they
are becoming morose and discontented, and have to be watched much
more carefully."[22]

Sinclair, taking his lead from the quartermaster in St. Augustine, began
swapping the less needed and unwanted rations for potatoes, onions,
milk, eggs, and special items for the sick. He also ordered land cleared
for gardens, and by summer's end in 1887 the Apaches were producing
vegetables for themselves with enough left over for sale.[23]

The prisoners also came up with an ingenious way to supplement
their diet with fresh meat. Often, the train through Mount Vernon col-
lided with a cow lolling on the tracks. Railroad regulations required that
fresh kill be buried immediately. After hitting a cow, the engineer blew a
"cattle alarm" to attract local workers to bury the carcass. The hungry
Apaches quickly learned to recognize the dead-cow whistle and raced
out to butcher the unfortunate animal before the burial party could
arrive. Although one side of the cow had been damaged, if butchered
quickly, the entire cow was edible.[24]

Finally, on October 12, 1887, the War Department ordered full army
rations for the prisoners. By November, eight months after the Apaches
arrived in Alabama, Dr. Walter Reed, assistant post surgeon, was able to
report, "It is believed that the ration now issued is adequate in all respects."
Following that, no complaints appear to have been made about the quantity of the prisoners' rations. By July 1889 Sinclair reported that the
Apaches' primary reason for doctor visits was stomach problems caused
by overeating.

By the end of 1890, the *Mobile Register* announced that a new dining
hall and kitchen had been completed. The newspaper noted that Lieutenant William W. Wotherspoon, who replaced Sinclair in June 1890,

thought it was essential for the Indians to have a good diet, and a central dining area would allow supervision of the Apaches' nutritional habits. The Indians apparently had the option of dining out or eating at home. By the middle of February 1891, Wotherspoon bragged that the barracks had a bakery for preparing the prisoners' bread, and "in a short time I shall have another cookhouse." As an afterthought he reported that "in addition to their personal gardens, some men began clearing land for a farm."[25]

Initially, to contend with the ration shortages, the Apaches revived their arts and crafts enterprise to raise money for food. Contrary to William Sinclair's observation that there was "no market here for their bows, arrows, and trinkets," a modest outlet for handmade Indian goods existed when the Indians arrived. It mushroomed after the prisoners settled in. The railroad had come through Mount Vernon in 1873, making the area a popular day-trip destination for Mobilians. Interpreter George Wratten noted that "the placing of the Indians at Mt. Vernon will add greatly to the attractiveness of that place as a Sunday school picnic resort." Also, well before any Apaches were on the scene, families from the coast retreated to the area in the summer to avoid the coastal diseases, creating a hefty seasonal gain in population.[26]

The Apaches' arrival was the biggest thing to happen in Mount Vernon since the military post had been built in the 1830s. Merchants in both Mount Vernon and Mobile rejoiced over the economic bonanza. The Apaches' trinkets-for-tourists trade began almost immediately. Ten days after the Indians arrived in the "piney woods of Alabama," the Alabama State Artillery, a Confederate veterans' group, and the Independent Order of Odd Fellows of Mobile sponsored two well-attended fund-raising excursions, sending up to a thousand tourists "to see the famous Apaches" on a single weekend. Nine days later the black churches of Mobile sponsored a large expedition, nine rail cars full, to see the Apaches and raise funds for the Colored Orphan's Home. So it went, a little business every day and crowds of tourists, often in the hundreds, on the weekends and holidays.[27]

The visits increased in number and size as civic, social, and church organizations planned special events to see the "Indian village" year-round. Schools throughout Mobile periodically held outings in Mount Vernon. Spring Hill College held a large picnic and reunion there every spring. And all this is not to mention train passengers buying crafts from Apache vendors on the station platform during the scheduled daily stops at Mount Vernon.

A Mobile reporter rhapsodized about Alabama's newest holiday destination: "The United States Garrison is near at hand, while the Indians are a novelty of which the visitor would never tire." The Mobilian's fascination with the Apaches and the increased passenger traffic to Mount Vernon were not lost on local railroad executives. By late June 1888 the railroad began to offer attractive excursion packages. It frequently arranged special tours and outings for "reputable" groups so that "the Indian camp could be visited and the peculiar traits and customs could be observed. . . . Apache curiosities would be displayed and offered for sale." The army cooperated and even encouraged the tours, apparently in an effort to bring tourist dollars into the Indian camp. "Major Sinclair opened the barracks to visitors and provided a place for dancing. Good music by the post band was featured."[28]

The tours were popular, often filling nine or ten railroad cars with three hundred or four hundred people. Arrangements could be made for visitors to stay overnight. Free passes to tour the Apache village were issued at the barracks. If the visitor was a newspaperman or a celebrity, an officer provided a deluxe guided tour.[29]

The Apaches, with little else to do, created a wide array of articles for sale: baskets, water jugs woven from oak strips, bows and arrows, leather belts, beaded handbags, cloth dolls, moccasins, and "other very handsome and ingenious Indian curiosities." Most items sold in the $1 to $5 range. One visitor observed that the Apaches spoke very poor English but had clearly mastered the word "dollar" when negotiating. A student from Spring Hill College noted that Geronimo "would condescend to give you his signature for one dollar, while a walking stick with his name upon it, he considered worth an additional fifty cents."[30] Other Apache entrepreneurs were quick to sense the commercial value of the name "Geronimo." Soon visitors had the good fortune of meeting several Geronimos hawking their wares.[31]

When Lieutenant Wotherspoon replaced Sinclair, he set about creating a variety of wage jobs around the military base and in the Indian village at $10 a month. The records show that he initially employed twenty-five men to make barrel staves and split shingles for roofs. Both men and women were put to work tending the community garden. During this period he began encouraging local farmers to employ the men as farm hands.[32]

Wotherspoon employed women for work as laundresses for the officers, farm hands, and housekeepers for the hospital. Most likely they also served as cooks when the mess hall went into operation. Wotherspoon's reports imply that the women were paid but do not indicate how many of them received wages or how much. Taking only the men's wages for about fifty months, from August 1890 until the prisoners were transferred to Fort Sill, Oklahoma, in October 1894, it is possible to extrapolate that the prisoners received at least $12,500 in wages. Certainly, out of 170 women, an equal number, at least twenty-five, were also drawing wages. Virtually all the letters women wrote to their children away at school mentioned with pride that "I am working." However, since the figures are obscure, whatever the women earned is not credited.[33]

By early 1893, all the men and women willing to work were employed as day laborers. A few took jobs with the railroad at the standard employee wage. Initially, money made from the tribal farm was put into an account to pay salaries and purchase items for the prisoners' benefit. In 1890 the slush fund held enough to throw a Christmas party and buy gifts for all the children.

A few of the leaders took on more prestigious positions. Eskiminzin, noted for his successful farm in Arizona, was a natural for the head farmer's position. Geronimo was employed as justice of the peace and for a while did double duty as the volunteer disciplinarian at the school. Chihuahua hired on as the school's janitor and ultimately replaced the grim-faced Geronimo as a milder-mannered enforcer. One unnamed Apache worked as a hospital orderly. Headmen such as Loco were paid for their duties as village leaders.[34]

Perhaps the most stable source of income for the Apaches was Company I of the Twelfth Infantry. Fully one-fourth of the Mount Vernon Barracks's $6,000 monthly payroll went to the Apaches in Company I. This all-Apache, regular army outfit was organized in May 1891. Wotherspoon enlisted forty-seven prisoners as the company's first recruits. Collectively the Apache soldiers brought home $1,500 a month from May 1891 until they left Alabama—a total contribution to the prisoner community of approximately $58,000. Ultimately, fifty-five Chiricahuas were carried on Company I's rolls.[35]

Possibly the most astounding thing about the Apaches' stay at Mount Vernon was their ability to turn a profit. Aside from their wage jobs, the prisoners' arts and crafts enterprise continued to grow throughout their time in Alabama. The Apaches kept no records of their profits, and no accounting was required by the army, but it is possible to deduce that on the tourist traffic alone, the prisoners raked in $25,000 in sales during their stay in the "heart of Dixie."

The tribal farm and personal gardens were also sources of income. As soon as the prisoners' gardens and the farm began producing, the Indians not only supplemented their rations but also sold vegetables to the post and began shipping the surplus to Mobile for sale there. The army managed the profits for the benefit of the prisoners, but no accounting records have been found.

Altogether, one can speculate that by combining profits and income from their wages and enterprises during their stay in Alabama, the Apaches brought home about $95,000, or some $2 million in modern dollars, exclusive of the women's wages and the sale of agricultural products. In addition, the army provided housing and rations for the Apaches, and the Indians had the best medical care plan in the country at that time, all at no charge. The prisoners were doing much better than most historians have claimed.[36]

With the issues of food, clothing, housing, and finances resolved, attention turned to the prisoners' schooling and their salvation. In his fourth annual address, President Cleveland provided some background: "Some charitable and kind people [the Massachusetts Indian Association] asked permission to send two teachers to the Indians for the purpose of instructing the adults as well as such children as should be found there. Such permission was readily granted, accommodations were provided for the teachers, and some portions of the buildings at the barracks were made available for school purposes. The good work contemplated has been commenced, and the teachers engaged are paid by the ladies with whom the plan originated."[37]

Two experienced teachers, Vincentine Booth, formerly an instructor at Carlisle, and Marion Stephens, recently from the Hampton Institute, were employed to organize and operate a school for the prisoners' children. The school opened on March 4, 1889, with only one student, Chief Loco's thirteen-year-old son, John Loco. The Indian parents were afraid that the women were part of a plan to spirit away another batch of children, similar to the St. Augustine takings. "Our only obstacle came from fear that we had come to take more of their boys and girls from them. . . . The arguments and appeals that were made to us on this account made us glad that this was not our errand."[38]

Once the parents' worries about another kidnapping were calmed, the schoolroom filled quickly, and by the fall of 1892 an additional room was added to the original one-room schoolhouse. The increase in students was due largely to the efforts and personalities of the Shepard sisters, Sophie and Sylvia, who replaced Booth and Stephens early on. The two managed to acquire a small organ that, when played, attracted both children and adults from around the community. Adult men began to attend classes on their days off. Women were apparently less keen on learning, probably because some of the older women discouraged it.

Wotherspoon cooperated with the Shepards to create a work-study curriculum for the older boys. It consisted of taking the youngsters out of school for half of each day to work at carpentry. John Loco, who had started his education with the nuns in St. Augustine, attended the Mount Vernon school faithfully until he was eighteen, when the Indians were moved to Oklahoma.[39]

As part of their work, the Shepard sisters included religious instruction for the Indian community. Participation in church activities closely matched school attendance, growing rapidly throughout 1889 and 1890. By mid-1890, twenty-five children attended Sunday school regularly. In February 1891, Mount Vernon's post chaplain, William Pearson, reported, "Each Sabbath morning during the month Sabbath School was held in the chapel which was largely attended." An afternoon service was held for the adults. Pearson praised it as a spiritual step forward for the Apaches when they demonstrated a "desire on the part of the men to marry in accordance with the customs of the Whites. There have been four such marriages. This involved giving up their custom of polygamy and what is of equal importance, their custom of divorce."[40]

In addition to the Shepards' classes and attendance in the post chapel, some began to attend other churches around the Mount Vernon area. Although many Apaches, including John Loco, converted to Christianity, many others, including his father, Chief Loco, were at best uncertain converts—at least in Alabama. One might legitimately question whether many of the prisoners were as interested in salvation as they were in a little Sunday entertainment. Loco and other older Apaches began attending nearby Negro churches. Their sudden interest in Christianity was apparently motivated by the lively Negro spirituals and dancing during the services. Old Chief Loco was especially fascinated by members of the congregations who held long pig bones between their fingers and clicked them in the fashion of musical spoons to provide rhythm for the hymns.[41]

By late 1890 the Apache village had the character of any non-Indian community around the country. Almost everyone spoke at least a little English. Some of the youngsters were fluent. Students who returned from Carlisle replaced most of the old-time professional interpreters such as Sam Bowman. George Wratten stayed on, but he was married to a Chiricahua woman. Everyone adopted "citizens' clothes," and a few matched the best styles of the day. Store-bought shoes replaced traditional moccasins. Commuting by rail to shop and sightsee in Mobile became routine. Football and baseball became the sports of choice. Men worked regular hours at wage jobs; craftsmen and vendors catered to a booming tourist industry; those with a bent for farming tended gardens and operated a community farm. Those not employed elsewhere drew government pay. Some families had savings accounts. Mothers struggled daily to get their children off to school. Adults attended adult education classes during their off hours. Many families went to church on Sunday. Everyone lived in heated houses. The women cooked on wood stoves. They "use tables, china, and knives and forks. They no longer burn up all their property when a death in the family puts them in mourning." The village had gravity-fed running water. No Indian tribe in the United States, before or since, ever raced into the modern world so quickly or with such gusto.[42]

Perhaps Kaahteney said it best when he told John Bourke in 1889, only three years after the capture of the entire tribe, "You saw me with General Crook [in 1886], and you talked with me; you saw how I was then; I had on a breechclout, and I had no shoes; I wore moccasins and a shirt made by the squaws; now I have a shirt, hat, shoes, and coat from the store. I don't wear a breechclout; I wear trousers."[43]

CHAPTER TWENTY-TWO

The Dark Side of Mount Vernon

The prosperity the Apaches enjoyed at Mount Vernon was edged with darkness. Brawls, assaults, common thefts, and drinking incidents often intruded on the usually peaceful village. The years 1887 to 1894 saw four murders, a rape, and marriage problems that resulted in two suicides. A terrible tuberculosis epidemic and persistent intestinal problems struck down prisoners of all ages. Although dysentery and tuberculosis had plagued the tribe for years, even in the Southwest, at Mount Vernon Apaches were dying in uncustomary numbers while in the government's care.[1]

Many army officials and physicians believed the Apaches were afflicted with a hopeless inherited ailment. Dr. Walter Reed concluded in 1889 that tuberculosis among the prisoners had proved "incurable," and "not one case has shown any improvement under treatment." When the newly founded Tuberculosis Association recommended improving the sanitary conditions of the sick, providing adequate nutrition, and isolating them, many of its recommendations, if not already in place at Mount Vernon, were quickly arranged.[2]

Tuberculosis is a capricious disease. It might take months or even years after exposure for the initial symptoms to develop. The victim may feel fine at first, with no symptoms. Once the disease surfaces, the sufferer might initially only lose a little weight, show a general lethargy, and have night sweats—things considered normal in the sultry Alabama heat. Often, the early symptoms unexpectedly vanish. When this happens, in about half the cases the disease returns months or years later, and in the other half it never returns at all. If the disease progresses, the victim develops a fever and an increasingly intense and bloody cough. No medical treatment for tuberculosis was known during this period. Patients who reached the advanced stage invariably died.[3]

Thus, most of the Apaches felt good much of the time and were able to carry on their usual activities. Although many may have been infected, the Apache village was not packed with lethargic, half-sick consumptives. They were not dying in legions, as some writers have intimated. The prisoners were a vibrant group living in a robust community and making the best of depressing and difficult circumstances. Nevertheless, when they left Mount Vernon on October 2, 1894, after eight years of incarceration there and at Fort Marion, 280 of their tribal members had died. That averaged to two or three deaths a month from all causes, and one or two a month from tuberculosis. In a group of fewer than five hundred people, two or three deaths a month were catastrophic and seriously affected the Apaches' emotional health. After his inspection in December 1889, Lieutenant Guy Howard noted, "There has been and is much sickness and many deaths, with resultant depression." When Lieutenant Wotherspoon arrived at Mount Vernon in June 1890, he found "these Indians in a most depressed condition." Walter Reed wrote of the "profound discouragement that has fallen upon the Apaches."[4]

A dramatic rise in the death rate among the prisoners in the year from July 1889 to July 1890, forty-three in all, prompted an appropriation of more than $1 million (in modern dollars) to construct a new and, it was hoped, healthier village in the fiscal year 1890–91.[5]

The army selected a better site for the new village, in the open on a sandy ridge less than a mile from the first village. The War Department furnished the building materials, and all-Apache Company I, most of the labor. In February 1891 Wotherspoon hired two professional carpenters to instruct and supervise amateur carpenters from Company I to build the new village. Unaware that many of the Apaches had studied carpentry in St. Augustine, Wotherspoon marveled at how quickly the men learned to use the tools.[6]

The new houses were of frame construction and had two rooms each, under a single roof. The rooms were larger than those of the original houses, fourteen feet square, with two doors, two larger windows, a fireplace, a wood-fired cookstove, and a Sibley stove for heat. They were set on raised foundations and painted outside. Every home had a finished interior. Each family received new furniture made by the men. The houses in the original log village, along with the old furniture, were burned to prevent contaminating the new community.[7]

The seventy-four houses in the new village were set facing one another along wide dirt streets. They were farther apart and in the open, away from the dense surrounding woods, which theoretically gave the places better ventilation. The Apaches moved into the improved housing in April 1891. Wotherspoon installed a number of amenities in the new village to improve the Indians' health. An eight-bed hospital was opened, twenty-four hours a day, seven days a week, exclusively for the prisoners. Several Sibley tents were erected to serve as isolation wards for the extremely sick.[8] Two large "swimming or bathing tanks and a number of steam bath houses (sweat houses) . . . tubs, scrubbing boards and soap have been provided." Wotherspoon's efforts to supply the very best for the Apaches drew the attention of Surgeon General Charles Sutherland: "Each family is provided with better quarters than many married soldiers at our posts. Few of our posts have reached the stage of swimming baths and steam bath houses."[9]

Initially, four wells were dug in convenient locations around the neighborhood. Later, gravity-fed water stations were installed throughout the village where the prisoners "got their water from a faucet connected by pipes to an elevated water tower." A new two-room schoolhouse was included in the community.[10] The homes were easier to clean. Sanitation was significantly improved, and along with it, the prisoners' morale. "The industry, skill and cheerfulness of the Indians cannot be too highly commended. . . . Their homes are neatly kept and in some cases pride is shown in this neatness, and [they have made] some attempts at decoration."[11]

The prisoners were comfortably settled in their new houses by April 26, 1891. Major William Borden took over as Mount Vernon's new post surgeon in the summer of that year. The major was enthusiastic and unshakably convinced that sanitation was the key to ending the deaths among the prisoners. He established stringent standards for cleanliness and the upkeep of the living quarters, and he enforced his requirements with weekly inspections and daily visits to the Apaches' homes. Wotherspoon described the inspections and the results:

A marked improvement in the neatness of their dwellings is apparent due to the weekly inspections (on Sundays) in addition to the daily visits . . . [by] an officer of the Medical Department [Borden] who accompanies the officer in charge of the weekly inspection at which time all Indians are at their houses for personal examination. I have already destroyed much useless material which might lead to the spread of disease. I cannot but think that this system must result in the greatest benefit to the people. . . . The entire camp [must] be swept each morning, immediately after reveille and all refuse gathered in carts, hauled off and burned. Each house is scrubbed with soap and sand once a week. . . . This inspection of the homes is minute. All houses found not up to standard are ordered cleaned and a second inspection follows. All bedding and clothing found not cleaned and all rags and dirt are ordered cleaned if fit for use; burned if not. . . . Rooms are not only regularly scrubbed and washed out but the walls, ceilings, shelving and all ledges are wiped, the dust collected and burned.[12]

At first, Wotherspoon believed that his $50,000 project had curbed the epidemic: "For the past four months there has been no decrease in members. I think much of this improvement is due to the new dwellings and the better mode of life adopted since moving into the village." He also concluded that the new houses had improved the prisoners' morale. Ironically, deaths in the camp that year jumped to fifty-three, the greatest number during the Apaches' entire stay in Florida and Alabama. But the epidemic had run its course, and losses began to show a slight downswing beginning the following year, 1892, dropping back to forty-five.[13]

Meanwhile, in Pennsylvania, youngsters at Carlisle Indian Industrial School were dying about as quickly as their families in Alabama. By May 24, 1889, two years after the first Apache children were taken at Fort Marion, twenty-seven students drafted for the Carlisle experience were dead from tuberculosis, and "two others will die within two or three days. Others are drooping and will take their places soon." Captain Richard Pratt, who founded the Carlisle school, viewed the extraordinary death rate among the Apache students as a blight on the school's reputation. He wrote, "The school ought not bear this affliction any longer."[14] He kept the students at Carlisle until they teetered at death's door. Then, to avoid besmirching the school's reputation, he shipped them home to die at Mount Vernon.[15] The arrival of a regular stream of dying children from Carlisle sent Indian parents in search of any visitor to Mount Vernon who they thought might help secure the youngsters' return. Chief Loco was among the anxious parents. In January 1888, Isabel B. Eustis, an educator and advocate of Indian rights, wrote of talking with Loco: "The intense love of their children is their most striking characteristic. . . . There was one request that a child should be returned [from Carlisle] . . . from old Loco, who was blind and wanted his boy [Dexter] to lead him." Loco was not blind, but pretending to be might secure Dexter's return.[16]

In July 1889, John Bourke and Charles Painter of the Indian Rights Association came to Mount Vernon to determine the Indians' preferences regarding moving to a reservation that would be purchased by northern philanthropists. Loco buttonholed the two about the return of his son and grandchildren from Carlisle:

> My son was taken five years ago to Carlisle school; if we get that farm I'd like to have him sent back to me; I'd like to have him come now if he could; he ought to have learned a good deal by this time, and I'll need him to help me on that farm, if we get it. I let him go to school because I thought I'd like to have him talk for me and write my letters for me; but I think he ought to be able to do all that now. I have four young relations at Carlisle; I want them well taken care of; if they get sick let them have good doctors, as I haven't many [children] left now; but I want my son to come back to me now. That's all I have to say. I mean what I say.[17]

There can be no doubt that the army's main concern at Mount Vernon was the Apaches' health. Virtually every communication from the day the Indians arrived, April 28, 1887, until the day they left, October 2, 1894, was full of discussions about diet, sick counts, treatments, hospital accommodations, preventive efforts, and deaths. But the army had other concerns, too. The three officers at Mount Vernon who successively had charge of the Indians—William Sinclair, William Wotherspoon, and John Cochran—also took a strong interest in the tribe's social welfare and showed a zest for nudging them into the twentieth century. Their endeavors to move the Apaches into modern society were, for the most part, remarkably successful. The army's efforts, however, ran into problems with the attempted prohibition of gambling and drinking.

The Indians came to Mount Vernon with a warning to the commanding officer that gambling had put Colonel Langdon at Fort Marion at odds with the influential women of St. Augustine. Major Sinclair at Mount Vernon, however, was apparently unable to envision problems in backwoods Alabama. Early in the Apaches' stay at Mount Vernon, the military turned a blind eye to Indian gambling. Soon, however, gambling became associated with drinking, and the army outlawed it, but eliminating the games proved impossible. Accounts of wagering appeared regularly in Mount Vernon's monthly reports throughout the Apaches' stay in Alabama. Finally, in February 1894, Wotherspoon reported, with little confidence, "I may add that the habit of gambling has been checked; at least, it is prohibited." Nevertheless, the games continued, and little was done to stop them unless an officer happened across a game in progress.[18]

Drinking was a different matter. Across the board, white America viewed liquor and Indians as a volatile mix—unhealthy for the Indians and dangerous for the whites. Because of their reputation in the Southwest, the Apaches carried a special onus. The close confinement in St. Augustine had slowed the flow but not stopped it. A few bottles slipped through Langdon's blockade at Fort Marion, although never enough for a large blowout. At Mount Vernon, with change in the Indians' pockets and newfound freedom, it was only a matter of time before an incident took place.

About four months after they arrived in Alabama, the prisoners were still living in Sibley tents in scattered locations around the post. A single guard in each camp kept a casual, if not lackadaisical, watch over the Indians. An order removing the guards was not issued until the Apaches were moved into log cabins.

In the late hours of August 23, 1887, the sentry watching Loco's camp reported a drunken scrimmage going on in the village. When a contingent of troops arrived at Loco's place, they found the Indians thoroughly drunk and embroiled in a ferocious free-for-all, wielding knives and swinging firewood clubs. It was an old-time drinking party gone bad.

Ramon, a prominent member of Loco's group, and his wife, Sounig, hosted the bash. They had bought a quantity of home brew from a local man and invited a crowd over to quaff a few. Things calmed when the soldiers arrived, but not before Ramon tried to knife one of the troopers. As punishment for arranging the affair and for the attack, Ramon and Sounig were sent to Fort Pickens to be held with Geronimo and his group, "doomed to fight mosquitoes on the Island of Santa Rosa." The two returned to Loco's village in May 1888 when the Apaches at Fort Pickens were transferred to Mount Vernon. A sergeant who escorted the couple to Pickens reported that Ramon acquired a "considerable amount of red liquor" from "people who live in the country round about Mount Vernon."[19]

As a result of such incidents, the military launched a campaign to stamp out drinking among the prisoners. Peddling strong spirits to the white soldiers at the barracks had been a mainstay of the local economy for more than fifty years. Despite federal law prohibiting the sale of alcohol to Indians, the legitimate liquor outlets, which ordinarily relied on the soldier trade, found that the Indians provided a profitable addition to their revenues. What was more, nearly everyone nearby was a bootlegger. Most of the rural folk in the area distilled their own and did not hesitate to sell a pint to improve the family's bottom line. Wotherspoon reported that "liquor has been found in the [Indians'] camp, obtained from "irresponsible Negroes against whom evidence is being gathered and proceedings will be taken as soon as possible."[20]

Because of the rising number of drinking incidents among the Indian troops, Wotherspoon was forced to close the post exchange to Apache soldiers on August 1, 1892.[21] It was a useless effort. If the Indian soldiers did not get their alcohol from the exchange, from bootleggers, or at the back doors of local gin mills, then there was always Mobile. While on a pass in the big city, Noche and Fatty, both members of Company I, were discovered by a policeman, unconscious in a doorway and "loaded to the guards with whiskey." Beside them was a toy wagon piled high with sweets and toys for children back at Vernon, potent drugs apparently recommended to treat tuberculosis or dysentery, bars of perfumed soap for the women, and nine quarts of Yellow Label whiskey, quality stuff. The two had undoubtedly sampled supplies intended for another big social event. The policeman tried to rouse the two by shouting, shaking them, and whistling, but with no luck. Finally the patrolman "took his club and catching Noche by the hair, drew his club around his head." Noche woke immediately, shouting and cursing. The two warriors then followed the policeman to the station, pulling their wagonload of gifts behind. They were not charged but were allowed to sober up and put on the return train to Mount Vernon that evening with their purchases—except for the two-plus gallons of whiskey.[22]

Probably the most serious incident involving liquor occurred on Sunday, March 12, 1893. Dutchy, George Crook's most reliable scout back in Arizona, and Dittoen, a youngster who enlisted in Company I after two years at Carlisle, were killed in a drunken fray near the train depot by two white privates from Company G, Michael Cooney and William Wise. There had been bad blood between Dutchy and Wise for weeks. On that Sunday evening, Dutchy threatened Wise, and a fight ensued. Dutchy apparently set things in motion when he tried to hit Wise with a two-by-four board with a protruding nail. Wise fended off the blow and somehow managed to seize the board. He then beat the two Company I men to death.

Wise and Cooney were tried in federal court in Mobile and initially pleaded guilty to the killings, but their defense attorney, J. Parker, in a "remarkable masterpiece of legal oratory," got the men off on a revised plea of self-defense. The two were quickly transferred to Jackson Barracks in New Orleans to "to prevent them from contact with the Apache soldiers at Mount Vernon." They were then dishonorably discharged and lost to history. Dutchy, who had not adjusted well to army life in Company I despite his previous experience as a scout, had been discharged before the fight. The Apaches buried him in the woods near the Indian village. Dittoen, still a soldier when he died, was given a military funeral and buried in the Mobile National Cemetery.[23]

By the end of 1890 Wotherspoon was at his wit's end with the drinking. "I have had trouble with the Indians on account of the ease with which they can get whiskey from the saloon keepers," he reported. In January 1891 he wrote, "Having found it impossible to get trustworthy evidence of such sales of whiskey . . . and the evil being on the increase, I employed a detective from Mobile who spent some days in gathering sufficient evidence to bring the principal offenders to trial."

Wotherspoon's detective, Henry Baker, a Mobile county constable, made his first arrests in February 1891. Eventually, eleven of fourteen cases that came to trial resulted in convictions. The two worst offenders, those who operated nearest the Indians' camp, were jailed for fifty to two hundred days. The others received substantial fines.[24]

Despite his limited success, Wotherspoon continued to fear that drinking would lead to raids and depredations by the prisoners. Most of the "raids," however, were little more than garden-variety drunken affairs involving only a few people. Walter Reed wrote in July 1890, "The general conduct of the Indians during the month has been good with the exception of two men and two squaws, who whilst under the influence of liquor which they obtained at a saloon in the forest, killed a calf belonging to a poor woman." Although similar "depredations" occurred from time to time, they were infrequent and involved only the theft of small livestock or poultry.[25] Nevertheless, the availability of liquor remained a constant worry for the military, which envisioned a Sherman-like march by the Apaches through Mississippi and westward. But the glory days of large war parties were a thing of the past, and dealing with unexceptional incidents became the order of the day.[26]

The entire prison period saw only one escape attempt—actually two attempts by the same man, Zes-cloya, probably a Yavapai. He was married to a Chiricahua woman and had been caught up in the sweep at Fort Apache. Louie, as he was called, was a large, unattractive, middle-aged man. His wife was in the last throes of tuberculosis, and Louie was casting about for a younger woman. He became smitten with Bekiva, a beautiful young thing with long black hair and bright eyes, straight as an arrow, and very mature—for a twelve-year-old. Small for her age, she looked to be nine or ten. Ziestoe, her mother, and Talusher, the father, were members of Loco's band and wanted nothing to do with Louie.[27]

On Saturday night, April 7, 1888, Louie slipped into the sleeping girl's cabin while her parents were visiting friends. He took her from her bed and carried her into the woods before she awoke. He was apparently planning to return to Arizona with his prize. Ziestoe reported her daughter missing the next morning. When Louie was also discovered gone, he was immediately suspected of kidnapping, and twenty-five troopers with a cadre of Apache scouts set out to run him down.

The trackers quickly found the fugitive and his victim concealed in an army supply wagon only ten miles from Mount Vernon, but they reckoned Louie had wandered about forty miles in an effort to elude the pursuers. Bekiva was returned to her parents that day. She had been raped seven times.

Bekiva testified against Zes-cloya during the trial, but he was released on a technicality. Major Sinclair immediately confined him in the post jail, as much to save him from the wrath of Loco's people as to punish him. Eventually Louie was sent into exile at Fort Pickens. He escaped for a second time a year later but was picked up by the Mobile police and subsequently sent to prison at Fort Adams in Rhode Island. Zes-cloya's sick wife lost the will to live after the incident and soon "died in despair."[28]

Along with the other deaths, two suicides took place during the Apaches' stay at Mount Vernon. They apparently had nothing to do with liquor. The first occurred in the spring of 1892. Fun, the hero who had saved the children from Geronimo's threats at Alisos Creek, killed himself "in a fit of jealous insanity, after shooting and slightly wounding his young wife."[29] Fun had recently joined the army, so his body was accompanied by "Sergeant Martin Grab and two privates for Company I, 12th Infantry to the National Cemetery in Mobile for interment."[30]

A murder-suicide happened two years later when Seeltoe, also a private in Company I, sank into a deep depression. Like Fun, Seeltoe suspected that his wife, Belle, was unfaithful. The marriage was going poorly for Belle, too. She began drowning her sorrows in bootleg whiskey, and on more than one occasion she landed in jail.

On April 18, 1894, Seeltoe, along with two other privates, Zele and Nah-to-ah-jun, drew the unusual duty of guarding Seeltoe's wife and

Arnold Kinzhuna, a recent returnee from Carlisle. Both Belle and Arnold were confined for overindulging. Apparently, while walking his post, Seeltoe spotted Belle talking with his fellow guard Nah-to-ah-jun, assumed the worse, and without hesitation squeezed off a quick shot through the jailhouse window. The shot missed and sent Belle running, but Seeltoe put a second shot through her lungs. She dropped on the spot. For good measure, he shot her again while she was laid out in the sand. He then wounded Nah-to-ah-jun. After a short chase, he sat down, took his shoe off, and put the rifle against his head. He pulled the trigger with his toe and blasted away "all of that portion [of his head] above the eyes and ears." Private Nah-to-ah-jun died in the post hospital that evening at about seven o'clock. Both were buried in Mobile's National Cemetery. Belle mounted an amazing recovery, survived the episode, and lived to a ripe old age.[31]

Although the Apache prisoners were treated kindly during their stay in Florida and Alabama, the incarceration proved cataclysmic for the tribe. A greater percentage of prisoners died at Mount Vernon than in any American prisoner-of-war camp in any war, ever. American prison camps during the American Revolution saw about a 17 percent death rate. During the Civil War, the worst prison camp in the country, the infamous Confederate camp at Andersonville, Georgia, lost about 30 percent of its prisoners to starvation and disease. The Union camp at Elmira, New York, was not far behind, with losses of 25 percent. A total of 280 Apache prisoners died during the eight years between the fall of 1886 and the fall of 1894, at Fort Marion, Mount Vernon Barracks, and Carlisle—about 55 percent of all prisoners.[32]

One might wonder how the Chiricahuas would have fared on their own in the West. A brief look at the years 1880 through 1882 shows that in October 1880, Victorio lost 79 killed and 68 captured at Tres Castillos. Then, in two days in April 1882, 95 Warm Springs Apaches and Chiricahuas were killed at Sierra Enmedio and Alisos Creek. Thirty-three more were lost to captivity. A few weeks later, another dozen or so were killed at Casas Grandes, and about 25 captured. In four days during a two-year period, 312 died or were taken into slavery and lost to the tribe forever—32 more than were lost over an eight-year period as prisoners. At that pace, it is not a stretch to conclude that the free Chiricahuas in the Southwest would have been annihilated by 1894. Chief Loco, of course, would argue that if Victorio had stayed at home in 1880, and if Geronimo had not raided incessantly and had left Loco's folks alone in 1882, then Loco would have been on his farm at Turkey Creek, and the Chihennes' only deaths would have been from natural causes. The imprisonment would have never happened, at least not for the Warm Springs band, and most likely their descendants would be living on their own reservation today.

CHAPTER TWENTY-THREE

"Loco Died, Causes Unknown"

By the last of 1888, the Apache prisoners were costing the government an average of about $62,000 annually and had become an ugly embarrassment for the Cleveland administration. They were dying at a disturbing rate in government custody. The army considered guarding the peaceful prisoners a nuisance, more akin to babysitting than proper duty for soldiers. Worst of all, the "bloody and murderous savages" were dressing like citizens, speaking English, and running their own businesses. They were walking the streets and making friends in St. Augustine and Mobile. For that matter, the citizens of Florida and Alabama were delighted to have the Indians as neighbors. Yet no one seemed to know what to do with them.[1] The question had been bandied about by practically everybody, but none of the suggested solutions seemed to gain traction. Because of President Cleveland's resistance to their release, Washington officials continued to keep the Apache question as deeply under wraps as possible. John Bourke observed, "It did not take me long to see that all the War Department wanted was quiet; it did not intend to do anything at all for the Chiricahuas, but it would avoid as much as possible any popular clamor. The only way to get anything out of these practical politicians is to fire hot shot and shell them."

Grover Cleveland continued to insist that the Chiricahuas were dangerous and that holding them as prisoners was necessary: "I am not at all in sympathy with those benevolent but injudicious people who are constantly insisting that these Indians should be returned to their reservation. Their removal was an absolute necessity if the lives and property of citizens upon the frontier are to be at all regarded by the Government. . . . This is true not only of those who, on the warpath have heretofore actually been guilty of atrocious murder, but their kindred and friends, who, while they remained upon their reservation, furnished aid and comfort to those absent with bloody intent."[2]

Despite the government's efforts to keep the Apache prisoner problem out of public view, articles about the unfair imprisonment of noncombatants and about the high death rate at Mount Vernon began appearing in newspapers around the country by 1889. In cooperation with the Indian Rights Association, the Indian Citizenship Committee of Boston enlisted a host of sympathizers to lobby for a suitable home for the prisoners. Dozens of suggestions for places to put them poured into the War Department and the White House. A beleaguered secretary of war, Redfield Proctor, commented, "There has certainly been no lack of a multitude of counselors."[3]

Climate ruled out most of the suggested locations. Dr. Walter Reed was positive "that a dry climate must be the first consideration. I cannot urge this too strongly. . . . I am now convinced that the principal factor in the causation of pulmonary disease amongst the Apaches is the excessive atmospheric moisture which prevails along the Gulf and Atlantic coasts."[4] After his investigation in December 1889, Lieutenant Guy Howard, son of General O. O. Howard, concluded that "their rapid dying is due in great part, to their location in the moist atmosphere of the seacoast." Guy Howard called for "prompt action to avoid positive inhumanity" and recommended the prisoners be moved by March 1, 1890.[5]

Eventually, Fort Sill, Oklahoma, and the Cherokee reservation in North Carolina surfaced as the two top contenders for places to relocate the prisoners. The Indian Rights Association and some people in the military showed a keen interest in the area adjacent to or on the Cherokee reservation in North Carolina's Smoky Mountains. In June 1889, Charles Painter, of the Indian Rights Association, and John Bourke visited the area and liked what they saw. After a talk with the Cherokee leaders, the two headed for Mount Vernon to meet with the Apaches about relocating. In late July 1889, Bourke introduced Painter to the prisoners assembled. Painter came to the point quickly:

> I was talking with the Secretary of War the other day and I told
> him that . . . some of my friends were ready to buy a place as a
> home for the Apaches, and I asked if these friends were ready to
> offer a suitable location, could he send an army officer to examine

and report. To this the Secretary agreed, so I went to Boston and saw my friends and when I came back he said he would send Captain Bourke with me to look at these places and we have come round by this place to have a talk with you before going back and making our report. . . . If you will tell me today that you are ready to give up the past, all the old life, ready to start in a new path, in the white man's way, then I can go back and tell this to my friends and I am pretty sure that Captain Bourke and I can find such a place as our friends can buy and the Government accept.[6]

In response, virtually all the leaders, including Geronimo, Naiche, and Chihuahua, pointed out that the Apaches were already on Painter's "new path" and said they definitely were agreeable to relocation. Loco's speech was somewhat similar to those of the others, but he emphasized that for his part, what Painter was calling for was what he had proposed and practiced for the past twenty years—give up the old ways and live quietly at peace:

It's a long time since I first followed in the footsteps of the white people and I am still doing it, trying to be as much like a white man as I can. It is twenty-five years or more since I first made peace with the white people, and I have tried hard to keep it. I have grown old among them. I like to be with the white people, and always did. My thoughts are more like those of a white man than an Indian; that's the reason I have been glad to grow old among them. I am so old and feeble now I can hardly stand up. . . . I know that we can make a living off a farm, because I used to make my living farming. I always like to be near the white people; they have always treated me well and seemed to like to have me near them, and I am grateful for their kindnesses to me. I am getting old and feeble now.[7]

Satisfied with the meeting, Painter left for Boston, where he raised enough money from wealthy contributors to purchase a twelve-thousand-acre tract inside the Cherokee reservation. The reservation lay about thirty-five straight-line miles from Asheville, North Carolina, which was touted as a "center for care of tuberculosis, having an optimum combination of barometric pressure, temperature, humidity and sunlight" to cure the afflicted. Nevertheless, the plan failed. North Carolina newspapers opposed accepting the Apaches. The war department's enthusiasm for the Cherokee idea faltered in the face of the negative publicity. Some officials worried that the Carolina mountains too closely resembled the Apaches' old haunts. Governor David Fowle ultimately killed the deal when he objected to the project "in very vigorous language," even though it was "especially observable that the intimate friends of the Indians, those well posted in their affairs, as well as the Cherokees themselves, are favorable to the reception and adoption of the now diminutive band of Apaches."[8]

Since at least as far back as the 1860s, people had been tendering proposals to move the Apaches to Indian Territory. With the North Carolina option dead, General Crook visited Mount Vernon in early 1890 and then stopped by Fort Sill. On January 6, 1890, he submitted a report on the visit, touting Oklahoma as the best destination for the Apaches.[9] Senator Henry Dawes introduced Joint Resolution 42 eighteen days later, granting the army the authority to relocate the Apaches, but its passage was confounded by politics until 1894.

Finally, on August 28, 1894, Captain Marion Maus and First Lieutenant Hugh Scott traveled to Mount Vernon to ease the Apaches into the idea of another move. After seeing the pristine military post and inspecting the Apache village with its amenities, Maus could not understand why the Apaches were dissatisfied. George Wratten explained that the Indians were afraid that everyone would die if they remained in Alabama. After their tour, Maus and Scott met with the leaders to discuss moving the Indians from Mount Vernon. The meeting was short. The leaders gave their reaction to the officers' comments.[10]

Loco made a short statement at the meeting, his last one recorded for history:

> I was tired and sick but since I heard what you say about a farm, I am getting better. I have known white people many years ago when I was a boy and now I am an old man and I have always been taken care of and well treated. I have nothing to talk about except a farm. I want a farm to live in and make crops. You (looking at George Wratten, the interpreter) have known me since I was a boy and you never heard anything wrong about me, that Loco did this or Loco did that. I have always done right. I have always been at peace and no white man can point to me and say there goes a bad man. I have grown old amongst the white people. My skin is dried up and drawn across the bones. I wanted peace and nothing but peace. We thought when

we came here we would do well but it is just like a road with a precipice on each side. They fall off on both sides. Nobody killed them. Sickness did it.[11]

Finally, twenty-one days after the Apache leaders met with Maus and Scott, orders came on September 18, 1894, to relocate the prisoners to Fort Sill, Indian Territory. The Apaches were to be accompanied by Lieutenant Allyn Capron and the all-Apache Company I. The prisoners moved back into Sibley tents while their houses were dismantled. Everything usable, such as doors and windows, was to be taken to Fort Sill for use in building new houses. Garden tools and seven hundred pounds of clothing were packed and made ready for shipment. After an unsuccessful effort to sell the gutted shells of houses left standing, the army burned the remains of the village. No evidence that the Apaches were ever in Mount Vernon was left. Each family was issued cooked rations for the train trip to Oklahoma, and army field rations were carried for use on the thirty-mile trip from the train terminal at Rush Springs to Fort Sill.[12]

At one o'clock on the afternoon of October 2, 1894, Loco and his people departed "one of the prettiest posts in the army." After the Apaches were off, Major George Russell, the new commanding officer at Mount Vernon, wired Washington, "The Indian business here is closed out. Praise the Lord!"[13]

Two days later, on October 4, 1894, a sorry lot of 259 Apaches arrived at the Rush Springs, Oklahoma, rail station, thirty-two miles from Fort Sill. Before they left Mount Vernon, Lieutenant Wotherspoon reported that "more than one-half of the men and nearly one-half of the women were unhealthy and crippled." These were all that were left of the Warm Springs and Chiricahua Apaches, except for about forty-five youngsters away in school at Carlisle.

Army cooks at Rush Springs welcomed the exiles with huge cauldrons of food. John Loco thought there must have been at least a hundred military wagons waiting to transport the Apaches and their belongings to a temporary campsite at Fort Sill.[14] After a hot meal, the soldiers helped the women, children, and the aged aboard the wagons. Many of the Apaches preferred to walk the entire distance to Fort Sill. The wagons and walkers began late in the afternoon but halted before nightfall, only a few miles from the depot, to make camp. The cold field rations, issued before they left Mount Vernon, were broken out and served up. During the meal, the howls of coyotes in the distance brought tears to many. It was the first time since they had left Arizona eight years before that they had heard coyotes.[15]

Early the next morning, an upbeat crowd continued the trip to Fort Sill. They arrived by mid-afternoon the next day and set up camp about a mile and a half from the main post. There, they soon built an old-style Apache rancheria of wickiups covered with surplus army canvas brought down from the recently closed Fort Supply. Several hundred Kiowas and Comanches, curious for a look at their ancient adversaries, were waiting to meet the prisoners at their campsite. Lieutenant Hugh Scott, who was to be in charge of the prisoners of war for their first three years at Fort Sill, had prepared the Plains Indians for the Apaches' arrival. They had come to welcome the newcomers. The "Lords of the Plains," elegantly bedecked in beaded buckskins and feathers for the occasion, later commented on the Apaches' poverty, noting that they had no livestock, little clothing, and not a single camp dog. Most of the Chiricahuas' personal belongings and store-bought clothes, along with their dismantled Mount Vernon houses, had been put on a separate freight train routed through New Orleans. While it was sidetracked in a freight yard there, an inexplicable fire destroyed most of the Apaches' goods.[16]

General Nelson Miles, now commanding the Department of the Missouri and again in charge of the Apaches, was at last able to report that "one officer, five white enlisted men, one interpreter, and 305 Apache Indians have been located on the Fort Sill Reservation." The count was corrected on December 12, 1894, to "17 men, nearly all old Indians or crippled, 126 women, 70 boys, 46 girls, 259 total instead of 304 as [Miles] reported."[17]

One day after their arrival, Dr. Charles LeBaron, medical officer in charge of the prisoners of war, wrote, "It is my opinion that the 24 hours that they have been here has made an appreciable improvement in their spirits. They seem more high and cheerful than usual and many have expressed to me their pleasure at being here and also stated that they could breathe easier and freer since their arrival."

Hugh Scott assumed charge of the Apaches upon their arrival. His instructions were "to settle them upon arable land on the military reservation of Fort Sill under control and protection of the garrison, to prevent their escape, and all access to intoxicating liquor and generally to make them self-supporting as soon as practicable." Lieutenant Scott wrote that the Indians were "delighted with the change from Mount Vernon Barracks."[18]

Although they had come to expect "some kind of roof" during their eight years in Alabama, by necessity the prisoners lived in tents and canvas-covered wickiups at Fort Sill for a little more than a year until new houses could be built. They remained camped together through that winter, but in the spring of 1895 Scott separated the prisoners into twelve tent-and-wickiup villages. By January 1897 most of the tents were gone, replaced by sixty-nine comfortable picket houses. The new houses were the best yet. Although of the same design as those in the first village in Alabama, they were of frame construction and had larger rooms and four windows instead of two. Tile chimneys provided almost smoke-free living quarters. Once again the Indians built much of their furniture, mainly beds and tables. The army purchased chairs, chinaware, and other household items in Lawton, Oklahoma, to replace those lost in the New Orleans fire. Wood-fired cookstoves were standard. The recognized leaders of the tribe were put in charge of each village, which consisted of the leader's family and personal following. The village headmen included Loco, Chihuahua, Chatto, Chiricahua Tom, Geronimo, Perico, Noche, Kayihtah, Kaahteney, Mangas, Toclanny, and Naiche. Loco's village, near Four Mile Crossing, just north of Heyle's Hole, was the largest, with forty people in nine homes. Other villages averaged about twenty-one residents.

At the same time they were building houses, the prisoners set to work clearing and plowing a large plain between Cache and Medicine Bluff Creeks for a tribal farm. Eventually, more than a thousand acres were cultivated. In time the Apaches' cattle herd grew to at least four thousand head. Some estimated that it was as large as "12,000 head, perhaps the biggest herd in the West at the present time." The cattle herd and the farm became the primary sources of employment and the mainstays of the tribal economy for the Apaches while at Fort Sill.[19]

Within the first year after their arrival, school arrangements for the children were also changed to the Apaches' satisfaction. Chief Loco's son Dexter and granddaughter, the shoeless Nahdoyah, with twelve other students finally returned to their families from the Carlisle School in November 1895. A few young people of the tribe voluntarily remained at Carlisle or at Hampton Normal Institute in Virginia, mostly in pursuit of professional skills such as blacksmithing and baking. The Indian Citizenship Committee of Boston discontinued the policy of furnishing teachers, but missionaries of the Dutch Reformed Church enthusiastically took up the task and ran a small school on the military base. The older children attended the Indian Office's Riverside School in Anadarko, only thirty miles away.[20]

In time, two Dutch Reformed preachers, Walter Roe and Frank Wright, brought the Christian religion to the Indian villages. It was apparently not an intense issue for the Apaches. Some continued with their old practices, but many converted. Most, perhaps hedging their bets with the divine, converted to Christianity but also continued the old traditions. Ultimately the missionaries acquired some land, built a school and a church, and convinced several notables to join the church, including Loco's son and grandson, John Loco and Raymond Loco.

During their first eighteen months at Fort Sill, the Apaches lived in wickiups and tents while they built houses. Although the winter of 1894–95 was the coldest in Fort Sill's history, Lieutenant Scott thought the outdoor living "seemed to have a beneficial effect on their health" and offered "hope of stamping out tuberculosis rife among them." In the first year that the Apaches were in Oklahoma, the death rate among the prisoners dropped to less than half that recorded during their worst year in Alabama, 1890–91. Still, tuberculosis continued to haunt the band for years at a reduced level.[21]

Although a few newspapers around the country, especially in Arizona, continued to depict the Apaches as unreconstructed spoliators, people in Oklahoma took little notice of the prisoners' activities. In January 1897, two years after they came to Fort Sill, Scott wrote, "Their conduct [in Oklahoma] has been so uniformly good that almost everybody has forgotten that they are here and no white man or Indian has had the slightest just cause for complaint."[22]

Nevertheless, on one occasion in 1898 the Apache prisoners' reputation returned to stalk them. On February 15, the Spanish-American War began with the sinking of the battleship *Maine* in Havana harbor. On April 19, 1898, virtually every soldier at Fort Sill was shipped out to Cuba, leaving two officers and a small contingent behind to guard federal property and tend the Apaches. Lieutenant Francis Beach found himself in command of both fort and prisoners, replacing Scott.

A young Apache woman, housekeeping for the Beach family, told the lieutenant's wife that with the army gone, the Apaches were making medicine and holding war dances. She claimed that Rogers Toclanny was eager to outdo Geronimo as a warrior and was plotting an uprising. A rumor also floated that in the absence of the troops, the Kiowas and Comanches were preparing to massacre the Apaches. A tribal war would surely ensue, putting the white women and children of the fort in the middle. Beach checked the rumors with the interpreter, George Wratten. Wratten could not say what the Comanches were up to but confirmed that the Apaches were restless. Beach immediately telegraphed Rush Springs for reinforcements before the troops embarked. By midnight a troop of the First Cavalry bounded onto post grounds. Their arrival reportedly quelled the "uprising" and calmed the women. A subsequent investigation of the affair proved that the young woman's allegations were untrue. In fact, while the women at the post armed themselves and huddled in defensive positions, most of the Apaches were dozing through another of Reverend Robert Chaat's long-winded sermons in the Dutch Reformed Church. Chaat, a Comanche Indian ordained by the Reformed Church, was known to the Apaches as "Ether" because of his sleep-inducing preachments.[23]

On June 30, 1895, Company I of the Twelfth Infantry was merged into another all-Indian company, Company L, Seventh Cavalry. The new company included the Apaches but was composed mostly of Kiowas and Comanches. The unit was finally mustered out on May 31, 1897. John Loco had signed up as a scout in the company when the Indians arrived at Fort Sill in 1894 and remained in that capacity until the company was closed down in 1897. Like most of the other Apache ex-soldiers, John went to work with the tribe's cattle herd and farm enterprise. Some others took employment with the Oklahoma City and Western Railroad or hired on as laborers at white-owned farms in the area.[24]

Chief Loco's health began slipping just after his eightieth birthday in 1903. John, his son by Clee-hn, had gradually taken over the village leadership from his father. John had the same charisma that attracted people to Loco and had been educated in church schools. Probably in early 1900, old Loco had turned his leadership entirely over to John. John, with the Shepard sisters' encouragement, had converted to Christianity at Mount Vernon and had developed a reputation as an inspirational lay preacher in his own right. He married a Chihenne woman, Marion Juan, the daughter of Pedro Juan, a member of Loco's band.[25]

Loco continued a quiet existence, confining most of his activities to lobbying for a reservation at Ojo Caliente and for a return of the tribe's children from captivity in Mexico. He remained in fragile health. After his four-year-old granddaughter, Ruth Loco, died of tuberculosis on January 1, 1905, he declined rapidly. He died a month later, on February 2, 1905. A simple coffin was constructed of boards taken from ammunition crates. An entry in Fort Sill's "Record of Medical History of the Post, 1903–1913" reads, "February 2, 1905, Loco died, Causes Unknown, age 82."[26]

Chiz-pah-odlee, Loco's oldest wife, had died in 1895, the year after the Apaches reached Oklahoma. Both Chiz-odle-netln, his second oldest wife, and Clee-hn, the youngest, lived on until 1909. They died within months of each other. Geronimo, Chief Loco's nemesis, died the same year. John Loco ran the affairs of the tribe until he relinquished them to Benedict Jozhe Jr., Loco's grandson. Jozhe represented the tribe for more than fifty years.[27]

Ultimately, the majority of the Apaches at Fort Sill voted to join the Mescalero Apache tribe. The old Mescalero reservation near Fort Stanton had been relocated to a new, more desirable place in 1882 and 1883. Old doubts about moving in with the Mescaleros were long forgotten. A few Chiricahuas refused to leave Oklahoma and instead requested that they be given allotments there. Those choosing to remain in Oklahoma were for the most part Loco's people, the Warm Springs Apaches, who, thanks to the late chief, had attended schools, acquired trades, and not only "showed the most susceptibility to white advice in respect to farming techniques, but they were also the ones who showed the most interest in Christian teachings. They were and are the church group among the Chiricahua Apaches."[28]

On April 30, 1913, Chandler Robbins, post surgeon for Fort Sill, noted in the post's medical record that "187 Apache Prisoners of War [were] released and turned over to the Interior Department and departed for Mescalero Agency, April 2, 1913, accompanied by 1st Lieutenant Thomas L. Ferenbaugh, M.C.U.S.A." Eighty-seven Apaches remained at Fort Sill, including Loco's son John, his family, some grandchildren, and other relatives. Chief Loco's older son, Dexter, moved to Mescalero.[29]

The Apaches who remained in Oklahoma moved off the military reservation on March 7, 1914, and settled on eighty-acre allotments chosen by themselves. To set them apart from those who returned to Mescalero, they were called Fort Sill Apaches.[30] The band was not officially organized as a tribe recognized by the federal government until October 30, 1976, when the Fort Sill Apaches voted to ratify a constitution and bylaws, under which they are presently governed.

Loco, the old warrior turned peacemaker, finally had his "good peace." He had seen his dream of a modern Warm Springs Apache tribe living in harmony with their neighbors become a reality. For him it had been a fifty-year struggle that he endured despite the Americans' double-dealing and his fellow Apaches' doubts and derision. He was the first leader to make peace with no conditions other than fair play. After he declared his peaceful intent in 1869, more Warm Springs people consistently followed him than any of the other, more prominent leaders. No evidence exists that he attacked a single American or Mexican after 1869, although who actually killed the victims of the 1877 outbreak from Camp Goodwin is unknown. While on the reservations in the Tularosa Valley and at Ojo

Caliente, Loco did gun down three Apaches in pursuit of a more tranquil existence for his band. He alone saved the tribe from annihilation by the Coyoteros in 1886.

Even though Chief Loco's greatest aspiration for his Warm Springs people was a carefree life at peace, he knew peace would not be enough for the band to survive. They needed to learn the workaday skills of modern life in mainstream America. He understood that a non-Indian education was the key to success in the dog-eat-dog world of the Americans. Consequently, by example, Loco became the Apaches' "education chief." He was among the first Chiricahua leaders to send a child to school from San Carlos in 1884. Another son was the first, and initially the only, student to attend school in Alabama in 1889.

Although others eventually joined him, Chief Loco led the way in the Warm Springs Apaches' rapid rise from their near Stone Age existence to becoming well-dressed, churchgoing farmers, ranchers, and business-men—educated on a par with most Americans and living in solid, warm houses. Although he did not live to see it all happen, he probably died secure in the knowledge that because of his life-long effort, the children were finally safe.

Notes

ABBREVIATIONS

AAAG	Acting Assistant Adjutant General
AAG	Assistant Adjutant General
ACIA	Acting Commissioner of Indian Affairs
AG	Adjutant General
AAAGDC	Acting Assistant Adjutant General in Washington, D.C.
AGDC	Adjutant General in Washington, D.C.
AGO	Adjutant General's Office
AGODC	Adjutant General's Office in Washington, D.C.
CIA	Commissioner of Indian Affairs
CO	Commanding Officer
IGO	Inspector General's Office
LR	Letters Received
LS	Letters Sent
NAMP	National Archives Microfilm Publication
NARA	National Archives and Records Administration
OIA	Office of Indian Affairs
SI	Secretary of the Interior
SW	Secretary of War

INTRODUCTION

1. Opler, *Apache Life-Way,* 334–35.

2. Sonnichsen, *Geronimo and the End of the Apache Wars,* 15–20; Raymond Loco (grandson of Chief Loco), interview by author, October 7, 1962.

3. Opler, *Apache Life-Way,* 9–55; Raymond, Norman, and Moses Loco (grandsons of Chief Loco) and Benedict Jozhe (grandson of Chief Loco and former chairman, Fort Sill Apache Tribe), interviews by author, 1962–74.

4. Raymond, Norman, and Moses Loco, interview by author, December 21, 1965.

5. Sonnichsen, *Geronimo,* 9–10.

6. *Fort Sill Record of Medical History of Post,* 1903–1913, in National Archives and Records Administration (NARA), Old War Records Division.

CHAPTER 1

1. Opler, *Apache Life-Way,* 337–39; Raymond Loco, interview by author, October 7, 1962.

2. Raymond, Norman, and Moses Loco, interview by author, August 15, 1962; John Bourke, "Diary," 1886.

3. Edwin R. Sweeney, correspondence with author, May 4, 2006; Opler, *Apache Life-Way,* 347, 430.

4. Sweeney, *Mangas Coloradas,* 272–73; Edwin R. Sweeney, correspondence with author, April 14, 2006.

5. Opler, *Apache Life-Way,* 2.

6. Sweeney, *Cochise,* 4–5; Barrett, *Geronimo,* 66.

7. Raymond, Norman, and Moses Loco, interview by author, August 15, 1962; Opler, *Apache Life-Way,* 466–69.

8. O. O. Howard to wife, September 8, 1872, in O. O. Howard Papers; Sweeney, *Cochise,* 143, quoting George Wratten to W. Holmes, May 4, 1907.

9. Raymond Loco, interview by author, January 9, 1968; Betzinez, *I Fought with Geronimo,* 6.

10. Raymond, Norman, and Moses Loco, interview by author, August 20, 1962.

11. Opler, *Apache Life-Way,* 224–25, 251–54.

12. Raymond, Norman, and Moses Loco, interview by author, August 20, 1962; Betzinez, *I Fought with Geronimo,* 33.

13. Betzinez, *I Fought with Geronimo,* 33; Boyer and Gayton, *Apache Mothers and Daughters,* 27–29.

14. Raymond and Moses Loco, interview by author, December 23, 1962; Betzinez, *I Fought with Geronimo,* 33; Davis, *The Truth about Geronimo,* 112.

15. Howard to wife, September 8, 1872, Howard Papers; Davis, *Truth about Geronimo,* 112, 115.

16. Clark, "The Victorio Raid."

17. Bourke and Painter report, July 5, 1889, in National Archives Microfilm Publication (NAMP) M689, R193; Bourke, "Special Report to Secretary of War," March 14, 1889, and Bourke to AAG, July 24, 1889, "Meeting with the following head men present, Chatto, Chihuahua, Kay-e-tennae, Ramon, Noche, Naiche, Loco, Zele, Nana, Geronimo," in NAMP M689, R193; Boyer and Gayton, *Mothers and Daughters,* 27–29; "Interview with Leon Perico," in Sol Tax Papers, Special Collection 5, Box 10, Folder 15; Davis, *Truth about Geronimo,* 112.

18. Dunn, *Massacres of the Mountains,* 324; Boyer and Gayton, *Mothers and Daughters,* 27–29.

19. Sweeney, *Mangas Coloradas,* 281; Edwin R. Sweeney, correspondence with author, April 30, 2000.

20. Boyer and Gayton, *Mothers and Daughters,* 27–29; Eve Ball, correspondence with author, April 15, 1972; Raymond Loco, interview by author, November 25, 1971; Alicia Delgadillo (Apache prisoner of war historian and genealogist), correspondence with author, January 11, 2001; Cruse, *Apache Days and After,* 41.

21. Furnas, *Life and Times of the Late Demon Rum,* 121; Unrau, *White Man's Wicked Water,* 11.

22. Rickey, *Forty Miles a Day on Beans and Hay,* 159.

23. Sweeney, *Mangas Coloradas*, 255, 262, 272–73.

24. Ibid., 289, quoting Michael Steck letter, August 12, 1853; Raymond Loco, interview by author, December 23, 1962.

25. Sweeney, *Mangas Coloradas*, 304, 309.

26. Ibid., 311.

27. Ogle, *Federal Control of the Western Apaches,* 38.

28. Sweeney, *Cochise,* 146–64, 205; Sweeney, *Mangas Coloradas,* 70–75, 130–36, 358–59, 123.

29. Betzinez, *I Fought with Geronimo,* 24.

30. Undated statement by Richard C. Patterson, in NARA, RG123, Indian Depredation claim number 8927.

31. Betzinez, *I Fought with Geronimo,* 24; Alicia Delgadillo, correspondence with author, August 15, 2001.

32. Lt. Henry F. Leggett to post adjutant, Fort McRae, August 21, 1868, in NARA, RG75, M234, letters sent (LS), Fort McRae, 1868; Undated statement by Patterson, NARA.

CHAPTER 2

1. Commissioner of Indian Affairs (CIA), Annual Report 1870, 623–25; Raymond and Moses Loco, interview by author, March 25, 1965.

2. Captain H. C. Corbin, 38th Infantry, to Lieutenant M. W. Saxton, post adjutant, Fort Bayard, April 2, 1869, in NARA, RG393, N107–109, 1869, letters received (LR), Department of the Missouri.

3. Raymond Loco, interviews by author, January 2, 1963, and November 24, 1964; Thrapp, *Victorio and the Mimbres Apaches,* 98–100, quoting Capt. John Gilmore to AAG, District of New Mexico, June 12, 1869, and Lt. Charles Drew to Major William Clinton, November 1, 1869; Drew to CIA, September 3, 1869, in CIA, Annual Report 1869; Sweeney, *Cochise,* 278.

4. Lt. Col. Cuvier Grover to Lt. George Getty, District of New Mexico, June 7, 1869, in NAMP, M1072, R4, LS, District of New Mexico; Thrapp, *Victorio,* 98, quoting Grover to Getty, July 2, 1869.

5. Drew to Clinton, November 1, 1869, in CIA, Annual Report 1869, Appendix K, 544; *Santa Fe New Mexican,* May 4 and 13, 1869; Sweeney, *Cochise,* 288; Drew to CIA, September 3, 1869, CIA.

6. Thrapp, *Victorio,* 98, quoting Grover to Getty, June 2, 1869.

7. CIA, Annual Report 1870–71, including Second and Third Annual Reports of the Board of Indian Commissioners.

8. Thrapp, *Victorio,* 98, quoting Gilmore to AAG, District of New Mexico, June 12, 1869; Sweeney, *Cochise,* 288–89, quoting Gilmore to AAAG, District of New Mexico, August 12, 1869.

9. Drew to CIA, September 3, 1869, CIA; Sweeney, *Cochise,* 288–89; Thrapp, *Victorio,* 98.

10. Drew to CIA, September 3, 1869, CIA.

11. Ibid.

12. Drew to CIA, September 3, 1869, and Drew to Clinton, December 1, 1869, in CIA, Annual Report 1869.

13. Raymond Loco, interview by author, January 2, 1963; Sweeney, *Cochise,* 288; Drew to CIA, September 3, 1869, Drew to Clinton, December 1, 1869, and Drew to Clinton, November 1, 1869, CIA.

14. Thrapp, *Victorio,* 101–103.

15. Ibid., 101.

16. Ibid., 103, quoting Drew to Clinton, October 11 and 23, 1869.

17. Drew to Clinton, December 1, 1869, CIA.

18. Thrapp, *Victorio,* 103–104.

19. Ibid., quoting Getty to Commander, Department of the Missouri, January 4, 1870.

20. Drew to Clinton, January 5, 1870, in CIA, Annual Report 1869, Appendix O, 107–109.

21. Ibid.

22. Ibid.

23. Sobel, *Panic on Wall Street,* 127–50; Kindleberger, *Manias, Panics, and Crashes,* 30, 35, 131.

24. Sobel, *Panic on Wall Street,* 150.

CHAPTER 3

1. Drew to Clinton, October 11, 1869, in CIA, Annual Report 1869.

2. Thrapp, *Victorio,* 105; Drew to Clinton, January 5, 1870, CIA.

3. Drew to Clinton, January 5, 1870, CIA.

4. Thrapp, *Victorio,* 126–28.

5. CIA, Annual Report 1870, 623–25.

6. General Order no. 10, November 21, 1871, in CIA, Annual Report 1870, 623–25.

7. Opler, *Apache Life-Way,* 326; Raymond Loco, interview by author, January 9, 1968; Rickey, *Forty Miles a Day,* 116–21.

8. Thrapp, *Victorio,* 129, 101–103.

9. Drew to Clinton, October 11, 1869, CIA; Sweeney, *Cochise,* 307.

10. Thrapp, *Victorio,* 136, quoting Orlando Piper to Major George Shorkley, February 29, 1872; *Las Cruces Borderer,* March 16, 1871; *Alta California,* April 8, 1871; Sweeney, *Cochise,* 307, quoting Piper to General John Pope, March 31, 1871.

11. Lt. Argalus Hennisee to CIA, August 31, 1870, in CIA, Annual Report 1870; Thrapp, *Victorio,* 131.

12. Hennisee to Clinton, October 31, 1870, in NAMP, M621, R12.

13. Colyer, "Report on the Apache Indians"; Vincent Colyer to Columbus Delano, December 17 and 23, 1870, Colyer to Edward D. Townsend, December 24, 1870, Delano to A. A. Sargent, December 19, 1870, Colyer to Townsend, December 24, 1870, Executive Order of December 23, 1870, and General Order no. 10, November 21, 1871, in NARA, LR, Office of Indian Affairs (OIA), 1824–1881, New Mexico Superintendency, 1848–1880.

14. CIA, Annual Report 1871, including *Third Annual Report of the Board of Indian Commissioners;* Thrapp, *Victorio,* 135, quoting Pope to Ely Parker, April 21, 1871; Edwin R. Sweeney, correspondence with author, January 18, 2001.

15. Thrapp, *Victorio,* 134; Worcester, *Apaches,* 209.

16. Thrapp, *Victorio,* 134; Worcester, *Apaches,* 209.

17. Judge Richard Hudson to Piper, July 18, 1871, in CIA, Annual Report 1871, Appendix Ab, no. 7.

18. Drew to CIA, September 3, 1869, CIA; Sweeney, *Cochise,* 265, 361, 288–89, quoting Drew to Clinton, January 5, 1870, and Lt. Col. Thomas Devin to Serburne, January 25, 1869.

19. Sweeney, *Cochise,* 264–339; Edwin R. Sweeney, correspondence with author, July 9, 2007.

20. Sweeney, *Cochise,* 265, 361, 288–89, quoting Drew to Clinton, January 5, 1870, and Devin to Serburne, January 25, 1869; Drew to CIA, September 3, 1869.

21. Piper to Shorkley, February 29, 1872, in NARA, RG393, LR, District of New Mexico; Moses Loco, interview by author, January 3, 1969; Sweeney, *Cochise,* 285, 307, quoting the *Las Cruces Borderer,* March 16, 1871, the *Alta California,* April 8, 1871, and Piper to Pope, March 31, 1871.

22. Thrapp, *Victorio,* 126–28.

23. CIA, Annual Report 1869, 104–109; Thrapp, *Victorio,* 106–107.

24. Thrapp, *Victorio,* 107–108; CIA, Annual Report 1870, 104–109.

25. Thrapp, *Victorio,* 106–108.

26. H. D. Hall to Clinton, June 5, 1870, in NARA, OIA, 1824–81, New Mexico Super-intendency, 1849–1880.

27. Loco descendants, interviews, 1963–1971.

CHAPTER 4

1. Thrapp, *Encyclopedia of Frontier Biography,* 35–36.

2. Thrapp, *Victorio,* 126–28, quoting Hennisee to Clinton, September 15, 1870.

3. Ibid., 127, quoting Hennisee to Clinton, September 16, 1870.

4. Ibid., 126–28, quoting Hennisee to Clinton, September 16, 1870.

5. Ibid., 98, quoting Grover to Getty, June 2, 1869; Raymond, Norman, and Moses Loco, interview by author, October 20, 1970.

6. Thrapp, *Victorio,* 98–99, quoting Clinton to Parker, August 5, 1869; AAAG District of New Mexico to CO, Fort Wingate, June 7, 1869, in NAMP, M1072, R4, LS, District of New Mexico.

7. Sonnichsen, *Geronimo,* 134, 135, 149; Thrapp, *Victorio,* 126 and 345n.

8. Raymond Loco, interview by author, October 21, 1970.

9. Thrapp, *Victorio,* 130–32, quoting William Arny, Report no. 8, November 21, 1870; Arny, *Indian Agent in New Mexico,* 54–58.

10. Sweeney, *Cochise,* 300–302, 339, quoting Arny to Parker, November 8, 1870; Raymond, Norman, and Moses Loco, interview by author, October 20, 1970.

11. Arny, *Indian Agent,* 54–58.

12. Raymond, Norman, and Moses Loco, interview by author, October 20, 1970; Sweeney, *Cochise,* 329, quoting the *Las Cruces Borderer,* November 1, 1871.

13. Sweeney, *Cochise,* 300–302, quoting Arny to Parker, November 8, 1870; Secretary of War (SW), Annual Report 1870, 15–16; Thrapp, *Victorio,* 133, quoting Pope to Parker, December 7, 1870.

14. Thrapp, *Victorio,* 133, quoting Piper to Pope, December 31, 1870; Sweeney, *Cochise,* 302–303, quoting Piper to Pope, January 31, 1871; Giese, *Forts of New Mexico,* 29.

15. Thrapp, *Victorio,* 131, citing Arny, Report no. 8.

16. Ibid., 127–130; Sweeney, *Cochise,* 300.

17. Thrapp, *Victorio,* 131, citing Arny, Report no. 8; Sweeney, *Cochise,* 300, quoting Arny to Parker, November 8, 1870.

18. Colyer, "Report," 45–46; Worcester, *Apaches,* 125–28.

19. Thrapp, *Victorio,* 138; Sladen, *Making Peace with Cochise,* 15; Edwin R. Sweeney, correspondence with author, August 25, 2002.

20. Colyer, "Report," 45–47.

21. Ibid.

22. Ibid.

23. Thrapp, *Victorio,* 138–39; Colyer, "Report," 45–47; Raymond Loco, interview by author, October 20, 1970.

24. Colyer to Pope, August 29, 1871, and Colyer to Delano, September 6, 1871, in U.S. Indian Office, *Executive Orders Relating to Indian Reserves,* 128.

25. Sweeney, *Cochise,* 330–31, quoting Piper to Lowrie, October 9, 1871.

26. Ibid., 330–32, quoting Col. Gordon Granger to Pope, October 12, 1871.

27. Ibid., quoting Granger to Pope, October 12, 1871, and Piper to Pope, October 19, 20, and 21, 1871.

28. Ibid., 329, quoting the *Las Cruces Borderer,* November 1, 1871.

29. Ibid., 332, quoting Britton Davis to AAG, Department of the Missouri, October 25, 1871.

30. Ibid., 332, quoting Piper to Granger, October 30, 1871.

31. Ibid., 332–33.

32. Ibid., 332–33, quoting Davis to AAG, October 25, 1871, and Colyer to Pope, November 7, 1871.

33. Thrapp, *Victorio,* 141, quoting Pope to ACIA, October 26, 1871.

34. Colyer, "Report," 45–46; *Army and Navy Journal,* December 9, 1871.

35. Colyer, "Report," 45–46.

36. Sweeney, *Cochise,* 332–33; Thrapp, *Victorio,* 140.

37. Thrapp, *Victorio,* 126–28, quoting Piper to Pope, December 31, 1871; Sweeney, *Cochise,* 332–35, quoting Piper to Colyer, January 27, 1871.

38. Sweeney, *Cochise,* 333; Thrapp, *Victorio,* 352n.

39. Thrapp, *Victorio,* 144–45, quoting Pope to Walker, March 23, 1872; Sweeney, *Cochise,* 336.

40. Thrapp, *Victorio,* 145, quoting Pope to Walker, March 23, 1872.

41. Sweeney, *Cochise,* 336–38, quoting Pope to Walker, March 18, 20, 28, 1872.

42. Raymond Loco, interview by author, October 20, 1970; Shorkley to AAG, District of New Mexico, April 18, 1872, in NARA, RG393, LR, Department of the Missouri, 1872; Thrapp, *Victorio,* 145.

43. Shorkley to AAG, April 18, 1872, NARA; Piper to Pope, March 28, 1872, in NARA, RG393, LR, New Mexico Superintendency; Thrapp, *Victorio,* 146, citing Pope to Walker, April 29, 1872.

44. CIA, Annual Report 1872, including Piper report, 302–303; Thrapp, *Victorio,* 144–45, quoting Piper to Pope, March 28 and 31, 1872, and Pope to CIA, May 9, 1872.

45. CIA, Annual Report 1872, 300–10; Devin to AAAG, Department of New Mexico, May 27, 1882, in NARA, Old Military Records Division, Miscellaneous Correspondence, AGO, 1871, 2456 AGO 1871; U.S. Congress, House Executive Document, 41st Congress, 2nd Session, 1902, no. 1, 549–51.

46. CIA, Annual Report 1872, 302–303; Devin to AAAG, Department of New Mexico, May 9 and 27, 1872; Sweeney, *Cochise,* 342.

47. SW to Secretary of the Interior (SI), January 28, 1873, in CIA, Annual Report 1873.

CHAPTER 5

1. Sweeney, *Cochise,* 300, 317, 319, quoting George Crook to AGO, July 10, 1871.

2. Sweeney, *Cochise,* 327–28.

3. Altshuler, *Latest from Arizona,* 152, quoting *San Francisco Evening Bulletin,* November 25, 1860.

4. Thrapp, *Victorio,* 136, quoting Piper to Pope, October 8, 1871.

5. Edwin R. Sweeney, correspondence with author, February 8, 2003; Israel, *Sears Roebuck Catalog;* Sladen, *Making Peace,* 14; John M. Shaw to CIA, July 14, 1876, in NARA, M234, R569.

6. Sladen, *Making Peace,* 6; Sweeney, *Cochise,* 309, 315–32, citing Piper to Pope, July 23, 1871, Pope to Parker, July 28, 1871, and Howard to Pope, October 11, 1872; Raymond Loco, interview by author, November 24, 1964.

7. Sweeney, *Cochise,* 319, 283; Sladen, *Making Peace,* 14.

8. Piper to Pope, August 21, 1871, in CIA, Annual Report 1871, Appendix Ab, no. 14, 82.

9. Ibid.

10. Sweeney, *Cochise,* 320, quoting Crook to AG, September 19, 1871.

11. Howard, *Autobiography,* vol. 2, 210–11; McFeely, *Yankee Stepfather,* 120, quoting Sherman to Howard, May 17, 1865.

12. Terrell, *Apache Chronicle,* 294; Weland, *O. O. Howard,* 100.

13. Sladen, *Making Peace,* 17–18 and 25–26; Howard, *My Life,* 161, 165.

14. Howard, *My Life,* 184–86.

15. Ibid., 124; Sladen, *Making Peace,* 25, 117, and Appendix A, Council of Mimbres Apaches, September 11, 1872.

16. CIA, Annual Report 1870, 623; Sweeney, *Cochise,* 297; Sladen, *Making Peace,* 134n21.

17. CIA, Annual Report 1874, 310–11; Thrapp, *Victorio,* 150, 157, quoting Howard to Piper, September 16, 1872.

18. Sweeney, *Cochise,* 301–302; Thrapp, *Victorio,* 212, 346 n56.

19. Sweeney, *Cochise,* 352; Thrapp, *Victorio,* 148; Sladen, *Making Peace,* 30–33; Ogle, *Federal Control,* 107, quoting Howard to Pope, September 5, 1872, and Howard to Francis Walker, November 7, 1872.

20. Sladen, *Making Peace,* 114.

21. Ibid., 113, and Appendix A, Council of Mimbres Apaches, September 11, 1872.

22. Ibid.

23. Sweeney, *Cochise,* 353; Sladen, *Making Peace,* 117 and 122; Thrapp, *Victorio,* 153.

24. Thrapp, *Victorio,* 151, quoting Howard to Walker, November 7, 1872; Sweeney, *Cochise,* 353.

25. Sladen, *Making Peace,* 65.

26. Howard, *My Life,* 207; Sladen, *Making Peace,* 65.

27. Frederick Coleman to AAAG, HQ, Fort Tularosa, October 17, 1872, in NARA, RG393; Thrapp, *Victorio,* 151, 155, quoting Howard to Walker, November 7, 1872.

28. Thrapp, *Victorio,* 151, 155, quoting Howard to Walker, November 7, 1872; Colyer, "Report," 45–47; Thrapp, *Victorio,* 138–39.

29. Raymond Loco, interview by author, October 20, 1970.

30. McFeely, *Yankee Stepfather,* 128, citing Eldridge to Donaldson, September 11, 1865.

31. Coleman to AAAG, January 12, 1873, in Benjamin Thomas Papers; Thrapp, *Victorio,* 148–49.

32. Sladen, *Making Peace,* 113 and Appendix A, Council of Mimbres Apaches, September 11, 1872; Coleman to AAAG, October 17, 1872, NARA; Thrapp, *Victorio,* 155.

33. Thrapp, *Victorio,* 152–53, quoting Howard to William W. Belknap, November 27, 1872; Benjamin Thomas to Edwin Dudley, April 18, 1874, and Dudley to Thomas, June 10, 1874, in Benjamin Thomas Papers; Coleman to AAAG, District of New Mexico, January 12, 1873, in NARA, RG393; Raymond Loco, interview by author, October 20, 1970.

34. Coleman to AAAG, District of New Mexico, January 12, 1873, NARA; Coleman to AAAG, District of New Mexico, January 12, 1873, Thomas Papers.

35. Thomas to Dudley, January 13, 1873, in Benjamin Thomas Papers.

36. Thrapp, *Victorio,* 149, quoting Howard to Coleman, forwarded by Dudley to CIA, March 15, 1873.

37. Thomas to Dudley, March 7, 1873, in Benjamin Thomas Papers.

38. Thrapp, *Victorio,* 152, quoting John Pope to Phil Sheridan, October 28, 1872; Ellis, *General Pope and U.S. Indian Policy,* 216.

39. Thrapp, *Victorio,* 152, quoting Sheridan to William T. Sherman, November 7, 1872.

40. Ibid., 145–51, citing Major William Price to AAAG, District of New Mexico, December 13, 1873; Thomas to Dudley, January 28 and August 5, 1873, in Benjamin Thomas Papers.

41. Thomas to Dudley, October 7, 1873, in Benjamin Thomas Papers.

42. CIA, Annual Report 1873, 291.

CHAPTER 6

1. CIA, Annual Report 1874, 310–11.

2. Thomas to Dudley, January 31, 1873, in Benjamin Thomas Papers.

3. CIA, Annual Report 1874, 275–76; Sladen, *Making Peace,* 15; Raymond, Norman, and Moses Loco, interview by author, March 27, 1965.

4. Interviews with U.S. Department of Agriculture Forest Service staff, Reserve, New Mexico, October 11, 2002.

5. CIA, Annual Report 1874, 310–11; Thomas to Dudley, November 10 and December 3, 1873, in Benjamin Thomas Papers.

6. Thomas report, January 31, 1874, and Thomas to Dudley, February 28, 1874, in Benjamin Thomas Papers; CIA, Annual Report 1874, 310–11.

7. CIA, Annual Report 1873, 275–76; Thomas to Dudley, January 22, 1873, in Benjamin Thomas Papers.

8. CIA, Annual Report 1873, 275–76; Thomas to Dudley, December 3, 1873, and January 1, 1874, in Benjamin Thomas Papers.

9. CIA, Annual Report 1874, 310–11; Henry Duane, M.D., reports for August, September 1873, in Benjamin Thomas Papers.

10. Sladen, *Making Peace,* 113 and Appendix A, Council of Mimbres Apaches, September 11, 1872.

11. Thomas monthly reports, January 1, 1874, and February 28, 1874, in Benjamin Thomas Papers; Rickey, *Forty Miles a Day,* 122–26.

12. Dr. James M. Lanig annual report, August 31, 1874, in Benjamin Thomas Papers.

13. CIA, Annual Report 1874, 310–11; Raymond Loco, interview by author, March 24, 1965.

14. Thomas reports, January 1, 1874 and February 28, 1874, Thomas Papers.

15. Ibid.

16. Coleman to AAAG, January 12, 1873, Thomas Papers.

17. Thomas to Dudley, June 30, 1874, in Benjamin Thomas Papers.

18. Thomas to CIA, August 31, 1874, including Lanig report, in Benjamin Thomas Papers.

19. Raymond, Norman, and Moses Loco, interview by author, March 27, 1965.

20. Raymond Loco, interview by author, March 24, 1965; CIA, Annual Report 1871, 68, including Colyer, "Report," 47.

21. Opler, *Apache Life-Way,* 477–78; Raymond, Norman, and Moses Loco, interview by author, March 27, 1965.

22. Opler, *Apache Life-Way,* 230.

23. U.S. Fish and Wildlife Service, "Mexican Spotted Owl," www.fws.gov/southwest/msowlfaq.htm (accessed October 22, 2002); Opler, *Apache Life-Way,* 230; Raymond Loco, interview by author, March 24, 1965.

24. David J. Regela, "New Mexico's San Francisco River: Heare [*sic*] There Be Dragons," *Paddler Magazine,* May–June 1999 (Paddlermagazine.com/issues/1999_3).

25. Opler, *Apache Life-Way,* 42, 118–22; Raymond Loco, interview by author, March 24, 1965.

26. Sladen, *Making Peace,* 52.

27. Ibid., 98–99.

28. Thomas report, August 31, 1874, including Lanig report, in Benjamin Thomas Papers.

29. Thomas reports for April 1873, May 31, 1873, January 1, 1874, and February 28, 1874, in Benjamin Thomas Papers; Thrapp, *Victorio,* 148, citing Howard to CIA, November 7, 1872.

30. Duane report, August 1873, Lanig report, August 31, 1874, Thomas Papers.

31. Tim Dye (former superintendent, Fort Apache Agency, Whiteriver, Arizona), interview by author, June 1974.

CHAPTER 7

1. Thomas report, May 31, 1873, Thomas Papers.

2. Ibid.

3. Thomas to Dudley, March 31, 1874, in Benjamin Thomas Papers.

4. Duane to Thomas, September 4, 1873, and Thomas report, including Lanig report, August 31, 1873, in Benjamin Thomas Papers.

5. Thomas to Dudley, August 7, 1873, in Benjamin Thomas Papers.

6. Thomas to Dudley, August 7, 1873, and Thomas to Price, June 26, 1873, in Benjamin Thomas Papers.

7. Thomas to Dudley, June 28, 1873, in Benjamin Thomas Papers.

8. Thomas to Price, June 26, 1873, and Thomas to Dudley, June 28 and August 7, 1873, Thomas Papers.

9. Thomas to Price, June 26, 1873, Thomas Papers.

10. Thomas to Dudley, July 25, 1873, in Benjamin Thomas Papers.

11. Ibid.

12. Ibid.

13. Price to Thomas, July 30, 1873, in Benjamin Thomas Papers.

14. Thomas to Price, July 30, 1873, and Price to Thomas, July 30, 1873, in Benjamin Thomas Papers.

15. Thomas to Dudley, July 30, 1873, Thomas Papers.

16. Ibid.

17. Thrapp, *Victorio,* 98–105, 129; Sweeney, *Cochise,* 277–78.

18. Thrapp, *Victorio,* 98–103; Raymond Loco, interview by author, September 18, 1964.

19. Thrapp, *Victorio,* 98–103.

20. Ibid., 144–45.

21. Thomas to Dudley, September 4, 1873, in Benjamin Thomas Papers.

22. Thrapp, *Victorio,* 158.

23. Ibid., 158; Thomas report, January 31, 1874, Thomas Papers.

24. Thomas to Price, July 30, 1873, Thomas Papers

25. Price to Thomas, July 30, 1873, Thomas Papers

26. Thomas to Dudley, August 7, 1873, Thomas Papers.

27. Thomas to Dudley, August 30, 1873, in Benjamin Thomas Papers

28. Opler, *Apache Life-Way,* 25, 181–84.

29. Edwin R. Sweeney, correspondence with author, February 2, 2002; Price to Thomas, July 24, 1873, and Thomas to Price, June 14 and July 11, 1873, in Benjamin Thomas Papers.

30. Thomas to Price, June 14, 1873, Thomas Papers.

31. Thomas to Dudley, monthly report, September 3, 1873, Thomas Papers.

32. Raymond Loco, interview by author, January 9, 1968.

33. Myatt, *Illustrated Encyclopedia of 19th Century Firearms,* 72–73.

34. Thomas reports, August 30, 1873, and September 3, 1873, Thomas Papers.

35. Ibid.

36. Opler, *Apache Life-Way,* 154, 168.

37. Thomas to Dudley, September 3, 1873, and September 4, 1873, Thomas Papers.

38. Thomas to Dudley, December 3, 1873, Thomas Papers.

39. Thomas to Dudley, January 1, 1874, Thomas Papers.

40. Thomas to Dudley, April 30 and August 5, 1874, in Benjamin Thomas Papers.

41. Thomas to Dudley, August 31, 1874, in Benjamin Thomas Papers.

42. "Panics of the Late Nineteenth Century," 773.

43. Thomas to Dudley, June 27, 1874, in Benjamin Thomas Papers; Thrapp, *Victorio,* 149, 158, 162, quoting Dudley to Edward P. Smith, December 2, 1873, Howard to Coleman, March 15, 1873, Dudley to CIA, March 15, 1873, and John Pope to Drum, January 9, 1874.

44. Thrapp, *Victorio,* 151, citing Howard to Walker, November 7, 1872.

45. Thomas to Dudley, May 5, 1873, in Benjamin Thomas Papers.

46. Thomas to Dudley, September 4, 1873, Thomas Papers.

47. Thrapp, *Victorio,* 161–65, quoting Dudley to Smith, March 6 and 28, 1874.

48. Ogle, *Federal Control,* 137.

49. U.S. Indian Office, *Executive Orders,* 76.

50. Thomas to Dudley, April 18, 1874, Thomas Papers.

51. Thomas to Dudley, May 30, 1874, in Benjamin Thomas Papers.

52. Dudley to Thomas, June 20, 1874, in Benjamin Thomas Papers.

53. Thomas to Smith, August 31, 1874, in Benjamin Thomas Papers.

54. Thomas to Dudley, October 7 and December 5, 1874, in Benjamin Thomas Papers.

55. Thrapp, *Victorio,* 168, quoting Dudley to Smith, June 30, 1874.

CHAPTER 8

1. Sweeney, *Cochise,* 292.

2. Shaw report, 333–35, in CIA, Annual Report 1875.

3. Thrapp, *Victorio,* 172, 176, citing Shaw to CIA, May 5, 1875, and Lt. Col. Edward Hatch to AAG, Fort Leavenworth, May 17 and 20, 1876; Ogle, *Federal Control,* 170–71.

4. Thrapp, *Victorio,* 174–75, quoting Shaw to CIA, April 17, 1876.

5. Ibid., 182, quoting Shaw to CIA, October 8, 1876.

6. Ibid., 175–76, quoting Shaw to CIA, October 8, 1876.

7. Raymond Loco, interview by author, January 2, 1969; Shaw to CIA, July 14 and 21 and September 30, 1876, in NARA, M234, R569.

8. Thrapp, *Victorio,* 176, quoting Hatch to AAG, Fort Leavenworth, May 20, 1876.

9. Ibid., 175–76, citing Hatch to AAG, Fort Leavenworth, April 17 and May 20, 1876, and Pope's endorsement to Hatch to AAG, Fort Leavenworth, May 20, 1876.

10. Ibid., 172–73, citing Shaw to CIA, March 24, 1876, Shaw to Stephen Elkins and Shaw to CIA, March 29, 1876, and Elkins to CIA, April 7 and 15, 1876.

11. Ibid., 172–73, 181, citing Shaw to CIA, March 24, 1876, and S. A. Gilpin to Shaw, September 4, 1876; Ogle, *Federal Control,* 171, citing Kemble to CIA, May 17, 1876.

12. Thrapp, *Victorio,* 171, 181, quoting Acting Commissioner S. A. Galpin to Shaw, September 4, 1876; Edwin R. Sweeney, correspondence with author, October 7, 2003.

13. Harte, "The San Carlos Indian Reservation," vol. 1, 388–89; Debo, *Geronimo,* 112–13; Clum, *Apache Agent,* 253.

14. Debo, *Geronimo,* 112–13; Edwin R. Sweeney, correspondence with author, July 9, 2007.

15. Clum, *Apache Agent;* Edwin R. Sweeney, correspondence with author, July 9, 2007.

16. Debo, *Geronimo,* 98; CIA, Annual Report 1876; Thrapp, *Victorio,* 180, quoting Shaw to CIA, June 23, 1876, and CIA to John Clum, March 20, 1877; Harte, "San Carlos," vol. 1, 354–57, quoting Clum to CIA, March 26, 1877.

17. Thrapp, *Victorio,* 180, quoting Shaw to CIA, June 16, 1876.

18. Ogle, *Federal Control,* 168–72, citing the *Arizona Citizen,* February 14 and March 17, 1877, and the *Arizona Miner,* March 9, 1877.

19. Opler, *Apache Life-Way,* 462–63; Thrapp, *Victorio,* 172, 177–78.

20. Undated correspondence between Balatchu and Morris Opler, in Morris Opler Papers, Kroch Library, Rare and Manuscript Collections, Cornell University.

21. Raymond Loco, interview by author, June 8, 1964.

22. Thrapp, *Victorio,* 177–78, quoting Shaw to CIA, May 8, 1876.

23. Debo, *Geronimo,* 98; Lummis, *General Crook,* 54.

24. Dunn, *Massacres,* 637; Debo, *Geronimo,* 103; Harte, "San Carlos," vol. 1, 354–57, citing Col. August Kautz to AG, March 26, 1877, and Gov. Anson Safford to CIA, March 18 and 19, 1877.

25. Thrapp, *Victorio,* 186, quoting Safford to CIA, March 18 and 19, 1877; Harte, "San Carlos," vol. 1, 354–57.

26. Harte, "San Carlos," vol. 1, 342, 360–61; Clum, *Apache Agent,* 251.

27. Harte, "San Carlos," vol. 1, 354–57, quoting Smith to Clum, March 20, 1877, and Clum to Smith, March 26, 1877; Clum, *Apache Agent,* 205.

28. Clum, *Apache Agent,* 204–205.

29. Thrapp, *Victorio,* 186, citing Clum to Hatch, April 2, 1877; Harte, "San Carlos," vol. 1, 354–57, quoting Clum to Smith, March 26, 1877.

30. Harte, "San Carlos," vol. 1, 358, 370–71; Clum, *Apache Agent,* 210; Debo, *Geronimo,* 103.

31. Harte, "San Carlos," vol. 1, 360–61; Clum, *Apache Agent,* 210–12; Thrapp, *Victorio,* 188, citing Clum to CIA, April 15, 1877.

32. Thrapp, *Victorio,* 187–88, quoting Clum to CIA, April 15, 1877.

33. Ogle, *Federal Control,* 174–75, citing CIA to Clum, April 17, 1877; Thrapp, *Victorio,* 188, citing Clum to CIA, April 15, 1877, and Clum to Major James Wade, April 21, 1877.

34. Thrapp, *Victorio,* 188, quoting Clum to Walter Whitney, April 20, 1877.

35. Ibid., quoting Whitney to Clum, April 20, 1877.

36. Clum, *Apache Agent,* 210–12, 215–16; *Grant County (New Mexico) Herald,* April 14, 1877; Thrapp, *Victorio,* 188–90, citing Clum to CIA, April 14 and 15, 1877.

37. Ogle, *Federal Control,* 173, citing Clum to AAG, April 2, 1877, and Clum to CIA, March 29, 1877; Debo, *Geronimo,* 103; Clum, *Apache Agent,* 219–20.

38. Debo, *Geronimo,* 107; Barrett, *Geronimo,* 133; Thrapp, *Victorio,* 188, quoting Clum to CIA, April 21, 1877.

39. Barrett, *Geronimo,* 133–34; Clum, *Apache Agent,* 229–36.

40. Ogle, *Federal Control,* 174–75, citing CIA to Clum, April 17, 1877, Clum to Wade, April 24, 1877, Hatch to AAG, April 27, 1877, and Clum to CIA, July 28, 1877.

41. Clum, *Apache Agent,* 229–36.

42. Ibid., 235.

43. Ogle, *Federal Control,* 174–75, citing CIA to Clum, April 17, 1877, Clum to Wade, April 24, 1877, Hatch to AAG, April 27, 1877, and Clum to CIA, July 28, 1877.

44. Clum, *Apache Agent,* 229–36.

45. Thrapp, *Victorio,* 188–89, quoting Clum to CIA, April 21, 1877, and Clum to Wade, April 21, 1877; Debo, *Geronimo,* 109.

46. Thrapp, *Victorio,* 189, quoting Clum to Smith, April 25, 1877.

47. Ibid., 190, citing Clum to CIA, May 1 and 7, 1877.

48. Clum, *Apache Agent,* 229–33, 245–49; Ogle, *Federal Control,* 173–75, citing Clum to CIA, May 1, 1877; Thrapp, *Victorio,* 189, quoting Clum to Smith, April 25, 1877; Debo, *Geronimo,* 110.

49. CIA, Annual Report, 1877, 430–31, including Clum report, September 18, 1877; Harte, "San Carlos," vol. 1, 370–71.

CHAPTER 9

1. Clum, *Apache Agent,* 245–49; Thrapp, *Victorio,* 190, quoting Clum to CIA, May 7, 1877; Centers for Disease Control and Prevention, "Small Pox Overview," www.cdc.gov/agent/overview/disease-facts.asp (accessed November 6, 2003).

2. Clum, *Apache Agent,* 245–49.

3. Ball, *Indeh,* 49.

4. Betzinez, *I Fought with Geronimo,* 54.

5. Clum, *Apache Agent,* 130.

6. Basso, *Western Apache Raiding,* 102–103, John Rope account.

7. Betzinez, *I Fought with Geronimo,* 44; Edwin R. Sweeney, correspondence with author, November 10, 2003.

8. *Arizona Star,* March 29, 1880; Thrapp, *Victorio,* 193; Debo, *Geronimo,* 112–16.

9. Harte, "San Carlos," vol. 1, 398–99, citing William Vandever to CIA, July 5 and 26, August 28 and 29, and September 10, 1877, citing Lemuel Abbott to CIA, August 11, 28, and 31, 1871, and quoting Abbott to AAG, Department of Arizona, August 21, 1877; *Tucson Citizen,* August 4, 1877; Thrapp, *Victorio,* 193.

10. Hart to CIA, August 1, 1877, in CIA, Annual Report 1877, 502–504.

11. Debo, *Geronimo,* 112.

12. Hart to CIA, August 1, 1877, CIA.

13. Harte, "San Carlos," vol. 1, 402, quoting Vandever to CIA, October 14, 1877; Debo, *Geronimo,* 112–13; Raymond Loco, interview by author, April 7, 1966.

14. *Grant County Herald,* September 22, 1877; Ogle, *Federal Control,* 190, quoting Hart to CIA, May 1, 1878; Harte, "San Carlos," vol. 1, 392–95.

15. CIA, Annual Report 1877, 416.

16. Harte, "San Carlos," vol. 1, 311–12, 400; Thrapp, *Victorio,* 194, quoting Whitney to CIA, May 8, 1877; Edwin R. Sweeney, correspondence with author, January 22, 2007.

17. Debo, *Geronimo,* 98; Harte, "San Carlos," vol. 1, 400; Sweeney, *Cochise,* 456 n21, citing Brief of Indian Affairs at San Carlos, 1878.

18. CIA, Annual Report 1877, 416; Ogle, *Federal Control,* 183, quoting Hart to Vandever, September 24, 1877.

19. CIA, Annual Report 1877, 416.

20. Harte, "San Carlos," vol. 1, 399–400, citing Abbott to AAG, Department of Arizona, August 21, 1877, John Kelton to AAG, Department of Arizona, and Major James Martin to AAG, Division of the Pacific, August 29, 1877; Thrapp, *Victorio,* 193–94, quoting Kautz to AG, September 28, 1877.

21. Thrapp, *Conquest of Apacheria,* 177–78; Thrapp, *Victorio,* 195, 207.

22. CIA, Annual Report 1877, 416; Thrapp, *Victorio,* 196, citing Kautz to AG, September 28, 1877; Raymond and Moses Loco, interview by author, April 6, 1966.

23. Harte, "San Carlos," vol. 1, 403–404; CIA, Annual Report 1877, 416.

24. CIA, Annual Report 1877, 416; Harte, "San Carlos," vol. 1, 403–404; Thrapp, *Victorio,* 196–97, citing Hart to CIA September 18, 1877.

25. Thrapp, *Victorio,* 199, citing Capt. Tillius C. Tupper report to Camp Grant Adjutant, September 18, 1877.

26. Ibid., 200–205, quoting Whitney to CIA Ezra Hayt, November 30, 1877, and Hatch to AAG, Fort Leavenworth, September 22, 1877.

27. Ibid., 200.

28. Ibid., 202 and 200, quoting Kautz to AAG, San Francisco, October 5, 1877, and Whitney to Hayt, January 9, 1878; Edwin R. Sweeney, correspondence with author, January 22, 2007.

29. Thrapp, *Victorio,* 200, quoting Thomas Keams to Capt. Horace Jewett, October 8, 1877.

30. Ibid., 203, quoting Jewett to AAAG, Santa Fe, October 11, 1877; CIA, Annual Report 1877, 416.

31. *Grant County Herald,* September 22, 1877.

32. Raymond Loco, interview by author, April 7, 1966; Thrapp, *Victorio,* 207.

33. Thrapp, *Victorio,* 199, citing Tupper report to Camp Grant Adjutant, September 18, 1877; *Grant County Herald,* September 22, 1877.

34. Thrapp, *Victorio,* 205, quoting Whitney to CIA Hayt, November 30, 1877.

35. *Arizona Star,* March 29, 1880.

36. Thrapp, *Victorio,* 200, quoting Keams to Jewett, October 8, 1877.

37. *Arizona Star,* March 29, 1880.

38. Thrapp, *Victorio,* 193–94, quoting Kautz to AG, September 28, 1877, and Abbott to AAG, Prescott, Arizona, September 22, 1877.

39. Harte, "San Carlos," vol. 1, 400.

40. Thrapp, *Victorio,* 195–96, quoting Vandever to CIA, September 12, 1877.

41. Ibid., 196, quoting Abbott to AAG, Prescott, September 22, 1877.

42. Ibid., 193–94, quoting Kautz to AG, September 28, 1877.

43. Dunn, *Massacres,* 641, quoting Col. Orlando Willcox.

44. Ibid., quoting Pope.

45. Raymond Loco, interview by author, April 7, 1966.

CHAPTER 10

1. CIA, Annual Report 1877, 416; U.S. Indian Office, *Executive Orders,* 71.

2. Kindleberger, *Manias, Panics, and Crashes,* 150.

3. SI, Annual Report, 1878, 440–41.

4. CIA, Annual Report 1877, 416; Thrapp, *Victorio,* 203, quoting Hatch to AAG, Fort Leavenworth, October 11, 1877.

5. Secretary of the Interior, Annual Report 1878, 440; Harte, "San Carlos," vol. 2, 473, quoting CIA to Watkins, March 25 and April 1, 1877; Thrapp, *Victorio,* 206, quoting Sherman and Sherman's endorsements to Loud to AAG, Fort Leavenworth, January 2, 1878.

6. Thrapp, *Victorio*, 206, quoting Sheridan's endorsement in Loud to AAG, Fort Leavenworth, January 2, 1878.

7. Ibid., quoting Hayt to SI, February 2, 1878, and SI to SW, February 5, 1878.

8. Ogle, *Federal Control*, 183–84, quoting Hatch to AAG, October 11, 1877, SW to SI, November 1, 1877, and Sheridan to AG, November 9, 1877; Terrell, *Apache Chronicle*, 330.

9. Thrapp, *Victorio*, 204, quoting Pope to Richard C. Drum, October 18, 1877.

10. Ibid.; Harte, "San Carlos," vol. 2, 537–40.

11. Thrapp, *Victorio*, 203, quoting Jewett to AAG, Santa Fe, October 11, 1877.

12. Debo, *Geronimo*, 116; Vandever report, October 23, 1877, in NARA, Inspectors File 1732.

13. First Lt. Martin Hughes to CO, Ojo Caliente, November 10, 1877, in NARA, M1088, RG393, LR, Post at Ojo Caliente.

14. Thrapp, *Victorio*, 205, quoting Whitney to CIA, November 10, 1877.

15. 1877 Statements of Loco, Nana, and Victorio to Captain Jewett, October 24, 1877, in NARA, M1088, RG393, R31, LR, District of New Mexico.

16. Ibid.

17. Thrapp, *Victorio*, 208, quoting Captain Charles Steelhammer, report on the Mimbres, in John S. Loud to AAG, Fort Leavenworth, August 18, 1878.

18. Ibid., and 204, 208, quoting Pope to Drum, October 18, 1877.

19. Ibid., 207, quoting Pope endorsement, Whitney to Hayt January 9, 1878.

20. Ibid., 200, quoting Whitney to brother, October 1, 1877.

21. Dunn, *Massacres*, 641, quoting Pope.

22. Thrapp, *Victorio*, 206, quoting Sheridan's endorsement, Loud to AAG, Fort Leavenworth, January 2, 1878.

23. Ibid., 207–208, quoting SI to SW, May 11, 1878, Pope endorsement, June 20, 1878, and Sheridan endorsement, June 24, 1878, Townsend to Commanding General, Chicago, July 22, 1878.

24. Ibid., 209, quoting Hart to CIA, September 9, 1878, and Loud to AAG, Fort Leavenworth, October 18, 1878.

25. CIA, Annual Report 1878; Report of Captain F. T. Bennett, 9th Cavalry, December 4, 1878, in NARA, RG75, LR by the CIA, 1824–1881, Arizona, R366; Thrapp, *Victorio*, 209, quoting Loud to AAG, Fort Leavenworth, October 18, 1878.

26. CIA, Annual Report 1878; Bennett report, December 4, 1878, NARA,; Thrapp, *Victorio*, 209, quoting Loud to AAG, Fort Leavenworth, October 18, 1878.

27. Undated correspondence between Balatchu and Opler, Opler Papers; Raymond Loco, interview by author, April 6, 1966.

28. CIA, Annual Report 1878; Bennett report, December 4, 1878, NARA; Thrapp, *Victorio*, 210–11; Harte, "San Carlos," vol. 2, 475.

29. Thrapp, *Victorio*, 210–11.

30. CIA, Annual Report 1878; Bennett report, December 4, 1878, NARA.

31. Harte, "San Carlos," vol. 2, 473; Thrapp, *Victorio*, 209.

32. CIA, Annual Report 1878; Bennett report, December 4, 1878, NARA.

33. Thrapp, *Victorio*, 211; Harte, "San Carlos," vol. 2, 475.

34. Thrapp, *Conquest*, 179–80; Thrapp, *Victorio*, 209–211; Harte, "San Carlos," vol. 2, 475.

35. Thrapp, *Conquest*, 180, quoting Pope to AG, Washington, D.C., February 12, 1879; Thrapp, *Victorio*, 209–11, quoting Agent Samuel A. Russell to CIA, August 21 and 22 and October 18, 1879; Sonnichsen, *Mescalero Apaches*, 162–63, quoting Solon Sombrero, June 8, 1955.

36. Thrapp, *Conquest,* 186, 190, quoting the *Arizona Star,* October 17, 1879.

37. Thrapp, *Victorio,* 301–307; Debo, *Geronimo,* 124.

38. CIA, Annual Report 1878; Thrapp, *Victorio,* 220, quoting Hatch to AAG, Fort Leavenworth, September 6, 1879, and Hatch to Hayt, September 6, 1879.

39. Raymond Loco, interview by author, April 6, 1966.

40. Harte, "San Carlos," vol. 2, 537–40, quoting ACIA to Adna R. Chaffee, March 8, 1880, Chaffee to CIA, March 12, April 1, and May 8, 1880, Hatch to AAG, Department of the Missouri, Fort Bayard, March 15, and endorsement by Pope at Fort Leavenworth, March 15, 1880; Thrapp, *Victorio,* 220, quoting Hatch to AAG, Fort Leavenworth, September 6, 1879, and Hatch to Hayt, September 6, 1879; Raymond, Norman, and Moses Loco, interview by author, April 7, 8, 1966.

CHAPTER 11

1. Harte, "San Carlos," vol. 2, 532–37, quoting Chaffee to CIA, December 31, 1879, and January 3, 1880, and SI to CIA, November 11, 1879.

2. Ibid., quoting Chaffee to CIA, April 14 and May 24 and 31, 1880.

3. Ibid., quoting SI to CIA, November 11, 1879, and Chaffee to CIA, December 31, 1879, and January 3 and April 22, 1880.

4. Betzinez, *I Fought with Geronimo,* 54.

5. U.S. Indian Office, *Executive Orders,* 14–15; Harte, "San Carlos," vol. 2, 517–18, quoting CIA to Chaffee, July 11, 1879, and the *Globe Silver Belt,* August 1, 8, 22, and 29, 1879.

6. Betzinez, *I Fought with Geronimo,* 54–55; Harte, "San Carlos," vol. 2, 517–18, quoting Chaffee to CIA, July 29, 1879; Chaffee to AAG, Department of the Missouri, January 11, 1882, in NARA, Old Military Records Division, RG75.

7. Harte, "San Carlos," vol. 2, 575, 584–88, quoting ACIA to SI, April 15, 1881.

8. Harte, "San Carlos," vol. 2, 565–73, quoting the *Globe Silver Belt,* July 31 and September 18, 1880, Joseph C. Tiffany to CIA, August 18, September 30, October 7, and November 20, 1880, and CIA to Tiffany, September 28, 1880.

9. Betzinez, *I Fought with Geronimo,* 54–55; Harte, "San Carlos," vol. 2, 584–88, citing ACIA to SI, April 15, 1881.

10. Betzinez, *I Fought with Geronimo,* 54.

11. Opler, "A Chiricahua Apache's Account," 363–64, quoting Sam Kenoi, n.d.

12. Harte, "San Carlos," vol. 2, 605–616, citing Connell, "The Apache, Past and Present."

13. Thrapp, *Conquest,* 212–16.

14. Cruse, *Apache Days,* 102–103, 114–21; Thrapp, *General Crook,* 8–28; Harte, "San Carlos," vol. 2, 605–606.

15. Raymond Loco, interview by author, June 21, 1971; Bourke, "Diary," April 7, 1883; Edwin R. Sweeney, correspondence with author, July 9, 2007.

16. Bourke, "Diary," April 7, 1883; Edwin R. Sweeney, correspondence with author, January 22, 2007; Thrapp, *General Crook,* 49; Thrapp, *Al Sieber,* 221.

17. Edwin R. Sweeney, correspondence with author, August 9, 2004; Betzinez, *I Fought with Geronimo,* 55; Loco family, interviews by author, January 3, 1969.

18. Thrapp, *Victorio,* 222; Harte, "San Carlos," vol. 2, 651–52; Loco family, interviews by author, January 3, 1969.

19. Edwin R. Sweeney, correspondence with author, August 9 and July 9, 2004; Betzinez, *I Fought with Geronimo,* 55; Loco family, interviews by author, January 3, 1969.

20. Thrapp, *Victorio,* 222; Harte, "San Carlos," vol. 2, 651–52.

21. Raymond Loco, interview by author, November 24, 1969; Betzinez, *I Fought with Geronimo,* 58; Edwin R. Sweeney, correspondence with author, June 14, 2004.

22. Undated correspondence between Balatchu and Opler, Opler Papers; Raymond, Norman, and Moses Loco, interviews by author, 1962–1971; Benedict Jozhe, interview by author, June 22, 1971.

23. Opler, "Chiricahua Apache's Account," 363–64; Raymond, Norman, and Moses Loco, interviews by author, 1962–1971; Benedict Jozhe, interview by author, June 22, 1971.

24. Barrett, *Geronimo,* 105–106.

25. Raymond Loco, interview by author, October 19–25, 1970.

26. Ball, *Victorio,* 136–38; "Interview with Leon Perico," in Sol Tax Papers, University of Chicago, Special Collection 5, Box 10, Folder 15.

27. Raymond Loco, interview by author, October 19–25, 1970.

28. Debo, *Geronimo,* 117; Benedict Jozhe, interview by author, June 22, 1971.

29. SW, Annual Report 1882, including report of Willcox, August 31, 1882; AG to SW, May 2, 1882, in NAMP, M689, R96–97, AGO; Charles Morton to AGO, May 30, 1882, in NAMP, M689, R97, AGO, LR, Report of the Chiricahua Outbreak.

30. Forsyth, *Thrilling Days in Army Life,* 79; Thrapp, *General Crook,* 72–73, quoting Benjamin to CO, Forts Bowie and Huachuca, January 1, 1882.

31. Debo, *Geronimo,* 138; Terrell, *Apache Chronicle,* 351.

32. Morton report, May 30, 1882, NAMP.

33. Thrapp, *General Crook,* 72–74, quoting Benjamin to Major David Perry at Willcox, Arizona, February 19, 1882, Willcox to AG, Washington, February 17, 1882, and Howard to Willcox and Willcox to Col. Ranald Mackenzie, February 20, 1882.

34. Harte, "San Carlos," vol. 2, 653, quoting Tiffany to CIA, February 15, 1882, Willcox to AG, Prescott, February 20, 1882, SI to Inspector Howard, March 2, 1882, Letters to Inspectors, and Connell, "The Apache, Past and Present"; Horn, *Life of Tom Horn,* 43, 143–45.

35. Thrapp, *General Crook,* 97, quoting Willcox to AAG, Division of the Pacific, April 21, 1882; Harte, "San Carlos," vol. 2, 650–51.

36. *Grant County Herald,* April 15, 1882.

37. Benedict Jozhe, interview by author, June 22, 1871.

38. Col. Luther Bradley to AG, Department of the Missouri, January 11, 1882, in NARA, RG75, Document 2512; Raymond Loco, interview by author, June 21, 1971.

39. Thrapp, *General Crook,* 64–65, quoting Guy Howard report, March 25, 1882, and Bradley to AG, Department of the Missouri, January 11, 1882.

40. Harte, "San Carlos," vol. 2, 650–51, 663–65, quoting Bradley to Adjutant, April 21, 1882, including Howard to Kirkwood, March 25, 1882.

41. Harte, "San Carlos," vol. 2, 651, quoting Sherman to SI, April 4, 1882.

42. Thrapp, *General Crook,* 97, quoting Willcox to AAG, Division of the Pacific, April 21, 1882; Galen Eastman to CIA, February 22, 1882, in NARA, RG75, Document 4407; Bradley to AAG, Department of the Missouri, January 11, 1882, and endorsement by Mackenzie on January 20, 1882, in NARA, RG75, Document 2512.

43. Eastman to CIA, February 22, 1882, and Bradley to AAG, Department of the Missouri, January 11, 1882, NARA; Benedict Jozhe, interviews by author, June 21–22, 1971.

CHAPTER 12

1. Crook, *Resume,* 10; Edwin R. Sweeney, correspondence with author, January 22, 2007.

2. Basso, *Western Apache Raiding,* Rope account, 143–44; Thrapp, *Conquest,* 237–38, quoting unnamed San Francisco newspaper.

3. S. D. Pangburn to Benjamin, AAG, Whipple Bks., April 19, 1882, in NARA, M689, R96–97.

4. Ibid.; Betzinez, *I Fought with Geronimo,* 55; Raymond Loco and Benedict Jozhe, interviews by author, June 21–22, 1971.

5. Betzinez, *I Fought with Geronimo,* 56.

6. Ibid.

7. Raymond Loco, interview by author, June 21, 1971; Sheridan to AG, May 19, 1882, in NAMP, M689, R96; *New Southwest and Grant County Herald,* May 13, 1882; Crook, *Resume,* 10; Betzinez, *I Fought with Geronimo,* 56.

8. Basso, *Western Apache Raiding,* 146; Pangburn to Benjamin, AAG, Whipple Bks., April 19, 1882, NAMP.

9. Basso, *Western Apache Raiding,* 146; Betzinez, *I Fought with Geronimo,* 56; Horn, *Life of Tom Horn,* 44; Thrapp, *Conquest,* 236.

10. Horn, *Life of Tom Horn,* 44–47; Larry Ball (Horn's biographer), correspondence with author, October 6, 2006; Thrapp, *General Crook,* 85n.

11. Horn, *Life of Tom Horn,* 44–47.

12. Ibid.

13. Debo, *Geronimo,* 143; Harte, "San Carlos," vol. 2, 661–63; SW, Annual Report 1882, including Willcox report, August 31, 1882; Erickson, *Trailing the Apache;* Thrapp, *General Crook,* 75, quoting Sieber to Willcox, June 8, 1882; Pangburn to Benjamin, AAG, Whipple Bks., April 19, 1882, and Irvin McDowell to AGO, April 29, 1882, in NAMP, M689, R96–97.

14. Thrapp, *General Crook,* 76, quoting Benjamin to CO at Ft. Apache, April 19, 1882; McDowell to AG, April 29, 1882, NAMP.

15. Pangburn to Benjamin, AAG, Whipple Bks., April 19, 1882, NAMP; Morton to AGO, May 30, 1882, NAMP.

16. Basso, *Western Apache Raiding,* 143–44; "History of Barrels," www.eresonant.com /pages/history/history-barrels.html (accessed September 5, 2005); U.S. Army, *Wagon Harness,* n.p.

17. Thrapp, *Conquest,* 217–30; Debo, *Geronimo,* 126–33; Sheridan to Drum, May 17, 1882, in NARA, RG75, Document 10908.

18. Basso, *Western Apache Raiding,* Rope account, 146–47.

19. Betzinez, *I Fought with Geronimo,* 58.

20. Ibid.; Raymond and Norman Loco, interview by author, June 18, 1966; Bradley to AAG, District of New Mexico, May 11 and 30, 1882, in NAMP, M1088, R47.

21. SW to SI, March 13, 1885, in NARA, RG92, Quartermaster Consolidated files, Indians, Chiricahua (1885).

22. Bradley to AAG, District of New Mexico, May 11 and 30, 1882 (Bradley's numbers do not add up), and Sheridan to Drum, May 17, 1882, in NAMP, M1088, R47; Pope to James Williams, AAG, Chicago, May 30, 1882, in NARA, RG75, Document 10908.

23. Pope to AAG, Chicago, May 15, 1882, Bradley to AAG, District of New Mexico, May 30, 1882, and McDowell to AGDC, July 21, 1882, in NAMP, M689, R96; Raymond Loco, interview by author, June 18, 1966; Edwin R. Sweeney, correspondence with author, June 14, 2004.

24. Smith, Fort Union, to AAG, District of New Mexico, May 22, 1883, in NAMP, 689, R96.

25. Bradley to AG, Department of the Missouri, June 3, 1884, and Bradley to AAG, District of New Mexico, May, 30, 1882, in NAMP, M689, R97.

26. Morton to AGO, May 30, 1882, NAMP; Horn, *Life of Tom Horn,* 47.

27. Betzinez, *I Fought with Geronimo,* 56–60; Raymond Loco, interview by author, June 18, 1966; Pangburn to Benjamin, AAG, Whipple Bks., April 19, 1882, NAMP; Morton to AGO, May 30, 1882, NAMP.

28. Pope to AGDC, April 28, 1882, in NAMP, M689, R96; Harte, "San Carlos," vol. 2, 662, quoting McDowell to AG, San Francisco, April 22 and 28 and May 3, 1882, and Connell, "The Apache Past and Present, II"; Thrapp, *General Crook,* 76, quoting Benjamin to CO, Ft. Apache, April 19, 1882; McDowell to AGODC, April 29, 1882, in NARA, LR, AGO.

29. Pope to AGDC, April 28, 1882, NAMP.; Raymond Loco, interview by author, June 18, 1966; Horn, *Life of Tom Horn,* 49.

30. Raymond, Norman, and Moses Loco, interview by author, June 18, 1966; Benedict Jozhe and Mildred Cleghorn (former chair, Fort Sill Apache Tribe), interviews by author, June 20, 1966; Betzinez, *I Fought with Geronimo,* 65; Pope to AGDC, April 28, 1882, NAMP.

31. Thrapp, *General Crook,* 81, 85; Dodge to SW, April 25, 1882, HQ, Division of the Pacific, to AGDC, April 27, 1882, and Pope to AAAGDC, April 28, 1882, in NAMP, M689, R96–97.

32. Sheridan to AGO, April 26, 1882, and McDowell, San Francisco, to AGODC, April 24, 1882, in NAMP, LR, AGO, M689, R96.

33. Raymond, Norman, and Moses Loco, interview by author, June 18, 1966.

34. Forsyth, *Thrilling Days,* 100.

35. Ibid., 85.

36. Ibid., 85–86.

37. Ibid.

38. Sheridan to Drum, April 25, 1882, in NARA, LR, AGO, M689, R96.

39. Erickson, "Trailing the Apache," n.p.

40. Ibid.

41. Ibid.; Forsyth, *Thrilling Days,* 107.

42. Forsyth, *Thrilling Days,* 108–109.

43. Raymond, Norman, and Moses Loco, interview by author, June 18, 1966; Benedict Jozhe and Mildred Cleghorn, interviews by author, June 20, 1966; Sheridan to Drum, April 25, 1882, including George Forsyth report, NARA; Betzinez, *I Fought with Geronimo,* 63; Forsyth, *Thrilling Days,* 107.

44. Sheridan to Drum, April 25, 1882, including Forsyth report, NARA; Betzinez, *I Fought with Geronimo,* 63; Forsyth, *Thrilling Days,* 107; Thrapp, *Conquest,* 244; Raymond, Norman, and Moses Loco, interview by author, June 18, 1966.

45. Betzinez, *I Fought with Geronimo,* 63.

46. Forsyth, *Thrilling Days,* 113.

47. Raymond, Norman, and Moses Loco, interview by author, June 18–21, 1966.

48. Ibid.; Horn, *Life of Tom Horn,* 57.

49. Raymond, Norman, and Moses Loco, interview by author, June 18–21, 1966; Benedict Jozhe and Mildred Cleghorn, interviews by author, June 20, 1966; Horn, *Life of Tom Horn,* 58.

50. Harte, "San Carlos," vol. 2, 663n, quoting Report of a Military Board of Officers, n.d.; Forsyth to AAG, District of New Mexico, April 25, 1882, Sheridan to Drum, April 25, 1882, and Sheridan to AGDC, April 26, 1882, in NAMP, M689, R96–97, LR, AGO.

CHAPTER 13

1. Horn, *Life of Tom Horn,* 58.

2. Heitman, *Historical Register and Dictionary of the United States Army,* 812, 973; Thrapp, *General Crook,* 86–87, quoting Willcox to AAG, Division of the Pacific, April 26, 1882; Thrapp, *Juh,* 32–33.

3. Thrapp, *General Crook,* 86–87, quoting Willcox to AAG, Division of the Pacific, April 26, 1882.

4. Horn, *Life of Tom Horn,* 59.

5. Ibid., 58–60; Goodwin, "Sherman Curley," n.p.; Thrapp, *General Crook,* 86–87, quoting Willcox to AAG, Division of the Pacific, April 26, 1882; William Rafferty's diary in the *Arizona Star,* May 17, 1882; Francis Darr's interview in the *Arizona Star,* May 26, 1882.

6. Thrapp, *General Crook,* 85–86, 90, quoting Willcox to AAG, Division of the Pacific, April 26, 1882.

7. Rafferty's diary in the *Arizona Star,* May 17, 1882; Darr's interview in the *Arizona Star,* January 22, 1882; Sieber, "Military and the Indians."

8. Opler, *Apache Life-Way,* 352–53; Ellyn Bigrope (director, Tribal Cultural Center, Mescalero Apache Tribe), correspondence with author, June 8, 2004.

9. On-site observations with Dan L. Thrapp, 1969; Rafferty's diary in the *Arizona Star,* May 17, 1882; Darr's interview in the *Arizona Star,* January 22, 1882; Sieber, "Military and the Indians."

10. Heitman, *Historical Register,* 223, 354, 714, 812, 966, 973.

11. On-site observations with Dan L. Thrapp, 1969; Rafferty's diary in the *Arizona Star,* May 17, 1882; Darr's interview in the *Arizona Star,* January 22, 1882; Thrapp, *General Crook,* 85–86, quoting Rafferty, Fort Bowie, to Perry, Fort Huachuca, May 14, 1882; Sieber, "Military and the Indians"; Thrapp, *Juh,* 32–33; Raymond Loco, interviews by author, June 18, 1966, and June 21–24, 1971.

12. *Grant County Herald,* reprinting an article from the *Tucson Citizen,* October 9, 1881; Raymond Loco, interviews by author, June 18, 1966, and June 21–24, 1971; Goodwin, "Sherman Curley," n.p.; Thrapp, *General Crook,* 85–86, 89; Rafferty's diary in the *Arizona Star,* May 17, 1882; Darr's interview in the *Arizona Star,* January 22, 1882; Sieber, "Military and the Indians."

13. Goodwin, "Sherman Curley," n.p.

14. Rafferty's diary in the *Arizona Star,* May 17, 1882; Darr's interview in the *Arizona Star,* January 22, 1882; Sieber, "Military and the Indians"; Horn, *Life of Tom Horn,* 63.

15. Rafferty's diary in the *Arizona Star,* May 17, 1882; Darr's interview in the *Arizona Star,* January 22, 1882; Sieber, "Military and the Indians"; Goodwin, "Sherman Curley," n.p.

16. Thrapp, *Al Sieber,* 232–33, quoting newspaper clipping, Los Angeles Public Library; Goodwin, "Sherman Curley," n.p.

17. Goodwin, "Sherman Curley," n.p.; Darr's interview in the *Arizona Star,* January 22, 1882.

18. Goodwin, "Sherman Curley," n.p.; Betzinez, *I Fought with Geronimo,* 69.

19. Rafferty's diary in the *Arizona Star,* May 17, 1882; Darr's interview in the *Arizona Star,* January 22, 1882; Sieber, "Military and the Indians."

20. Horn, *Life of Tom Horn,* 63–65; Betzinez, *I Fought with Geronimo,* 70.

21. Raymond Loco, interview by author, June 18, 1966; Horn, *Life of Tom Horn,* 63–65; Betzinez, *I Fought with Geronimo,* 69.

22. Betzinez, *I Fought with Geronimo,* 69.

23. Thrapp, *Al Sieber,* 234; Goodwin, "Sherman Curley," n.p.; Betzinez, *I Fought with Geronimo,* 69.

24. McDowell to AGDC, including Tupper field report, May 1, 1882, in NAMP, M689, R96; on-site observations with Dan L. Thrapp, 1969.

25. Ibid.; Raymond, Norman, and Moses Loco, interviews by author, June 21–22, 1971.

26. Horn, *Life of Tom Horn,* 66.

27. Thrapp, *Al Sieber,* 236.

28. Ibid.

29. Ibid.; Benton, "Sgt. Neil Erickson and the Apaches," 124–25.

30. Benton, "Sgt. Neil Erickson," 125–26.

31. Betzinez, *I Fought with Geronimo,* 70.

32. Rickey, *Forty Miles a Day,* 244, 276, 292; Forsyth, *Thrilling Days,* 113.

33. Forsyth, *Thrilling Days,* 115; Benton, "Sgt. Neil Erickson," 125.

34. Forsyth, *Thrilling Days,* 115.

35. Goodwin, "Sherman Curley," n.p.; Betzinez, *I Fought with Geronimo,* 69.

36. Goodwin, "Sherman Curley," n.p.; Betzinez, *I Fought with Geronimo,* 69; Forsyth, *Thrilling Days,* 115.

CHAPTER 14

1. Cruse, *Apache Days,* 136; Forsyth, *Thrilling Days,* 115; Betzinez, *I Fought with Geronimo,* 70–72.

2. Raymond Loco, interview by author, December 26–27, 1963; Betzinez, *I Fought with Geronimo,* 71–72.

3. Ibid.

4. Rafferty to Perry, Fort Huachuca, May 14, 1882, in NARA, M689, R96, LR, AGO; Goodwin, "Sherman Curley," n.p.; Benton, "Sgt. Neil Erickson," 121–30; Erickson, "Trailing the Apache," n.p; Forsyth, *Thrilling Days,* 119.

5. Garcia report in the Official Mexican Government Newspaper, May 19, 1882, in NARA, M689, R96–97, LR, AGO; Edwin R. Sweeney, correspondence with author, January 25, 2005, and July 9, 2007.

6. Erickson, "Trailing the Apache," n.p.

7. Thrapp, *Al Sieber,* 239, quoting Lt. Thomas Cruse to Davis, October 8, 1927; Betzinez, *I Fought with Geronimo,* 71–72.

8. Edwin R. Sweeney, correspondence with author, December 30, 2004; Raymond Loco, interview by author, December 27, 1963.

9. Betzinez, *I Fought with Geronimo,* 70–72; Horn, *Life of Tom Horn,* 67.

10. Betzinez, *I Fought with Geronimo,* 70–72.

11. Thrapp, *Al Sieber,* 238; Thrapp, *General Crook,* 92, citing report of Brigadier Jose Guillermo Carbo, CO, First Mexican Military Zone, to Mexican Secretary of War and Maritime; Benton, "Sgt. Neil Erickson," 121–30.

12. Betzinez, *I Fought with Geronimo,* 71–72.

13. Thrapp, *Al Sieber,* 239, quoting Cruse to Davis, October 8, 1927.

14. Benton, "Sgt. Neil Erickson," 121–30.

15. Forsyth, *Thrilling Days,* 118–19.

16. Thrapp, *Al Sieber,* 238–39, quoting Crook, "The Apaches Tell Their Story," and Crook to AAG, Division of the Pacific, March 28, 1883; Bourke, "Diary," March 28, 1883.

17. Betzinez, *I Fought with Geronimo,* 73–74; Edwin R. Sweeney, correspondence with author, August 9, 2004.

18. Frasca and Hill, *The .45–70 Springfield,* 350–69; Edwin R. Sweeney, correspondence with author, August 9, 2004; Myatt, *Encyclopedia,* 101–104.

19. Bourke, "Diary," April 7, 1883; Benton, "Sgt. Neil Erickson," 121–30; Myatt, *Encyclopedia,* 101–104; Frasca and Hill, *.45–70 Springfield,* 369.

20. Davis, *Truth about Geronimo,* 8; CO, Fort Davis, Texas, to AG, Department of Texas, May 20, 1882, in NAMP, M689, R96.

21. Raymond Loco, interviews by author, December 26–27, 1963, and June 18–22, 1966; Betzinez, *I Fought with Geronimo,* 73–74.

22. Raymond Loco, interview by author, June 18–22, 1966; Crook to AGO, March–June 1883, in NARA, M689, R173; Betzinez, *I Fought with Geronimo,* 73–74.

23. Raymond Loco, interview by author, December 26–27, 1963; Betzinez, *I Fought with Geronimo,* 74.

24. Tupper to Perry, Fort Huachuca, May 14, 1882, in NAMP, 689, R96.

25. Betzinez, *I Fought with Geronimo,* 72; Rafferty to Perry, Fort Huachuca, May 14, 1882, NARA.

26. Betzinez, *I Fought with Geronimo,* 73.

27. Benton, "Sgt. Neil Erickson," 121–30.

28. Tupper to Perry, May 14, 1882, NAMP.

29. Benton, "Sgt. Neil Erickson," 121–30; Erickson, "Trailing the Apache," n.p.; CO, Fort Davis, Texas, to AG, Dept. of Texas, May 20, 1882, relaying Stephen Mills's information, NAMP; Rafferty to Perry, Fort Huachuca, May 14, 1882, NARA.

30. Goodwin, "Sherman Curley," n.p.; Raymond Loco, interviews by author, December 26–27, 1963, and June 18–22, 1966; Ellyn Bigrope, correspondence with author, September 28, 2004; Sheridan to AG Drum, May 19, 1882, in NAMP, M689, R96; Griswold, "Fort Sill Apaches," n.p.

31. Rafferty to Perry, Fort Hauchuca, May 14, 1882, NARA; Benton, "Sgt. Neil Erickson," 121–30; *New Southwest and Grant County Herald,* May 13, 1882; Goodwin, "Sherman Curley," n.p.; Sheridan to AG Drum, May 19, 1882, NAMP.

32. Erickson, "Trailing the Apache," n.p.

33. *New Southwest and Grant County Herald,* May 13, 1882; Benton, "Sgt. Neil Erickson," 121–30; Erickson, "Trailing the Apache," n.p.

34. Thrapp, *General Crook,* 92, citing report of Brigadier Jose Guillermo Carbo, CO, First Mexican Military Zone, to Mexican Secretary of War and Maritime; Thrapp, *Conquest,* 248–49, and *Victorio,* 310–11.

35. Britton Davis report, 1884, "List of Chiricahua Captured in Mexico in the 1880s," in NARA, RG94, M689, R177; Bailey, *Indian Slave Trade in the Southwest,* 129.

36. Bailey, *Indian Slave Trade,* 38–44, 177; Tinker-Salas, *In the Shadow of Eagles,* 63.

37. Bourke, "Diary," May 19, 1883.

38. Dunn, *Massacres,* 325.

39. "Mistresses in Mexico," *International Encyclopedia of Sexuality: Mexico,* www.Worldpolicy.org/globalrights/mexico (accessed September 3, 2004).

40. Thrapp, *Conquest of Apacheria,* 305, quoting Crook to AGO, Army, April 7, 1885.

41. Thrapp, *Al Sieber,* 238, n23; Thrapp, *Victorio,* 241–42, n34.

42. Heitman, *Historical Register,* 223, 354, 430, 973, 812, 714; Thrapp, *Al Sieber,* 326, 368, 400.

43. Barrett, *Geronimo,* 116.

44. Goodwin, "Sherman Curley," n.p.; Debo, *Geronimo,* 432.

45. SW to SI, June 14, 1883, in NARA, 1883 AGO 2453; Crook to AGO, March–June 1883, NARA; Bourke, "Diary," October 30, 1882.

46. Bourke, "Diary," May 8, 1884; Opler, *Apache Life-Way,* 293, 305, 475; Raymond, Norman, and Moses Loco, interviews by author, December 26, 1863, and June 18–22, 1966.

47. Davis report, 1884, "List of Chiricahua Captured in Mexico in the 1880s," NARA.

48. Bourke, "Diary," October 30, 1882; Raymond, Norman, and Moses Loco, interviews by author, December 26, 1863, and June 18–22, 1966; Betzinez, *I Fought with Geronimo,* 75; Thrapp, *Victorio,* 237, quoting Crook to AAG, Division of the Pacific, March 28, 1883.

CHAPTER 15

1. Betzinez, *I Fought with Geronimo,* 72; Raymond Loco, interview by author, June 18–22, 1966.

2. Forsyth, *Thrilling Days,* 117–18.

3. Betzinez, *I Fought with Geronimo,* 69–77.

4. Ibid., 74–75; Raymond, Norman, and Moses Loco, interviews by author, December 26–27, 1963, and June 18–22, 1966.

5. Betzinez, *I Fought with Geronimo,* 74–75; Raymond, Norman, and Moses Loco, interview by author, December 26–27, 1963; Bourke, "Diary," October 30, 1882.

6. Opler, *Apache Life-Way,* 2; Raymond Loco, interview by author, June 18–22, 1966; Betzinez, *I Fought with Geronimo,* 15, 76.

7. Edwin R. Sweeney, correspondence with author, May 17, 2005; Betzinez, *I Fought with Geronimo,* 76–77.

8. Betzinez, *I Fought with Geronimo,* 77.

9. Ibid., 3; Kraft, *Gatewood and Geronimo,* 13–14.

10. Betzinez, *I Fought with Geronimo,* 3.

11. Edwin R. Sweeney, conversation with author, October 24, 2007; Debo, *Geronimo,* 154; Betzinez, *I Fought with Geronimo,* 77–9.

12. Bourke, "Diary," October 30, 1882; Betzinez, *I Fought with Geronimo,* 77–78.

13. Edwin R. Sweeney, conversation with author, May 8, 2005; Debo, *Geronimo,* 154; Raymond, Norman, and Moses Loco, interview by author, December 26–27, 1963; Thrapp, *Conquest,* 273, quoting unidentified Chicago newspaper, March 30, 1883.

14. Betzinez, *I Fought with Geronimo,* 81–83.

15. Ibid.; Bourke, "Diary," October 30, 1882, and May 3 and March 30, 1883; Debo, *Geronimo,* 15.

16. Bourke, "Diary," including article in unidentified newspaper, May 3, 1883.

17. Ibid., October 30, 1882, quoting conversation between Crook and Eshkebenti.

18. Ibid., March 30, April 7, and May 3, 1883; Thrapp, *Conquest,* 273.

19. Bourke, "Diary," April 7, 1883.

20. Thrapp, *Victorio,* 209; Raymond Loco, interview by author, January 4, 1869.

21. Thrapp, *Conquest,* 265, 273, quoting Crook to AAG, Division of the Pacific, March 28, 1883; Betzinez, *I Fought with Geronimo,* 101–102; Bourke, "Diary," March 30, April 7, and May 3, 1883.

22. Debo, *Geronimo,* 159–60; Bourke, *Apache Campaign,* 31; Betzinez, *I Fought with Geronimo,* 103; Bourke, "Diary," April 4–7, 1883.

23. Simmons, *Massacre on the Lordsburg Road,* 109–13.

24. Thrapp, *General Crook,* 115–16; Terrell, *Apache Chronicle,* 362; Debo, *Geronimo,* 159–60; Simmons, *Massacre,* 24, quoting Bourke, "Diary."

25. Simmons, *Massacre,* 157.

26. Ibid., 136; *Albuquerque Tribune Online,* March 31, 2004.

27. Simmons, *Massacre*, 141–42.

28. Bourke, *Apache Campaign*, 128; Betzinez, *I Fought with Geronimo*, 118–20; Kraft, *Gatewood and Geronimo*, 31; Simmons, *Massacre*, 182–83.

29. Raymond Loco, interview by author, January 4, 1869.

30. SW, Annual Report, 1883, 174; Bourke, *Apache Campaign*, 26–27; Simmons, *Massacre*, 157, quoting Daly, "The Geronimo Apache Campaign," and *Arizona Historical Review* 3 (July 1930).

31. Thrapp, *General Crook*, 141–42, quoting General Bonifacio Topete, Report to Mexican Minister of War and Marine, May 1, 1883.

32. Betzinez, *I Fought with Geronimo*, 110; Thrapp, *Conquest*, 280–81, quoting the *Arizona Star*, May 12, 1883.

33. Betzinez, *I Fought with Geronimo*, 110.

34. Thrapp, *Conquest*, 280–81, quoting the *Arizona Star*, May 12, 1883; Thrapp, *General Crook*, 141–42, quoting Topete report, May 1, 1883.

35. Bourke, *Apache Campaign*, 32–33.

36. Betzinez, *I Fought with Geronimo*, 110–11; Bourke, "Diary," April 7, 1883.

37. Betzinez, *I Fought with Geronimo*, 110–11.

38. *Arizona Star*, May 12, 1883; Betzinez, *I Fought with Geronimo*, 110–12; Thrapp, *General Crook*, 141–42, quoting Topete report, May 1, 1883; Edwin R. Sweeney, conversation with author, June 5, 2005.

39. *Arizona Star*, May 12, 1883; Betzinez, *I Fought with Geronimo*, 110–12; Thrapp, *General Crook*, 141–42, quoting Topete report, May 1, 1883; Bourke, "Diary," April 7, 1883.

40. Parker West, San Carlos, to AAG, Department of Arizona, May 29, 1883, in NAMP, M689, R173; Sheridan to Drum, May 17, 1882, NARA; Norman Loco, interview by author, June 21, 1971; Betzinez, *I Fought with Geronimo*, 58.

41. West to AAG, Department of Arizona, May 29, 1883, NAMP.

42. Report of Parker West, attachment to a letter from SW to SI, June 25, 1883, in NARA, RG75, Document 11691; Bourke, *Apache Campaign*, 115–16.

43. Willcox to SI, June 16, 1883, in NAMP, M689, R173; SI to SW, June 14, 1883, and Document 11691, West report, June 25, 1883, NARA.

CHAPTER 16

1. Bourke, *Apache Campaign*, 37, 56–57; SW, Annual Report 1883, 174.

2. Bourke, *Apache Campaign*, 72–75; Thrapp, *Sierra Madre*, 106, 145.

3. Bourke, *Apache Campaign*, 94–95.

4. Goodwin, "Sherman Curley," n.p.; Thrapp, *General Crook*, 121.

5. Thrapp *Conquest*, 290, quoting the *Arizona Star*, June 21, 1883; Thrapp, *General Crook*, 162–63; Bourke, *Apache Campaign*, 118.

6. Bourke, *Apache Campaign*, 104–15; Kraft, *Gatewood and Geronimo*, 34; Terrell, *Apache Chronicle*, 368; Harte, "San Carlos," vol. 2, 722.

7. Bourke, *Apache Campaign*, 119; Davis, *Truth about Geronimo*, 69; Thrapp, *General Crook*, 162.

8. Bourke, *Apache Campaign*, 118–19; Thrapp, *Conquest*, 265, quoting Crook to AAG, Division of the Pacific, March 28, 1883.

9. Bourke, *Apache Campaign*, 120–22, 125.

10. Porter, *Paper Medicine Man*, 164; Bourke, *Apache Campaign*, 125; Debo, *Geronimo*, 190–92; Thrapp, *General Crook*, 169; Betzinez, *I Fought with Geronimo*, 123; Undated interview

with Balatchu, in Morris Opler Papers, Kroch Library, Rare and Manuscript Collections, Cornell University; Bourke, *Apache Campaign,* 125–26.

11. Betzinez, *I Fought with Geronimo,* 123; Opler, *Apache Life-Way,* 230–37; Thrapp, *General Crook,* 169; Basso, *Western Apache Raiding,* 171.

12. Betzinez, *I Fought with Geronimo,* 122.

13. Basso, *Western Apache Raiding,* 171.

14. Debo, *Geronimo,* 189–92, quoting Goodwin, "Experiences," *Arizona Historical Review,* 72.

15. Ibid.; Bourke, *Apache Campaign,* 108–109; Crook to Division of the Pacific, July 23, 1883, 176–78, in SW, Annual Report 1883; Thrapp, *Al Sieber,* 286.

16. Bourke, *Apache Campaign,* 108–109.

17. Basso, *Western Apache Raiding,* 171–72, quoting Rope; Raymond Loco, interview by author, January 3, 1869.

18. Davis, *Truth about Geronimo,* 72.

19. Harte, "San Carlos," vol. 2, 723.

20. Wilcox to CIA, August 15, 1884, and Wilcox to SI, June 16, 1883, in NAMP, M689, R173; Memorandum from SW and SI, June 7, 1883, in NAMP, M689, R174.

21. Harte, "San Carlos," vol. 2, 723–24.

22. Ibid., 720, quoting Beaumont to SI, June 16, 1883; SI to SW, June 14, 1883, in NAMP M689, R173.

23. Crook to AAG, June 6, 1885, and SW to SI, June 15, 18, and 19, 1883, in NAMP, M689, R174.

24. Betzinez, *I Fought with Geronimo,* 122–23.

25. Memorandum from SW and SI, June 7, 1883, SW to SI, June 15 and 19, 1883, and SI to SW, June 18, 1883, in NAMP, M689, R174; Bourke, "Diary," July 24, 1883; Harte, "San Carlos," vol. 2, 728–30.

26. Davis, *Truth about Geronimo,* 69–73.

27. Edwin R. Sweeney, correspondence with author, July 9, 2007; Davis, *Truth about Geronimo,* 85–86; Harte, "San Carlos," vol. 2, 744.

28. Davis, *Truth about Geronimo,* 85–86; Thrapp, *General Crook,* 176.

29. Davis, *Truth about Geronimo,* 107–21.

30. Betzinez, *I Fought with Geronimo,* 122–23.

31. Harte, "San Carlos," vol. 2, 793; Betzinez, *I Fought with Geronimo,* 122–23.

32. Emmet Crawford to Crook, March 21, 1884, in NARA, RG393, LR, Arizona 1884.

33. Radbourne, "Captain Hatfield and the Chiricahuas," 143, quoting Frazer, *Apaches of the White Mountain Reservation, Arizona* (Philadelphia: IRA, 1885); Davis, *Truth about Geronimo,* 105–11; Edwin R. Sweeney, correspondence with author, July 28, 2005.

34. Davis, *Truth about Geronimo,* 107, 133–35; Edwin R. Sweeney, correspondence with author, July 9, 2007.

35. Davis, *Truth about Geronimo,* 131–33; Radbourne, "Captain Hatfield," 144, quoting "An Apache Dance," *Outing Magazine,* June 1893, 189–91.

36. Davis, *Truth about Geronimo,* 133–35; Edwin R. Sweeney, correspondence with author, July 9, 2007.

37. Davis, *Truth about Geronimo,* 133–135; Harte, "San Carlos," vol. 2, 781–82; Wilcox to CIA, August 15, 1884, in Senate Executive Document 117, 49th Congress, 2nd session; Crook to AAG, June 6, 1885, in NAMP, M689, R178.

38. Crook to AG, November 23, 1883, and Pope to AG, January 9, 1884, in NAMP, M689, R174.

39. Davis, *Truth about Geronimo,* 133–35.

40. Debo, *Geronimo,* 228–29; Betzinez, *I Fought with Geronimo,* 125; Edwin R. Sweeney, correspondence with author, August 5, 2005; Bourke, *On the Border,* 466; Crawford to Crook, August 2, 1884, in NAMP, M689, R175.

41. Sonnichsen, *Geronimo,* 76, quoting "A Chiricahua Apache's Account of the Geronimo Campaign of 1886, by Samuel E. Kenoi," recorded by Morris E. Opler.

42. Raymond Loco, interview by author, November 23, 1964; Crawford to Crook, December 17, 1883, in NAMP, M689, R175; Harte, "San Carlos," vol. 2, 803–804.

CHAPTER 17

1. Davis to Crawford, September 26, 1884, in NARA, RG393, LR, San Carlos.

2. CIA to SI, March 13, 1885, in NARA, RG92, Box 895, Indians, Chiricahua (1885), Quartermaster Consolidated Files.

3. Raymond, Norman, and Moses Loco, interview by author, December 23, 1963; Edwin R. Sweeney, correspondence with author, July 9, 2007; Davis, *Truth about Geronimo,* 140.

4. *Albuquerque Journal,* July 7, 1885.

5. Raymond, Norman, and Moses Loco, interview by author, December 23, 1963; Belle Kazshay (Mescalero Apache tribal member), interview by author, November 18, 1971.

6. Bradley to Crook, July 5, 1885, and Charles B. Gatewood to Crook, August 1 and 8, 1885, in NARA, RG393, LR, Department of Arizona, 1885; Debo, *Geronimo,* 230, 28n.

7. C. D. Ford to CIA, January 21, 1885, in NAMP, M689, R177; Debo, *Geronimo,* 207, quoting SW to SI, January 25, 1884, and Pope to AG, January 24, 1884.

8. Opler, "Chiricahua Apache's Account," 71–73; Betzinez, *I Fought with Geronimo,* 129.

9. Waddell and Everett, *Drinking Behavior among Southwestern Indians,* 3, 149, 158, 160; Opler, *Apache Life-Way,* 368, 436.

10. Edwin R. Sweeney, correspondence with author, July 9, 2007.

11. Davis, *Truth about Geronimo,* 139–40.

12. Crook to AAG, June 5, 1885, War Department to SI, February 26, 1885, Ford to CIA, April 11 and May 15 and 27, 1885, and Pope to AG, San Francisco, May 21 and 23 and August 26, 1885, in NAMP, M689, R178; Davis, *Truth about Geronimo,* 115, 139–43; Harte, "San Carlos," vol. 2, 805–806, quoting Frank Armstrong, Indian Inspector, to SI, August 26, 1885; Thrapp, *Conquest,* 311–14, quoting Crook to Editor, *Clifton Clarion,* May 18, 1885; Kraft, *Gatewood and Geronimo,* 85–87; John Pope to AAG, May 23, 1885, in NAMP, M689, R177.

13. George Roach to Roberts, July 9, 1885, in NARA, RG393, LR, Department of Arizona, 1885.

14. William W. Wotherspoon to post adjutant, March 31, 1892, in NAMP, M689, R196; Barrett, *Geronimo,* 49–50.

15. Crawford to Crook, December 17, 1883, in NAMP, M689, R175; Crook to AAG, December 22, 1884, in NAMP, M689, R176,; Wilcox to SI, June 4, 1883, in Arizona Historical Society, microfilm, San Carlos Indian Agency, Roll 3.

16. Simmons, *Massacre,* 176.

17. Harte, "San Carlos," vol. 2, 805–806, quoting Armstrong to SI, August 26, 1885.

18. Betzinez, *I Fought with Geronimo,* 122; Raymond, Norman, and Moses Loco, interview by author, December 27, 1963; Davis, *Truth about Geronimo,* 72, 83–86.

19. Barrett, *Geronimo,* 140; Debo, *Geronimo,* 246, quoting Crook Letterbook I, 227–28, and Crook to AAG, Division of the Pacific, September 19, 1886; Kraft, *Gatewood and Geronimo,* 106–12, 126, quoting Crook to Nelson Miles, September 17, 1885.

20. Pierce to AAG, Department of Arizona, July 11, 1885, in NARA, RG393, LR, Department of Arizona, 1886.

21. Ogle, *Federal Control,* 233–34; Faulk, *The Geronimo Campaign,* 71–73; Debo, *Geronimo,* 248; Thrapp, *Conquest,* 334–35, quoting Crook to AAG, Division of the Pacific, November 25, 1885; Kraft, *Gatewood and Geronimo,* 111–12.

22. Kraft, *Gatewood and Geronimo,* 106–12, quoting Gatewood Collection, Arizona Historical Society.

23. Ibid., quoting Sanchez in Gatewood Collection, Arizona Historical Society.

24. Ibid., 109–11.

25. Sheridan to SW, July 7, 1886, in NARA, RG75, Document 18268.

CHAPTER 18

1. Crook, *Resume,* 10; Davis, *Truth about Geronimo,* 213–19; Bourke, *On the Border with Crook,* 480.

2. Crook to Sheridan, April 17, 1886, in NAMP, M689, R179.

3. Senate Executive Document no. 117, 67–74.

4. Ibid.

5. Horn, *Life of Tom Horn,* 157; Thrapp, *Victorio,* 131.

6. Sheridan to SW, July 7, 1886, NARA.

7. Crook to Division of the Pacific, September 27, 1883, in SW, Annual Report 1883, 169.

8. Raymond and Norman Loco, interview by author, December 27, 1963.

9. *Army and Navy Journal,* September 25, 1886; Edwin R. Sweeney, correspondence with author, October 24, 2006.

10. Bourke, "Diary," May 1, 1886, to March 5, 1887; "Apaches Before Secretary Lamar," *Washington Evening Star,* July 19, 1886; Raymond Loco, interview by author, November 21, 1971.

11. Bourke, "Diary," May 1, 1886, to March 5, 1887.

12. "Apaches Before Secretary Lamar," *Washington Evening Star,* July 19, 1886; Raymond Loco, interview by author, November 21, 1971.

13. Indian Claim Settlement no. 8043, in NARA, RG217, Second Auditor's Records.

14. *Washington Evening Star,* July 19, 1886; "Chaco Safe from Harm," *Washington Post,* July 23, 1886.

15. Bourke, "Diary," May 1, 1886, to March 5, 1887.

16. Radbourne, "Captain Hatfield," 172, quoting Roberts to James Lockett, April 11, 1886; Bourke, "Diary," May 1, 1886, to March 5, 1887.

17. Notes from a Conference between SW and the Apache Delegation, July 26, 1886, in NAMP, M689, R187.

18. "Apaches at the White House—Their Conference with the Great Father," *Washington Evening Star,* July 28, 1886.

19. Ibid.

20. Indian Claim Settlement no. 8043, NARA.

21. Bourke, "Diary," May 1, 1886, to March 5, 1887; Porter, *Paper Medicine Man,* 216.

22. Brodsky, *Grover Cleveland,* 34, 162, 172–74.

23. Senate Executive Document no. 117, 55.

24. Ibid., 67–74; Senate Executive Document no. 35, 4–13, 35–48; Porter, *Paper Medicine Man,* 218; Skinner, *The Apache Rock Crumbles,* 141.

25. Strover, "The Apaches' Last Trek." Articles published under the name William Strover were apparently written by Lieutenant Lewis Strother. Heitman, *Historical Register,* 933; Faulk, *Geronimo Campaign,* 160–61.

26. AAG to Loomis Langdon, Commanding St. Francis Barracks, September 7, 1886, in NAMP, M689, R185; Strover, "Apaches' Last Trek"; Raymond and Norman Loco, interview by author, December 27, 1963; Porter, *Paper Medicine Man,* 223. Accounts vary from 381 to 385 prisoners.

27. Strover, "Apaches' Last Trek."

28. Senate Executive Document no. 117, 75, AG to General John Schofield, September 21, 1886; East, "Apache Prisoners at Castillo de San Marcos"; AGO to CO Mount Vernon Barracks, Alabama, 1886–87, in NARA, LR, 1886 and 1887, AGO; Strover, "Last of Geronimo"; Strover, "Apaches' Last Trek."

29. Strover, "Apaches' Last Trek;" Drum to Commissary General, December 6, 1886, and AGO to CO, Mount Vernon Barracks, in NARA, 1359, AGO 1887.

30. White, *The American Railroad Passenger Car,* xiii, 26.

31. Raymond Loco, interview by author, December 27, 1963.

32. White, *American Railroad Passenger Car,* 400–404; Raymond Loco, interview by author, December 27, 1963.

33. White, *American Railroad Passenger Car,* 14, 99, 429–30.

34. Raymond and Norman Loco, interviews by author, December 27, 1963, and April 3, 1975; Mildred Cleghorn, interview by author, October 1, 1967; White, 14, 99, 429–30; Goodwin, *Western Apache,* 563–64.

35. Strover, "Apaches' Last Trek"; Senate Executive Document no. 117, 17–25; Skinner, *Apache Rock,* 266, quoting the *Pensacolian,* October 2, 1886.

36. Skinner, *Apache Rock,* 267, quoting Miles to Redfield Proctor, cited in Wratten, 449–551.

37. Strover, "Last of Geronimo."

38. Senate Executive Document no. 117, 23–25; Skinner, *Apache Rock,* 79.

39. Strover, "Apaches' Last Trek."

40. Debo, *Geronimo,* 301; Porter, *Paper Medicine Man,* 223; Strover, "Apaches' Last Trek."

41. *Florida Times Union,* September 20, 1886.

42. *Army and Navy Journal,* September 25, 1886.

43. Debo, *Geronimo,* 309–11.

CHAPTER 19

1. Porter, *Paper Medicine Man,* 229, quoting Bourke, "Diary."

2. U.S. National Park Service, *History of Castillo de San Marcos,* 42–43, 55–59; Interviews with Castillo de San Marcos National Monument staff, November 11, 2005.

3. Davis, "Tardy Reminiscence," 77–83; Horace Caruthers to SI, January 20, 1887, in NAMP, M689, R188; East, "Apache Prisoners," 5–30.

4. East, "Apache Prisoners," 30; Skinner, *Apache Rock,* 56, quoting the *Pensacolian,* April 17, 1886.

5. Debo, *Geronimo,* 326, quoting inspector general, March 11, 188, endorsed by Langdon; Graff and Schlesinger, *Grover Cleveland,* 150–60.

6. Skinner, *Apache Rock,* 85, quoting the *Pensacolian,* September 18, 1886.

7. East, "Apache Prisoners," 32; Debo, *Geronimo,* 279, citing the *Pensacolian,* September 18, 1886; Skinner, *Apache Rock,* 53, quoting the *Florida Times-Union,* n.d.

8. Debo, *Geronimo,* 279, quoting the *Pensacolian,* September 18, 1886; U.S. National Park Service, "The Apache; Geronimo! Apache Prisoners at Fort Pickens," *Gulf Island National Seashore,* www.nps.gov/guis/extended/fla/history/apache.htm (accessed September 30, 2005); Senate Executive Document no. 117, 18–20.

9. *Army and Navy Journal,* June 19, 1886.

10. Langdon report, July 4, 1886, included with Langdon to William Endicott, August 21 and 23, 1886, in NAMP, M689, R188.

11. Langdon to Endicott, August 21 and 23, 1884, NAMP; Senate Executive Document no. 35, 40–45.

12. Webb, "Paper Read before the Duchess County Medical Society"; Langdon to AG, September 29, 1886, in NAMP, M689, R188.

13. Tentsmiths, "Sibley Tents," www.tentsmiths.com/ushist.com (accessed January 10, 2006); Caruthers to SI, January 20, 1887, NAMP.

14. Welsh, *Apache Prisoners in Fort Marion,* 13; Imbrie, "Biography of Herbert Welsh."

15. Welsh, *Apache Prisoners,* 187; Imbrie, "Biography."

16. Webb, "Paper"; *Army and Navy Journal,* September 25, 1886; Bourke to SW, "Report of Visit to Mount Vernon Barracks, Alabama, and Vicinity," April 19, 1887, in NAMP, M689, R189; Porter, *Paper Medicine Man,* 228, quoting Bourke, "Diary."

17. Welsh, *Apache Prisoners,* 10–20.

18. Webb, "Paper."

19. Porter, *Paper Medicine Man,* 228, quoting Bourke, "Diary."

20. Langdon to AG, September 29, 1886, NAMP; National Institute of Health, "Carbolic Acid," *Medlineplus Medical Encyclopedia,* www.nilm.nih.gov/medlineplus/encyclopedia (accessed December 6, 2005); Welsh, *Apache Prisoners,* 10–14.

21. East, "Apache Prisoners," 35; Debo, *Geronimo,* 316, quoting Senate Executive Document no. 73, 49th Congress, 2nd Session; Opler, *Apache Life-Way,* 133; Amy Harper (interpretive ranger, Castillo de San Marcos National Monument) and Charles Tingley (library manager, St. Augustine Historical Society), interviews, September 12–13, 2007.

22. Debo, *Geronimo,* 323, quoting Langdon reports, January 7, June 28, and August 9, 1886, and January 1887.

23. William Sinclair to AAG, monthly reports, May 26, 1887, and September 30, 1887, in NAMP, M689, R190; Blossom Haozous (daughter of George Wratten), interview by author, October 3, 1963; East, "Apache Prisoners," 35; Welsh, *Apache Prisoners,* 10–20.

24. Sinclair to AAG, monthly report, May 26, 1887, NAMP.

25. Welsh, *Apache Prisoners,* 14–16; Raymond and Norman Loco, interview by author, October 1, 1963.

26. Welsh, *Apache Prisoners,* 14–16; East, "Apache Prisoners," 25.

27. East, "Apache Prisoners," 25–30; Raymond and Norman Loco, interview by author, October 1, 1963.

28. East, "Apache Prisoners," 30.

CHAPTER 20

1. Senate Executive Document no. 117, 1–10; Debo, *Geronimo,* 324–25, quoting Ayres to Sheridan, March 25, 1887; *Army and Navy Journal,* September 25, 1886.

2. *Army and Navy Journal,* September 25, 1886; East, "Apache Prisoners," 37; Skinner, *Apache Rock,* 120.

3. Betzinez, *I Fought with Geronimo,* 146.

4. Langdon reports, August 20 and 23, 1886, in NAMP, M689, R186.

5. Ibid.

6. East, "Apache Prisoners," 17; Langdon to AAG, October 1, 1886, in NAMP, M689, R186; Raymond, Norman, and Moses Loco, interview by author, October 1, 1963; East and Mancy, "Arizona Apaches as Guests in Florida," 294–300.

7. Welsh, *Apache Prisoners,* 14–15; Van Campen, *St. Augustine; Army and Navy Journal,* September 25, 1886.

8. Betzinez, *I Fought with Geronimo,* 146; Skinner, *Apache Rock,* 121, quoting the *Pensacola Commercial,* October 3, 1886.

9. Skinner, *Apache Rock,* 56.

10. Welsh, *Apache Prisoners,* 14; Betzinez, *I Fought with Geronimo,* 146.

11. Raymond and Norman Loco, interview by author, October 1, 1963; Langdon to AAG, October 1, 1886, NAMP; *Florida Times Union,* April 18, 1886; Betzinez, *I Fought with Geronimo,* 146.

12. Welsh, *Apache Prisoners,* 13; Charles Tingley, interview by author, September 12, 2007; Interviews with Castillo de San Marcos National Monument staff, June 15, 1964.

13. Langdon to AAG, October 1, 1886, NAMP; Raymond and Norman Loco, interview by author, October 1, 1963; Interviews with Castillo de San Marcos National Monument staff, June 15, 1964.

14. Raymond and Norman Loco, interview by author, October 1, 1963; Betzinez, *I Fought with Geronimo,* 146.

15. Skinner, *Apache Rock,* 59, quoting *Frank Leslie's Illustrated Newspaper,* July 21, 1886.

16. Betzinez, *I Fought with Geronimo,* 146.

17. Porter, *Paper Medicine Man,* 228, quoting Bourke, "Diary"; Skinner, *Apache Rock,* 138–39, East, "Apache Prisoners," 24.

18. Langdon to AAG, October 1, 1886, NAMP; Raymond and Norman Loco, interview by author, October 1, 1963; Skinner, *Apache Rock,* 123.

19. Raymond and Norman Loco, interview by author, October 1, 1963; East and Mancy, "Arizona Apaches," 294–300; Helen Schmidt (staff, Saint Augustine Historical Society), interview by author, June 15, 1964; Langdon to AAG, October 1, 1886, NAMP.

20. Langdon to AAG, August 15, 1886, in NAMP, M689, R184,.

21. East, "Apache Prisoners," 17; Betzinez, *I Fought with Geronimo,* 146.

22. Welsh, *Apache Prisoners,* 15; Skinner, *Apache Rock,* 138, quoting the *Pensacola Commercial,* March 23, 1887.

23. East, "Apache Prisoners," 20; Skinner, *Apache Rock,* 137.

24. Raymond Loco, interview by author, November 23, 1963; AAG report to SW, March 17, 1887, in NAMP, M689, R191; CIA, Annual Report 1887; Debo, *Geronimo,* 318–19.

25. Debo, *Geronimo,* 318–19; Raymond Loco, interview by author, November 23, 1963.

26. Betzinez, *I Fought with Geronimo,* 149.

27. East, "Apache Prisoners," n.p.; Benedict Jozhe, interview by author, June 22, 1971; AAG to SW, March 17, 1887, in NAMP, M689, R191; CIA, Annual Report 1887; Debo, *Geronimo,* 318–9, quoting Ayres to AG, April 26, 1887; Skinner, *Apache Rock,* 138, quoting the *Pensacola Commercial,* March 23, 1887.

28. Caruthers to SI, January 20, 1887, NAMP; Davis, "Tardy Reminiscence."

29. Davis, "Tardy Reminiscence"; Teller to SW, March 21, 1887, in NAMP, M689, R189.

30. Turcheneske, *Chiricahua Apache Prisoners of War,* 16; Welsh, *Apache Prisoners,* 18; Imbrie, "Biography," n.p.

31. Debo, *Geronimo,* 324, quoting Ayres to Sheridan, March 25, 1887.

32. Bourke to SW, April 19, 1887, NAMP; Porter, *Paper Medicine Man,* 234.

33. *Philadelphia Record,* April 5, 1887; Skinner, *Apache Rock,* 167–68.

34. Skinner, *Apache Rock,* 131, quoting *Frank Leslie's Illustrated Newspaper,* April 2, 1887.

35. Skinner, *Apache Rock,* 152, quoting the *Pensacola Daily Commercial,* May 12, 1887; Porter, *Paper Medicine Man,* 234; Welsh, *Apache Prisoners,* 20; Turcheneske, *Chiricahua Apache Prisoners,* 21–30.

36. Porter, *Paper Medicine Man,* 232.

37. Ibid.

38. Turcheneske, *Chiricahua Apache Prisoners,* 15–17; Skinner, *Apache Rock,* 157, quoting the *Mobile Register,* April 22, 1887.

39. Bourke to SW, April 19, 1887, NAMP.

40. Ayres to AAG, April 27, 1887, in NAMP, M689, R189.

41. East, "Apache Prisoners," 30; Skinner, *Apache Rock,* 164, quoting the *Florida Times-Union,* April 27, 1887.

42. Webb, "Paper"; Imbrie, "Biography," n.p.; Raymond Loco, interview by author, November 23, 1963.

CHAPTER 21

1. Skinner, *Apache Rock,* 177; Alabama Forestry Commission, www.forestry.state.al.us (accessed February 8, 2006).

2. Bourke to SW, April 19, 1887, NAMP; on-site visits by author, 1965 and 1984.

3. "Mount Vernon Climate," www.city-data.com/Mount-Vernon-Alabama.html (accessed February 8, 2006); Bourke to SW, April 19, 1887, NAMP; Sam Bowman to Herbert Welsh, July 26, 1887, in NAMP, M689, R187.

4. Skinner, *Apache Rock,* 167–68, citing the *Mobile Daily Register,* April 30, 1887; Raymond Loco, interview by author, October 20, 1970.

5. Sinclair to Drum, June 30, 1887, in NAMP, M689, R190; Skinner, *Apache Rock,* 167–168.

6. Debo, *Geronimo,* 338; Skinner, *Apache Rock,* 171–72, citing the *Mobile Register,* June 26, 2887.

7. Skinner, *Apache Rock,* 239; Bourke to AAG, "Report on a Conference with the Headmen and Leaders of the Apache Prisoners," July 24, 1889, in NAMP, M689, R192.

8. Bourke to AAG, July 24, 1889, NAMP; Debo, *Geronimo,* 338.

9. Skinner, *Apache Rock,* 239, quoting the *New York Times,* May 11, 1890.

10. Ibid., 225–26, quoting the *Mobile Register,* June 19, 1888.

11. Ibid., 227–30, quoting Albert E. Wratten, "George Wratten, Friend of the Apaches," 97; Debo, *Geronimo,* 352, quoting the *Plattsburg Republic,* February 25, 1893.

12. Skinner, *Apache Rock,* 168, quoting the *Mobile Register,* May 1 and 10, 1887.

13. Raymond Loco, interview by author, October 20, 1970; Skinner, *Apache Rock,* 344, quoting the *Mobile Register,* January 17 and 19, 1893.

14. Skinner, *Apache Rock,* 344, quoting the *Mobile Register,* January 17 and 19, 1893.

15. Ibid., 172, quoting the *Mobile Register,* June 26, 1887.

16. Unsigned report, IGO, "Report of Conditions at Mount Vernon Barracks," April 30, 1887, in NAMP, M689, R189; Sinclair, monthly report, September 30, 1887, NAMP.

17. IGO, "Report of Conditions," April 30, 1887, NAMP; Mrs. Isabelle B. Eustis [teacher at Hampton] to Mrs. Hemenway, January 5, 1888, in NAMP, M689, R191; "Isabelle B. Eustis," *Southern Workman* (Hampton Institute, Hampton, Va.) 55 (1926): 53 (Hampton Institute Library).

18. Shepard, "The Apache School."

19. Shepard, "November Report of the Apache School."

20. Sinclair to AAG, monthly report, May 26, 1887, NAMP; Debo, *Geronimo,* 346, quoting AAG to Commanding General, Division of the Atlantic, March 19, 1887.

21. Sinclair to AAG, monthly report, May 26, 1887, NAMP.

22. Borden, "Vital Statistics of an Apache Indian Community," 4; Sinclair to AAG, May 26, 1887, NAMP.

23. Debo, *Geronimo,* 348; Borden, "Vital Statistics," 5–6.

24. Skinner, *Apache Rock,* 226, quoting Dr. J. Glenn in the *Alabama Christian Advocate,* May 8, 1966.

25. Dr. Walter Reed, Assistant Surgeon, monthly medical report, November 30, 1887, in NAMP, M689, R190; Skinner, *Apache Rock,* 301, quoting the *Mobile Register,* February 7, 1891; Wotherspoon report, July 31, 1889, in NAMP, M689, R190; Wotherspoon report, February 15, 1891, in NAMP, M689, R198.

26. Skinner, *Apache Rock,* 168–69, quoting the *Mobile Register,* April 23, 1887.

27. Sinclair to AAG, monthly report, May 26, 1887, NAMP; Skinner, *Apache Rock,* 169–75, quoting the *Mobile Register,* May 1, 10, and 15, 1887.

28. Skinner, *Apache Rock,* 244, quoting the *Mobile Register,* April 20, 1888.

29. Bricknell, *Spring Hill College Album;* Skinner, *Apache Rock,* 172, 228, quoting the *Mobile Register,* June 26, 1887.

30. Skinner, *Apache Rock,* 172, quoting the *Mobile Register,* June 26, 1887; Debo, *Geronimo,* 352; Bricknell, *Spring Hill College Album.*

31. Brennon, "Through the Years"; Benedict Jozhe, interview by author, February 29, 1972.

32. Skinner, *Apache Rock,* 301, quoting Albert Wratten, "George Wratten, Friend of the Apaches," 512; Debo, *Geronimo,* 349.

33. Eustis to Hemenway, January 5, 1888, NAMP; "Isabelle B. Eustis," 53–55.

34. Wotherspoon, monthly report, January 31, 1891, in NAMP, M689, R196; *Washington Evening Star,* January 29, 1894; Skinner, *Apache Rock,* 341, quoting the *Mobile Register,* March 14, 1888; Debo, *Geronimo,* 349, quoting Joseph Edgerton, "Letter to the Editor," *Plattsburg Republican,* February 25, 1893.

35. Unsigned, undated report, "Status of Indian Prisoners at Mount Vernon, Alabama", in NAMP, M689, R195; Wotherspoon, monthly reports, March 31 and September 30, 1892, in NAMP, M689, R196; Sinclair, "Special Report on Apache Indian Prisoners and Company I, 12th Infantry at Mount Vernon Barracks," December 31, 1893, in NAMP, M689, R197.

36. Welsh, *Apache Prisoners,* 13; Derk, *Value of a Dollar,* 2, 11; "What Is Its Relative Value in U.S. Dollars?" www.eh.net/hmit/compare (accessed February 10, 2006).

37. University of Southern California, American Presidency Project, "President Cleveland's Fourth Annual Message," Washington, D.C., December 3, 1888, www.americanpresidency.org (accessed February 9, 2005).

38. Raymond Loco, interview by author, October 22, 1970; Eustis to Hemenway, January 5, 1888, NAMP; "Isabelle B. Eustis," 53; Sinclair, monthly report, February 18, 1889, in NAMP, M689, R192; Booth and Stephens, "Apache Mission."

39. Wotherspoon, monthly reports, September 1890 through 1893, in NAMP, M689, R196. Debo, *Geronimo,* 355; William Pearson, Mount Vernon Post Chaplin, to AGDC, December 31, 1891, in NAMP, M689, R196; Shepard, "November Report of the Apache School, Alabama"; Raymond Loco, interview by author, October 20, 1970.

40. Pearson to AGDC, December 31, 1891, NAMP.

41. Pearson to AGDC, February 28, 1891, in NAMP, M689, R196; Shepard, "November Report"; Benedict Jozhe, interview by author, February 29, 1972; Raymond Loco, interview by author, February 22, 1971.

42. John Clum, interview, *Washington Evening Star,* January 29, 1894, in NAMP, M689, R196; Wotherspoon, monthly report, February 28, 1891, NAMP.

43. Bourke to AAG, July 24, 1889, NAMP.

CHAPTER 22

1. Borden, "Vital Statistics," 14; Guy Howard report, December 23, 1889, in NAMP, M689, R194; Wotherspoon to post adjutant, December 1, 1892, in NAMP, M689, R196.

2. Reed, monthly medical report, November 31, 1889, in NAMP, M689, R191; New Jersey Communicable Disease Service, "History of Tuberculosis," www.state.nj.us/health/ (accessed February 15, 2005).

3. Taber, *Taber's Cyclopedic Medical Dictionary,* T-56; Chester Haworth, M.D., correspondence, February 10, 2005.

4. Wotherspoon, "Special Report on Apache Prisoners," January 1, 1894, in NAMP, M689, R197; Howard report, December 23, 1889, NAMP; Wotherspoon, monthly report, August 1890, in NAMP, M689, R191.

5. Senate Executive Document no. 41, vol. 2686; Borden, "Vital Statistics," 6.

6. Wotherspoon, monthly report, February 28, 1891, NAMP.

7. Skinner, *Apache Rock,* 302–303, citing the *Mobile Register,* February 7, 1891; Debo, *Geronimo,* 350.

8. Skinner, *Apache Rock,* 302, quoting the *Mobile Register,* February 7, 1891.

9. Wotherspoon, monthly report, June 30, 1892, NAMP.

10. Captain Marion P. Maus, "Report of an interview with the Apache Prisoners concerning their wishes to be removed to some other locality," August 29, 1894, in H. L. Scott Papers.

11. Wotherspoon, June 30, 1892, NAMP.

12. Ibid.

13. Wotherspoon to post adjutant, June 30, 1892, in NAMP, M689, R196; Borden, "Vital Statistics," 6, 10.

14. John Cochran, Assistant Surgeon, to AAG, "Special Report on Conditions in the Indians Industrial School, Carlisle, Pa., July 1, 1889", in NAMP, M689, R192; Bourke, "Special Report to Secretary of War," March 14, 1889, NAMP; Richard Pratt to CIA, May 18 and 24, 1889, in NAMP, M689, R192.

15. Debo, *Geronimo,* 318; Wotherspoon, monthly report, November 30, 1890, NAMP.

16. Eustis to Hemenway, January 5, 1888, NAMP; "Isabelle B. Eustis," 53.

17. Bourke to AAG, "Report of a Conference," July 24, 1889, NAMP.

18. Skinner, *Apache Rock,* 338, quoting the *Mobile Register,* September 8, 1892; Wotherspoon to post adjutant, monthly reports, December 31, 1892, and February 1894, NAMP.

19. Skinner, *Apache Rock,* 192–93, quoting the *Mobile Register,* August 24, 1887, and the *Pensacola Daily Commercial,* August 24, 1887.

20. Ibid., 338, quoting the *Mobile Register,* September 8, 1892; Wotherspoon, "Special Report on Apache Indian Prisoners and Company I, 12th Infantry," December 31, 1893, in NAMP, M689, R197.

21. Skinner, *Apache Rock,* 338, quoting the *Mobile Register,* September 8, 1892.

22. Ibid., 366, quoting the *Mobile Register,* July 15, 1892.

23. Ibid., 355–65, quoting the *Mobile Register,* March 16, 1893; Post Returns, Mount Vernon Barracks, March 1893, in NARA.

24. Wotherspoon, "Special Report on Apache Indian Prisoners," December 31, 1893, NAMP; Skinner, *Apache Rock,* 301–303, quoting Albert Wratten, *Wratten,* 512, and the *Mobile Register,* February 7, 1891.

25. Skinner, *Apache Rock,* 222, quoting Albert Wratten, *Wratten,* 376–77.

26. Reed, monthly medical report, July 31, 1890, in NAMP, M689, R194; Post Returns, Mount Vernon Barracks, 1887, in NARA; Wotherspoon, "Special Report on Apache Prisoners," January 1, 1894, NAMP.

27. Edwin R. Sweeney, correspondence with author, February 26, 2006; Skinner, *Apache Rock,* 242–251, quoting the *Mobile Register,* April 10, 13, and 14, 1888.

28. Skinner, *Apache Rock,* 242–51, quoting the *Mobile Register,* July 4, 10, 13, and 14, 1888.

29. Wotherspoon to post adjutant, March 31, 1892, NAMP.

30. Wotherspoon to post adjutant, March 31, 1892, and Wotherspoon to Kelton, March 28, 1892, in NAMP, M689, R196.

31. Lieutenant Charles Ballou, monthly report, April 18, 1894, in NAMP, M689, R197; Skinner, *Apache Rock,* 372, citing the *Mobile Register* quoting Ballou, April 19 and 20, 1894.

32. Wotherspoon, "Special Report on Apache Prisoners," January 1, 1894, NAMP; Borden, "Vital Statistics," 10.

CHAPTER 23

1. Langdon to AAG, October 24, 1886, in NAMP, M689, R184.

2. Porter, *Paper Medicine Man,* 265, quoting Bourke to Welsh, March 12, 1891; University of Southern California, "President Cleveland's Fourth Annual Message"; Alabama State Archives, *New York Evening Post,* December 12, 1889.

3. Bourke, "Special Report to Secretary of War," March 14, 1889, NAMP; Welsh to SW, June 20, 1890, in NAMP, M689, R194.

4. Debo, *Geronimo,* 343; Reed to Whipple, November 18, 1889, Surgeon General's Endorsement, November 30, 1889, and SW to President Cleveland, January 13, 1889, in NAMP, M689, R194.

5. Skinner, *Apache Rock,* 268–69, quoting Albert Wratten, *Wratten,* 261–63; Howard report, December 23, 1889, NAMP.

6. Bourke, "Special Report to Secretary of War," March 14, 1889, and Bourke to AAG, July 24, 1889, NAMP.

7. Bourke and Painter report, July 5, 1889, Bourke, "Special Report to Secretary of War," March 14, 1889, and Bourke to AAG, July 24, 1889, NAMP.

8. U.S. National Park Service, "Asheville, NC, as a Health Retreat," *National Registry of Historic Places,* www.cr.nps.gov/nr/travel/Asheville/health/htm (accessed March 3, 2006); Goodman, "Apaches as Prisoners of War," 150–77.

9. Debo, *Geronimo,* 344; Skinner, *Apache Rock,* 280.

10. Proctor to President Cleveland, January 13, 1889, and Sen. Henry Dawes to Proctor, June 28, 1890, in NAMP, M689, R194; Maus, "Report of an interview," August 29, 1894, Scott Papers.

11. Maus, "Report of an interview," August 29, 1894, Scott Papers.

12. Davis, AGODC, "Report on Apache Prisoners," May 1895, in NAMP, M689, R198.

13. Ibid., and Russell, CO, Mount Vernon Barracks, to Davis, November 23, 1894.

14. Wotherspoon, "Special Report on Apache Prisoners," January 1, 1894, NAMP; Raymond Loco, interview by author, December 23, 1963.

15. Charles LeBaron, Surgeon to the Apache Prisoners of War at Fort Sill, report to Lieutenant Hugh Scott, October 5, 1894, in NAMP, M689, R198; Raymond Loco, interview by author, December 23, 1963; Mildred Cleghorn, interview by author, October 1, 1967.

16. SW, Annual Report 1895, 298–99; Nye, *Carbine and Lance,* 296–302; Scott to AG, Department of the Missouri, November 7, 1894, and LeBaron to Scott, October 5, 1894, in NAMP, M689, R198.

17. Miles to AGODC, October 12, 1894, in NAMP, M689, R198; Davis to AGO, "Apache Prisoners of War," January 23, 1895, in NAMP, M689, R199.

18. LeBaron to Scott, October 5, 1894, and Scott to AG, Department of the Missouri, November 7, 1894, August 1, 1896, and January 30, 1887, in NAMP, M689, R198.

19. Miles to AGODC, October 12, 1894, NAMP; Davis to AGO, January 23, 1895, NAMP.

20. Scott to AG, August 1, 1897, in H. L. Scott Papers; Davis to AG, December 23, 1896, in NAMP, M1066, R199.

21. Scott to AG, January 30, 1897, in NAMP, M689, R199; Betzinez, *I Fought with Geronimo,* 167; Turcheneske, *Chiricahua Apache Prisoners,* 42.

22. Scott to AG, January 30, 1897, in H. L. Scott Papers.

23. Nye, *Carbine and Lance,* 298–99; Turcheneske, *Chiricahua Apache Prisoners,* 69–70; Betzinez, *I Fought with Geronimo,* 182; Raymond Loco, interview by author, December 23, 1967.

24. Scott to Miles, "Annual Report Concerning the Apache Prisoners of War for the Year Ending June 31, 1897," in NAMP, M689, R200; Betzinez, *I Fought with Geronimo,* 198; Descendants of Apache Prisoners, *Historical Trip,* 9.

25. Raymond Loco, interview by author, December 23, 1963.

26. Ibid.; *Fort Sill Record of Medical History of Post,* 1903–1913, NARA.

27. Ibid.; Gillette Griswold (director, Missile and Artillery Museum, Fort Sill, Oklahoma), interview by author, March 3, 1972.

28. Opler to Office of Indian Affairs, "Memorandum re Organization of Fort Sill Apaches," 1936, in NARA.

29. *Fort Sill Record of Medical History of Post,* 1903–1913, NARA; Raymond Loco, interview by author, March 20–26, 1975.

30. Major George Goode, In Charge of the Prisoners of War, to War Department, March 7, 1914, in H. L. Scott Papers.

Bibliography

ARCHIVAL SOURCES

Bureau of Indian Affairs
    Probates of Margaret Loco, January 9, 1930, Juanita Loco, October 9, 1931, John Loco, January 14, 1947, and Marion Loco, November 4, 1947.
    Revised Membership Roll of the Fort Sill Apache Band Remaining in Oklahoma, November 17, 1913.
O. O. Howard Papers, Bowdoin College, Brunswick, Maine.
National Archives and Records Administration
    Department of Arizona Letterbooks.
    Microfilm Publication 666, Letters Received by the Office of the Adjutant General (Main Series), 1871–1880.
    Microfilm Publication 1066, Adjutant General's Office 1883, Microcopy 689, Rolls 173–202, Papers relating to the surrender of Geronimo and the disposition of the Apache prisoners of war.
    Microfilm Publication 1749, Adjutant General's Office 1882, Rolls 96–97, Papers relating to outbreaks in Arizona and New Mexico by Chiricahua Apaches.
    Microfilm Publication 2180, Adjutant General's Office 1882, Roll 101, Papers related to the threatened starvation of Indians of the Mescalero Reservation, New Mexico.
    Microfilm Publication 2809, Adjutant General's Office 1882, Roll 108, Papers relating to the boundaries of the White Mountain Reservation, Arizona Territory, and the Mescalero Apache Reservation, New Mexico Territory.
    Record Group 75, Bureau of Indian Affairs
    "Documents Relating to the Arizona and New Mexico Superintendencies."
    "Carlisle School Records."
    "Employee Records, San Carlos Agency, San Carlos, Arizona."
    Record Group 92, "Reports of Persons and Articles Hired for the Years 1880–1895 by the A. A. Quartermaster, U.S. Army": Fort Apache, San Carlos, and Fort Bowie, Arizona; Fort

341

Cummings and Fort Wingate, New Mexico; Fort Marion, Florida; Mount Vernon, Alabama; and Fort Sill, Oklahoma.

Record Group 94, Document File 4327-1881, "Papers Relating to the Apache Troubles, 1879–1883."

Record Group 123, Indian Depredation claim number 8927, *Richard C. Patterson v. United States and Apache Indians,* including statements by Richard C. Patterson, Joseph D. Emerson, and Samuel Creevy, testimony in support of Patterson's depredation claim, 1882.

Record Group 217, "Second Auditor's Records, Indian Claim Settlement no. 8043, Confirmed August 9, 1886," Federal Records Center, Suitland Maryland, 1886.

Oklahoma Historical Society, "Documents Relating to the Kiowa-Apache Prisoners of War," Indian Archives File no. 5782.

Morris Opler Papers, Kroch Library, Rare and Manuscript Collections, Warm Springs Apache, no. 14, Cornell University, Ithaca, N.Y.

H. L. Scott Papers and other documents relating to the Fort Sill Apaches, Fort Sill Museum, Fort Sill, Oklahoma.

Sol Tax Papers, "Interview with Leon Perico," n.d., Special Collections, Box 10, Folder 15, University of Chicago.

Benjamin Thomas Papers, 1872–74, Fray Angelico Chavez History Library, Santa Fe, New Mexico.

BOOKS AND ARTICLES

Able, Annie Heloise, ed. *The Official Correspondence of James S. Calhoun while Indian Agent at Santa Fe and Superintendent of Indian Affairs in New Mexico.* Washington, D.C.: Government Printing Office, 1915.

Adjutant General's Office. *Chronological List of Actions, etc., with Indians from January 1, 1866 to January 1891.* Washington, D.C.: Adjutant General's Office, 1891.

Alberta, Sister Mary, SSJ. "A Study of the Schools Conducted by the Sisters of St. Joseph of the Diocese of St. Augustine, Florida, 1886–1940." Master's thesis, Florida State University, 1940.

Alexander, David. *Arizona Frontier Military Place Names, 1846–1912.* Las Cruces, N.M.: Yucca Tree Press, 1998.

Altshuler, Constance Wynn., ed. *Latest from Arizona! The Hesperian Letters, 1859–1861.* Tucson: Arizona Pioneers' Historical Society, 1969.

Arnold, Elliott. *The Camp Grant Massacre.* New York: Simon and Schuster, 1976.

Arny, W. F. M. *Indian Agent in New Mexico: The Journal of Special Agent W. F. M. Arny, 1870.* Edited by Lawrence R. Murphy. Reprint, Santa Fe: Stagecoach Press, 1967.

Bailey, L. R. *Indian Slave Trade in the Southwest: A Study of Slave-taking and Traffic in Indian Captives.* Los Angeles: Westernlore Press, 1966.

Ball, Eve, with Nora Henn and Lynda Sanchez. *Indeh: An Apache Odyssey.* Provo, Utah: Brigham Young University Press, 1980.

———. *In the Days of Victorio: Recollections of a Warm Springs Apache.* Tucson: University of Arizona Press, 1970.

Barney, James M. "The Early Annals of Wickenburg County." Unpublished manuscript, Wickenburg, Arizona, Public Library, 1942.

Barrett, S. M. *Geronimo, His Own Story.* Edited by Frederick W. Turner III. Reprint, New York: E. P. Dutton, 1970.

Basso, Keith. *Portraits of the Whiteman*. Cambridge: Cambridge University Press, 1979.

———, ed. *Western Apache Raiding and Warfare*. Tucson: University of Arizona Press, 1971.

Benton, Colonel C. B. "Sgt. Neil Erickson and the Apaches." In *Westerners Brand Book*. Los Angeles: Corral, 1948.

Betzinez, Jason, with Wilbur Nye. *I Fought with Geronimo*. Harrisburg, Pa.: Stackpole, 1959.

Bigelow, Lt. John, Jr. *On the Bloody Trail of Geronimo*. Foreword, introduction, and notes by Arthur Woodward. Reprint, Los Angeles: Westernlore Press, 1968.

Booth, Vincentine, and Marion Stephens. "The Apache Mission." *Lend a Hand* 4 (1889). Boston: J. Stilman Smith.

Borden, William C. "The Vital Statistics of an Apache Indian Community." *Boston Medical and Surgical Journal*, July 6, 1893.

Bourke, John Gregory. *An Apache Campaign in the Sierra Madre*. Introduction by J. Frank Dobie. Reprint, New York: Charles Scribner's Sons, 1958.

———. "Diary of John G. Bourke, 1882–1887." Copy on file at the University of New Mexico Library, Albuquerque.

———. *On the Border with Crook*. Chicago: Rio Grande Press, 1891 (reprint 1962).

Boyer, Ruth M., and Narcissus D. Gayton. *Apache Mothers and Daughters*. Norman: University of Oklahoma Press, 1992.

Brennon, Peter A. "Through the Years: Mount Vernon, Alabama." *Montgomery Advocate*, August 29, 1948.

Bricknell, William E. *Spring Hill College Album*. Mobile, Ala.: Spring Hill College, 1891.

Brodsky, Alyn. *Grover Cleveland: A Study in Character*. New York: St. Martin's Press, 2000.

Brown, Robert L. *Saloons of the American West*. Denver: Privately printed, 1978.

Cash, Joseph. "The Reservation Indian Meets the White Man." In *Red Men and Hat-Wearers*, edited by Daniel Tyler, 43–112. Privately published, 1976.

Clark, Charles M. "The Victorio Raid." *Arizona Silver Belt* (Miami, Ariz.), October 20, 1900.

Clum, John. *Apache Days and Tombstone Nights: John Clum's Autobiography, 1877–1887*. Edited by Neil B. Carmony. Silver City, N.M.: High-Lonesome Books, 1997.

———. "Geronimo, Part I." *New Mexico Historical Review* 3, no. 1 (January 1928): 23.

Clum, Woodworth. *Apache Agent: The Story of John P. Clum*. Boston: Houghton Mifflin, 1936.

Colyer, Vincent. "Report on the Apache Indians of Arizona and New Mexico for 1871." *Third Annual Report of the Board of Indian Commissioners*, included in *Annual Report of the Commissioner of Indian Affairs 1871*. Washington, D.C.: Government Printing Office, 1871.

Commissioner of Indian Affairs. *Annual Reports 1849–1909*. 60 vols. Washington, D.C.: Government Printing Office, 1849–1909.

Conway, John. *The Apache Wars*. Derby, Conn.: Monarch Books, 1961.

Cozzens, Peter. *The Army and the Indian: Eyewitnesses to the Apache Wars, 1865–1890*. Harrisburg, Pa.: Stackpole Books, 2001.

Cremony, John C. *Life among the Apaches, 1850–1868*. Glorieta, N.M.: Rio Grande Press, 1969.

Crook, George. *General George Crook: His Autobiography*. Edited by Martin F. Schmitt. Norman: University of Oklahoma Press, 1960.

———. *Resume: Operations against Apache Indians, 1882 to 1886*. Washington, D.C.: Government Printing Office, 1887.

Cruse, Thomas. *Apache Days and After*. Edited by Eugene Cunningham. Caldwell, Idaho: Caxton Printers, 1941. Reprint, Lincoln: University of Nebraska Press, 1987.

Danese, Sister Mary Jerome, SSJ. "The Growth, Development, and Expansion of the Educational Activities of the Sisters of Saint Joseph in the Diocese of Saint Augustine, Florida, from the years 1886–1960." Master's thesis, Catholic University, 1960.

Davis, Britton. *The Truth about Geronimo.* Edited by M. M. Quaife. New Haven, Conn.: Yale University Press, 1929.

Davis, Curtis Carrol. "Tardy Reminiscence: Some Recollections of Horace Caruthers, 1824–1894." *Westchester County (N.Y.) Historical Bulletin* 24, no. 3 (July 1948).

Debo, Angie. *Geronimo: The Man, His Time, His Place.* Norman: University of Oklahoma Press, 1976.

Derk, Scott. *The Value of a Dollar: Prices and Incomes in the United States, 1860–1889.* Detroit: Manly, 1994.

Descendants of Apache Prisoners. *A Historical Trip covering the Journey of Chiricahua Apache Imprisonment, 1886–1913.* Mescalero, N.M.: Mescalero Apache Tribe, 1982.

Downey, Fairfax. *Indian Fighting Army.* New York: Bantam Books, 1957.

———, and Jacques Jacobsen Jr. *The Red Bluecoats.* Fort Collins, Colo.: Old Army Press, 1973.

Dunn, Jacob. *Massacres of the Mountains: A History of the Indian Wars of the Far West, 1815–1875.* New York: Archer House, 1886.

East, Omega G. "Apache Prisoners at Castillo de San Marcos." Unpublished manuscript. St. Augustine, Fla.: U.S. National Park Service, n.d.

———, and Albert C. Mancy. "Arizona Apaches as Guests in Florida." *Florida Historical Quarterly* 30, no. 3 (January 1952): 294–300.

Ellis, Richard N. *General Pope and U.S. Indian Policy.* Albuquerque: University of New Mexico Press, 1970.

Erdoes, Richard. *Saloons of the Old West.* New York: Gramercy Books, 1979.

Erickson, Neil, as told to Leonard M. Cowley. "Trailing the Apache." Unknown publication, August 1931.

Faulk, Odie B. *The Geronimo Campaign.* New York: Oxford University Press, 1969.

Forsyth, George. *Thrilling Days in Army Life.* New York: Harper and Brothers, 1900. Reprint, Lincoln: University of Nebraska Press, 1994.

Frasca, Albert J., and Robert H. Hill. *The .45–70 Springfield.* 2 vols. Riverside, Calif.: Frasca Publishing, 1980, 1997.

Furnas, C. C. *The Life and Times of the Late Demon Rum.* New York: Capricorn Books, 1973.

Giese, Dale F. *Forts of New Mexico.* Silver City, N.M.: Privately published, 1995.

Goodman, David. "Apaches as Prisoners of War, 1886–1894." Ph.D. dissertation, Texas Christian University, 1968.

Goodwin, Grenville. *Among the Western Apache.* Edited by Morris Opler. Tucson: University of Arizona Press, 1973.

———. "Experiences of an Indian Scout." *Arizona Historical Review* 7, no. 1 (January 1936).

———. "Sherman Curley, Western Apache Scout account." Granville Goodwin Collection, Arizona State Museum, n.d.

———. *The Social Organization of the Western Apache.* Tucson: University of Arizona Press, 1961.

Graff, Henry F., and Arthur M. Schlesinger. *Grover Cleveland.* New York: Henry Holt, 2002.

Griffith, A. Kinney. *Mickey Free, Manhunter.* Caldwell, Idaho: Caxton Printers, 1969.

Grimes, William. *Straight Up or on the Rocks: A Cultural History of American Drink.* New York: Simon and Schuster, 1993.

Griswold, Gillett M. "The Fort Sill Apaches: Their Vital Statistics, Tribal Origins, Antecedents. Fort Sill, Oklahoma." Unpublished manuscript. Fort Sill, Okla.: Fort Sill Museum, 1970.

———, compiler. "Apache Indian Cemetery, Fort Sill, Oklahoma: Numerical List of Deceased." Fort Sill, Okla.: Fort Sill Museum, 1961.

Harte, J. Bret. "The San Carlos Indian Reservation 1872–1886: An Administrative History." 2 vols. Ph.D. dissertation, University of Arizona. Ann Arbor, Mich.: University Microfilms, 1972.

Heitman, Francis Bernard. *Historical Register and Dictionary of the United States Army, from Its Organization, September 29, 1789, to March 2, 1902,* vol. 1. Washington, D.C.: Government Printing Office, 1903.

Hill, Charles E. *Leading American Treaties.* New York: Macmillan, 1922.

Hodge, Frederick Webb. *Handbook of American Indians North of Mexico.* 2 vols. New York: Rowman and Littlefield, 1965.

Horn, Tom. *Life of Tom Horn: Government Scout and Interpreter, Written by Himself.* Norman: University of Oklahoma Press, 1964.

Howard, Guy. "Report, March 25, 1882." Arizona Historical Society microfilm, San Carlos Indian Agency, Roll 3.

Howard, Oliver Otis. *Autobiography of Oliver Otis Howard, Major General United States Army.* 2 vols. New York: Baker and Taylor, 1908.

———. *My Life and Experiences among Our Hostile Indians.* Hartford, Conn.: A. D. Worthington, 1907. Reprint, New York: Da Capo Press, 1972.

Humfreville, Lee J. *Twenty Years among Our Hostile Indians.* New York: Hunter, 1899. Reprint, Mechanicsburg, Pa.: Stackpole Books, 2002.

Imbrie, Andrew W. Unpublished biography of Herbert Welsh. Berkeley, Calif., n.d.

Israel, Fred L., ed. *Sears Roebuck Catalog, 1897.* New York: Chelsea House, 1968.

Kappler, Charles J. *Indian Affairs: Laws and Treaties,* vol. 2. Washington, D.C.: Government Printing Office, 1904.

———. *Names of Graduates of the Carlisle Indian School.* Carlisle, Pa.: Carlisle Indian Press, 1914.

Khera, Sigrid. *The Yavapai of Fort McDowell.* Fountain Hills, Ariz.: Fort McDowell Mohave-Apache Indian Community, 1979.

Kindleberger, Charles P. *Manias, Panics, and Crashes: A History of Financial Crises.* 4th ed. New York: John Wiley and Sons, 2000.

Kraft, Louis. *Gatewood and Geronimo.* Albuquerque: University of New Mexico Press, 2000.

Kvasnicka, Robert M., and Herman J. Viola. *The Commissioners of Indian Affairs, 1824–1977.* Lincoln: University of Nebraska Press, 1979.

Leupp, Francis E. *Notes of a Summer Tour among the Indians of the Southwest.* Philadelphia: Indian Rights Association, 1897.

Lockwood, Frank C. *The Apache Indians.* New York: Macmillan, 1938.

Lummis, Charles F. *General Crook and the Apache Wars.* Edited by Turbese Lummis Fiske. Flagstaff, Ariz.: Northland Press, 1966.

———. *The Land of Poco Tiempo.* New York: Charles Scribner's Sons, 1893. Reprint, Albuquerque: University of New Mexico Press, 1969.

Mancall, Peter C. *Deadly Medicine: Indians and Alcohol in Early America.* Ithaca, N.Y.: Cornell University Press, 1995.

Marion, J.H. *Notes on Travel through the Territory of Arizona.* Edited by Donald M. Powell. Prescott: Office of the *Arizona Miner,* 1870. Reprint, Tucson: University of Arizona Press, 1965.

McFeely, William S. *Yankee Stepfather: General O. O. Howard and the Freedmen.* New Haven, Conn.: Yale University Press, 1968.

Meketa, Charles, and Jacqueline Meketa. *One Blanket and Ten Days Rations.* Globe, Ariz.: Southwest Parks and Monuments Association, 1980.

Mowry, Sylvester. *The Far Western Frontier.* Edited by Ray Billington. Reprinted from 1864 edition of *Arizona and Sonora.* New York: Arno Press, 1973.

Myatt, Major F. *The Illustrated Encyclopedia of 19th Century Firearms.* New York: Crescent Books, 1979.

Nye, W. S. *Carbine and Lance: The Story of Old Fort Sill.* Norman: University of Oklahoma Press, 1937.

Ogle, Ralph Hedrick. *Federal Control of the Western Apaches, 1848–1886.* Albuquerque: University of New Mexico Press, 1970.

Opler, Morris K. *An Apache Life-Way: The Economic, Social, and Religious Institutions of the Chiricahua Indians.* New York: Cooper Square Publishers, 1965.

———. "A Chiricahua Apache's Account of the Geronimo Campaign of 1886." *New Mexico Historical Review* 13, no. 4 (October 1938).

———. "Memorandum re Organization of Fort Sill Apaches." Unpublished memorandum, Office of Indian Affairs, 1936.

"Panics of the Late Nineteenth Century." *Gale Encyclopedia of U.S. Economic History.* Edited by Thomas Carson. Detroit: Gayle Group, 1999.

Porter, Joseph C. *Paper Medicine Man: John Gregory Bourke and His American West.* Norman: University of Oklahoma Press, 1986.

Radbourne, Allan. "Captain Hatfield and the Chiricahuas." In *Ho, for the Great West: The Silver Jubilee Publication of the English Westerners' Society,* 71–81. London: English Westerners' Society, 1980.

———. *Mickey Free: Apache Captive, Interpreter, and Indian Scout.* Tucson: Arizona Historical Society, 2005.

Rickey, Don, Jr. *Forty Miles a Day on Beans and Hay.* Norman: University of Oklahoma Press, 1963.

Robbins, Chandler S., Bertel Bruun, and Herbert S. Zim. *Birds of North America.* New York: Golden Press, 1966.

Schellie, Don. *Vast Domain of Blood: The Story of the Camp Grant Massacre.* Los Angeles: Westernlore Press, 1968.

Schroeder, Albert H. "A Study of the Apache Indians." Unpublished manuscript, Santa Fe, N.M., 1962.

Secretary of the Interior. Annual Reports, 1870–1915. Washington, D.C.: Government Printing Office, 1870–1915.

Secretary of War. Annual Reports, 1870–1915. Washington, D.C.: Government Printing Office, 1870–1915.

Seymore, Flora W. *Indian Agents of the Old Frontier.* New York: D. Appleton-Century, 1941.

Shapard, John. "The Sierra Enmedio Fight." *True Frontier Magazine* 43 (August 1975): 29.

Shepard, Sophia. "The Apache School." *Lend a Hand* 4 (1889). Boston: J. Stilman Smith.

———. "November Report of the Apache School, Alabama." *Lend A Hand* 10 (1893). Boston: J. Stilman Smith.

———. "Report of the Apache School, Alabama." *Lend a Hand* 5 (1890). Boston: J. Stilman Smith.

Sieber, Al. "Military and the Indians." *Prescott Weekly Courier,* May 27, 1882.

Simmons, Marc. *Massacre on the Lordsburg Road: A Tragedy of the Apache Wars.* College Station: Texas A&M University Press, 1997.

Skinner, Woodward B. *The Apache Rock Crumbles.* Pensacola, Fla.: Skinner Publications, 1997.

Sladen, Joseph Alton. *Making Peace with Cochise: The 1872 Journal of Captain Joseph Alton Sladen.* Edited by Edwin R. Sweeney. Norman: University of Oklahoma Press, 1997.

Sloane, Eleanor. *The Butterfield Overland Mail across Arizona.* Tucson: Arizona Pioneers' Historical Society, 1958.

Sobel, Robert. *Panic on Wall Street: A History of America's Financial Disasters.* New York: Macmillan, 1968.

Sonnichsen, C. L. *Geronimo and the End of the Apache Wars.* Lincoln: University of Nebraska Press, 1986.

———. *The Mescalero Apaches.* Norman: University of Oklahoma Press, 1958.

Stanley, F. *The Apaches of New Mexico 1540–1940.* Pampa, Tex.: Privately printed, 1962.

Stout, Joseph A., Jr. *Apache Lightning: The Last Great Battles of the Ojo Calientes.* New York: Oxford University Press, 1974.

Strover, William, "The Apaches' Last Trek." *Arizona Magazine,* May 1919.

———. "Last of Geronimo and His Band." *Washington National Tribune,* July 24, 1894.

Swanton, John R. *The Indian Tribes of North America.* Washington, D.C.: Government Printing Office, 1953.

Sweeney, Edwin R. *Cochise: Chiricahua Apache Chief.* Norman: University of Oklahoma Press, 1991.

———. *Mangas Coloradas: Chief of the Chiricahua Apaches.* Norman: University of Oklahoma Press, 1998.

———. *Merejildo Grijalva.* El Paso: University of Texas at El Paso, 1992.

Taber, Clarence Wilbur. *Taber's Cyclopedic Medical Dictionary.* 11th ed. Philadelphia: F. A. Davis, 1970.

Taylor, John. *Bloody Valverde: A Civil War Battle on the Rio Grande, February 21, 1862.* Albuquerque: University of New Mexico Press, 1995.

Terrell, John Upton. *Apache Chronicle: The Story of the People.* New York: World Publishing, 1972.

Thompson, Gerald. *The Army and the Navajo.* Tucson: University of Arizona Press, 1976.

Thrapp, Dan L. *Al Sieber, Chief of Scouts.* Norman: University of Oklahoma Press, 1964.

———. *The Conquest of Apacheria.* Norman: University of Oklahoma Press, 1967.

———. *General Crook and the Sierra Madre Adventure.* Norman: University of Oklahoma Press, 1972.

———. *Juh: An Incredible Indian.* El Paso: Texas Western Press, 1973.

———. *Victorio and the Mimbres Apaches.* Norman: University of Oklahoma Press, 1974.

———, ed. *Dateline Fort Bowie: Charles Fletcher Lummis Reports on an Apache War.* Norman: University of Oklahoma Press, 1979.

———, ed. *Encyclopedia of Frontier Biography.* 3 vols. Lincoln: University of Nebraska Press, 1991.

Tinker-Salas, Miguel. *In the Shadow of Eagles: Sonora and the Transformation of the Border during the Porfiriato.* Berkeley: University of California Press, 1997.

Turcheneske, John Anthony, Jr. *The Chiricahua Apache Prisoners of War: Fort Sill 1894–1914.* Niwot: University Press of Colorado, 1997.

Turner, Katharine C. *Red Men Calling on the Great White Father.* Norman: University of Oklahoma Press, 1951.

Unrau, Richard. *White Man's Wicked Water: The Alcohol Trade and Prohibition in Indian Country, 1802–1892.* Lawrence: University of Kansas Press, 1996.

U.S. Army, Quartermaster's Department. *U.S. Army Wagon Harness (Horse and Mule).* Washington, D.C.: Government Printing Office, 1877.

U.S. Congress. House Executive Document, 41st Congress, 2d Session. Washington, D.C.: Government Printing Office, 1902.

U.S. Indian Office. *Executive Orders Relating to Indian Reserves from May 14, 1855, to July 1, 1902*. Washington, D.C.: Government Printing Office, 1902.

U.S. National Park Service. *The History of Castillo de San Marcos, St. Augustine, Florida*. St. Augustine: Historic Print and Map Company, 2005.

U.S. Senate. Executive Documents nos. 35, 83, and 88, 51st Congress, 1st Session, vol. 16. Washington, D.C.: Government Printing Office, 1889.

———. Executive Document no. 41, vol. 2686, 51th Congress, 2nd Session. Washington, D.C.: Government Printing Office, 1891.

———. Executive Document no. 117, vol. 16, 49th Congress, 2nd Session, Part 3. Washington, D.C.: Government Printing Office, 1887.

Utley, Robert M. *Frontiersmen in Blue: The United States Army and the Indian, 1848–1865*. New York: Macmillan, 1967.

———. *The Indian Frontier of the American West, 1846–1890*. Albuquerque: University of New Mexico Press, 1984.

Van Campen, J. T. *St. Augustine: Florida's Colonial Capitol*. St. Augustine, Fla.: St. Augustine Historical Society, 1959.

Waddell, Jack O., and Michael W. Everett, eds. *Drinking Behavior among Southwestern Indians*. Tucson: University of Arizona Press, 1980.

Warfield, Col. H. B. *Apache Indian Scouts*. Privately printed, 1964.

———. *Cibicu Creek Fight in Arizona, 1881*. Privately printed, 1971.

———. *Cooley: Army Scout, Arizona Pioneer, Wayside Host, Apache Friend*. Privately printed, 1966.

———. *With Scouts and Cavalry at Fort Apache*. Tucson: Arizona Pioneers' Historical Society, 1965.

Webb, DeWitt. "Paper read before the Duchess County Medical Society of New York, September 1887." St. Augustine, Fla.: St. Augustine Historical Society Library.

Weland, Gerald. *O. O. Howard, Union General*. Jefferson, N.C.: McFarland, 1995.

Welsh Herbert, *The Apache Prisoners in Fort Marion, St. Augustine, Florida*. Philadelphia: Indian Rights Association, 1887.

Welty, Raymond L. "Supplying the Frontier Military Posts." *Kansas Historical Quarterly* 7, no. 2 (May 1938).

White, John H., Jr. *The American Railroad Passenger Car*. Baltimore: John Hopkins University Press, 1978.

Wood, Leonard. *Chasing Geronimo: The Journal of Leonard Wood, May–September 1886*. Edited by Jack Lane. Albuquerque: University of New Mexico Press, 1970.

Worcester, Donald E. *The Apaches: The Eagles of the Southwest*. Norman: University of Oklahoma Press, 1979.

NEWSPAPERS

Albuquerque Journal, 1885

Alta California, 1871

Arizona Silver Belt (Globe/Miami, Ariz.), 1879, 1880, 1883, 1900

Army and Navy Journal (Washington, D.C.), 1870–86

Bowdoin Orient (Bowdoin College, Brunswick, Me.), 2001

Clifton Clarion (Ariz.) 1885

Florida Times Union (Jacksonville), 1886–87

Frank Leslie's Illustrated Newspaper (New York, N.Y.), 1886–87

Hampton Institute Southern Workman (Hampton, Va.), 1893, 1926

Las Cruces Borderer (N.M.) 1871

Mobile Register (Ala.), 1886–94

Montgomery Advocate (Ala.), 1886–94

Grant County Herald, later the *New Southwest and Grant County Herald* (Silver City, N.M.), 1877–82

New York Evening Post, 1889

New York Times, 1887–90

The Pensacolian (Fla.), 1886–94

Pensacola Commercial (Fla.), 1886–94

Philadelphia Record, 1887

Phoenix Gazette, 1883

Phoenix Herald, 1883

Plattsburg Republic (N.Y.), 1893

Prescott Weekly Courier (Ariz.), 1882

Santa Fe New Mexican, 1869

Tucson Citizen (Ariz.), 1887, 1881

Arizona Star (Tucson), 1883

Washington (D.C.) Evening Star, 1886–87

Washington (D.C.) National Tribune, 1886–87

Washington Post, 1886–87

INTERVIEWS AND PERSONAL COMMUNICATIONS

Ball, Eve. Author, Ruidoso, N.M. 1965–78.

Bigrope, Ellyn. Director, Tribal Cultural Center, Mescalero Apache Tribe. 2001–2007.

Chino, Wendell. Late chair, Mescalero Apache Tribe, Mescalero, N.M. 1966, 1973, 1978.

Cleghorn, Mildred. Former chair, Fort Sill Apache Tribe, Apache, Oklahoma. 1962–81.

Delgadillo, Alicia. Apache prisoner of war historian and genealogist, Tucson, Ariz. 2001–2007.

Dye, Tim. Former superintendent, Fort Apache Agency, Whiteriver, Ariz. 1976.

Griswold, Gillett. Director, Missile and Artillery Museum, Fort Sill, Okla. 1963–78.

Haozous, Blossom. Daughter of George Wratten, Apache, Okla. 1969, 1973, 1975.

Harper, Amy. Interpretive ranger, Castillo de San Marcos National Monument, St. Augustine, Fla. 2007.

Hawley, Albert. Former superintendent, Fort Apache Agency, Phoenix, Ariz. 1965, 1969.

Jozhe, Benedict. Chief Loco's grandson and former chair, Fort Sill Apache Tribe. 1961–78.

Kazshay, Belle. Mescalero tribal member. 1971.

Loco, Moses. Chief Loco's grandson, Apache, Okla. 1961–1978.

Loco, Norman. Chief Loco's grandson, Apache, Okla. 1961–78.

Loco, Raymond. Chief Loco's grandson, Apache, Okla. 1960–78.

Lupe, Ronnie. Chairman, White Mountain Apache Tribe, Whiteriver, Ariz. 1969.

Naiche, Amelia. Naiche's daughter, Mescalero, New Mexico. 1966.

Robinson, R. E. Former superintendent, Fort Apache Agency, Whiteriver, Ariz. 1967.

Savilla, Agnes. Former chair, Colorado River Indian Tribes, Parker, Ariz. 1968.

Schmidt, Helen. Staff, St. Augustine Historical Society, St. Augustine, Fla. 1964.

Staff, Department of Agriculture, Forestry Service, Reserve, N.M. October 11, 2002.
Staff, National Park Service, Castillo de San Marcos National Monument, St. Augustine, Fla. 1964, 2003, 2004, 2005, 2007.
Sweeney, Edwin R. Author. 2001–2007.
Thrapp, Dan L. Author and journalist. 1968–1976.
Tingley, Charles. Library manager, St. Augustine Historical Society. 2007.

Index

Page numbers for photographs and maps are in *italics*.

Abbott, Lemuel, 103, 106, 110

Acoma, N.Mex., 10, 16–17

African Americans, Apache contact with, 278, 282, 290

Alamocito, N.Mex., 43

Alamosa River, N.Mex., 10

Albuquerque, N.Mex., 229

Albuquerque Journal, 210

Alchesay (Coyotero scout), 217

Alcohol/alcoholism: at Ft. Marion, 263; on Navajo reservation, 150; prevalence in U.S. and Apache culture, 16; prohibitionist efforts, 263, 288; selling whiskey to Indians, 38–40, 289–90. *See also* Drunkenness

Alisos Creek, Sonora, 175–82, 200–201, 293

Anadarko, Okla., 301

Ancient City. *See* St. Augustine, Fla.

Animas Mountains, *151*

Apache culture: abuse of women in, 72, 153, 208, 212–13; bathing and personal hygiene, 69–70, 231, 256, 286; caring for widows and children in, 17; ceremonial dances, 14; children in, 5, 287; cutting hair in mourning, 186; "ghost sickness" and spirits in, 68–69, 71, 200–201; impact of incarceration on, 284–85; impact of white encroachment on, 22; marriage in, 82; murder in, 3–4, 15–16, 80; personal names in, 7, 10; polygamy and divorce, 282; refusal to eat pork, 34, 256; revenge for losses, 88, 168, 185, 193, 215, 217–18; role of Principal Chief in, 78–79, 145; slaves in, 15–16, 22, 184; as tourist attraction, 251–52, 260–63, 278–79; white man's perspective of, 231; witches in, 12, 168. *See also* Rituals

Apache lifestyle: adaptation to employment and work, 140–42; at Ft. Marion, 250–58; on Indian time, 147; at Mount Vernon, 272–83; peace agreements in, 4–5; as prisoners, 284–85; raiding and warfare, 3–4, 88; reservation idleness, 72, 261–64; seasonal migration, 64–65; selling and trading for goods, 18–22, 261–62; *tiswin* in, 212; winter preparations, 27, 30, 206–207. *See also* Reservation life

"Apache Loco" (Crazy Apache, Loco), 7. *See also* Loco, Chief

Apache Pass, Ariz., 18

Apache police. *See* Indian police

Apache reservation: Army selection of sites, 43–49; Loco's surrender and plea for, 24–31; relocation to Tularosa, 49–55

Apachería, white encroachment in, 17, 22

Apache scouts: Loco enlistment as, 11; reservation employment as, 141; use against own peoples, 4; women as, 221

Apache warrior culture, 11–12

Aravaipa Apaches, 47
Arizona Star, 110, 123, 194
Armstrong, Frank C., 214
Army and Navy Journal, 205, 253
Arny, William, 35–36, 44–49, 51, 63
Ash Creek, 106, 109, 205
Asheville, N.C., 297–98
Ash Flats, Ariz., 152
Ast-te-wah-lah (Warm Springs man), 157
Atlantic and Pacific Railroad, 226–31
Ayres, John, 59, 62
Ayres, Romeyn, 251–53, 271

Baker, Henry, 291
Balatchu (Chihenne man), 10, 92
Ball, Eve, 145
Barrett, S. M., 144
Bascom, George, 18
Bascom affair of 1861, 18, 37
Baseball in reservation life, *243*, 263
Bathing and personal hygiene, 69–71, 228–29, 231, 253–56, 286
Battleship *Maine*, 302
Batuco Mountains, 191
Bavispe, Sonora, 184
Beach, Francis, 302
Bear power, 12–13
Bear sickness, 11
Beauford, Clay, 93–94, 96, 98
Bedonkohe Apaches, 10, 22, *249*
Bekiva (Warm Springs girl), 292
Belknap, William, 50, 54
Belle (Warm Springs woman), 292–93
Bennett, Frank T., 119–22
Bernard, Reuben, 143
Betzinez, Jason, 11–12, 18, 20, 101, 139–44, 153, 156–57, 161, 170–73, 176–81, 187–89, 191–94, 201–205, 208, 212–14, 230, 259–66
Beveridge, Louise, 222
Beveridge Hotel (Washington, DC), 222
Bey-ih-tsun (daughter of Loco), 209
Biddle, James, 201
Big Burro Mountains, *9*
Binday (Chiricahua man), *247*
Black Friday market collapse of 1869, 30–31
Black Point Mountain, 162
Black Range, *9*, 10, 12, 107

Blair, Thomas, 42
Blake, John ("Bo"), 170
Blankets. *See* Clothing and blankets
Board of Indian Commissioners, 25
Bonito (White Mountain leader), 74, 142, 146, 191–92, 198, 213
Bonneville, Benjamin, 17
Booth, Vincentine, 281
Borden, William, 286
Bosque Redondo reservation, N.Mex., 43
Bounty hunters, 32–33, 123
Bourke, John, 7, 150, 185–86, 191, 198–200, 202, 207, 221–25, 257, 263, 267–70, 283, 288, 295–97
Boutwell, George, 31
Bowman, Sam, 206, 221, 231, 256, 272, 282
Bradley, Luther, 148–50, 157
Brevoort, Elias, 39–40
Brown, George, 261
Bureau of Indian Affairs, 91
Bureau of Refugees, Freedmen, and Abandoned Lands, 58
Burro Springs, N.Mex., 107
Bylas (White Mountain chief), 152

Cadette (Mescalero leader), 53
Camp Goodwin, Ariz., *8*, 102, 109
Camp Grant, Ariz., 4, 47. *See also* Fort Grant, Ariz.
Camp Thomas, Ariz., 44
Cañada Alamosa, N.Mex.: Chihennes encampment near, 32–36; Cochise raiding and peace overtures, 37–38; "cornfield treaty" of 1867, 18–21; as illegal trade center, 88; illegal whiskey trade, 38–40; as reservation site, 43–48
Cañon de los Embudos, Mex., 219
Capron, Allyn, 299
Carbon dioxide poisoning, 228–29
Carlisle Indian Industrial School, *235*; abduction of children to, 264–66; children sent from Ft. Marion, 254; deaths of children at, 287; Loco's children sent to, 211, 287–88; Loco visit to, 225; return of children from, 301. *See also* Education
Carr, Eugene, 142
Caruthers, Horace, 254, 257, 267, 272
Caruthers, Horace (Mrs.), 264

Casas Grandes, Chihuahua, *151*, 174, 189–90, 293

Cash-for-scalps, 32–33, 123, 183–84

Castillo de San Marcos (Fort Marion), 250

Central Chiricahuas (Cochise Chiricahuas), 4, 10. *See also* Chokonen Apaches

Ceroso, Louis, 177

Chaat, Robert ("Ether"), 303

Chaffee, Adna, 123–25, 139–40

Chastine (Chihenne leader), 27

Chatto (Chiricahua leader), *138*, 146, 153, 178, 190–92, 194, 198–99, 204, 213, 221–24, *242*, *247*, 250, 301

Cherokee Reservation, N.C., 296–98

Chicil (Chiricahua man), *247*

Chihennes (the Red Paint People): bands combine for survival, 22; conflict with Chokonen, 38; Eastern Chiricahua group, 10; Loco and Victorio leadership, 14–17, 108–109; Loco removal as Principal Chief, 76–83; outbreak from San Carlos, 104–11; promise of Ojo Caliente reservation, 59–63; relocation to Ojo Caliente, 83–86, 115–18; relocation to San Carlos, 95–104, 119–25; relocation to Tularosa, 43–53; Treaty of Fort Thorn, 17. *See also* Warm Springs band

Chihuahua (Chiricahua leader), 146, 190–91, 198, 204, 212–13, 219, *239*, 252–53, 259, 264, 271, 275, 280, 297, 301

Chihuahua, Eugene, 101

Chihuahua, Mex., 10, 20, 32–33, 184

Chihuahua, Ramona (daughter of Chihuahua), 193

Children: abduction to Carlisle School, *235*, 264–66, 281; activities at Ft. Marion, 263–64; in Apache culture, 5, 287; as Apache slaves, 15; as battle casualties, 178–79; at Ft. Sill, 301; Geronimo's killing of, 180; girls coming of age, 263; growing up in the "better families," 11; health and medical problems, 70–71; reservation schools, 211; school at Mt. Vernon, 281–82; taken as hostages, 19–20, 192–93; taken as slaves, 123, 182–86

Chilson, George, 73

Chiricahua (Chokonen) Reservation: Chihenne overwintering/visits to, 67, 74, 79; creation of, 60–63; death of Cochise and closing of, 83–85; tribal removal and closing of, 89–93, 105

Chiricahua Apaches, *249*; acceptance of reservation life, 4–6; bands and divisions of the tribe, 10–11; delegation to Washington, DC, 221–25; finding a reservation site for, 45; refusal to stop raiding, 211–12; remnant bands combining for survival, 22; reputation as troublemakers, 5, 202–203, 214–15; total removal to Florida, 219–20, 224–32

Chiricahua Jim (Chiricahua man), *247*

Chiricahua Mountains, *8*, 60–61, 162

Chiricahua Outbreak of 1885, 208, 214–15

Chiva (Chevo/Cheever, Chihenne leader), 46, 52, 59, 107

Chiz-odle-netln (second wife of Loco), *135*, 148, 196–97, 209, 211, 221, 225, 303

Chiz-pah-odlee (first wife of Loco), *133*, 148, 151, 157, 196–97, 209–11, 221, 303

Chokonen Apaches (Cochise Chiricahua): bands combine for survival, 22; Central Chiricahua group, 10; continued raiding and attacks, 37–38; creation of a reservation for, 60–63; refusal to relocate, 52; tribal removal to San Carlos, 89–93, 105

Cholera, 253, 269

Cibecue Creek affair of 1881, *8*, 142–43, 148, 211

Civil War, 18

Clark, Charles, 13–14

Clee-hn (youngest wife of Loco), 183, 209–10, 221, 265, 303

Cleveland, Grover, 221, 224–25, 251–53, 268, 270, 281, 295

Clifton, Ariz., 107

Clinton, William, 24, 28–31, 38–40, 43

Clothing and blankets: adaptation to store-bought, 274–76, 282–83; Apache lifestyle and, 23, 27; failure of government issue, 28–31, 65–66, 206–207; losses escaping hostilities, 187–88, 210–11; sold by corrupt agent, 89–90; traded for food, 277; traded for whiskey, 39

Cloverdale, N.Mex., *9*, *151*, 162–65

Clum, John P., 90–91, 93–99, 101–103, 110, 112, 120–22, *130*

Clum, Woodworth, 98

Cochise (Chokonen leader): Bascom affair of 1861, 18, 37; death of, 84; government manhunt to find, 55–59; Loco's peace efforts and, 23, 76; observation about Tularosa Valley, 46; peace overtures, 37–38, 60–63; refusal to relocate, 52; U.S. peace efforts with, 4

Cochise Chiricahua. See Chokonen Apaches

Cochran, John, 288

Coleman, Frederick, 59, 67

Colored Orphan's Home, 278

Colyer, Vincent, 4, 36, 47–51, 55–57, 63, 124

Comanches, 300, 302–303

Company I, Twelfth Infantry. See U.S. Army Twelfth Infantry

Concentration and consolidation policies. See Tribal removal and relocation; U.S. Government Indian policy

Conjunctivitis (eye diseases), 71

Conklin, John, Jr., 270

Cook, G. W., 86

Cooney, Michael, 290–91

Coonie (Chiricahua man), 247

Corbin, Henry, 22–23, 27

"Cornfield treaty" of 1867. See Treaty of Cañada Alamosa of 1867

Corrosero (Chihenne leader), 16

Coyotero Apaches, 17; during Chiricahua outbreak of 1885, 216–18; finding a reservation site for, 45; during the Loco Outbreak, 153–55; relocation to San Carlos, 91; residing at San Carlos, 103–104

Crawford, Emmet, 202, 211

Crazy Apache. See Loco, Chief

Creevy, Sam, 18–19

Crook, George, 4, 55–57, 155, 194, 198–207, 212–13, 216, 219–20, 223, 298

Cruse, Thomas, 16

Cuba, 302

Cuchillo Negro (Chihenne leader), 10–11, 16–17

Cullah (Araviapa policeman), 101

Curley, Sherman (Apache scout), 167–68, 182

Daly, Henry W., 194

Darr, Francis, 164–68, 170–71

Date Creek reservation, 91

Davidson, Robert, 252

Davis, Britton, 13, 201, 204, 212–13

Davis, Nelson, 50

Dawes, Henry, 257, 298

Deaths/death rates: alcohol poisoning, 156; in Apache culture, 68–71; children at Carlisle, 287; drunken fights, 284; at Ft. Marion, 266, 271; at Ft. Sill, 302; from hostilities in the West, 293–94; impact of incarceration on, 293–94; at Mount Vernon, 296; suicide, 174, 247, 284, 292–93; tuberculosis, 285–87. See also Diseases

Debo, Angie, 180

Delano, Columbus, 36, 49–50, 57

Delgadito (Tudeevia, Chinenne leader), 16–17, 20

Delgadito Janeros (Gila Apache), 17

Devin, Thomas, 38, 52, 53

Dewey Flats, Ariz., 151, 156–57

Diseases: allegations of prostitution and syphilis, 211; cholera, 253, 269; health issues at Mt. Vernon, 284–88; health issues in Florida, 253, 255, 266, 269; lack of winter housing and clothing, 65–66, 257; malaria and dysentery, 58, 102, 124, 253, 255, 266; malnutrition, 277; smallpox, 101–102; tuberculosis, 157, 255, 265–66, 271, 284, 302; water and personal hygiene, 69–70; whooping cough and diseases, 70–71. See also Deaths/death rates

Ditteen (Apache soldier), 290–91

Dodge, Henry, 17

Dorst, Joseph, 221–22, 224–26, 231, 250

Dos Cabezos Mountains, 8

Doubtful Canyon, 8, 151, 159–62

Douglas, Ariz., 201

Dragoon Mountains, 8, 60, 91

Drew, Charles E., 23–33, 36, 39–41, 44, 56, 60, 76

Dreyfus, 19

Drunkenness: among women, 213–14; beating and abuse of women, 72, 208, 212–13; illegal trading in whiskey, 35; Loco incidents of, 15–16, 39–40, 213–14; during the Loco Outbreak, 156–57, 189–91; at Mount Vernon, 289–91. See also Alcohol/alcoholism

Duane, Henry, 66

Dudley, Edwin, 61–62, 83–85
Dunn, Jacob, 184
Dutch Reformed Church, 301–302, 303
Dutchy (Chiricahua scout), 199, 290–91
Dysentery, 255, 266, 284, 290

Eagle Creek, 158, 205–206
Eastern Chiricahuas (Mimbres, Gila, Copper
    Mine, Mogollon, Mimbreño, Ojo Caliente
    bands), 10. *See also* Chihennes
Eastman, Galen, 150
Education: activities at Ft. Marion, 263–66;
    children sent to Carlisle, *235*; at Ft. Sill,
    301; Loco's peace efforts and, 305; at
    Mount Vernon, 275, 281–82; for
    reservation children, 211; Riverside School
    (Anadarko), 301. *See also* Carlisle Indian
    Industrial School
Eighth Cavalry. *See* U.S. Army Eighth Cavalry
Elias Gonzales massacre of 1844, 18
Elkins, Stephen, 89
Emerson, Joseph D., 18–19
Emporia, Kans., 225
Endicott, William, 223–25, 252, 261, 267–70
Erickson, Neil, 161, 174, 179, 182–83
Escondido Mountain, 107
Eskiminzin (Aravaipa leader), 280
Eskinya (Skinya, Chihenne leader), 97
Esquerra, Concepción, 221
Esquirre [Esquine] (Chihenne leaders), 115
Eustis, Isabel B., 287
Eye diseases (conjunctivitis), 71

Face paint, 202
Farming: Chihenne adaptation to, 59–60, 142;
    making *tiswin* from corn, 212; at Mount
    Vernon, 283; at San Carlos, 207–209, 211;
    at Tularosa, 45, 67–68; Warm Springs band
    and, 6, 11, 297, 304
Fatty (Apache soldier), 290
Fawn (Chiricahua man), *247*
Ferenbaugh, Thomas L., 304
First California Volunteers, 18
First Cavalry. *See* U.S. Army First Cavalry
Fisk, Clinton, 139, 141
Fisk, Jim, 30–31
Flagler, Henry, 251
Forbes, Florissa, 223

Ford, Charles, 207
Forsyth, George, 146, 153, 159–62, 165,
    173–75, 181–82, 185, 187, 200
Fort Adams, R.I., 292
Fort Apache, Ariz., *8*, 13–14, 56–58, 122, 142,
    147, 155, 159, 203–12, 215–17, 220,
    224–27
Fort Bayard, N.Mex., *9*, 25
Fort Bowie, Ariz., *8*, 219
Fort Craig, N.Mex., *9*, 22–30, 33–34
Fort Cummings, N.Mex., *9*
Fort Fillmore, N.Mex., *9*, 147
Fort Grant (formerly Camp Grant), Ariz., *8*
Fort Leavenworth, Kan., 214, 225–26
Fort Marion, Fla., *233*; abduction of children
    from, 264–66; Apache adaptation to,
    259–61, 271; Chiricahua total removal to,
    224–32; diet and clothing, 256–57;
    enforced idleness of life at, 261–64; health
    and disease issues at, 254–56, 266;
    inadequacies as a prison, 250–54; transfer of
    Chihuahua's group to, 219–20
Fort McLane, N.Mex., *9*, 18
Fort McRae, N.Mex., *9*, 23–31
Fort Pickens, Fla., 231, 252, 269, 289
Fort Selden, N.Mex., *9*
Fort Sill, Okla.: Apache adaptation to,
    301–302; arrival of Apaches at, 299–300;
    Indian baseball at, 263; Loco at, 11–12;
    relocation of Apaches to, 296; rumors of
    Apache uprising, 302–303. *See also* Indian
    Territory
Fort Sill Apaches, 304
Fort Stanton, N.Mex., 43–46, 50–51, 77, 83,
    114, 304
Fort Sumner, N.Mex., 43
Fort Supply, Okla., 300
Fort Thomas, Ariz., *8*, 122, 147, 155, 159, 197
Fort Thorn treaty of 1855, 10, 44
Fort Tularosa, N.Mex., *9*, 58
Fort Union, N.Mex., 107, 157, 209–10
Fort Webster, 15
Fort West, N.Mex., *9*
Fort Wingate, N.Mex., 106–13, 143, 157
Four Mile Crossing, Okla., 301
Fourth Cavalry, 159–61
Fowle, David, 298
Francisco (Chihenne leader), 96

Francisco (interpreter), 20, 48
Frank Leslie's Illustrated Newspaper, 262–63, 268
Frazer, Robert, 206
Free, Mickey, 206, 221, 279
Freedman's Bureau, 58
Frenger, Frank, 40
Fun (Chihenne man), *247*, 292

Galena (Mex.) slaughter of 1846, 18
Galeyville, Ariz., *8*, 164
Galpin, S. A., 90
Gambling in reservation life, *246*, 257, 263, 288–89
García, Lorenzo, 177–80, 183–87, 195–96
Gatewood, Charles B., 211, 215, 217–18
Gavinda (Chihenne leader), 74–75, 78
Geronimo, *131*, *239*, *240*, *247*; breakout of 1885, 213–15; as celebrity, 252, 279; death of, 303–304; employment at Mt. Vernon, 280; at Ft. Pickens, 269, 289; at Ft. Sill, 279–80; as heavy drinker, 189; kidnap of Chihenne from San Carlos, 143–51; killing of Apache children, 180; Loco's peace efforts and, 293–94; peace overtures by, 4; refusal to change, 6, 14–15, 92–93, 208, 211–12; at San Carlos, 95–100, 205–208; surrender of, 219; as tribal leader, 301; Warm Springs band contempt for, 185, 188
Getty, George, 23–31
Ghosts and evil spirits, 68–69, 71, 201
Gila Apaches, 17, 45
Gila County, 148
Gila Mountains, *8*
Gila River, 44, 107, *151*, 152, 161
Gilmore, John, 23–25
Gilson (Mr.), 156
Globe, Ariz., *8*, 104
Globe Silver Belt, 208
Gómez, Victor, 221
Gonzales, Elias, 18
Goodrich (Private), 170
Goody (Chiricahua man), 199
Goody, Talbot (grandson of Loco), 266
Gordo (Chihenne leader), 52, 59, 96
Goso (Chiricahua warrior), 231
Gould, Jay, 30–31
Grab, Martin, 292

Granger, Gordon, 49, 51–52
Grant, Ulysses S., 30–31, 50, 56, 84
Grant County Herald, 108–109, 148
Grant peace policy, 4, 25
Gregg, Irwin, 52
Grijalva, Merejildo (Apache scout), 199
Grover, Cuvier, 23–24, 76
Guadeloupe Mountains, *9*

Hackney, Aaron, 208
Hall, H. D., 40–41
Hampton Normal Institute, 301
Hanos, Mex. *See* Janos, Chihuahua, Mex.
Harris Bijou Theatre (Washington, DC), 223
Hart, Henry L., 104
Hatch, Edward, 87–89, 94, 107, 113–15, 119, 124
Hatfield, Charles, 173, 182
Havana Harbor, Cuba, 302
Hayes, Rutherford B., 118
Hayt, Ezra, 113–14, 118–19, 121
Health. *See* Bathing and personal hygiene; Deaths/death rates; Diseases
Henley, Austin, 92–93
Hennissee, Argalus, 33, 35–36, 42–49, 54, 60, 63
Heyle's Hole, Okla., 301
Hiralchiddy (Chihenne leader), 115, 119, 121
Hoag, Ezra, 102–103, 105, 108–109, 148
Holbrook, Ariz., 226–27
Horache (Chihenne leader), 52
Horn, Tom, 154, 162, 165, 171
Horseshoe Canyon fight, 159–62
Horse thieves, 32
Hot Springs Reservation, *9*; creation of, 83–85; proposal for, 60–61; sale as public lands, 112; as sanctuary for troublemakers, 91–93; Victorio breakout from, 120–23. *See also* Chihennes; Ojo Caliente
Howard, Charles, 147–49
Howard, Guy, 284–85, 296
Howard, Oliver O. ("Bible Toting"), 4, 57–64, 71, 269
Huachinera, Sonora, 195
Huachinera Mountains, *151*, 173, 177, 194–95
Hudson, Richard, 37, 47
Huerra (wife of Mangas), 260
Hughes, Martin, 115

Hugo, William, 99
Hunter, Pendleton, 41

Illegal trading: Apache involvement in, 33–35;
    efforts to control, 42–43; Indian Agent
    corruption and, 86–87; in Mexico, 189; for
    whiskey, 35, 38–40, 263, 289–90. *See also*
    Trading with the Apache
Independent Order of Odd Fellows
    (I.O.O.F.), 278
Indian Agents: alcoholism and ineptness,
    103–104; corruption and mismanagement,
    87–89, 150; refusal to distribute supplies,
    65–67
Indian Association, Massachusetts, 281
Indian Citizenship Committee of Boston,
    267, 269, 296, 301
Indian delegations to Washington DC, 52, 58,
    61, 77, 118, 221–26, 231–32
Indian Office: bureaucratic struggles of, 25,
    43, 59; Carlisle school abduction of
    children, 264–66; creation of reservations,
    46–47; half-ration program, 33–36;
    inaction in providing food, 30–31;
    reservation closures, 90–91; tribal removal
    and relocation, 89–91, 119; Tularosa corn-
    planting program, 67–68. *See also* Bureau of
    Indian Affairs
Indian police, 92–99, 105–106, 119, 121–24,
    141–42, 147, 153–55, 168, 174
"Indian Pride," 231
Indian Rights: Boston Indian Citizenship
    Committee, 267, 269, 296, 301; Herbert
    Welsh as activist for, *236*, 254, 262, 267–70;
    Isabel B. Eustis as activist, 287;
    Massachusetts Indian Association, 281;
    Robert Frazer as activist for, 206
Indian Rights Association, 206, 267–70, 288,
    296
Indian scouts. *See* Apache scouts
Indian Territory, 113–15, 118, 148, 225,
    298–99. *See also* Fort Sill, Okla.
Ironquill (pseudonym). *See* Ware, Eugene Fisk
Itan (Chihenne leader), 16–17
'It'eedee (daughter of Loco), 182–86

Jackson Barracks (New Orleans), 291
Jacksonville, Fla., 229–31, 251–52, 261

Jacksonville *Florida Times-Union*, 230, 264–65,
    270
Janos, Chihuahua, Mex., 105, *151*, 174, 177
Janos Plain, *151*, 166, 173–74
Janos River, 174–75, 177, 200
Jeffords, Thomas, 39–40, 53, 56, 60, 83, 110
Jewett, Horace, 108
Jlin-tay-i-tith (Stops-His-Horse). *See* Loco,
    Chief
Johnson massacre of 1837, 18
Joint Resolution 42, 298
Jones, Roger, 251
Josannie. *See* Ulzanna
Josecito (Chihenne leader), 17
Jose Nuevo (Chihenne leader), 16–17
Jozhe, Benedict, Jr. (grandson of Loco), 266,
    304
Jozhe, Benedict, Sr., 266
Jozhe, Mabel (Nahdoyah, granddaughter of
    Loco), 266, 301
Juan, Marion. *See* Loco, Marion Juan
Juan, Pedro (Warm Springs man), 303
Juan Navajo (Navajo leader), 108
Juh (Nednai leader), 93, 142–44, 147–48, 152,
    188–91, 194, 199–200, 204

Kaahteney (Chiricahua leader), 146, 178, 190,
    204, 221, 223, *242*, 283, 301
Kaitah (Chiricahua scout), 208
Kansas City, Mo., 229
Kautz, August, 92–94, 106–107, 110–11
Kayihtah (Chokonen leader), 301
Keams, Thomas, 108, 110, 116
Kemble, John, 89–90
Kenaididlg (granddaughter of Loco), 221
Kenoi, Sam, 141, 212
Keogh, Pat, 164, 166, 173
Kinzhuna, Arnold, 293
Kiowas, 300, 302–303
Kirkwood, Samuel J., 148–49

Labadi, Lorenzo, 43
Laceris (Chihenne leader), 16–17
Lamar, Lucius, Jr., 220, 224
Lamar, Lucius, Sr., 222–25
Langdon, Loomis L., *234*, 253, 271, 288
Lanig, James M., 66–67, 69–70, 73
Las Cruces Borderer, 46, 50

Las Vegas, N.Mex., 230

Laudanum, 174

Lawton, Okla., 301

LeBaron, Charles, 300

Leeds, William, 119

Leggett, Henry, 21

Lesinsky, Henry, 107

Lidayisil (Stops-His-Horse). *See* Loco, Chief

"Limper." *See* Non-i-thian

Lincoln, Robert, 148

Little Burro Mountains, *9*

Livestock: horse and cattle rustling, 33, 72–73, 93–94; starvation leading to eating of, 30; theft by "peaceful" Apaches, 35, 87; theft of Apache horses, 32

Loco, Bey-ih-tsun (daughter), 209

Loco, Chief (Jlin-tay-i-tith, Lidayisil), *126, 127, 128, 137, 239, 244, 247*; as band leader and visionary, 5–6; birth, 10–11; death of, 183, 303; as heavy drinker, 15–16, 39–40, 77, 154; name variations (Locs, Losho, Loshio, Losio), 10, 15, 23; personal names of, 7, 10; physical description, 10–13; relations with the white man, 13–15; removal as Principal Chief, 76–83; reservation proposals, 26–31; resistance to Tularosa reservation, 49–54; search for "good peace," 99–100, 116–17, 206, 297, 304–305; surrender at Ft. Craig, 22–25, 76

Loco, Chief, wives of. *See* Chiz-odle-netln; Chiz-pah-odlee; Clee-hn

Loco, Dexter (son), 225, 287–88, 301, 304

Loco, John (son), *126, 248, 249*; as Army scout, 303; escape from Alisos Creek, 181; evasion of Carlisle snatches, 265–66; recollections of bear attack, 13; as student at Mt. Vernon, 281–82; taste for fancy clothes, 275–76; as tribal leader, 303–304

Loco, Marion Juan (wife of John), *238, 248, 249*, 303

Loco, Moses (grandson), 13

Loco, Raymond (grandson), 13

Loco, Ruth (granddaughter), 303

Loco Outbreak: ambush at Alisos Creek, 176–86, 200–201; ambush at Sierra Enmedio, 164–72; Apache planning for, 143–50; Chiz-odle-netln escape to San Carlos, 196–97; entry into Mexico, 162–63; escape from Alisos Creek, 187–88; escape from Sierra Enmedio, 172–75; Horseshoe Canyon fight, 160–62; kidnap from San Carlos, 152–60; Loco surrender to Crook, 199–200; Madeira Mountains ambush, 194–96; McComas family murders, 192–94, 214; return to San Carlos, 200–208; Sierra Madre campaign, 198–99

Loco Viejo (female relative of Loco), 182

Locs/Losho/Loshio/Losio. *See* Loco, Chief

Lopez (Chihenne leader), 23, 27, 59

Louie (Zes-cloya, Yavapai man), 291–92

Louisville and Nashville Railroad, 229–30

Macfeely, Robert, 256

MacGowan, Alexander, 147–48

Mackenzie, Ranald S., 149

Madeira Mountains, 194–96

Malaria, 58, 102, 124, 253, 255, 266

Mangas (son of Mangas Coloradas), 15, 115, 146, 202, 205, 213, 231–32, 301

Mangas Coloradas, 4–5, 15–18, 143

Manifest Destiny, 3–4

Mariana (Navajo chief), 108, *132*, 148–49, 157, 209

Marriage: in Apache culture, 82; customs of polygamy and divorce, 282; intermarriage between bands, 148; intermarriage with white men, 108; to provide for widows, 17

Martin, James, 106

Massacre of 1871 (near Camp Grant), 4

Massai (Chiricahua Apache), 230, 232

Master Car Builders Association, 228

Mather, Sara Ann, 264

Maus, Marion, 219, 298

May, Jake, 60

McComas, Charles C., 192–94

McComas, Charley, 192–94, 214

McComas, Hamilton C., 192

McComas, Jennie, 192

McComas family murders, 192–94, 214

McCrary, George, 113

McDonald, David, 159–61

McDowell, Irvin, 106

McIntosh, Archie Sunday, 205

Medicine man, Loco with "bear power" as, 12–13

Meriwether, David, 17

Merritt, Charles, 121

Mescalero Apaches: as Army scouts, 218; Chihenne relocation with, 52–53, 83, 114, 123, 304; Ft. Sill Apaches join with, 304; reservation at Ft. Stanton, 43–46, 50, 77; tribal removal and relocation, 148

Mescalero reservation, 230, 304

Mesilla, N.Mex., 7, *9*, 147

Mestas, Stanislaus, 152

Mexican Apaches. *See* Nednai Apaches

Mexican army: Alisos Creek ambush, 176–82; capture and treatment of women, 182–86; Casas Grandes massacre, 189–90; encounter with Loco, 13; Madeira Mountains ambush, 194–96; naming of Loco, 7

"Mexican Orchestra," 223

Mexico: ambush at Alisos Creek, 176–86, 200–201; ambush at Sierra Enmedio, 165–75; Casas Grandes massacre, 189–90; Chihuahua cash-for-scalps policy, 32–33; Chiricahua outbreak of 1885, 214–15; Geronimo kidnap party entry into, 162–64; Indian slaves in, 184, 210–11; kidnap of Loco's band to, 143–51; U.S. Army "hot pursuit" policy, 194; U.S. Army pursuit into, 164–65, 187; U.S. Army Sierra Madre campaign, 198–208

Miles, Nelson, *136*, 220–21, 224–26, 252, 268, 300

Miller (Private), 170, 174

Mills, Stephen, 164–67, 265–66

Mimbreño Apaches, 10

Mimbres Apaches, 24, 45

Mimbres Mountains, 59–60

Mimbres River, *9*, 44

Ming, Dan, 122

Mobile, Ala., 290–91

Mobile and Birmingham Railroad, 277

Mobile Register, 269, 274

Moctezuma District, Sonora, 194

Mogollon Apaches, 10, 45, 68–69

Mogollon Mountains, *9*, 107

Mohave Indians, 104

"Mongollon" ancient tribe, 68

Montoya, Juan, 42–43

Montoya, Ramón, 206

Morality, of raiding and warfare, 3

Morton, Charles, 146

Mountain Spirit Dance, 263

Mount Vernon, Ala., *237*, *245*; Apaches as tourist attraction, 278–79; deterioration of mental health, 284–85; drunkenness, 289–91; employment and wages, 279–81; food shortages, 276–78; gambling, 288–89; housing and clothing, 273–74, 285–87; relocation of Apaches to, 269–73

Mount Vernon, Ill., 229–30

Mount Vernon Barracks, Ala., 269–70, 272, 274, 280

Mrs. Mather's Female Seminary, 264

Murphy (Waycross police chief), 230

Nahdoyah (granddaughter of Loco). *See* Jozhe, Mabel

Nah-thle-tla (wife of Tudeevia), 20–21

Nah-to-ah-jun (Apache soldier), 292–93

Naiche (son of Cochise), 4, 11, 91–92, 102, 105, 142–44, 146–47, 153, 178, 189–90, 204, 208, 211, 213, 219, *239*, *242*, *247*, 252, 297, 301

Nana (Chihenne leader), 11, 17–18, 52, 76, 79, 107, 115, *129*, 142, *239*, *247*

Natanes Butte, Ariz., 106, 109, 205

Navajo Bosque Redondo reservation, 43

Navajo reservation (near Ft. Wingate): Chiz-pah-odlee escape to, 157; Warm Springs band relocation to, 43, 113–14, 116, 148–50; Warm Springs outbreak of 1877, 108

Nednai Apaches: bands combine for survival, 22; joining Warm Springs band, 191; in Mexico, 188–91; signing of Treaty of Fort Thorn, 17; Southern Chiricahua group, 10

New Mexico Volunteers, 86

New Orleans, La., 291, 300–301

The New Southwest and Grant County Herald, 183

New York Times, 274

Ninth Cavalry. *See* U.S. Army Ninth Cavalry

Noch-ay-del-klinne (White Mountain medicine man), 142

Noche (Apache soldier), 290

Nolgee (Chiricahua leader), 93, 98

Non-i-thian ("the Limper," son of Tudeevia), 20

North Beach, Fla., 253, 262, 266, 270
North River, Fla., 253, 255

Ojo Caliente, 9; as Chihenne homeland, 51;
    peace agreement in 1869, 5; as reservation
    site, 43–44, 59–64, 303. See also Chihennes;
    Hot Springs Reservation
Oklahoma. See Fort Sill, Okla.; Indian
    Territory
Opler, Morris, 10, 68, 82, 141, 166
Outbreak of 1877, 104–11
Outbreak of 1882. See Loco Outbreak
Outbreak of 1885, 214–18
Owl spirits, 68–69

Pah-gotzin-kay Mountain, 195–97
Painter, Charles, 288, 296–97
Pajarita (son-in-law of Victorio), 75, 79–82
Pajarita Chiquito (son of Cuchillo Negro),
    79–81
Parker, Ely, 24–31, 40, 44–46
Parker, J., 290–91
Patterson, Richard C., 18–19, 34–35
Peace agreements: Cochise overtures for,
    37–38; as gesture/tactical maneuver, 4;
    warfare while negotiating, 17–18. See also
    Treaties
Peaches (Apache scout), 154, 192, 194, 198
Pearson, William, 282
Pedro (Coyotero chief), 154
Pensacola, Fla., 251–52
Perico (Chihenne warrior and scout), 15, 242,
    247
Perico, Leon, 145
Perry, David, 147, 168
Philadelphia Record, 268
Pierce, Francis E., 215
Pierson, Ed, 153, 155
Pinary Apaches. See Nednai Apaches
Pionsenay (Chokonen troublemaker), 104–105
Piper, Orlando, 36–38, 46–53, 55–59, 61–62,
    76–78, 86, 145
Plains Indians, 250, 300
Poisoned whiskey incident of 1857, 18
Ponce (Chihenne leader), 16, 62, 96
Pope, John, 36, 63, 111–14, 117–18, 124–25,
    149, 207
Pope, Nathaniel, 37, 46–59

Pork rations, 34, 256
Pratt, Richard, 265–66, 287
Prescott, Ariz., 122, 194
Prescott Miner, 91
Price, William, 73–76, 78, 80, 210–11
Proctor, Redfield, 296
Prostitution: allegations at San Carlos, 211;
    Apache women forced into, 184–86
Puberty (girls coming of age), 263

Quah-day-lay-thay-go (Mojave scout), 160
Quintana Roo, Mex., 22

Raffaille (Chihenne leader), 79, 81
Rafferty, William, 164–74, 177–78, 181–82
Raiding: in Apache lifestyle, 3; Chiricahua
    refusal to stop, 211–12; Chiricahua return
    to, 91–93; Geronimo outbreak of 1885,
    214–15; during the Loco Outbreak,
    191–94; as means of survival, 11; at Mount
    Vernon, 291; refusal of Geronimo to end,
    6; to supplement government rations,
    34–36, 87–89; to trade for whiskey, 35,
    38–39; Victorio rampage of 1880, 123
Railroads: Atlantic and Pacific Railroad,
    226–31; Louisville and Nashville Railroad,
    229–30; Mobile and Birmingham
    Railroad, 277; Savannah, Florida, and
    Western Railroad, 270; Southern Pacific
    Railroad, 8, 9, 159
Ramon (Warm Springs man), 289
Ration issue day: at Ft. Marion, 261;
    recollections of Loco on, 11–12; role of
    Principal Chief on, 78; at San Carlos
    Agency, 13–14
Rations/rationing: Army refusal to provide,
    23–24; complaints at Tularosa, 65–67; at Ft.
    Marion, 256, 271; half-ration program,
    33–37; Indian Agent corruption and, 87–89;
    Indian efforts to supplement, 140–42,
    256–57, 262; at Mount Vernon, 276–78; at
    San Carlos, 103–104, 207–208; Treaty of
    Fort Thorn and, 17
Red Paint People. See Chihennes; Warm
    Springs band
Reed, Walter, 277, 284–85, 291, 296
Religion: at Ft. Sill, 301–302; at Mount
    Vernon, 282

Reservation life: baseball in, *243*, 263; Chiricahua adaptation to, 4–6, 208; enforced idleness at Ft. Marion, 261–64; gambling in, *246*, 257, 263, 288–89; impact on emotional health, 284–85; role of Principal Chief in, 78–79; wage jobs and, 140, 142, 209, 279–81, 283; Warm Springs band at San Carlos, 205–209, 211; work and employment, 140–42
Reyes, Bernardo, 177, 184
The Rhymes of Ironquill (Ware), 192
Richards, James, 219
Richmond, N.Mex., 160–61
Rinon (Chihenne leader), 16–17
Rio Grande, *9*, 24, 44, 59, 72, 87
Rituals: Mountain Spirit Dance, 263; mourning at time of death, 186, 283; in rearing and training children, 5; sweat-baths, 69, 286; victory celebrations, 165–66
Riverside School (Anadarko, Okla.), 301
Roach, George, 213–14
Robbins, Chandler, 304
Roe, Walter, 301–302
Rope, John, 102, 153, 177, 201–202
Ross, William, 57
Rush Springs, Okla., 299
Russell, George, 299

Safford, Anson, 93–94, 152
Safford, Ariz., *8*
Saks and Company (Washington, DC), 222
Salvador (son-in-law to Loco), 24, 29, 34
San Antonio, Tex., 231, 252
San Carlos Agency, *8*, 13–14
San Carlos Reservation, *8*; Chihenne outbreak of 1877, 104–11; Chiricahua outbreak of 1885, 214–15; Chiz-odle-netln escape from Mexico, 196–97; delegation to Washington, DC, 221–25; Geronimo's kidnap of Loco band, 143–51; Loco Outbreak of 1882, 152–60; relocation of Chihenne to, 95–104; relocation of Chokonen to, 89–94; return of Warm Springs band to, 198–208; as Utopia, 101
San Carlos River, 202
Sanchez (Coyotero leader), 216–18
Sanchez (Sancho, Chihenne man), 73, 78, 88, 121, 146

Sands, George, 158
San Francisco Mountains, 108
San Francisco River, 45, 69
San Jose, N.Mex., 29, *151*
San Simon Valley, 162
Santa Catalina Mountains, *8*
Santa Fe, N.Mex., 17, 24, 33, 49, 88–89, 116
Santa Fe New Mexican, 24
Santa Lucía, as reservation site, 44
Savannah, Florida, and Western Railroad, 270
Scalps, cash for, 32–33, 123, 183–84
Schofield, George W., 158
Schools. *See* Carlisle Indian Industrial School; Education
Schurz, Carl, 112–13, 119
Scott, Hugh, 298, 300–302
Scouts. *See* Apache scouts; U.S. Army
Seeltoe (Apache soldier), 292–93
Seminoles, 250
Separ, N.Mex., *151*
Settlers in Apachería: conflict for business and profit, 4; encroachment on Apache population, 17, 22; fear of Chiricahua, 218
Seventh Cavalry, 303
Sey-konne. *See* Siki
Shaw, John M., 86–95
Sheever. *See* Chiva
She-ga (wife of Geronimo), 215
Shepard, Sophie, 275, 281–82
Shepard, Sylvia, 281–82
Sheridan, Philip, 51, 63, 113, 118–19, 218–21, 225, 253, 267–68
Sherman, William, 113, 119, 149–50
Shnowin (Chihenne man), 20
Shorkley, George, 29, 38, 40, 53
Sieber, Al, 155, 158, 162, 165–67, 169–70, 173, 185, 201–202, 220
Sierra Enmedio, Chihuahua, *9*, *151*, 164–72, 176–77, 185–87, 293
Sierra Huachinera. *See* Huachinera Mountains
Sierra Madre, 190
Siki (Seykonne, stepdaughter of Loco), 123, 210–11, 260
Silver City, N.Mex., 94, 98–99, 183, 192
Silver Springs, Ariz., 201
Sinclair, William, *246*, 274, 276–77, 279, 288, 292
Sisters of St. Joseph, 264

Sixth Cavalry. *See* U.S. Army Sixth Cavalry

Skinya. *See* Eskinya

Sladen, Joseph, 59, 69–70

Slaves: in Apache culture, 15; Chihenne women and children, 123; Chiricahua women and children, 22; Loco treatment of, 15–16; for sale in Mexico, 182–86

Slim Jim (Apache scout), 173, 182

Smallpox, 101–102

Smith, Edward P., 83, 93–94

Smith, Tom, 157

Snaggle Tooth Ponce, 80

Society for the Preservation of Education, 264

Socorro, N.Mex., *9*, 43–46, 139

Sogotal, 153–54, 168, 174

Sonora, Mex.: Apache raiding in, 78, 87–89; as Chiricahua homeland, 10, 37, 63; as Cochise sanctuary, 55; selling Indian slaves in, 184

Sonora Apaches. *See* Nednai Apaches

Sonoran National Guard, 177, 179

Sounig (Warm Springs woman), 289

Southern Chiricahuas (Mexican Apaches, Pinary Apaches), 10. *See also* Nednai Apaches

Southern Pacific Railroad, *8*, *9*, 159

Spanish-American War, 302

Speedy (Apache warrior), 193

St. Augustine, Fla.: Apache freedom of movement in, 259–60; Apache relocation to Alabama, 270; Apaches as tourist attraction, 251–52, 260–63; Ft. Marion and, 250–58

St. Augustine Ladies Sewing Society, 257

Steck, Michael, 17

Steelhammer, Charles, 117

Steen, Enoch, 15

Stephens, Marion, 281

Sterling, Albert, 153–55

Stevens, George, 152

St. Francis Barracks, Fla., 250

St. Louis, Mo., 229–30

Stops-His-Horse. *See* Loco, Chief

Streeter, Zeb, 52–53

Strover, William, 226–27, 229–30

Suicides, 174, *247*, 284, 292–93

Sutherland, Charles, 286

Sweat baths, 69, 286. *See also* Bathing and personal hygiene

Sweeney, Edwin R., 37

Sweeney, Martin, 94, 103–104

Talusher (Warm Springs man), 292

Tange (Thomaso). *See* Hiralchiddy

Tarahumara scouts, 123

Tax, Sol, 15, 145

Taylor, Daniel, 223

Taza (son of Cochise), 91, 105

Teller, Henry, 267

Terrazas, Joaquín, 123, 183

Terry, Alfred, 226

Thirteenth Infantry, 148–49

Thirty-eighth Infantry, 23, 27

Thomas, Benjamin Morris, 59, 61–67

Thompson Canyon, N.Mex., 192

Thrapp, Dan, 78

Tiffany, Joseph C., 139–41, 144, 146, 211

Tiswin: in Apache culture, 212; drunkenness from, 15–16, 72, 74, 212–13; efforts to control, 42, 208; introduction to Navajo, 150; punishment for making, 154

Toclanny, Rogers (Apache scout), 171, *242*, 302

Toggi (Chihenne leader), 119–21, 143

Tomascito (Chihenne leader), 76

Tombstone, Ariz., *8*, *151*, 192

Tonto Apaches, 104

Topete, Bonifacio, 195

Torres, Lorenzo, 195

Touey, Timothy, 167–69, 185

Trading with the Apache: "cornfield treaty" of 1867, 18–21; criminal activity associated with, 32–33; at Ft. Marion, 261–62; at Mount Vernon, 274, 279–81. *See also* Illegal trading

Treaties, American undermining of, 4–5. *See also* Peace agreements

Treaty of Acoma of 1852, 10, 15–17

Treaty of Cañada Alamosa of 1867 ("cornfield treaty"), 18–21

Treaty of Fort Craig of 1855, 20–21

Treaty of Fort Thorn of 1855, 10, 17

Tres Castillos massacre, 123, 143, 183, 191–92, 210, 293

Tribal removal and relocation: Chihenne to San Carlos, 95–104, 119–25; Chihenne to Tularosa Valley, 47–54; Chokonen to San

Carlos, 89–94; Cleveland total removal policy, 224–32, 295–96; cost of relocation, 54, 100, 113–14; relocation to Ft. Sill, 299–300; relocation to Mount Vernon, 269–71; reservation closing and consolidation, 112–13, 148–49; Warm Springs band with Navajos, 148–50. *See also* Fort Marion, Fla.; Fort Pickens, Fla.; Fort Sill, Okla.; Mount Vernon, Ala.

Tribolett, Bob, 219

The Triplets (at San Carlos), 154

Trujillo, José, 20, 42–44, 55–57

Tuberculosis, 157, 255, 265–66, 271, 284

Tucson, Ariz., 4, *8*, 84, 104

Tudeevia (Delgadito), 16–17, 20

Tularosa Mountains, *9*

Tularosa Reservation, *9*; Chihenne adaptation to, 64–65; drunkenness, 72–73; lack of housing and supplies, 65–67; shootout over Pajarita reign of terror, 79–82; tribal removal and closing of, 83–85; Victorio breakout, 74–79

Tularosa River, 45, 49

Tularosa Valley: Chihenne relocation to, 51–53; cost of relocation, 54; ghosts and evil spirits of, 10, 68–69; Loco arrival at, 53; "Mongollon" ancient tribe, 68; as proposed reservation site, 45–46; suitability for farming, 67; winter weather, 65–67

Tupper, Tillius C., 107, *134*, 164–74, 176

Turevia (son of Cuchillo Negro), 79–81

Turkey Creek, Ariz., *8*, 205–209, 215–16, 294

Twelfth Infantry. *See* U.S. Army Twelfth Infantry

Ulzanna (Josannie, brother of Chihuahua), 216–17, 219

U.S. Army: Apache as army scouts, 4, 141; Apache as army soldiers, 280; Loco enlistment as scout, 11; prevalence of alcoholism, 16, 289–90; surrender of Loco's band to, 23–31; women as army scouts, 221

U.S. Army First California Volunteers, 18

U.S. Army First Cavalry, 13, 142–43, 183–84, 302–303

U.S. Army Fourth Cavalry, 159–61

U.S. Army Sixth Cavalry, 158, 164, 173, 201

U.S. Army Seventh Cavalry, 303

U.S. Army Eighth Cavalry, 53, 73, 210

U.S. Army Ninth Cavalry, 107, 115, 119, 142

U.S. Army Twelfth Infantry, *242*, 280, 285, 290–92, 299, 303

U.S. Army Thirteenth Infantry, 148–49

U.S. Army Thirty-eighth Infantry, 23, 27

U.S. Army Indian campaigns: attack on Loco's band, 22–23; "hot pursuit" policy, 194; intrusion into Mexico, 165–75, 181–87; to punish and subdue, 17–18; Sierra Madre campaign, 198–208

U.S. Bureau of American Ethnology, 222

U.S. Government: Black Friday market collapse, 30–31; undermining peace efforts, 6

U.S. Government Indian policy: Cleveland total removal policy, 224–32, 295–96; creation of reservation system, 47, 51; failure of Apache taming policy, 148; Grant peace policy, 4, 25; Hayes Indian policy, 118; Indian delegations to Washington DC, 52, 58, 61, 77, 118, 221–26, 231–32; Indian rights activism and, 267–71; Joint Resolution 42, 298; subsistence rationing, 33–37

Vandever, William, 103–104, 110, 114–15, 119

Veinte Realles (Chihenne leader), 16

Victorio (Chihenne leader): breakout from Hot Springs, 120–23; breakout from Tularosa, 74–79; conflicts with Loco, 14–15; death of, 123; Loco's peace efforts and, 23; physical description, 11; replacement of Loco as chief, 76–79; resistance to relocation, 49–54; shootout over Pajarita reign of terror, 79–82; Treaty of Acoma of 1852, 16–17

Wade, James, 94, 96–99, 107, 226, 231

Wage jobs for Indians, 140, 142, 209, 279–81, 283

Walker, Francis, 60–61

Walker, George, 80

Warden (Mr.), 264

Ware, Charles, 192–94, 214

Ware, Eugene Fisk, 192–94, 214

Warfare in Apache lifestyle, defined, 3. *See also* Raiding

Warm Springs band, *249*; as Army scouts, 215, 221; delegation to Washington, DC, 221–25; relocation to Mount Vernon, 269–71; relocation to Navajo reservation, 148–50; removal to Florida, 225–32; at San Carlos, 95–104, 198–208; San Carlos census of 1884, 190–91; as tourist attraction, 251–52, 260–63, 278–79; at Tularosa, 47–54, 64–67. *See also* Chihennes; Loco Outbreak

Washington (son of Victorio), 123

Washington, DC, Indian delegations to, 52, 58, 61, 77, 118, 221–26, 231–32

Washington Evening Star, 221–22, 224

Watkins, E. C., 113–14, 117, 119

Waycross, Ga., 229–30

Weapons: bow and arrow, 11–12; Remington Rolling Block rifles, 179; Winchester & Marlin repeating rifles, 179–80

Webb, DeWitt, 255–56

Welsh, Herbert, *236*, 254, 256, 262, 267–70

West, Parker, 197

Western Apaches: delegation to Washington, DC, 58; killing of Henry Dodge, 17; relations with the Chihenne, 104, 202–203

Whipple Barracks, Ariz., 194

White Mountain reservation, 91, 205–206

White Mountains, *8*, 205

Whitney, Walter, 90, 95–98, 107, 109, 115, 118

Whittington, J. H., 41

Whooping cough, 70–71

Wickenburg, Ariz., 91

Wilcox, P. P., 197, 202–203, 207, 211–12, 214

Willcox, Ariz., *8*, 201

Willcox, Orlando, 110–11, 142, 147, 149

Wingfield, Edward, 15

Wise, William, 290–91

Witches, in Apache culture, 12, 168

Women: acceptance into St. Augustine society, 260, 264; affection for children, 5; as Army scouts, 221; as battle casualties, 167, 169, 171–74, 178–79, 181, 193; beating and abuse of, 72, 153, 208, 212–13; captured as hostages, 20–21; caring for widows in Apache culture, 17; in ceremonial dances, 14; drunkenness, 213–14; marriage to white men, 108; as military prisoners, 209–10; as slaves in Apache culture, 15–16, 184; taken as slaves, 123, 182–86, 210–11; as U.S. prisoners, *238*; wage jobs for, 279–81; as witches in Apache culture, 12, 168

Women's Indian Rights Association, 267, 269

Women's National Indian Association, 269

Wotherspoon, William Wallace, *241*, *246*, 277–80, 282, 285–91, 299

Wratten, George, *247*, 274, 278, 282, 298, 302

Wright, Frank, 301–302

Wright, Henry, 121

Yanoza (Apache scout), *242*, *247*

Yaqui River, 190

Yavapais, 91, 104, 291

Yellow Fever, 253, 269

Yuma Indians, 104

Zele (Bedonkohe leader), 143, 152–53, 204, 213, 216, 273, 292–93

Zes-cloya. *See* Louie

Ziestoe (Warm Springs woman), 292